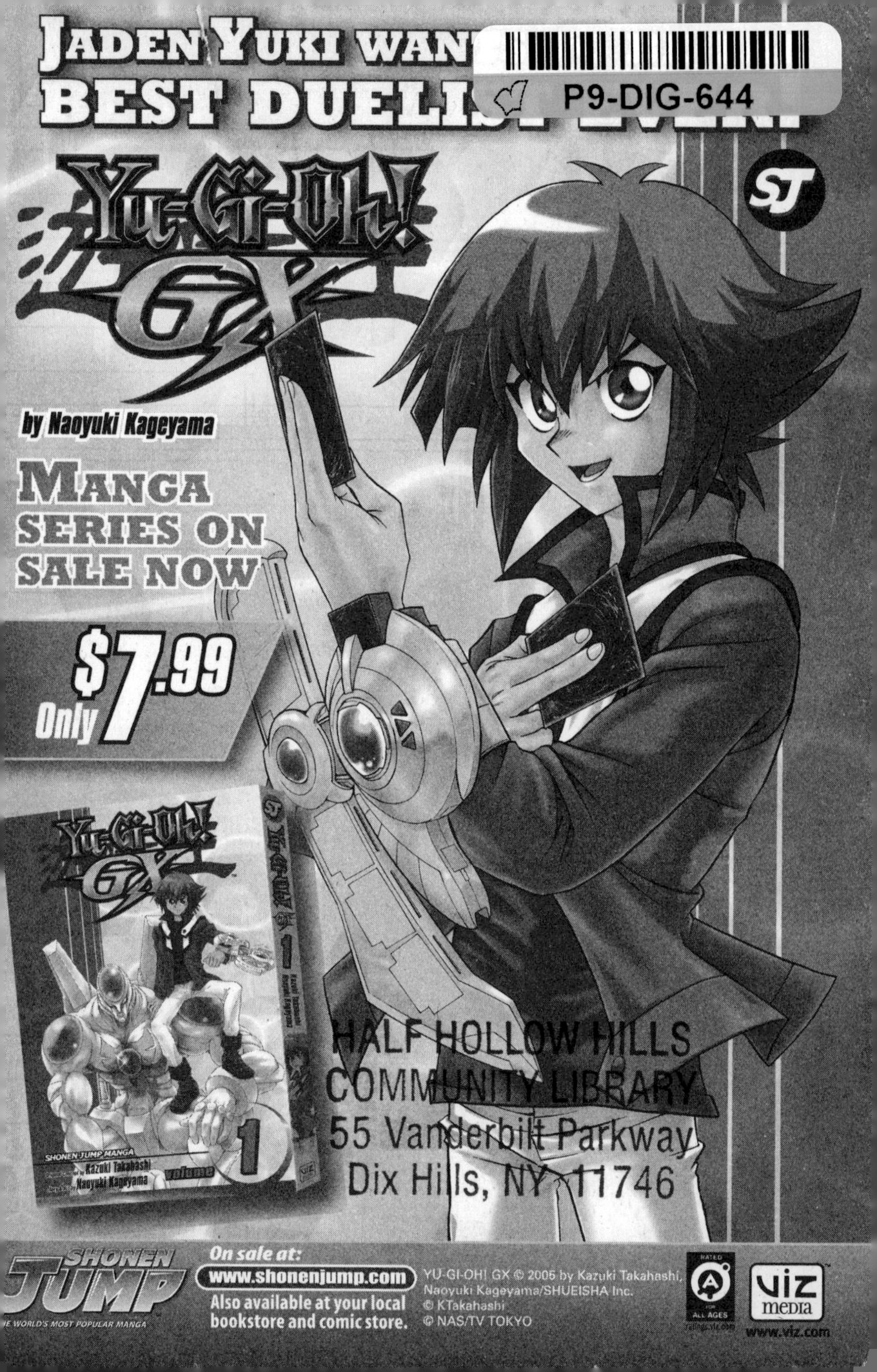

JADEN YUKI WAN
BEST DUELI
SJ
YU-GI-OH! GX
by Naoyuki Kageyama
MANGA SERIES ON SALE NOW
Only $7.99
YU-GI-OH! GX
SHONEN JUMP MANGA
Kazuki Takahashi
Naoyuki Kageyama
volume 1
SHONEN JUMP
THE WORLD'S MOST POPULAR MANGA
On sale at:
www.shonenjump.com
Also available at your local bookstore and comic store.
YU-GI-OH! GX © 2006 by Kazuki Takahashi, Naoyuki Kageyama/SHUEISHA Inc.
© KTakahashi
© NAS/TV TOKYO
RATED A FOR ALL AGES
ratings.viz.com
VIZ media
www.viz.com

IN THE NEXT VOLUME...

Yusei enters the D1 Grand Prix, hoping for a chance to duel Jack Atlas. There are new rivals and new duels to fight, and the competition will be fierce. Can Yusei battle his way to the top, or is he destined to crash and burn?

COMING FEBRUARY 2012!

5D's TRACKS

THE 8TH

BY SATOMASA

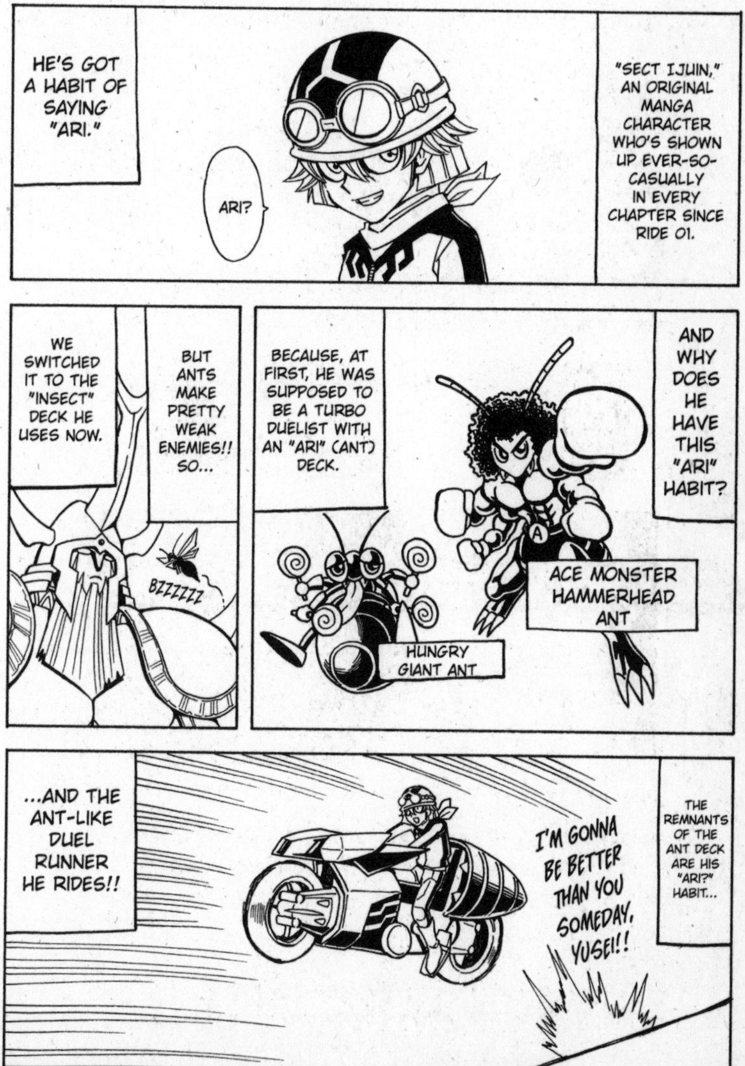
"SECT IJUIN," AN ORIGINAL MANGA CHARACTER WHO'S SHOWN UP EVER-SO-CASUALLY IN EVERY CHAPTER SINCE RIDE 01.
ARI?
HE'S GOT A HABIT OF SAYING "ARI."
AND WHY DOES HE HAVE THIS "ARI" HABIT?
BECAUSE, AT FIRST, HE WAS SUPPOSED TO BE A TURBO DUELIST WITH AN "ARI" (ANT) DECK.
ACE MONSTER HAMMERHEAD ANT
HUNGRY GIANT ANT
BUT ANTS MAKE PRETTY WEAK ENEMIES!! SO...
WE SWITCHED IT TO THE "INSECT" DECK HE USES NOW.
BZZZZZZ
THE REMNANTS OF THE ANT DECK ARE HIS "ARI?" HABIT...
I'M GONNA BE BETTER THAN YOU SOMEDAY, YUSEI!!
...AND THE ANT-LIKE DUEL RUNNER HE RIDES!!

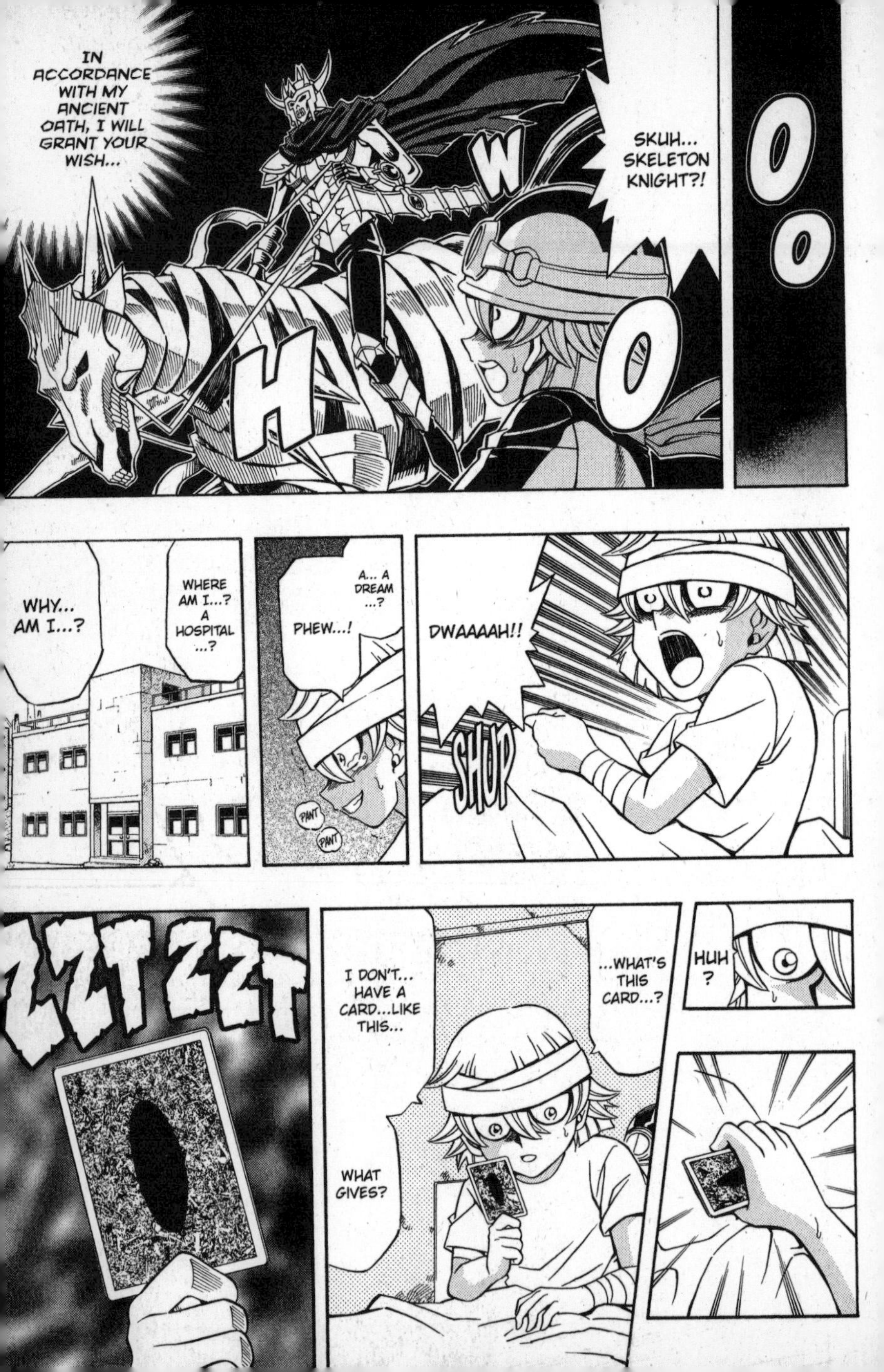
WHOOOO
SKUH... SKELETON KNIGHT?!
IN ACCORDANCE WITH MY ANCIENT OATH, I WILL GRANT YOUR WISH...
DWAAAAH!!
SHUP
A... A DREAM ...?
PHEW...!
PANT
PANT
WHERE AM I...? A HOSPITAL ...?
WHY... AM I...?
HUH ?
...WHAT'S THIS CARD...?
I DON'T... HAVE A CARD...LIKE THIS...
WHAT GIVES?
ZZT ZZT

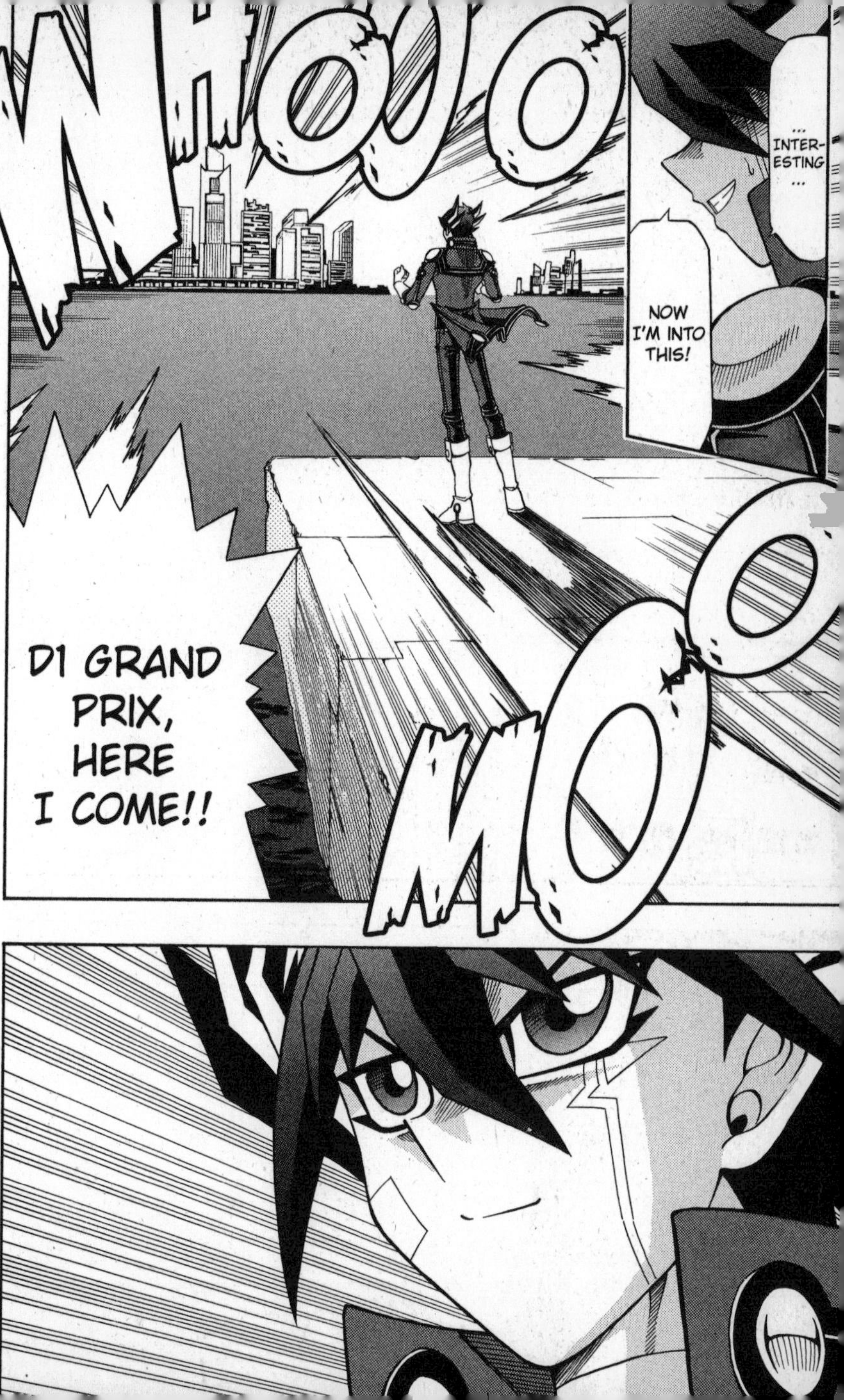
...INTERESTING...
NOW I'M INTO THIS!
WHOOO
D1 GRAND PRIX, HERE I COME!!
OOOW

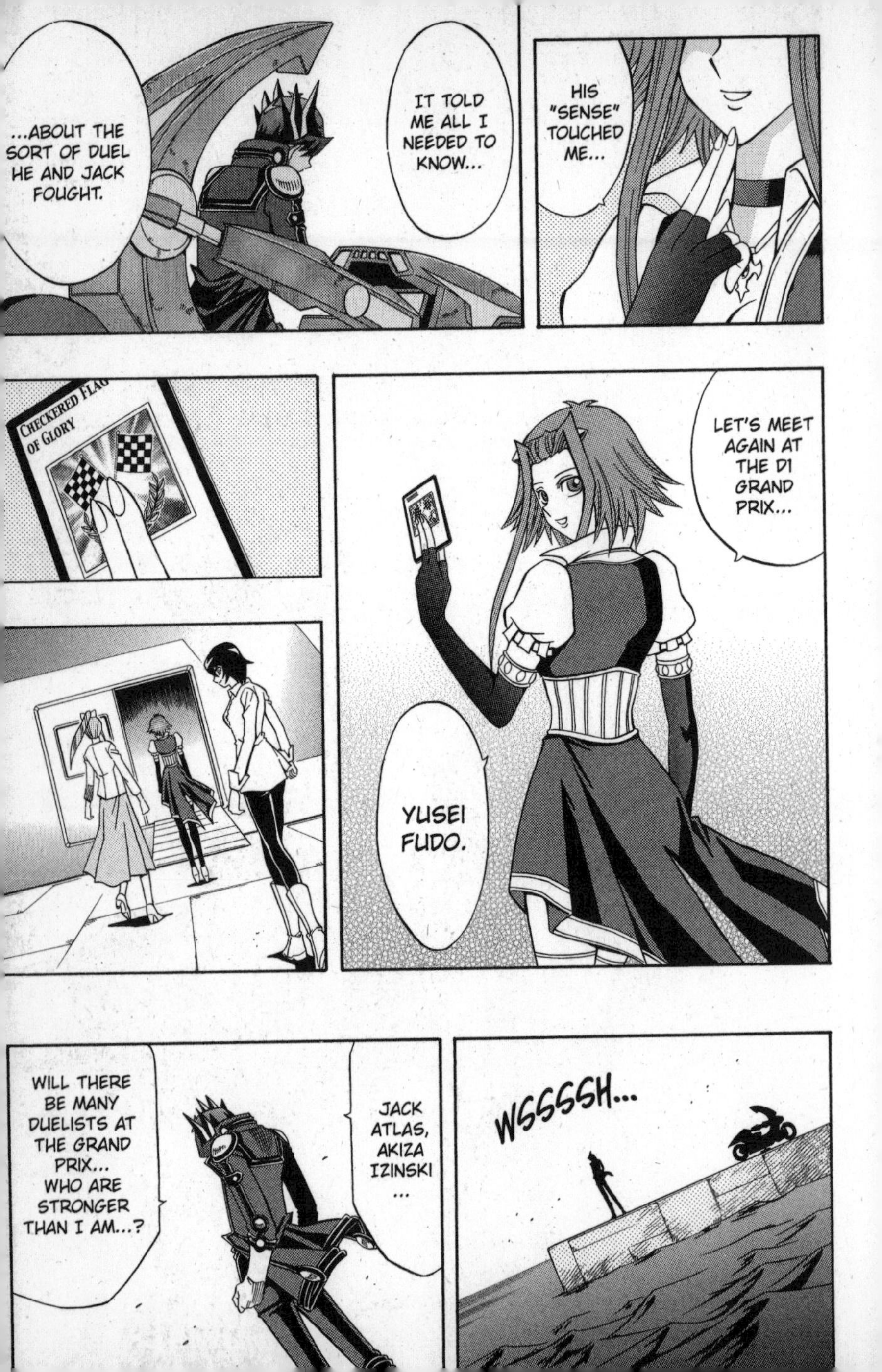
HIS "SENSE" TOUCHED ME...
IT TOLD ME ALL I NEEDED TO KNOW...
...ABOUT THE SORT OF DUEL HE AND JACK FOUGHT.
LET'S MEET AGAIN AT THE D1 GRAND PRIX...
YUSEI FUDO.
CHECKERED FLA
OF GLORY
WSSSSH...
JACK ATLAS, AKIZA IZINSKI ...
WILL THERE BE MANY DUELISTS AT THE GRAND PRIX... WHO ARE STRONGER THAN I AM...?

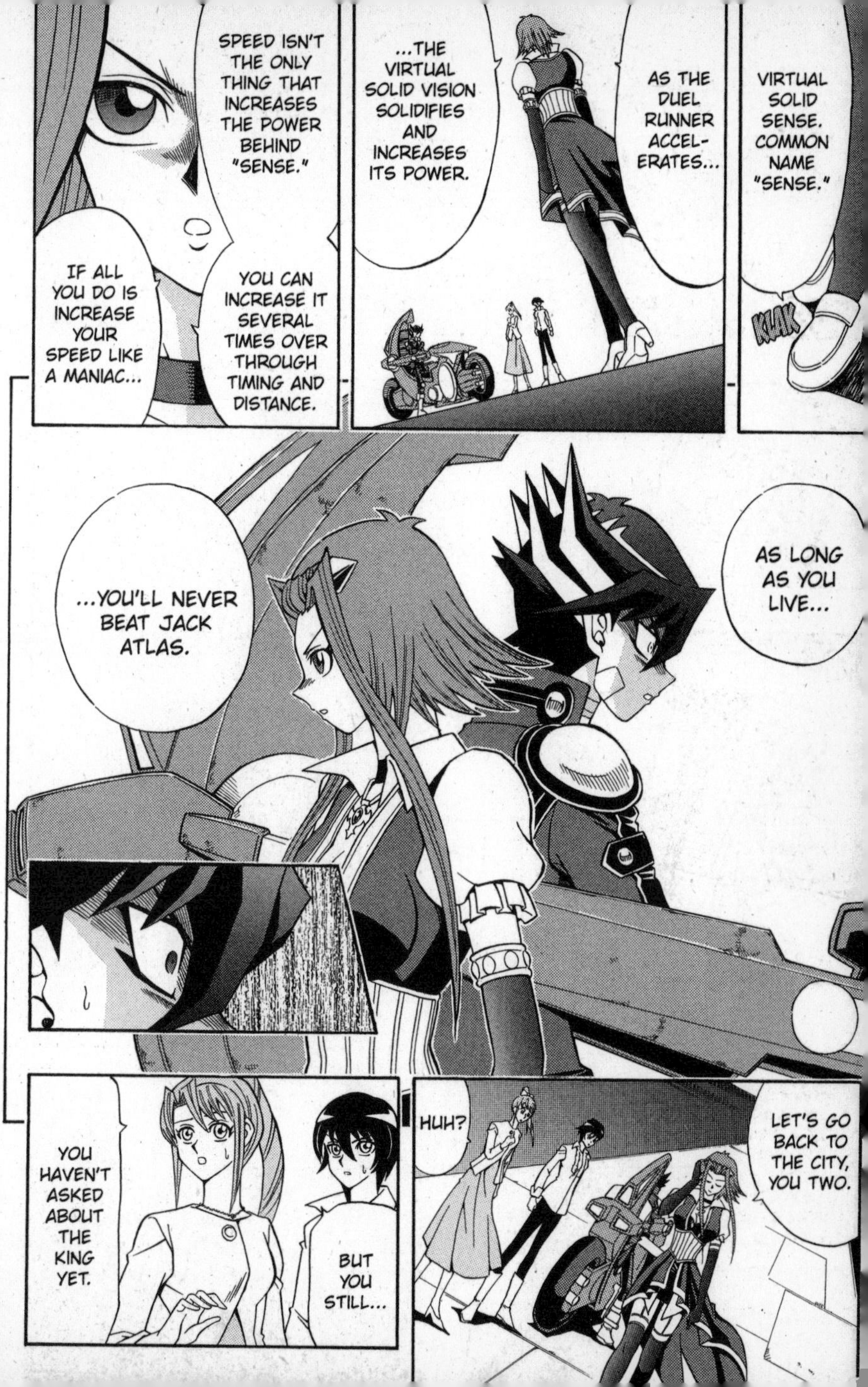
VIRTUAL SOLID SENSE. COMMON NAME "SENSE."
KLAK
AS THE DUEL RUNNER ACCEL-ERATES...
...THE VIRTUAL SOLID VISION SOLIDIFIES AND INCREASES ITS POWER.
SPEED ISN'T THE ONLY THING THAT INCREASES THE POWER BEHIND "SENSE."
YOU CAN INCREASE IT SEVERAL TIMES OVER THROUGH TIMING AND DISTANCE.
IF ALL YOU DO IS INCREASE YOUR SPEED LIKE A MANIAC...
AS LONG AS YOU LIVE...
...YOU'LL NEVER BEAT JACK ATLAS.
LET'S GO BACK TO THE CITY, YOU TWO.
HUH?
BUT YOU STILL...
YOU HAVEN'T ASKED ABOUT THE KING YET.

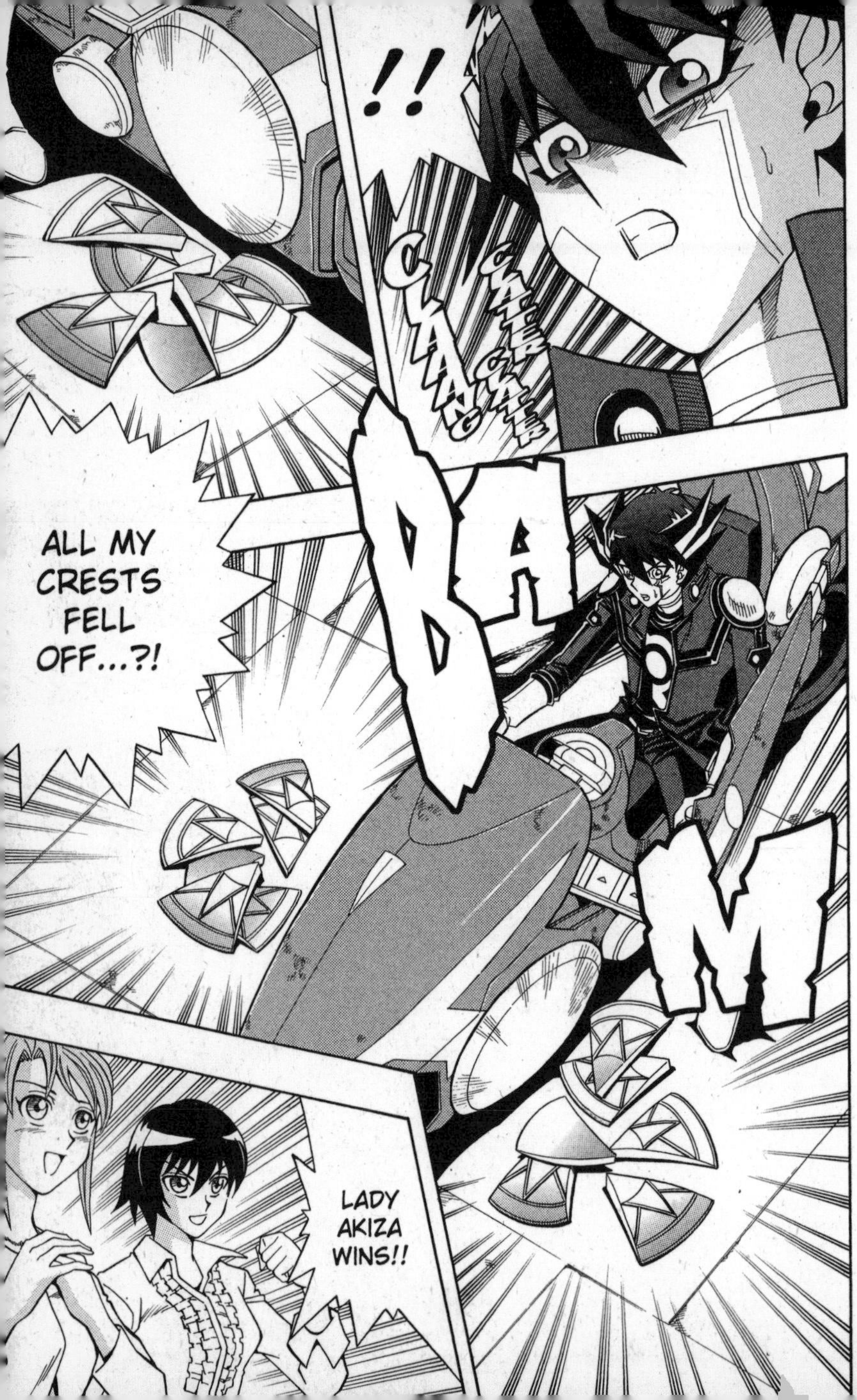
!!
CLANG
CLATTER CLATTER
BAM
ALL MY CRESTS FELL OFF...?!
LADY AKIZA WINS!!

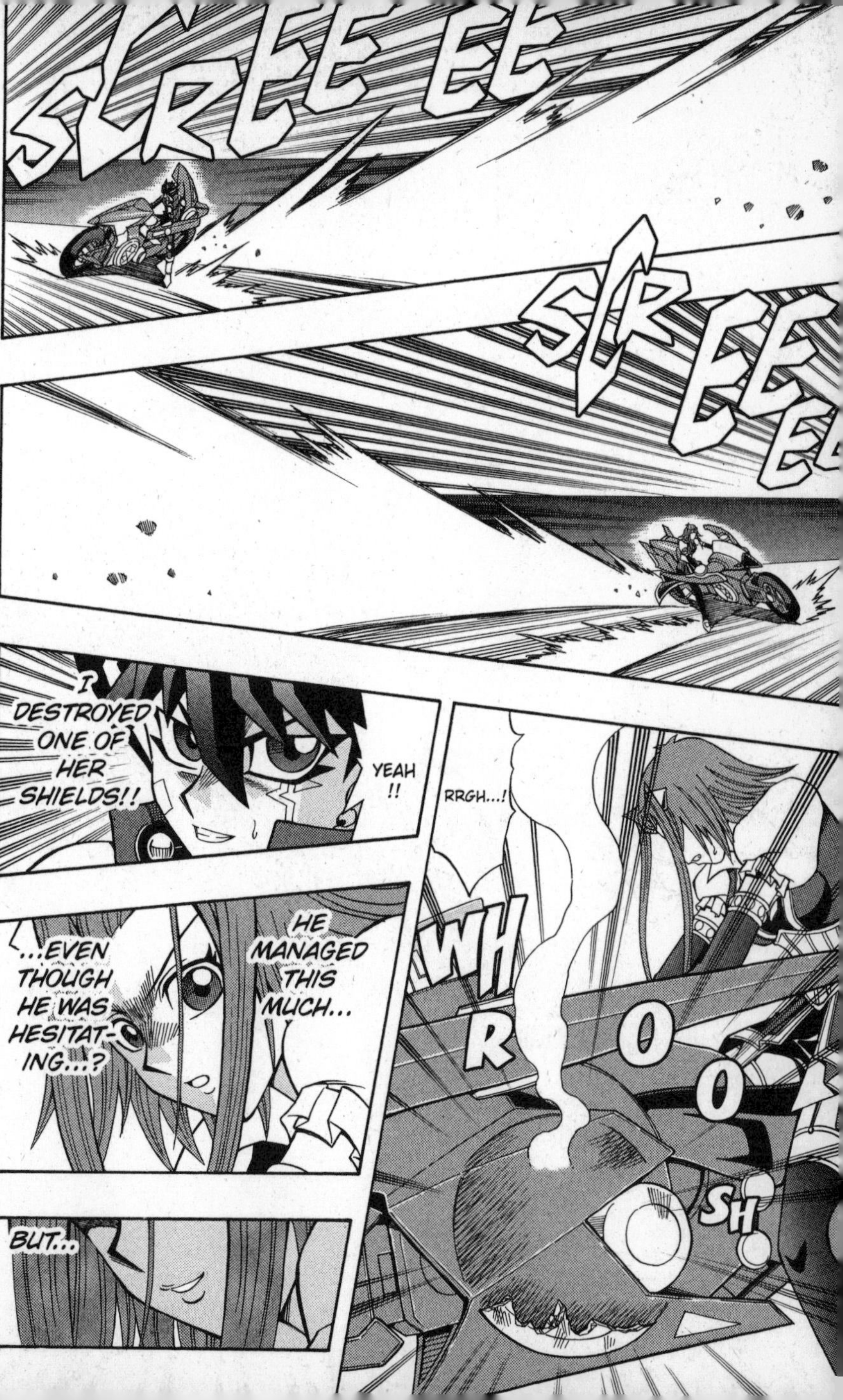
SCREE EE
SCREEEE
RRGH...!
WHROOOSH
I DESTROYED ONE OF HER SHIELDS!!
YEAH!!
HE MANAGED THIS MUCH...
...EVEN THOUGH HE WAS HESITATING...?
BUT...

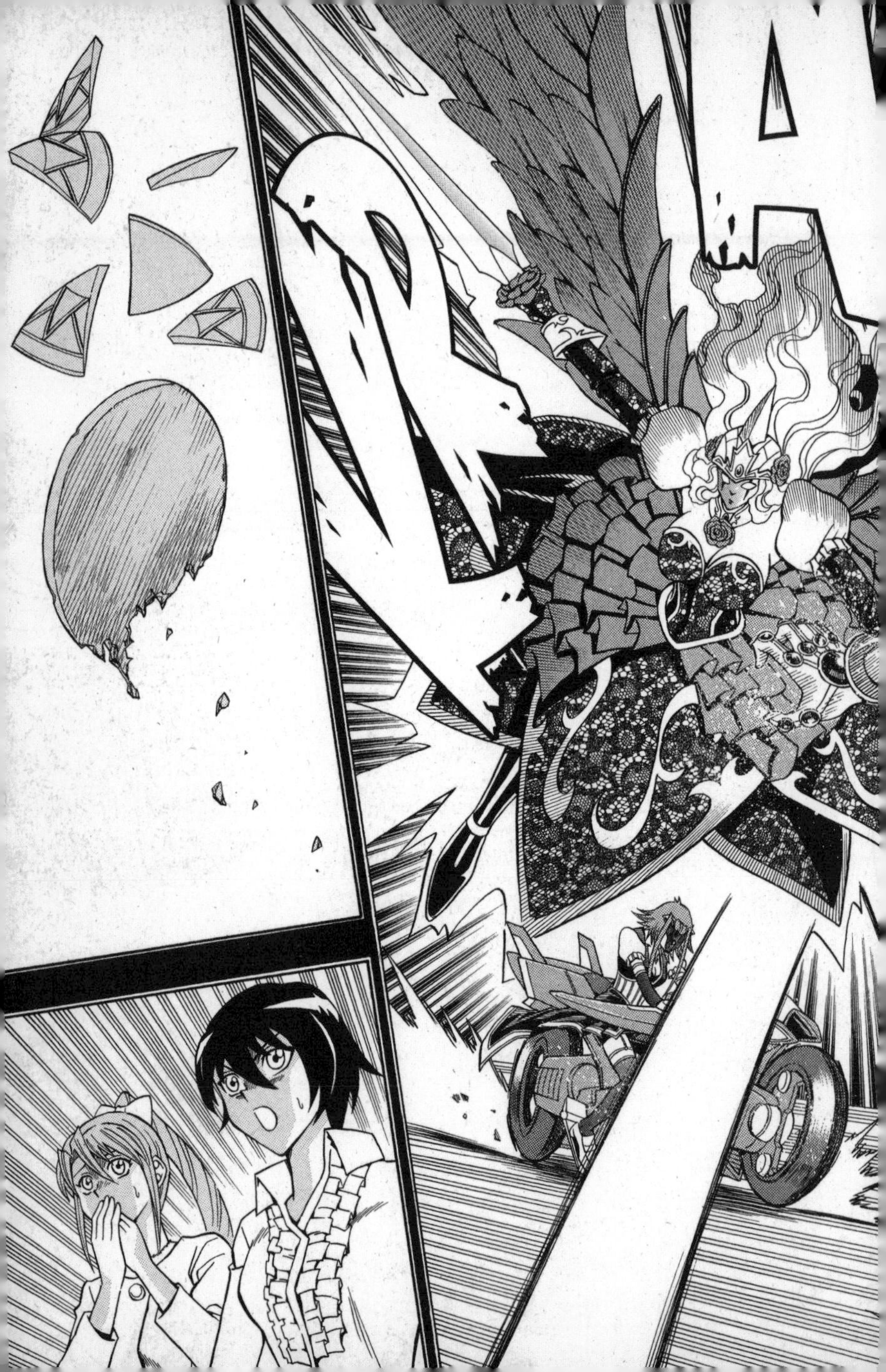

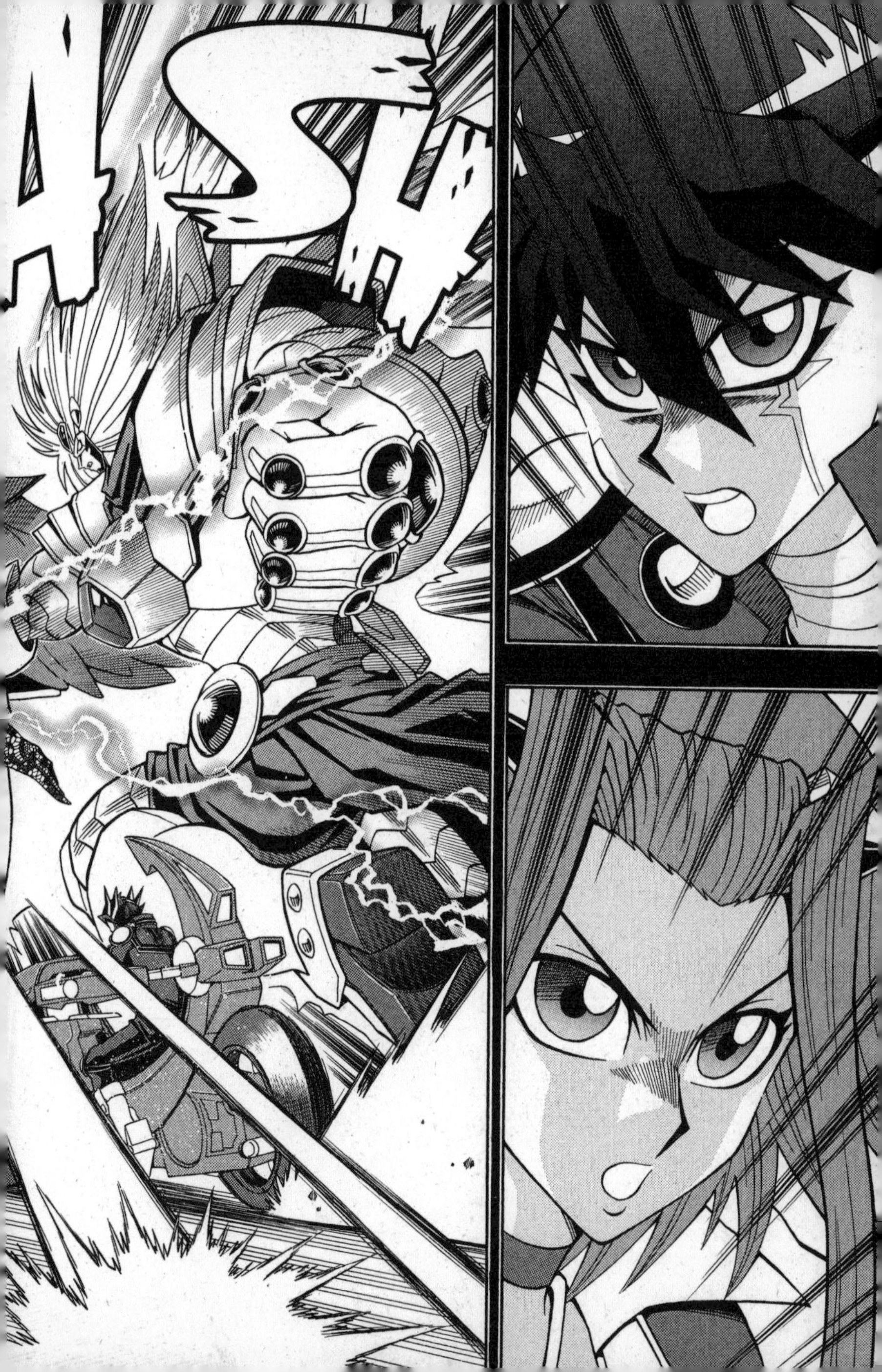
ASH

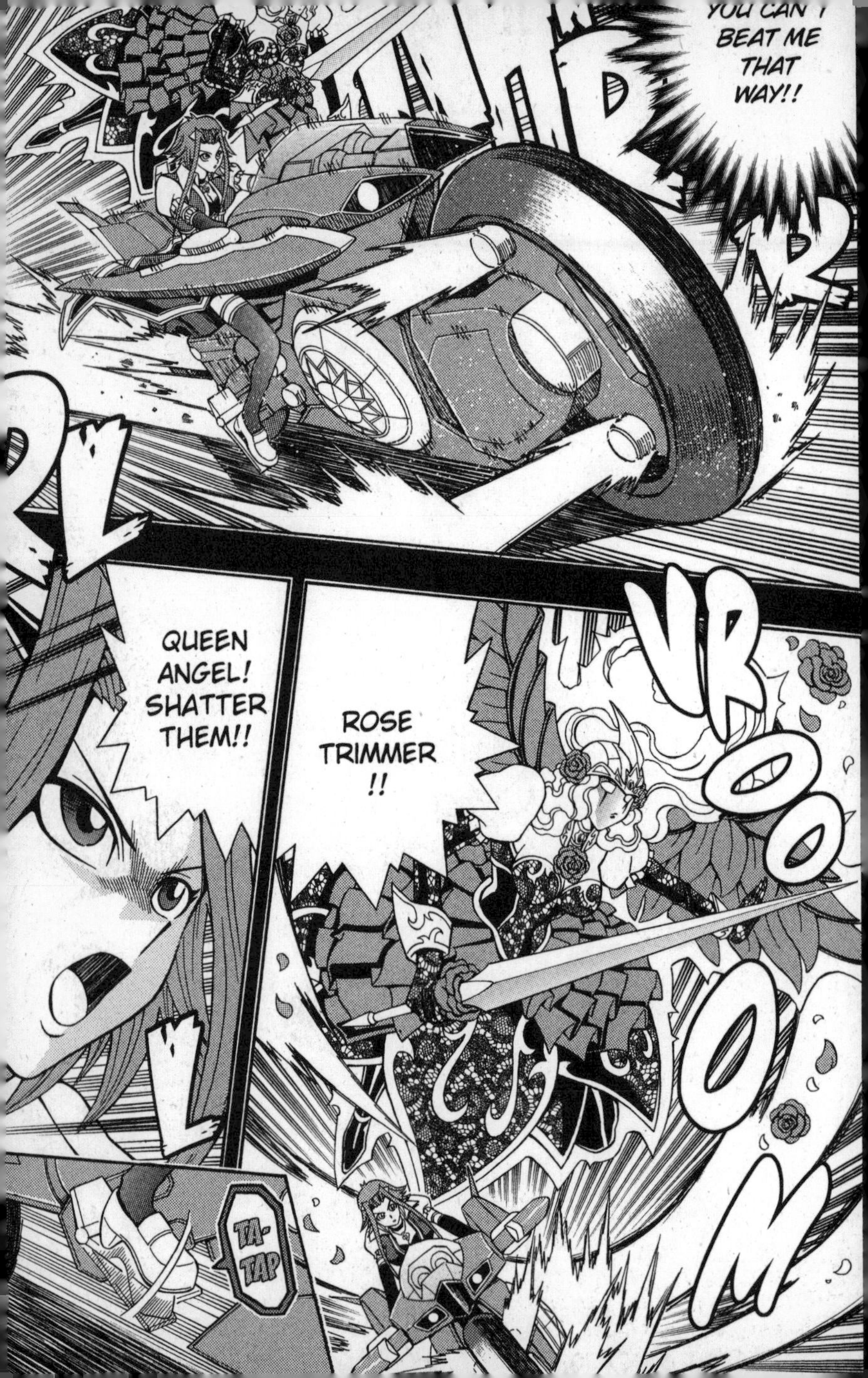
YOU CAN'T BEAT ME THAT WAY!!
VROOOOM
ROSE TRIMMER !!
QUEEN ANGEL! SHATTER THEM!!
TA-TAP

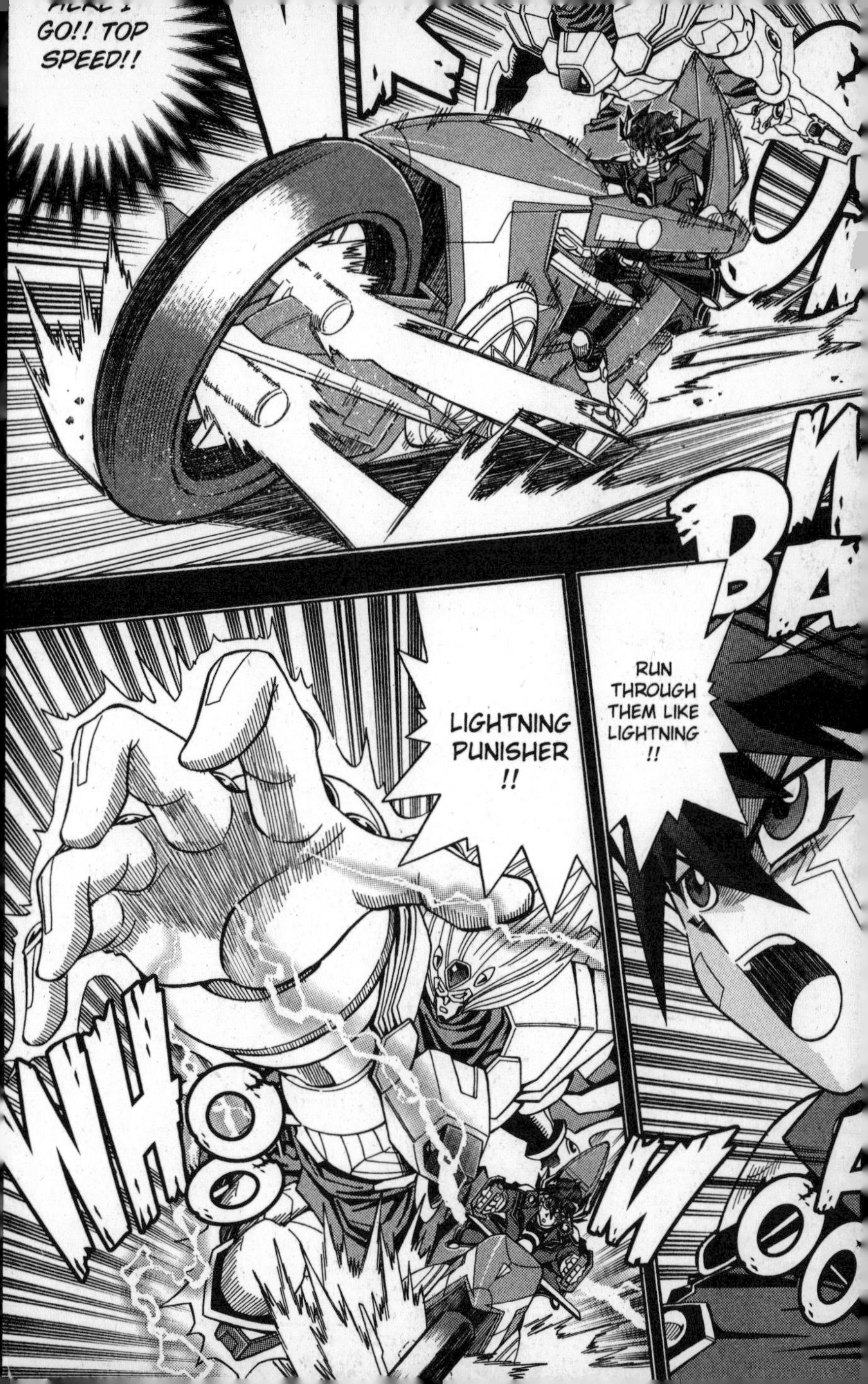
GO!! TOP SPEED!!
RUN THROUGH THEM LIKE LIGHTNING !!
LIGHTNING PUNISHER !!

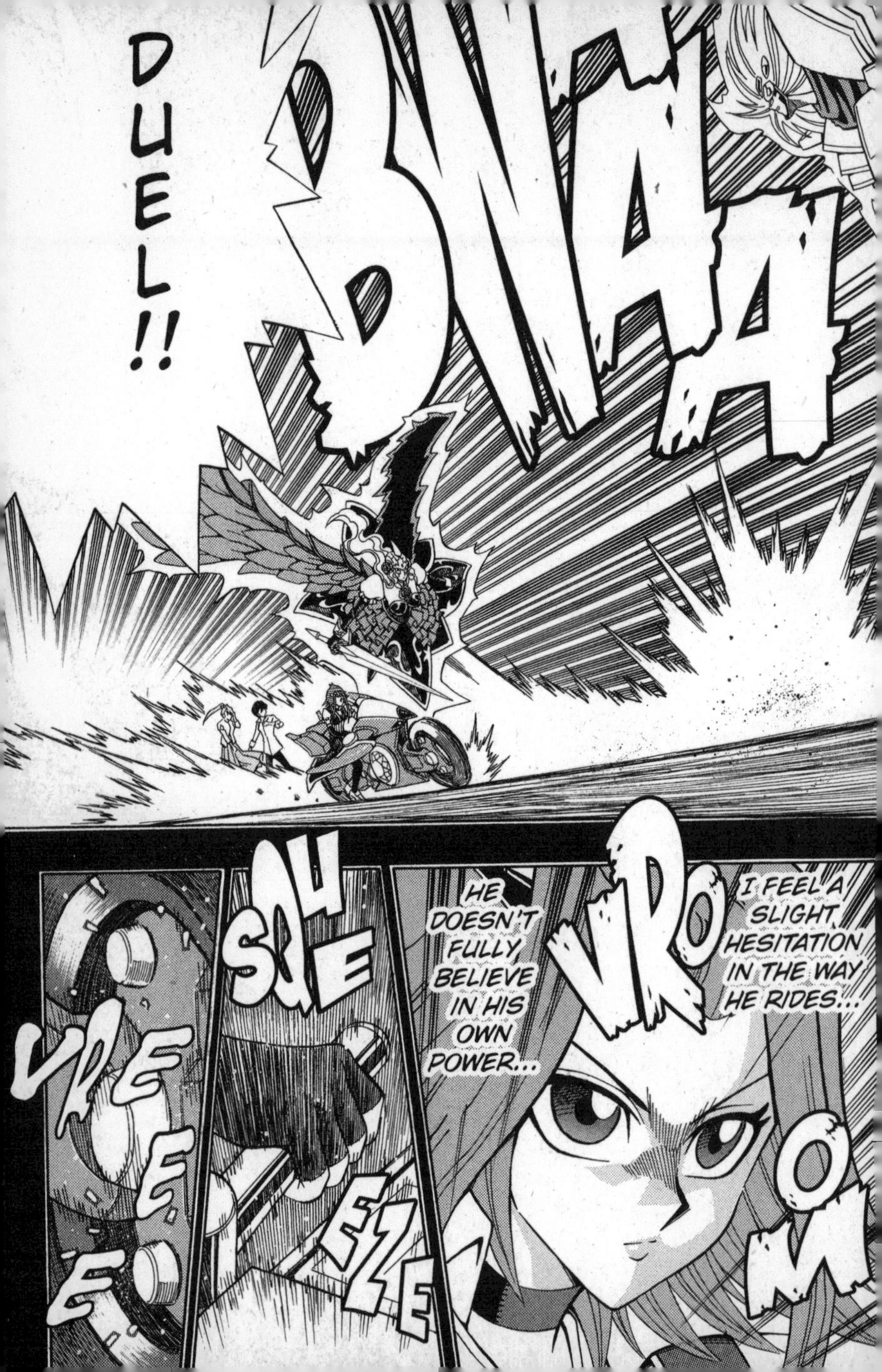
DUEL!!
I FEEL A SLIGHT HESITATION IN THE WAY HE RIDES...
VROOM
HE DOESN'T FULLY BELIEVE IN HIS OWN POWER...
SQUEEZE

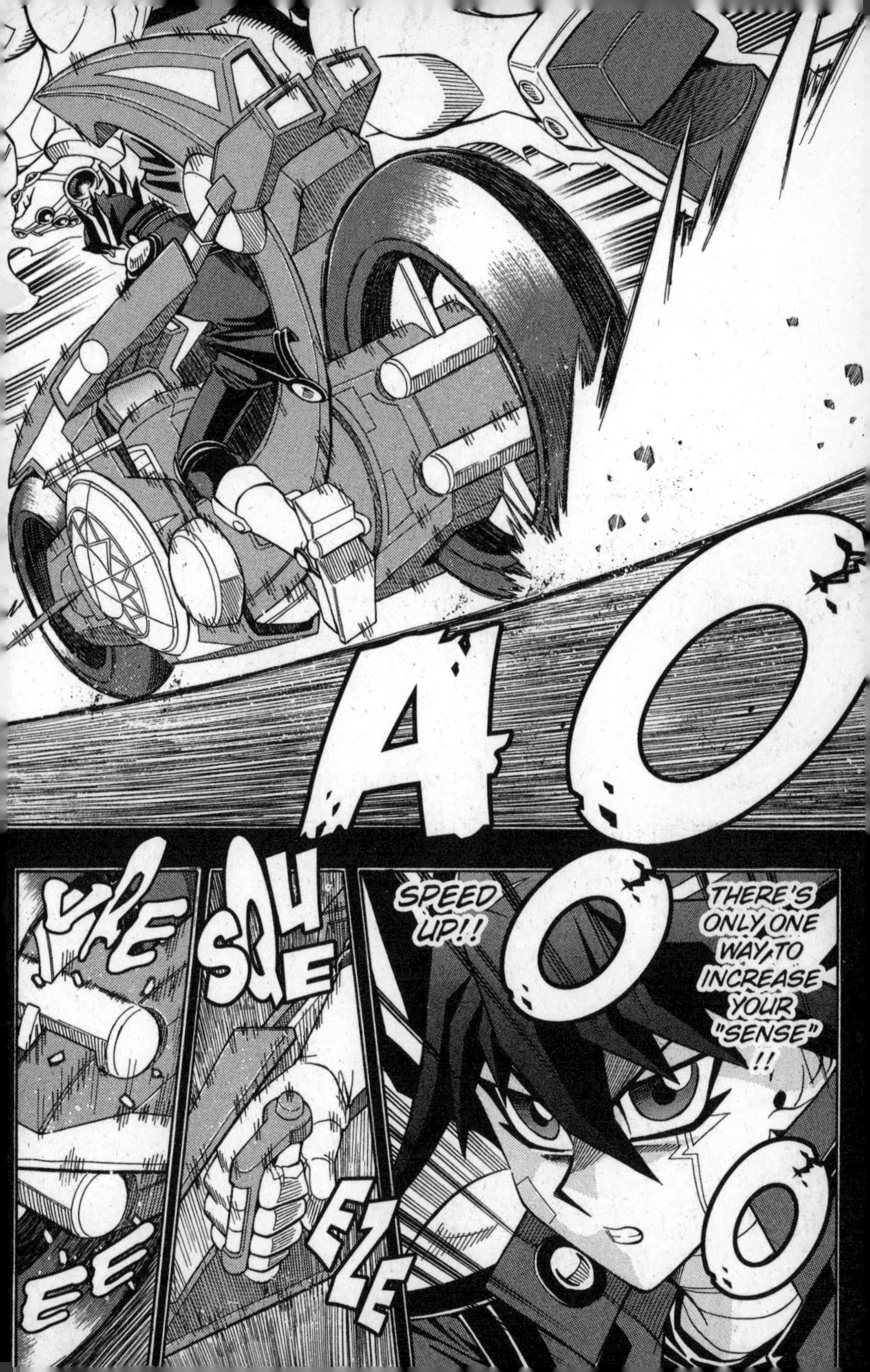

4000
THERE'S ONLY ONE WAY TO INCREASE YOUR "SENSE"!!
SPEED UP!!
SQUEEZE

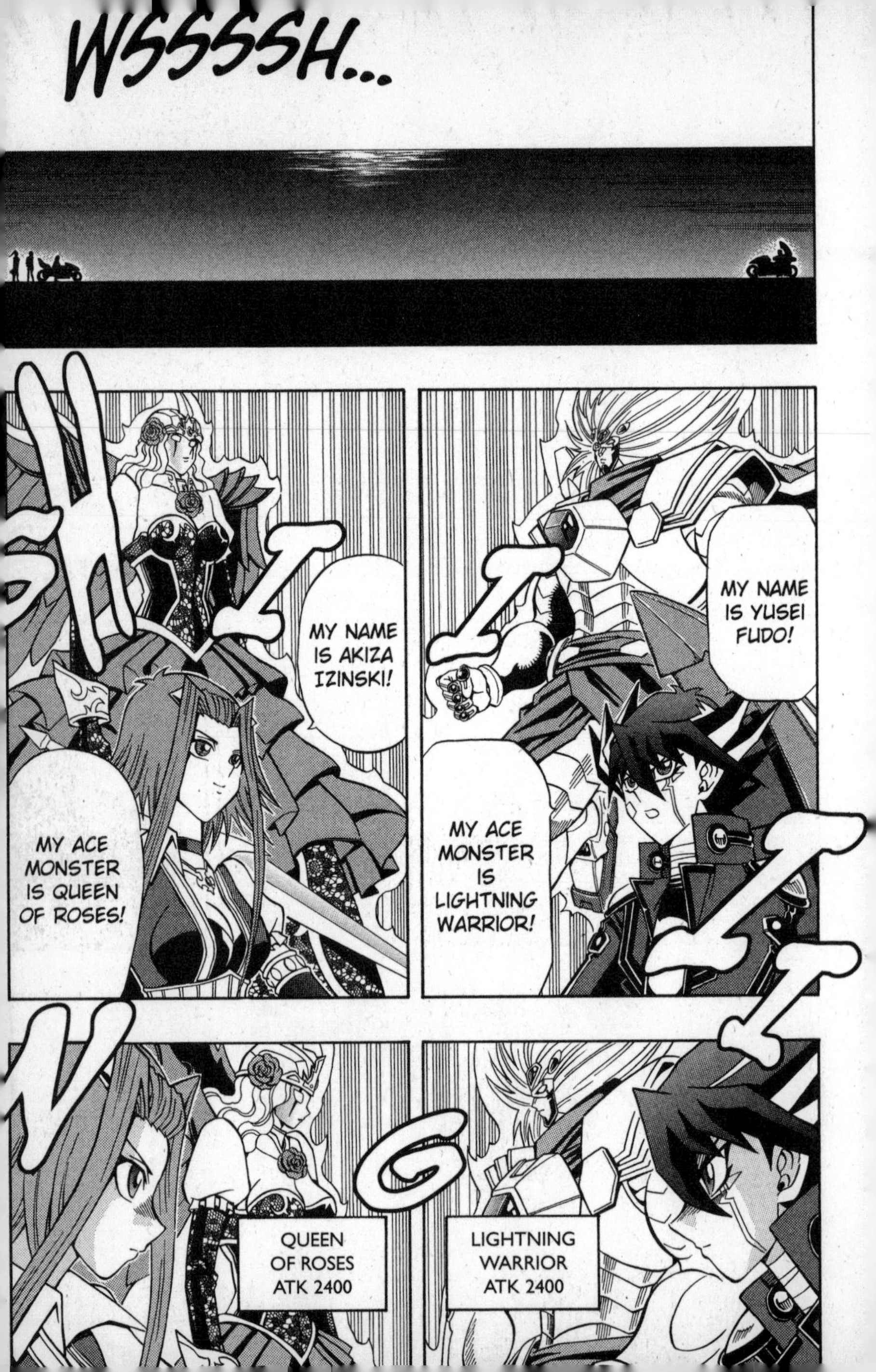
WSSSSH...
MY NAME IS YUSEI FUDO!
MY ACE MONSTER IS LIGHTNING WARRIOR!
MY NAME IS AKIZA IZINSKI!
MY ACE MONSTER IS QUEEN OF ROSES!
LIGHTNING WARRIOR ATK 2400
QUEEN OF ROSES ATK 2400

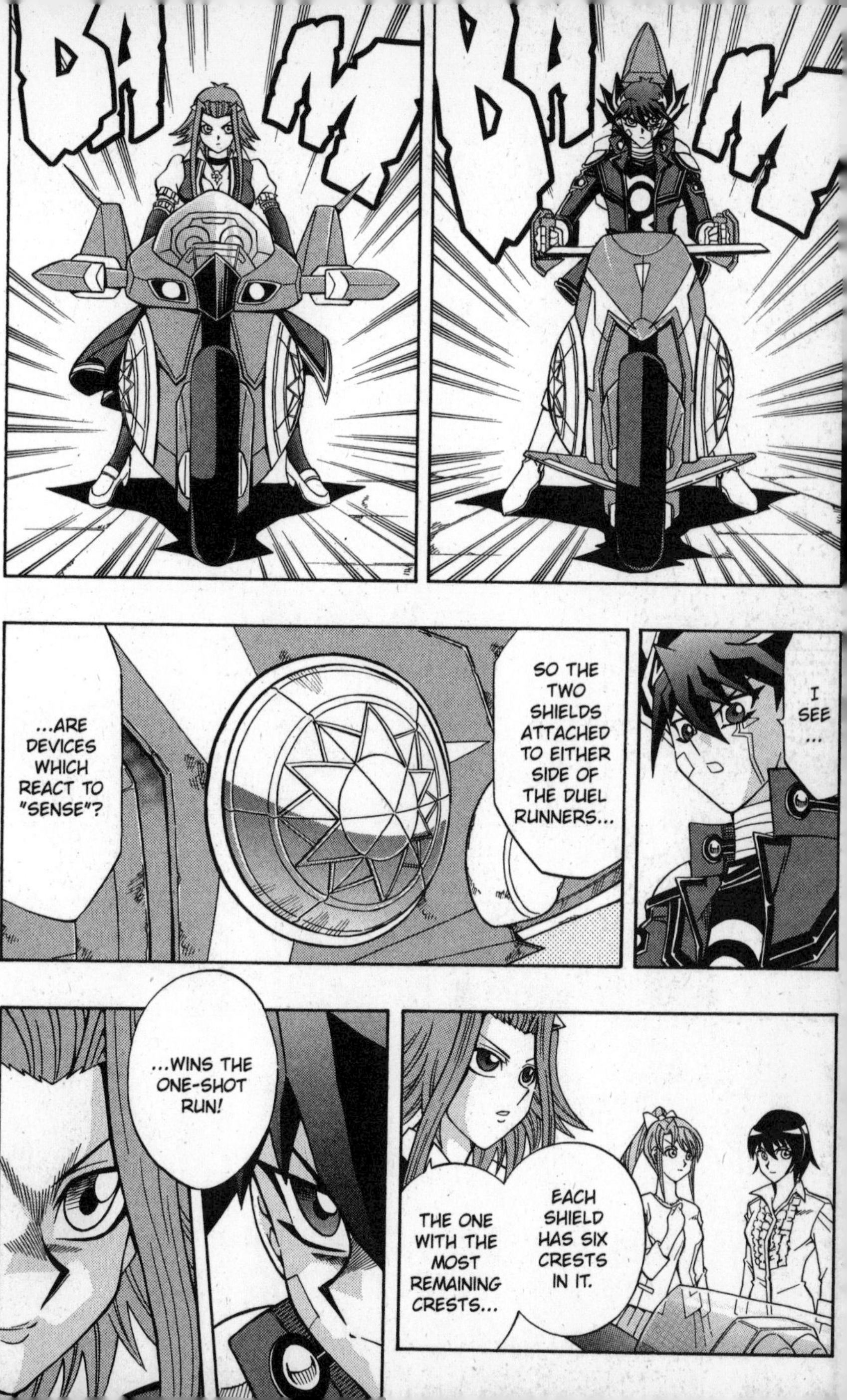
BAM
BAM
I SEE...
SO THE TWO SHIELDS ATTACHED TO EITHER SIDE OF THE DUEL RUNNERS...
...ARE DEVICES WHICH REACT TO "SENSE"?
EACH SHIELD HAS SIX CRESTS IN IT.
THE ONE WITH THE MOST REMAINING CRESTS...
...WINS THE ONE-SHOT RUN!

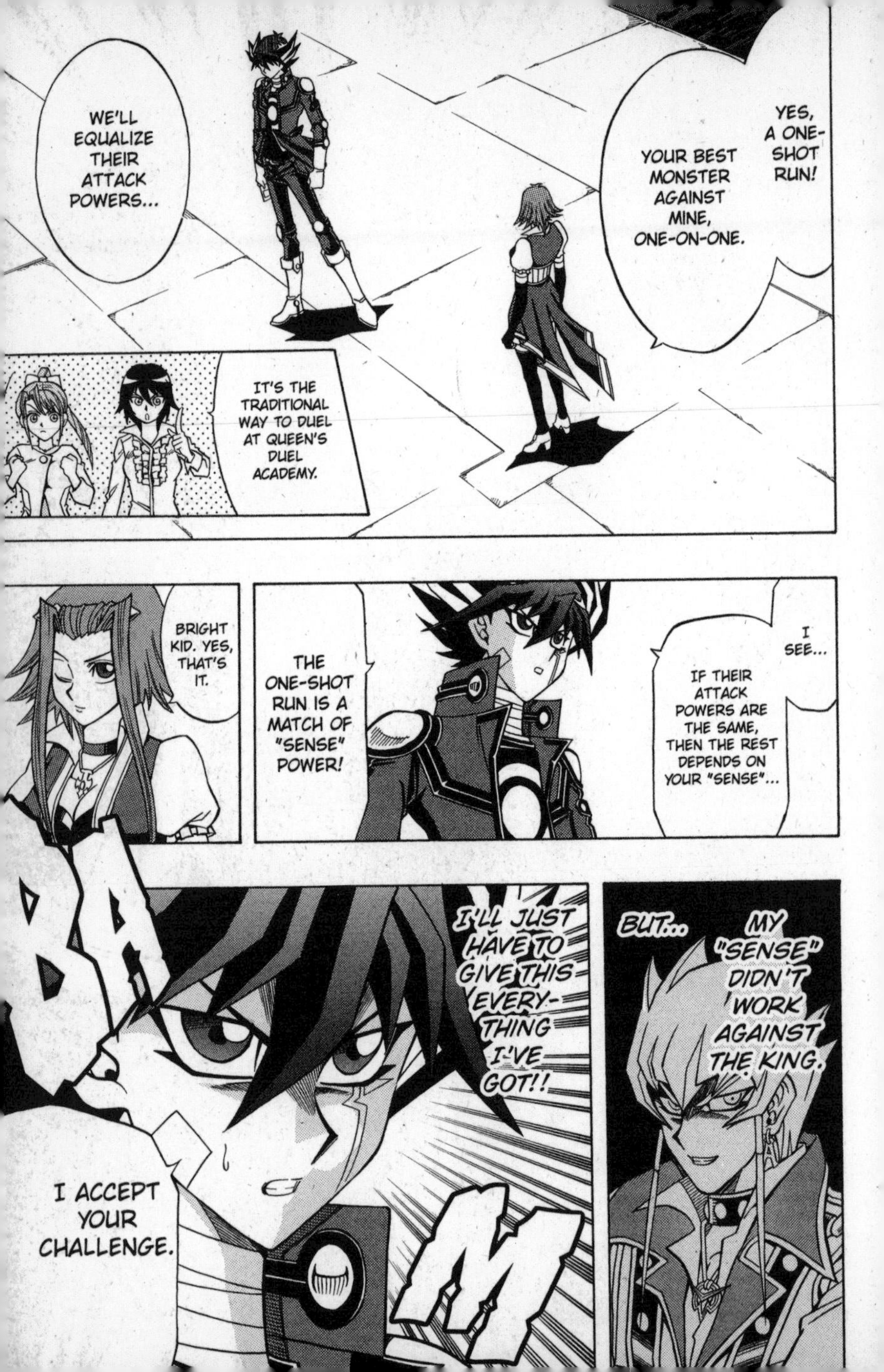
YOUR BEST MONSTER AGAINST MINE, ONE-ON-ONE.
YES, A ONE-SHOT RUN!
WE'LL EQUALIZE THEIR ATTACK POWERS...
IT'S THE TRADITIONAL WAY TO DUEL AT QUEEN'S DUEL ACADEMY.
I SEE...
IF THEIR ATTACK POWERS ARE THE SAME, THEN THE REST DEPENDS ON YOUR "SENSE"...
THE ONE-SHOT RUN IS A MATCH OF "SENSE" POWER!
BRIGHT KID. YES, THAT'S IT.
BUT...
MY "SENSE" DIDN'T WORK AGAINST THE KING.
I'LL JUST HAVE TO GIVE THIS EVERYTHING I'VE GOT!!
I ACCEPT YOUR CHALLENGE.

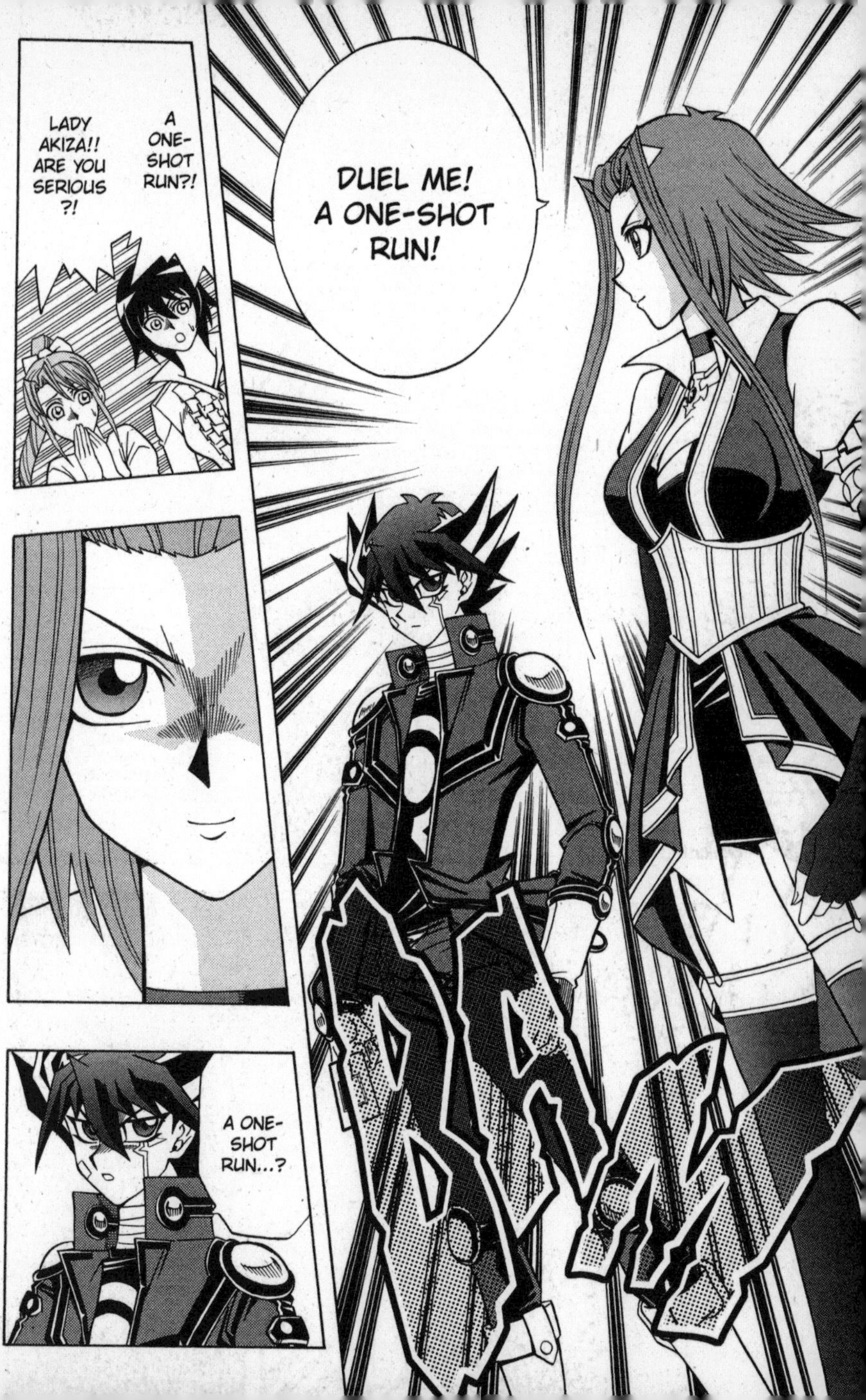
DUEL ME! A ONE-SHOT RUN!
A ONE-SHOT RUN?!
LADY AKIZA!! ARE YOU SERIOUS?!
A ONE-SHOT RUN...?

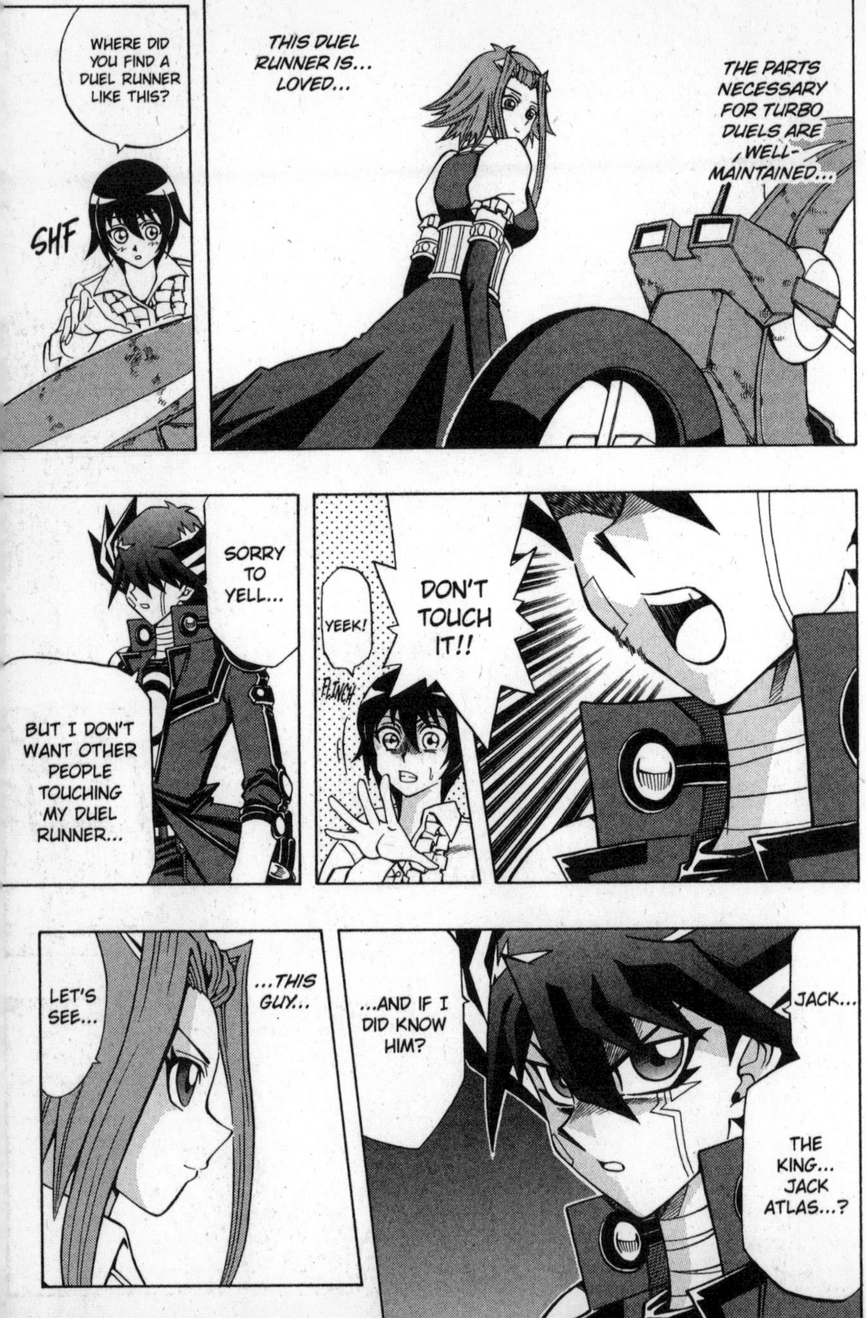
THE PARTS NECESSARY FOR TURBO DUELS ARE WELL-MAINTAINED...
THIS DUEL RUNNER IS... LOVED...
WHERE DID YOU FIND A DUEL RUNNER LIKE THIS?
SHF
DON'T TOUCH IT!!
YEEK!
FLINCH
SORRY TO YELL...
BUT I DON'T WANT OTHER PEOPLE TOUCHING MY DUEL RUNNER...
JACK...
...AND IF I DID KNOW HIM?
THE KING... JACK ATLAS...?
...THIS GUY...
LET'S SEE...

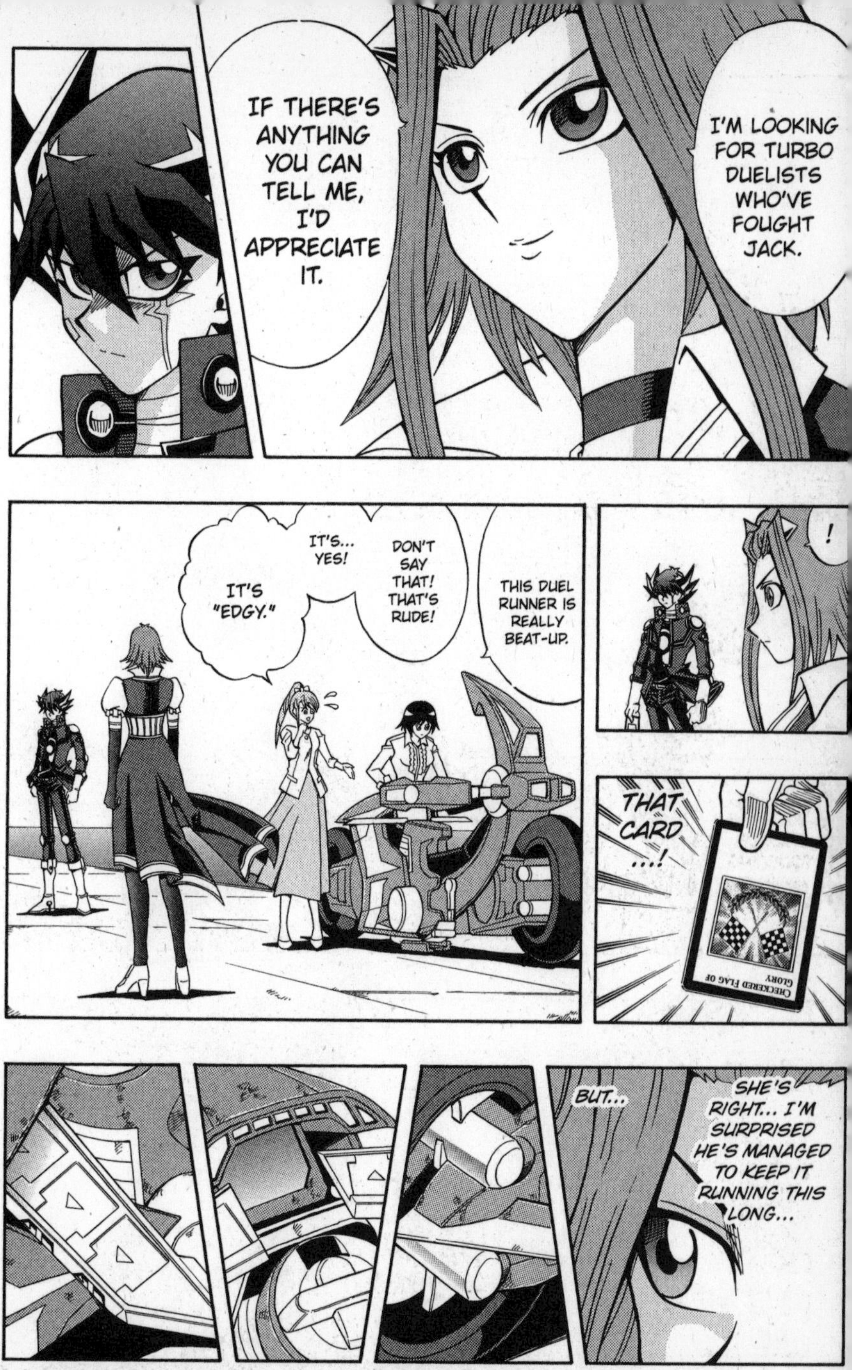
I'M LOOKING FOR TURBO DUELISTS WHO'VE FOUGHT JACK.
IF THERE'S ANYTHING YOU CAN TELL ME, I'D APPRECIATE IT.
!
THAT CARD ...!
CHECKERED FLAG OF GLORY
THIS DUEL RUNNER IS REALLY BEAT-UP.
DON'T SAY THAT! THAT'S RUDE!
IT'S... YES!
IT'S "EDGY."
SHE'S RIGHT... I'M SURPRISED HE'S MANAGED TO KEEP IT RUNNING THIS LONG...
BUT...

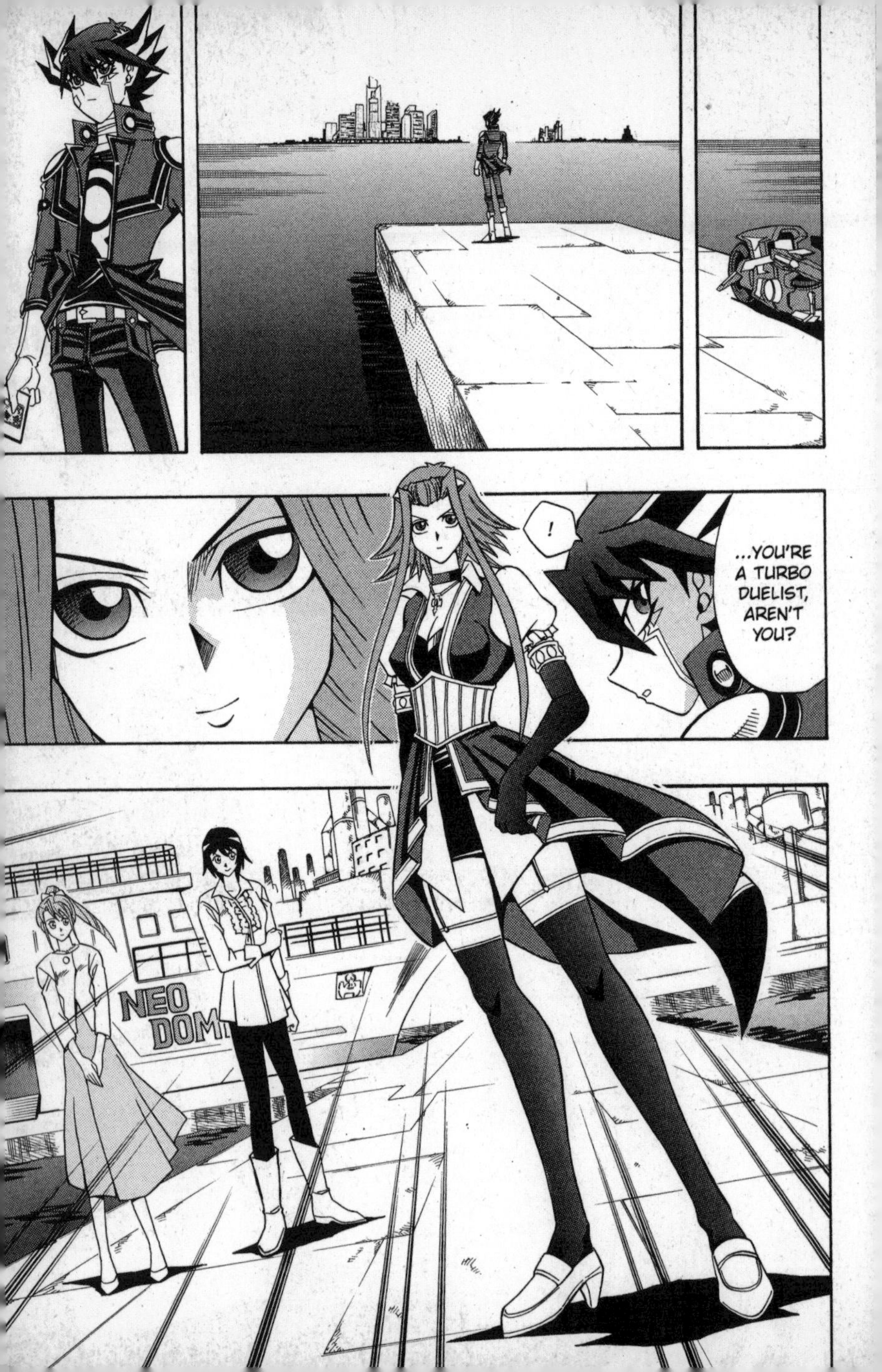
...YOU'RE A TURBO DUELIST, AREN'T YOU?
!
NEO DOM

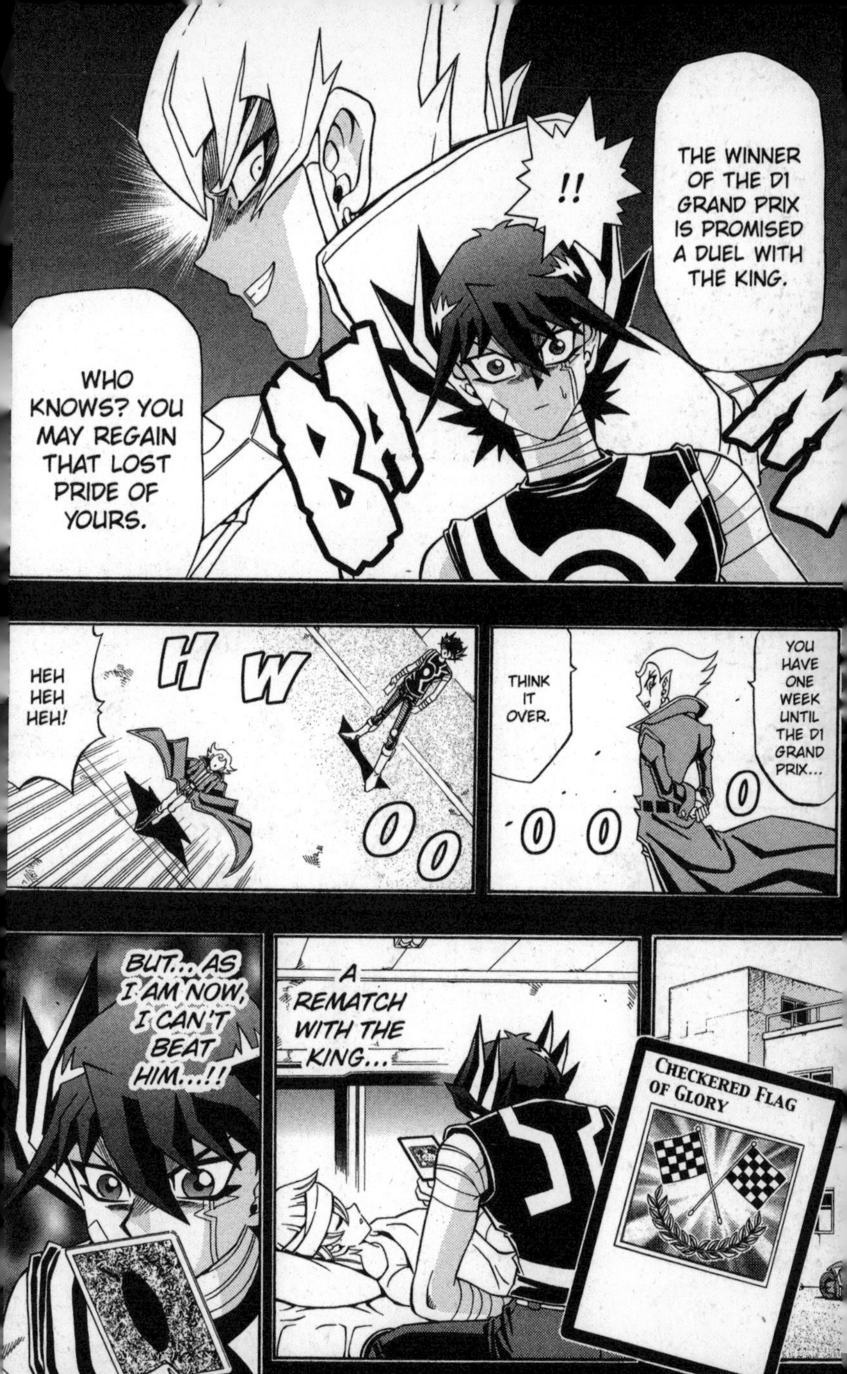
THE WINNER OF THE D1 GRAND PRIX IS PROMISED A DUEL WITH THE KING.
!!
BA
WHO KNOWS? YOU MAY REGAIN THAT LOST PRIDE OF YOURS.
YOU HAVE ONE WEEK UNTIL THE D1 GRAND PRIX...
THINK IT OVER.
HEH HEH HEH!
HW
CHECKERED FLAG OF GLORY
A REMATCH WITH THE KING...
BUT... AS I AM NOW, I CAN'T BEAT HIM...!!

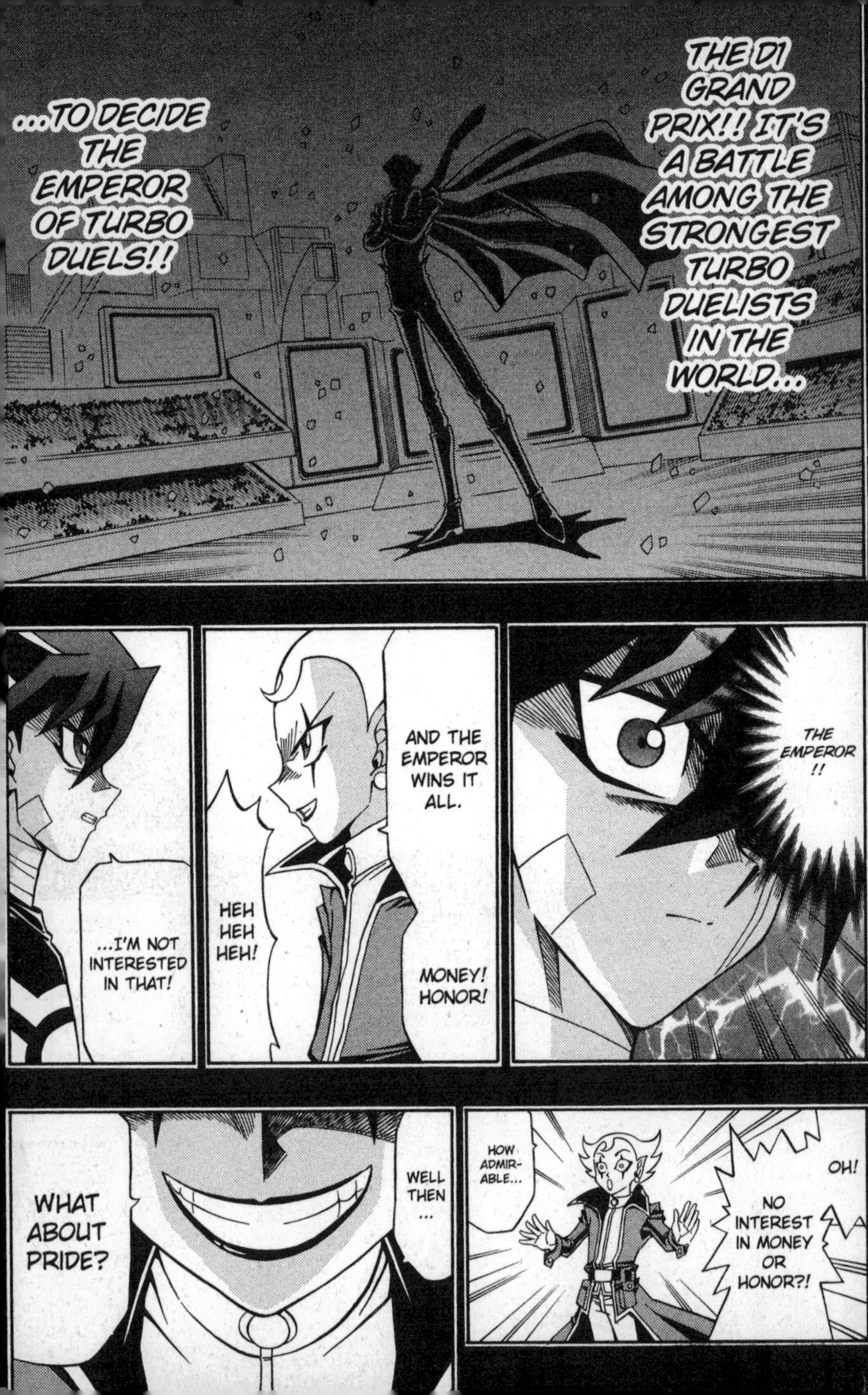
THE D1 GRAND PRIX!! IT'S A BATTLE AMONG THE STRONGEST TURBO DUELISTS IN THE WORLD...
...TO DECIDE THE EMPEROR OF TURBO DUELS!!
THE EMPEROR!!
AND THE EMPEROR WINS IT ALL.
MONEY! HONOR!
HEH HEH HEH!
...I'M NOT INTERESTED IN THAT!
OH!
NO INTEREST IN MONEY OR HONOR?!
HOW ADMIR-ABLE...
WELL THEN...
WHAT ABOUT PRIDE?

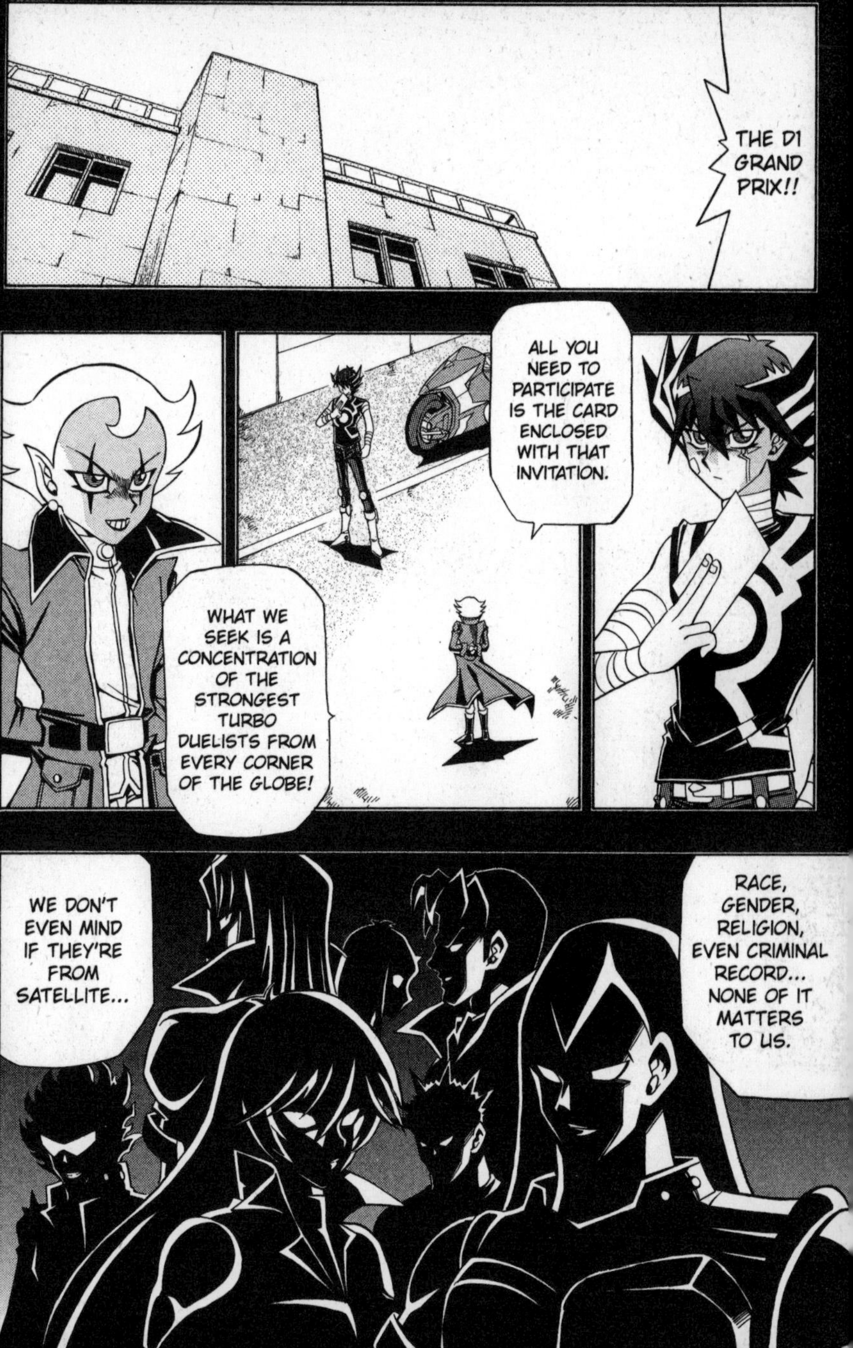
THE D1 GRAND PRIX!!
ALL YOU NEED TO PARTICIPATE IS THE CARD ENCLOSED WITH THAT INVITATION.
WHAT WE SEEK IS A CONCENTRATION OF THE STRONGEST TURBO DUELISTS FROM EVERY CORNER OF THE GLOBE!
RACE, GENDER, RELIGION, EVEN CRIMINAL RECORD... NONE OF IT MATTERS TO US.
WE DON'T EVEN MIND IF THEY'RE FROM SATELLITE...

RIDE-08

ONE-SHOT RUN!!

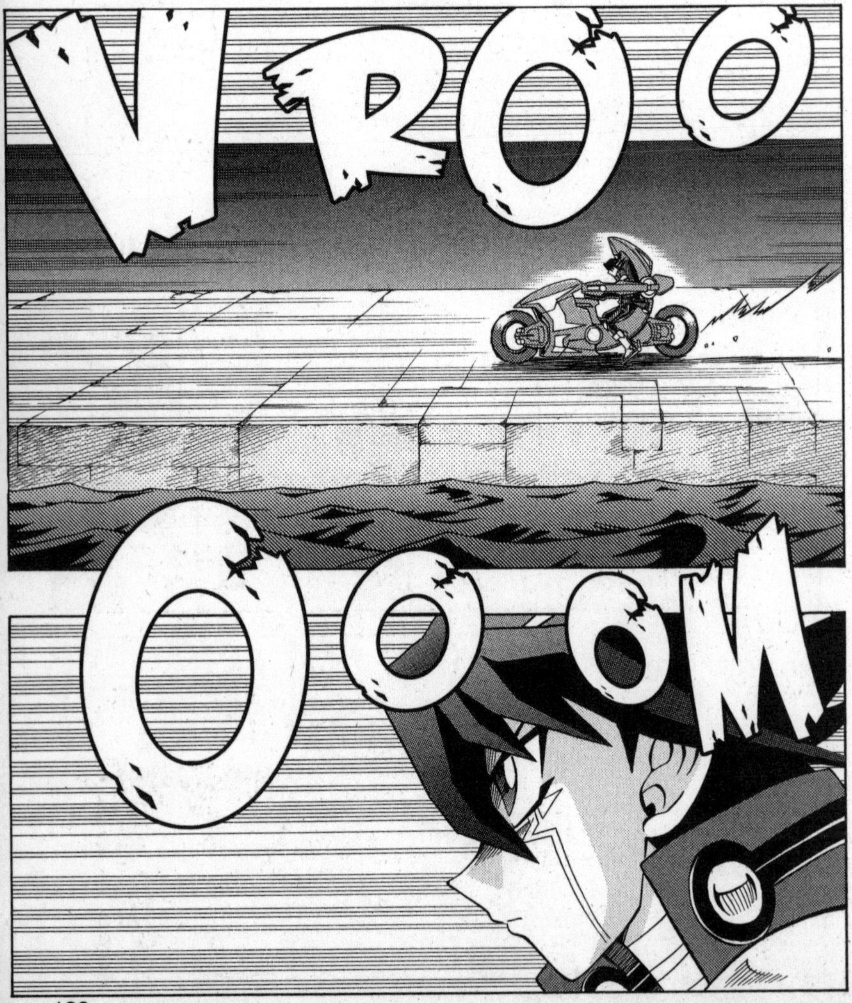
VROOOOOOM

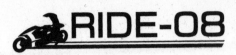

5D's TRACKS

THE 7TH

BY SATOMASA

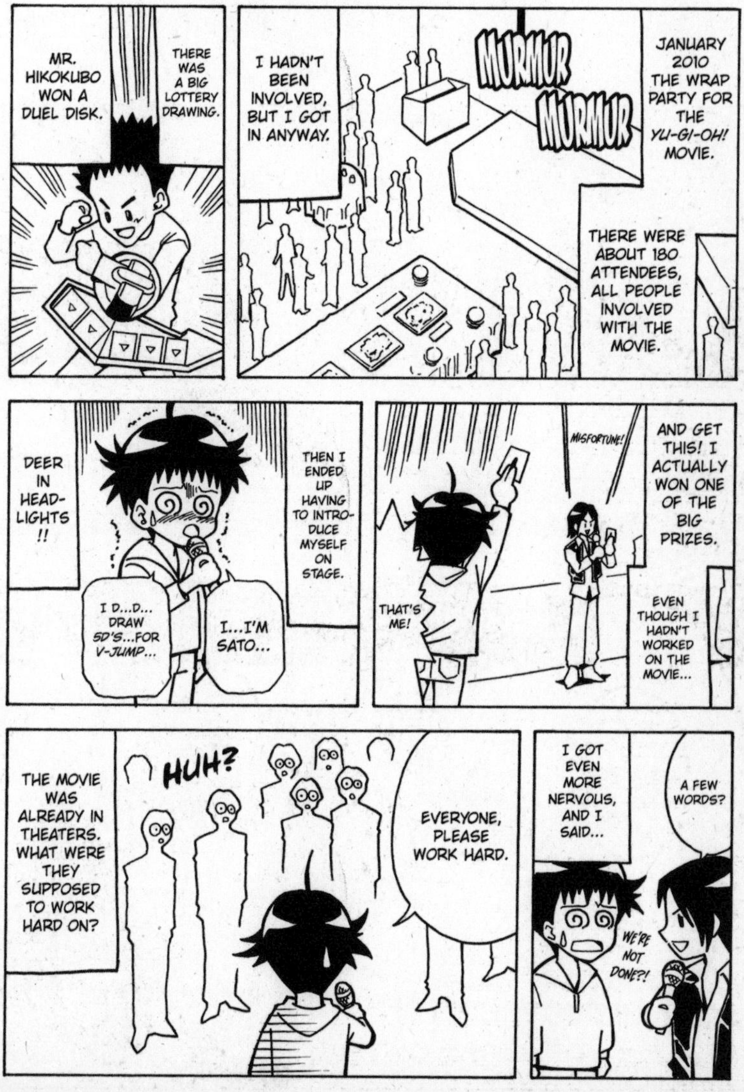

JANUARY 2010 THE WRAP PARTY FOR THE YU-GI-OH! MOVIE.
MURMUR
MURMUR
I HADN'T BEEN INVOLVED, BUT I GOT IN ANYWAY.
THERE WERE ABOUT 180 ATTENDEES, ALL PEOPLE INVOLVED WITH THE MOVIE.
THERE WAS A BIG LOTTERY DRAWING.
MR. HIKOKUBO WON A DUEL DISK.
AND GET THIS! I ACTUALLY WON ONE OF THE BIG PRIZES.
MISFORTUNE!
EVEN THOUGH I HADN'T WORKED ON THE MOVIE...
THAT'S ME!
THEN I ENDED UP HAVING TO INTRODUCE MYSELF ON STAGE.
DEER IN HEADLIGHTS!!
I...I'M SATO...
I D...D... DRAW 5D'S...FOR V-JUMP...
A FEW WORDS?
I GOT EVEN MORE NERVOUS, AND I SAID...
WE'RE NOT DONE?!
EVERYONE, PLEASE WORK HARD.
HUH?
THE MOVIE WAS ALREADY IN THEATERS. WHAT WERE THEY SUPPOSED TO WORK HARD ON?

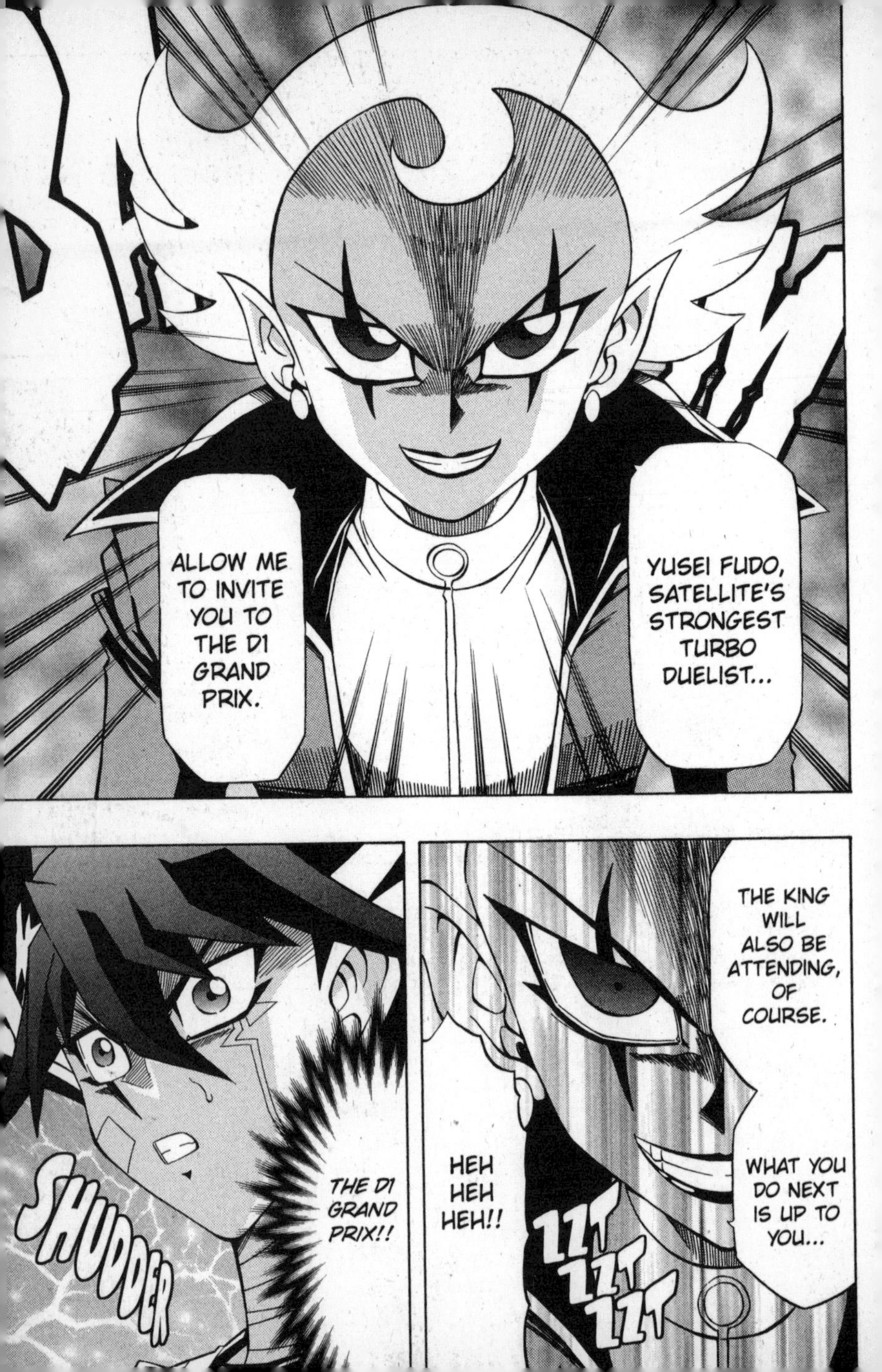
YUSEI FUDO, SATELLITE'S STRONGEST TURBO DUELIST...
ALLOW ME TO INVITE YOU TO THE D1 GRAND PRIX.
THE KING WILL ALSO BE ATTENDING, OF COURSE.
WHAT YOU DO NEXT IS UP TO YOU...
ZZZT ZZZT ZZZT
HEH HEH HEH!!
THE D1 GRAND PRIX!!
SHUDDER

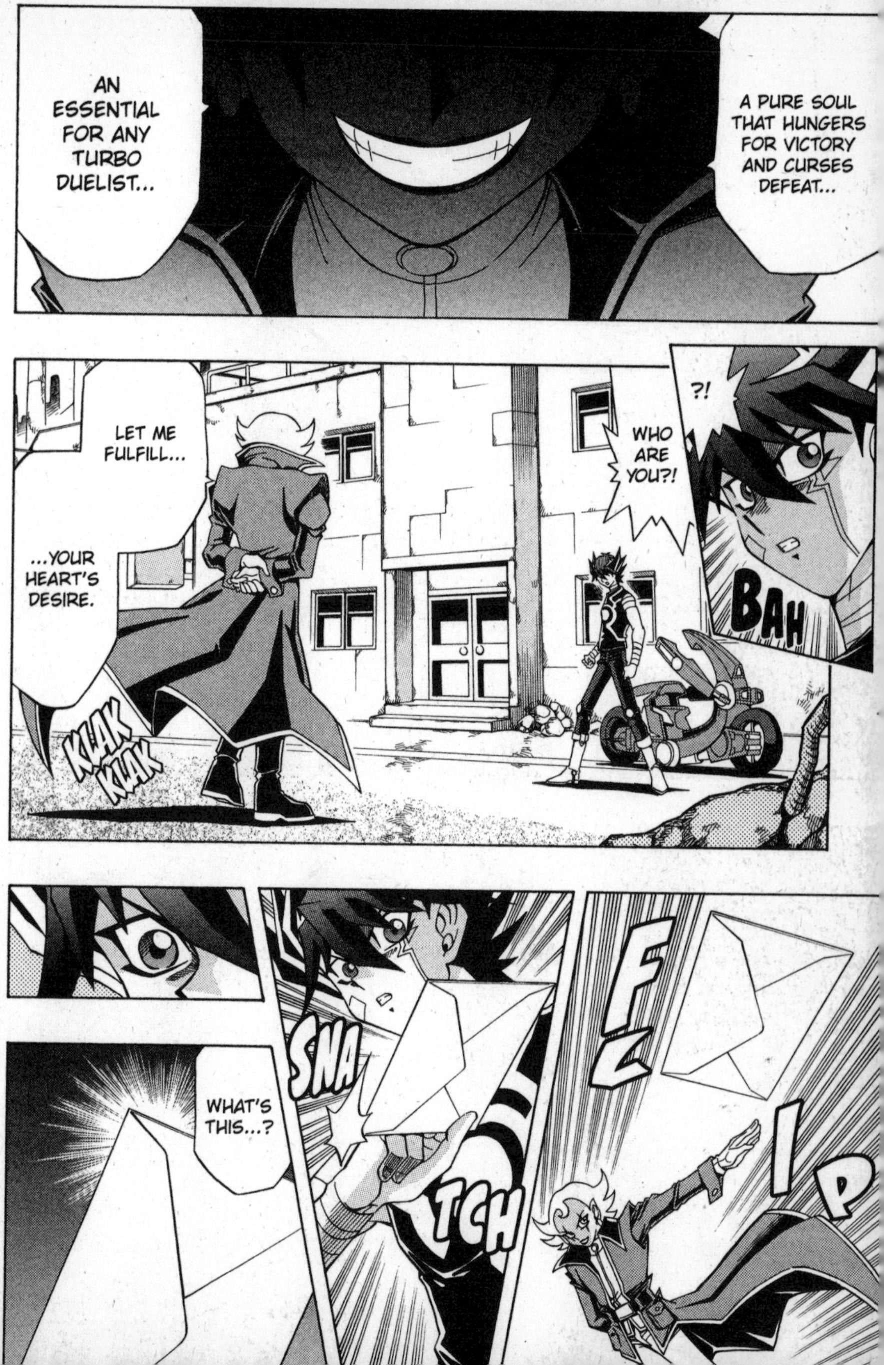
A PURE SOUL THAT HUNGERS FOR VICTORY AND CURSES DEFEAT...
AN ESSENTIAL FOR ANY TURBO DUELIST...
?!
BAH
WHO ARE YOU?!
LET ME FULFILL...
...YOUR HEART'S DESIRE.
KLAK KLAK
FLIP
SNATCH
WHAT'S THIS...?

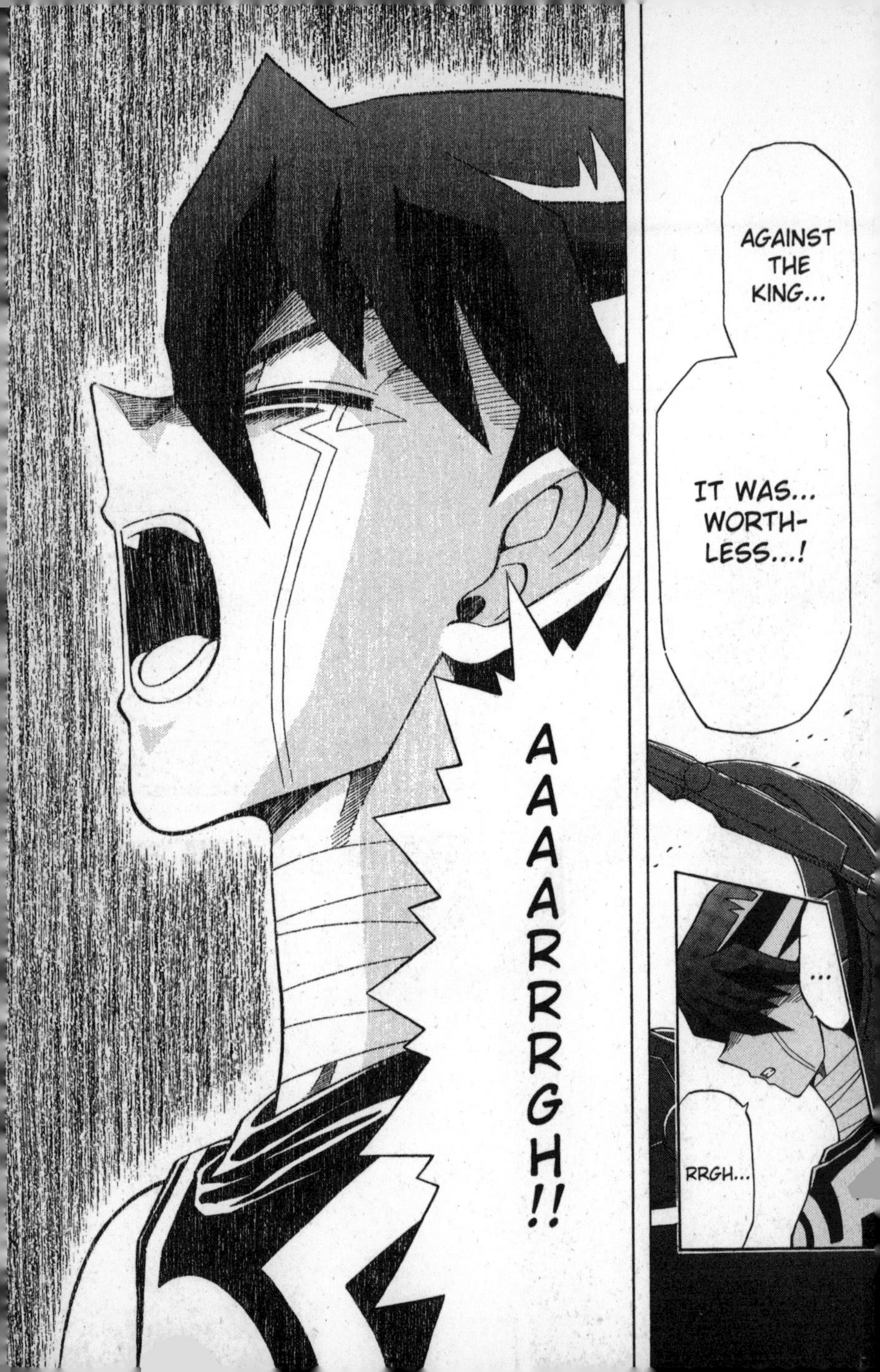
AGAINST THE KING...
IT WAS... WORTH-LESS...!
...
RRGH...
AAAARRRGH!!

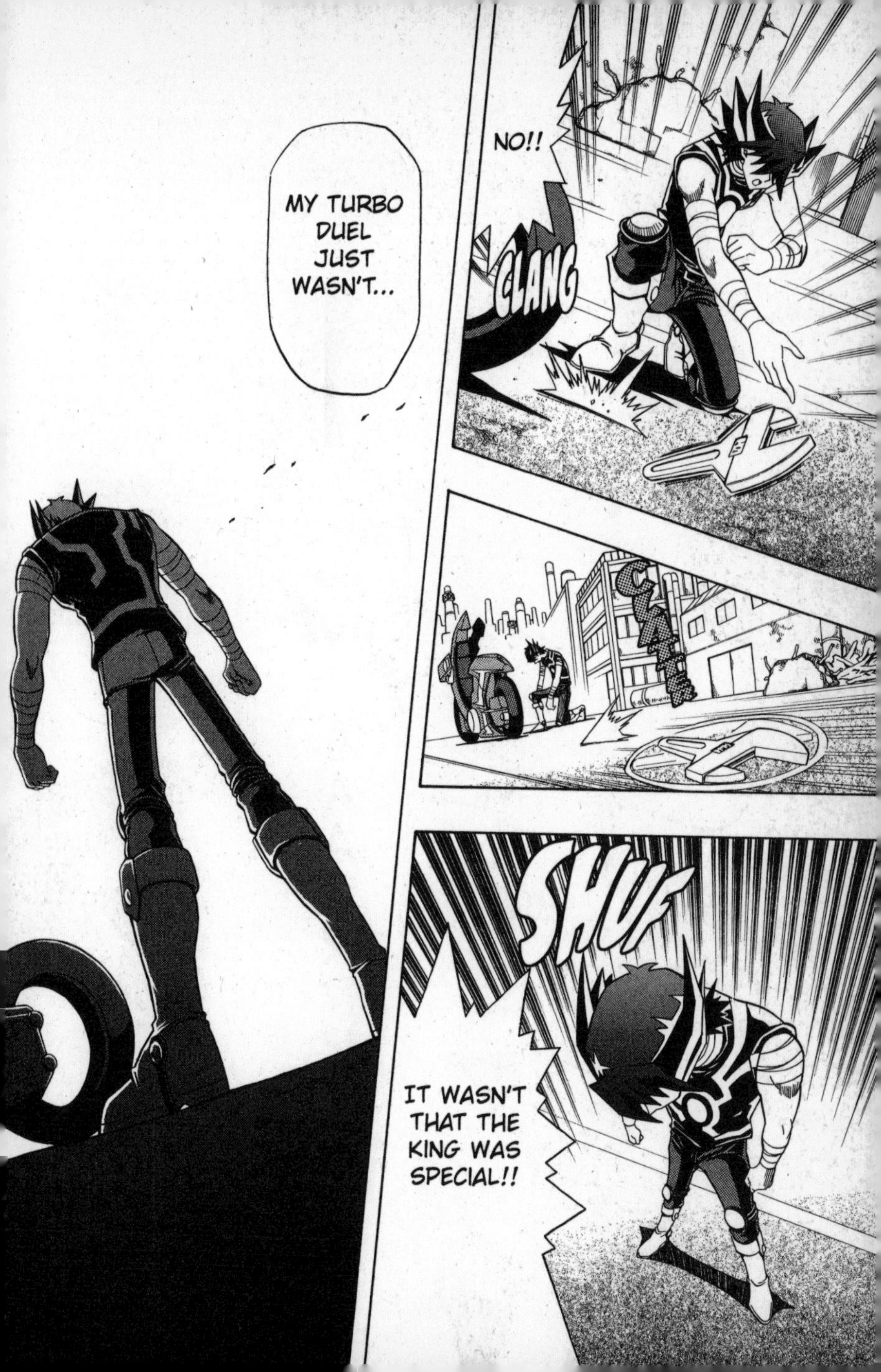
NO!!
CLANG
SHUF
IT WASN'T THAT THE KING WAS SPECIAL!!
MY TURBO DUEL JUST WASN'T...

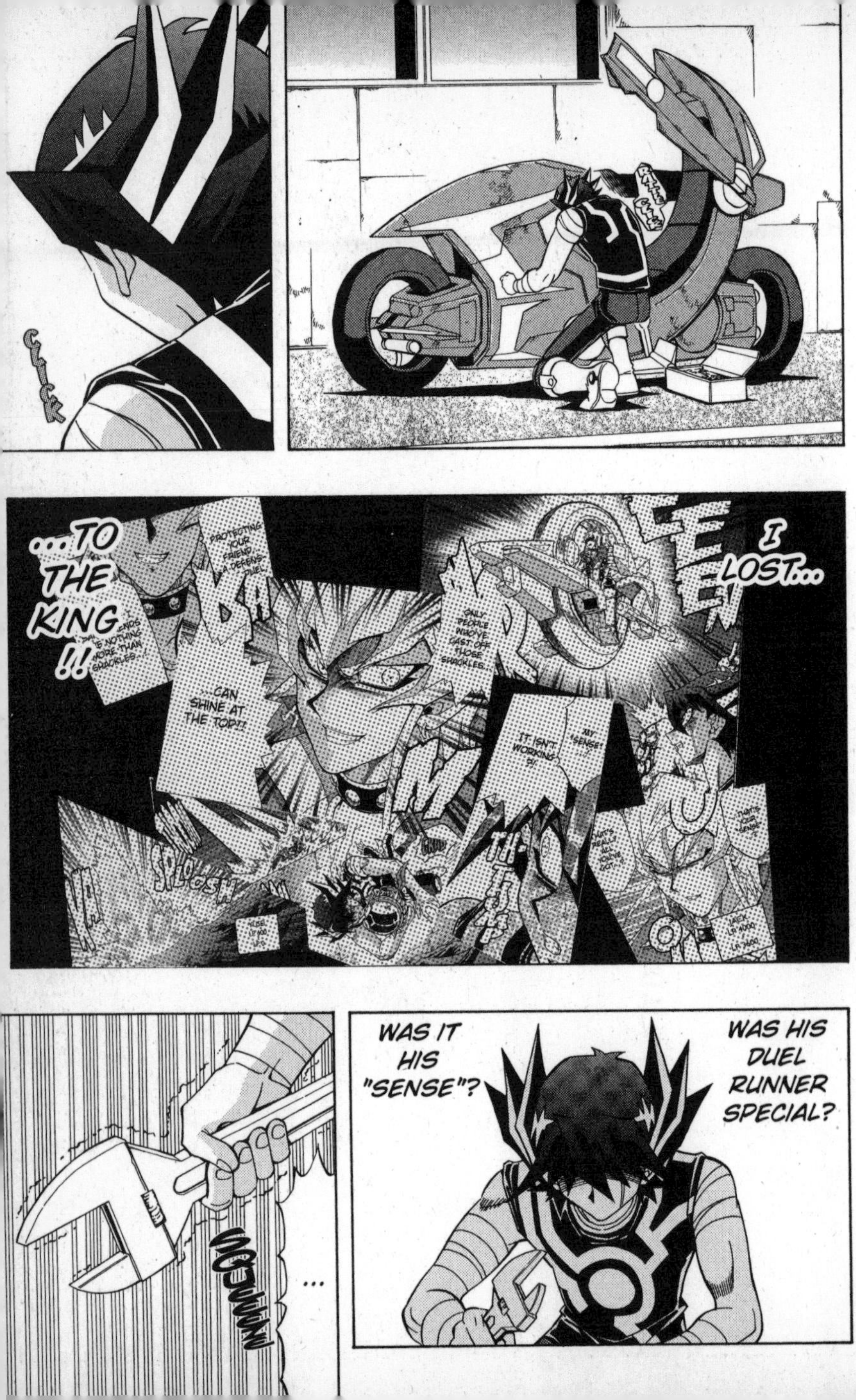
CLICK
I LOST...
...THAT'S YOUR "SENSE"?
THAT'S REALLY ALL YOU'VE GOT...?
MY "SENSE"
IT ISN'T WORKING?!
ONLY PEOPLE WHO'VE CAST OFF THOSE SHACKLES...
...CAN SHINE AT THE TOP!!
PROTECTING YOUR FRIEND... A DEFENSIVE DUEL.
IS NOTHING MORE THAN SHACKLES...!
...TO THE KING!!
SPLOOSH
WAS HIS DUEL RUNNER SPECIAL?
WAS IT HIS "SENSE"?
...

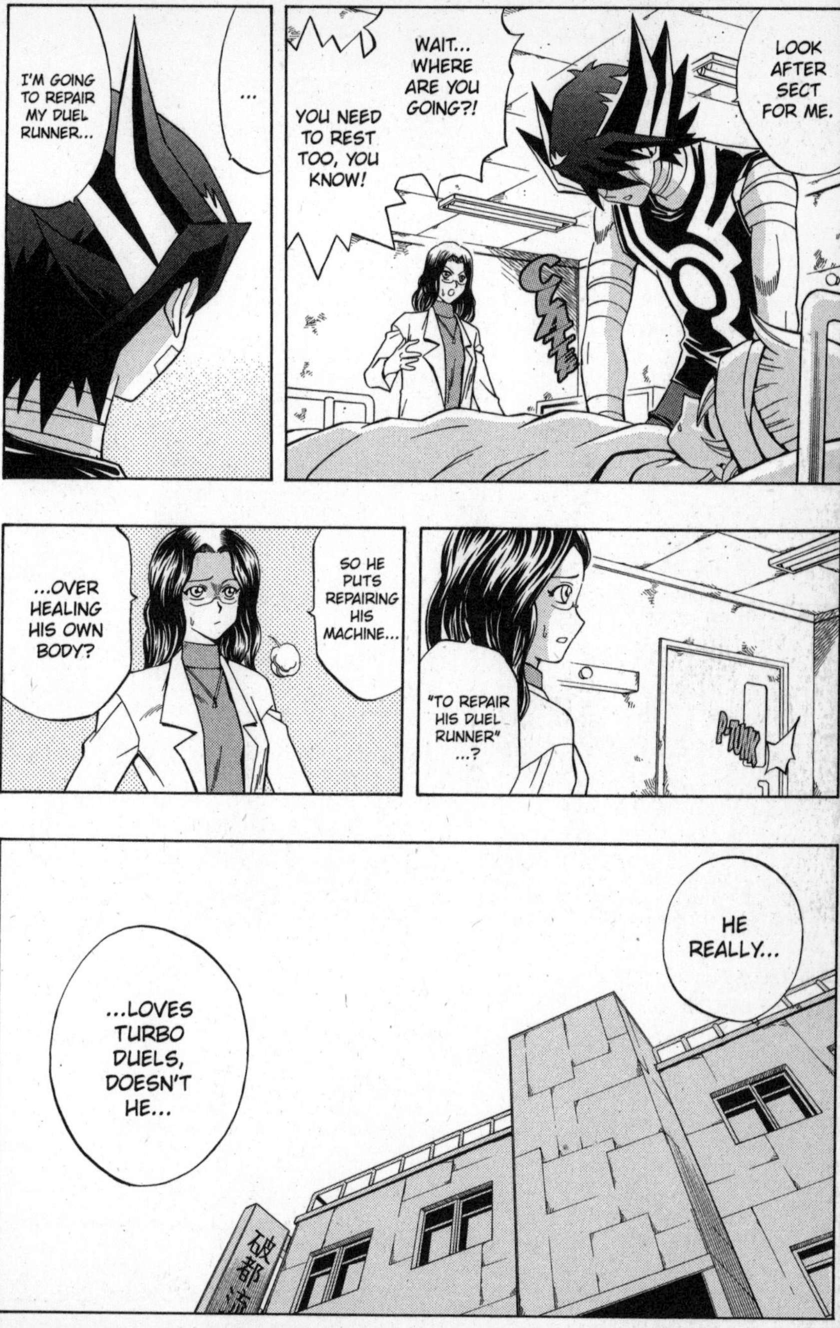
LOOK AFTER SECT FOR ME.
WAIT... WHERE ARE YOU GOING?!
YOU NEED TO REST TOO, YOU KNOW!
...
I'M GOING TO REPAIR MY DUEL RUNNER...
"TO REPAIR HIS DUEL RUNNER" ...?
P-TUNK
SO HE PUTS REPAIRING HIS MACHINE...
...OVER HEALING HIS OWN BODY?
HE REALLY...
...LOVES TURBO DUELS, DOESN'T HE...

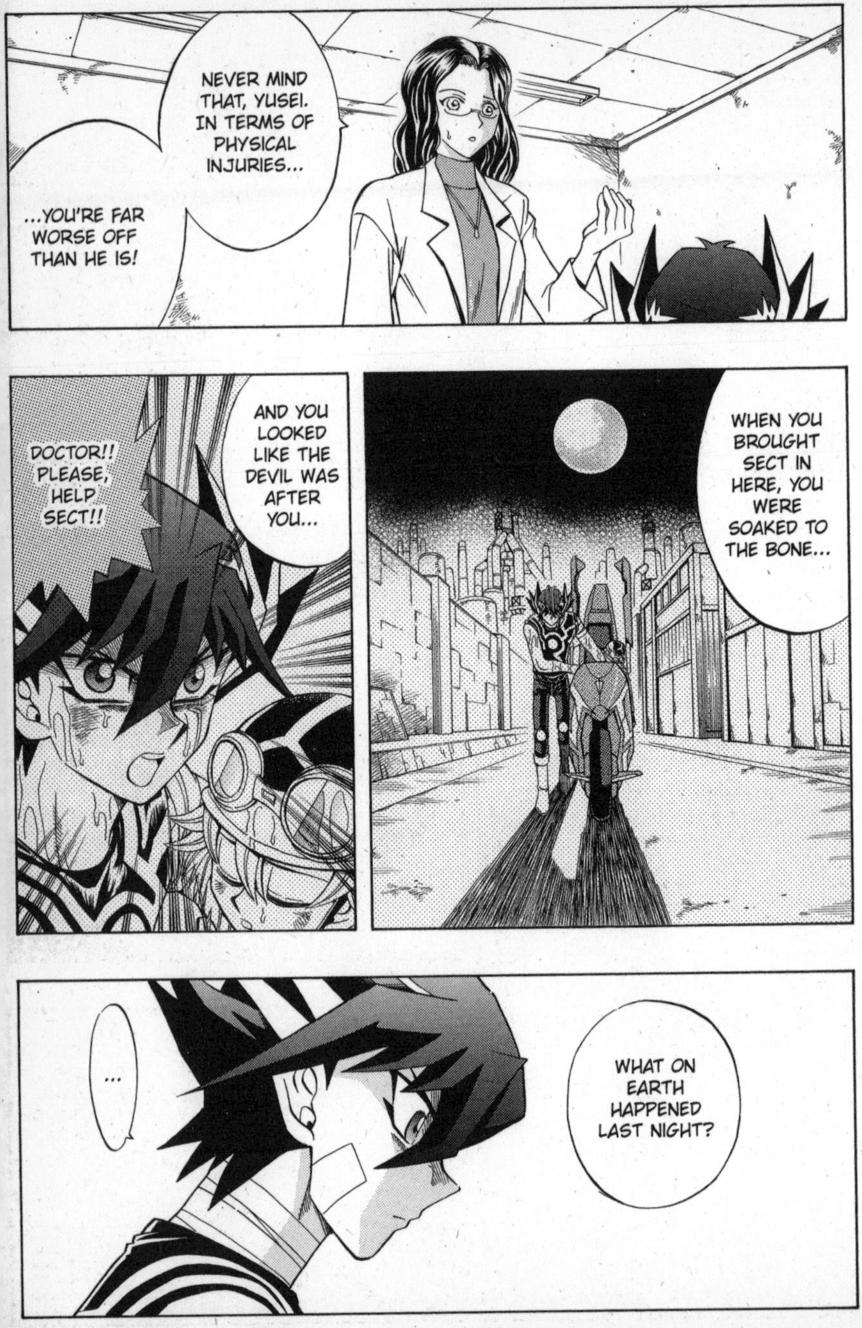
NEVER MIND THAT, YUSEI. IN TERMS OF PHYSICAL INJURIES...
...YOU'RE FAR WORSE OFF THAN HE IS!
WHEN YOU BROUGHT SECT IN HERE, YOU WERE SOAKED TO THE BONE...
AND YOU LOOKED LIKE THE DEVIL WAS AFTER YOU...
DOCTOR!! PLEASE, HELP SECT!!
WHAT ON EARTH HAPPENED LAST NIGHT?
...

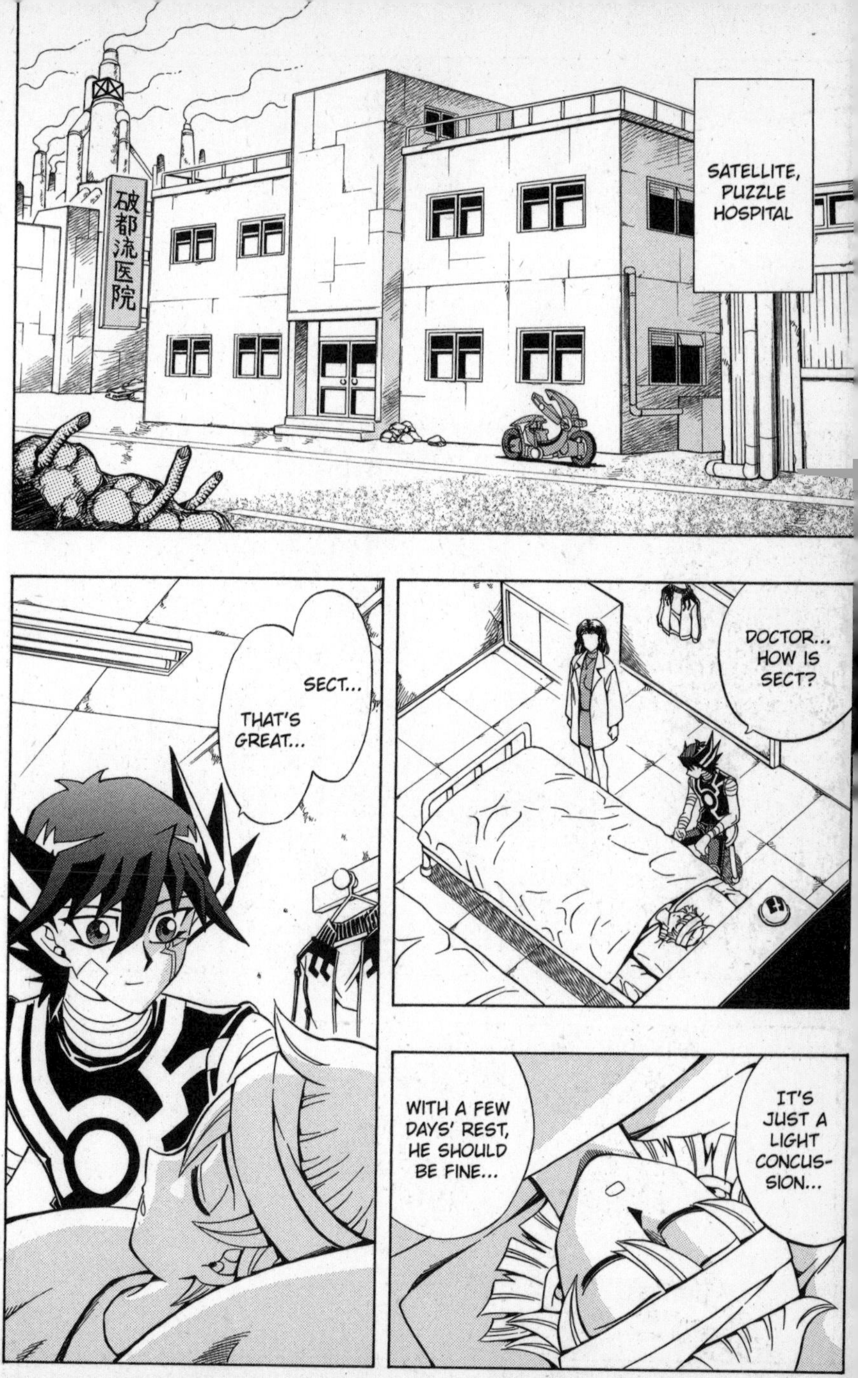
SATELLITE, PUZZLE HOSPITAL
破都流医院
DOCTOR... HOW IS SECT?
IT'S JUST A LIGHT CONCUS-SION...
WITH A FEW DAYS' REST, HE SHOULD BE FINE...
SECT...
THAT'S GREAT...

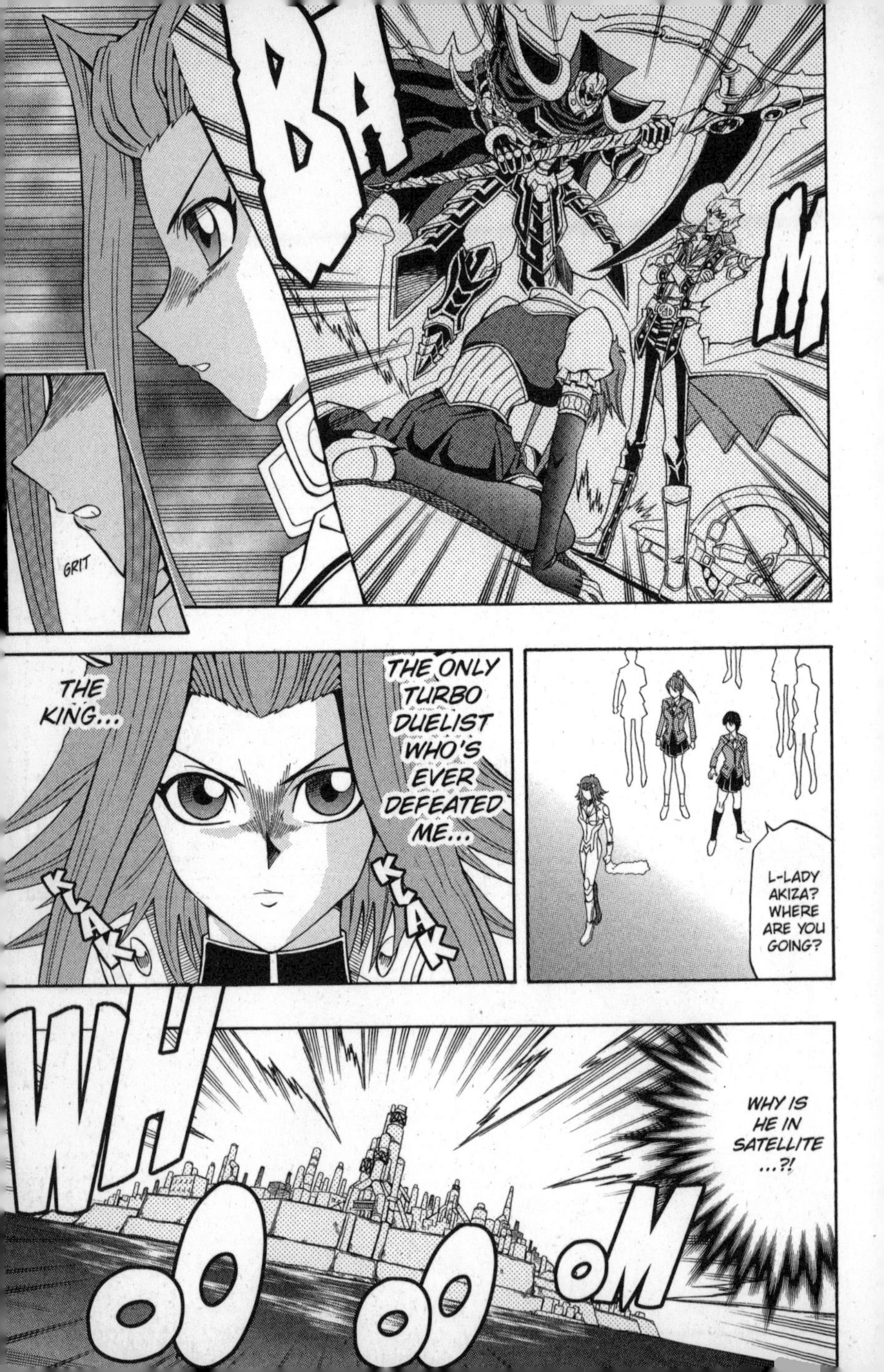
BA
M
GRIT
L-LADY AKIZA? WHERE ARE YOU GOING?
THE ONLY TURBO DUELIST WHO'S EVER DEFEATED ME...
THE KING...
KLAK
KLAK
WHY IS HE IN SATELLITE ...?!
WHOOOOOM

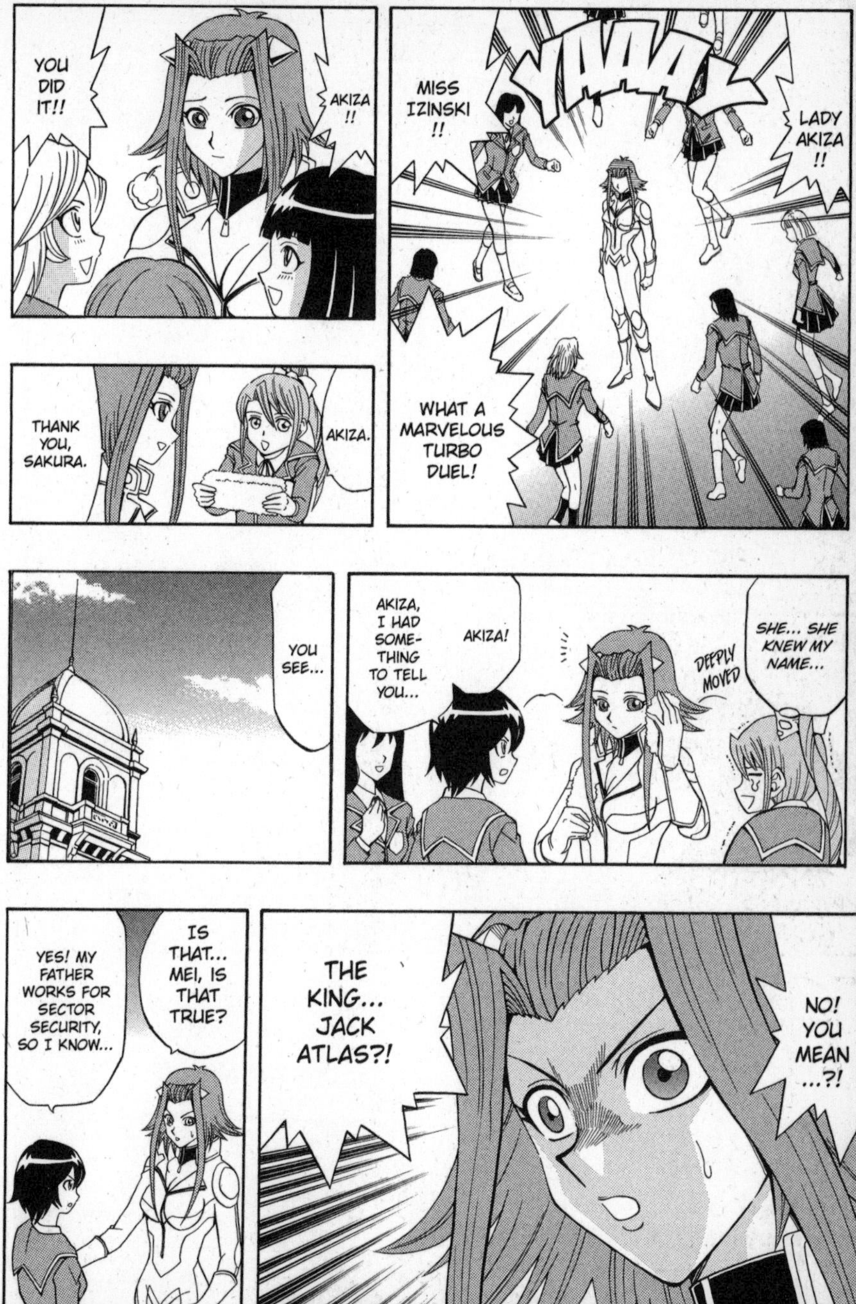
YAAA
LADY AKIZA !!
MISS IZINSKI !!
WHAT A MARVELOUS TURBO DUEL!
AKIZA !!
YOU DID IT!!
AKIZA.
THANK YOU, SAKURA.
SHE... SHE KNEW MY NAME...
DEEPLY MOVED
AKIZA!
AKIZA, I HAD SOME-THING TO TELL YOU...
YOU SEE...
NO! YOU MEAN ...?!
THE KING... JACK ATLAS?!
IS THAT... MEI, IS THAT TRUE?
YES! MY FATHER WORKS FOR SECTOR SECURITY, SO I KNOW...

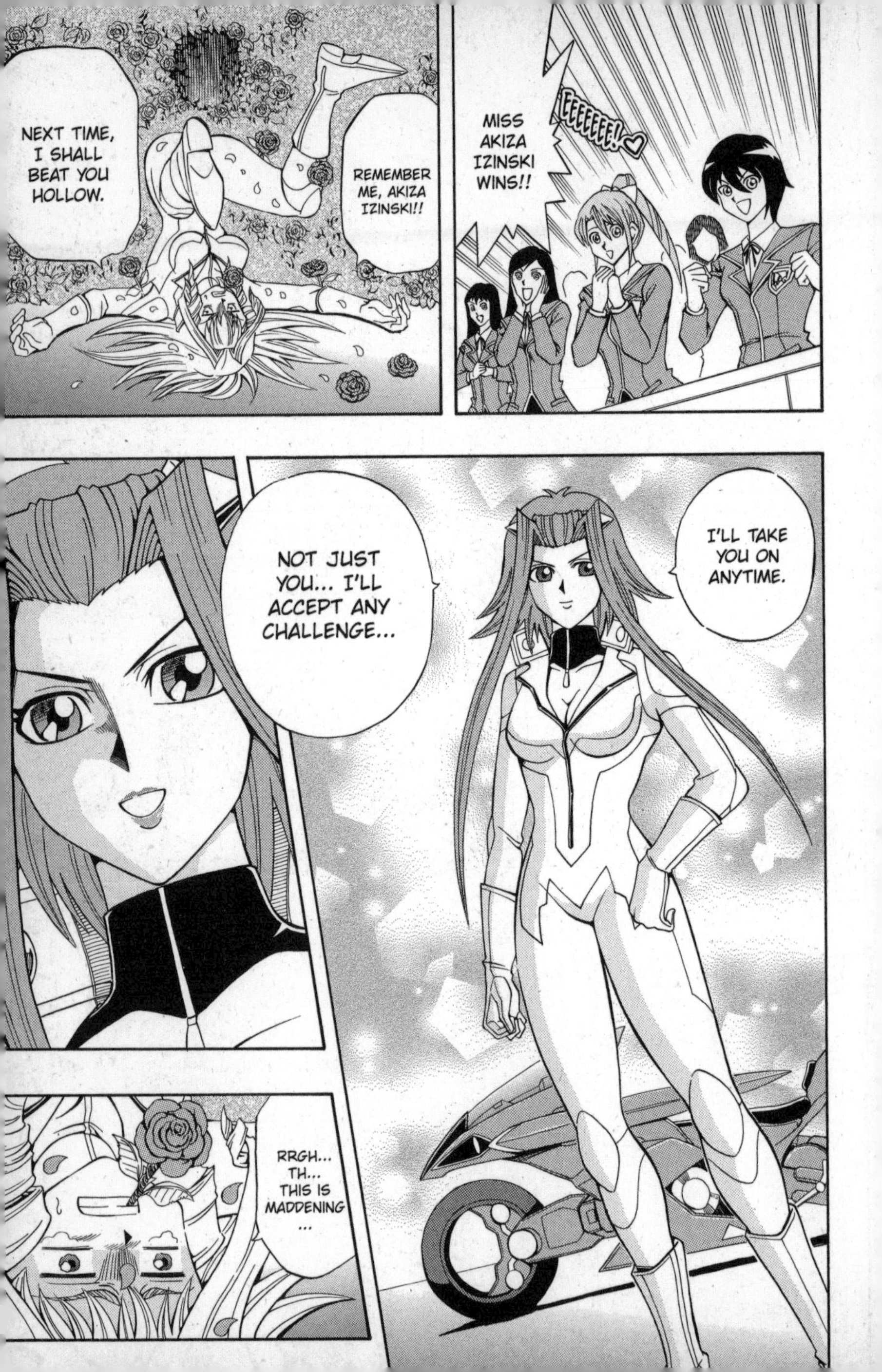
EEEEEEE!!♡
MISS AKIZA IZINSKI WINS!!
REMEMBER ME, AKIZA IZINSKI!!
NEXT TIME, I SHALL BEAT YOU HOLLOW.
I'LL TAKE YOU ON ANYTIME.
NOT JUST YOU... I'LL ACCEPT ANY CHALLENGE...
RRGH... TH... THIS IS MADDENING ...

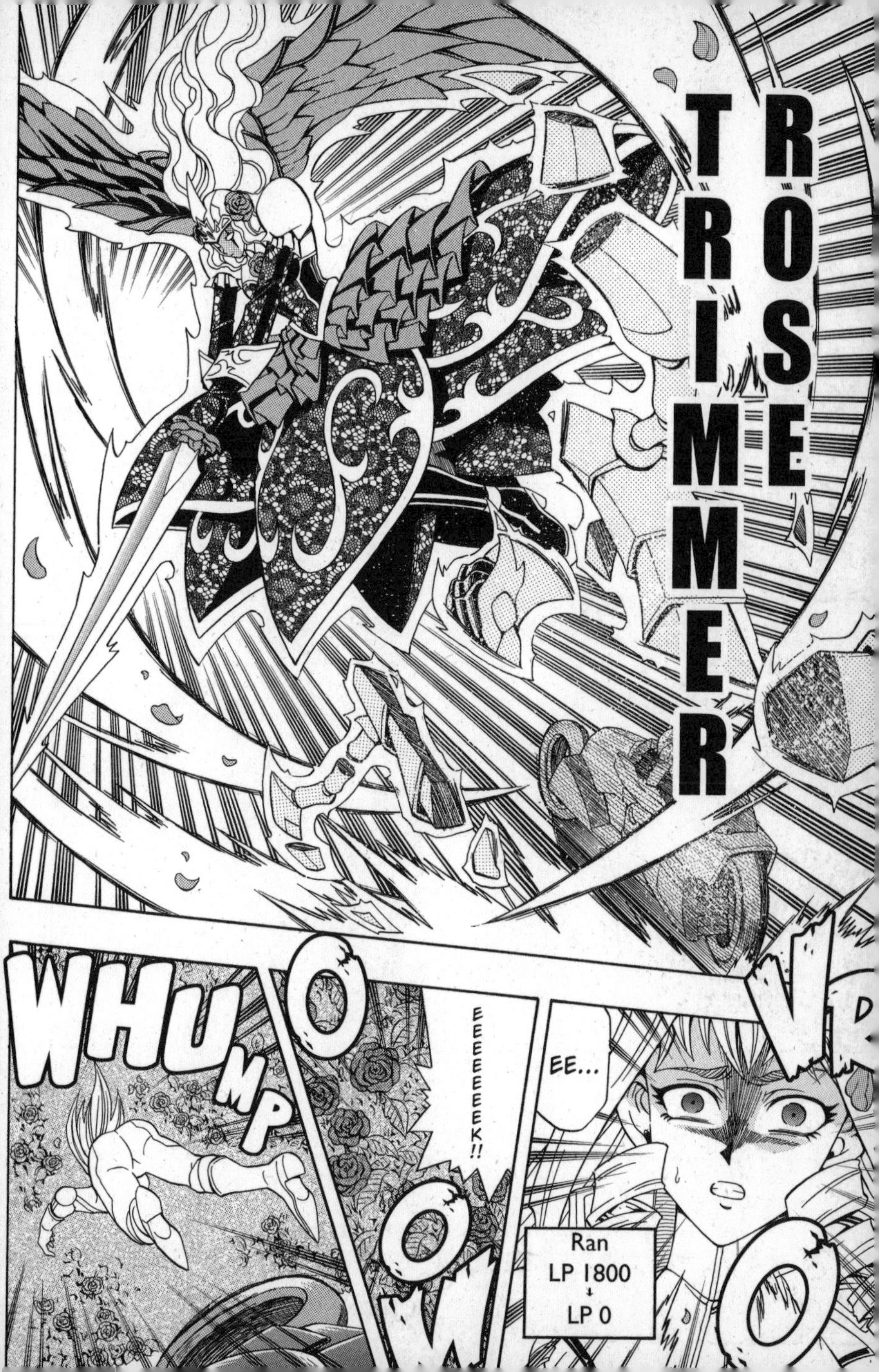
ROSE TRIMMER
EE...
EEEEEEEEEK!!
Ran
LP 1800
↓
LP 0
WHUMP

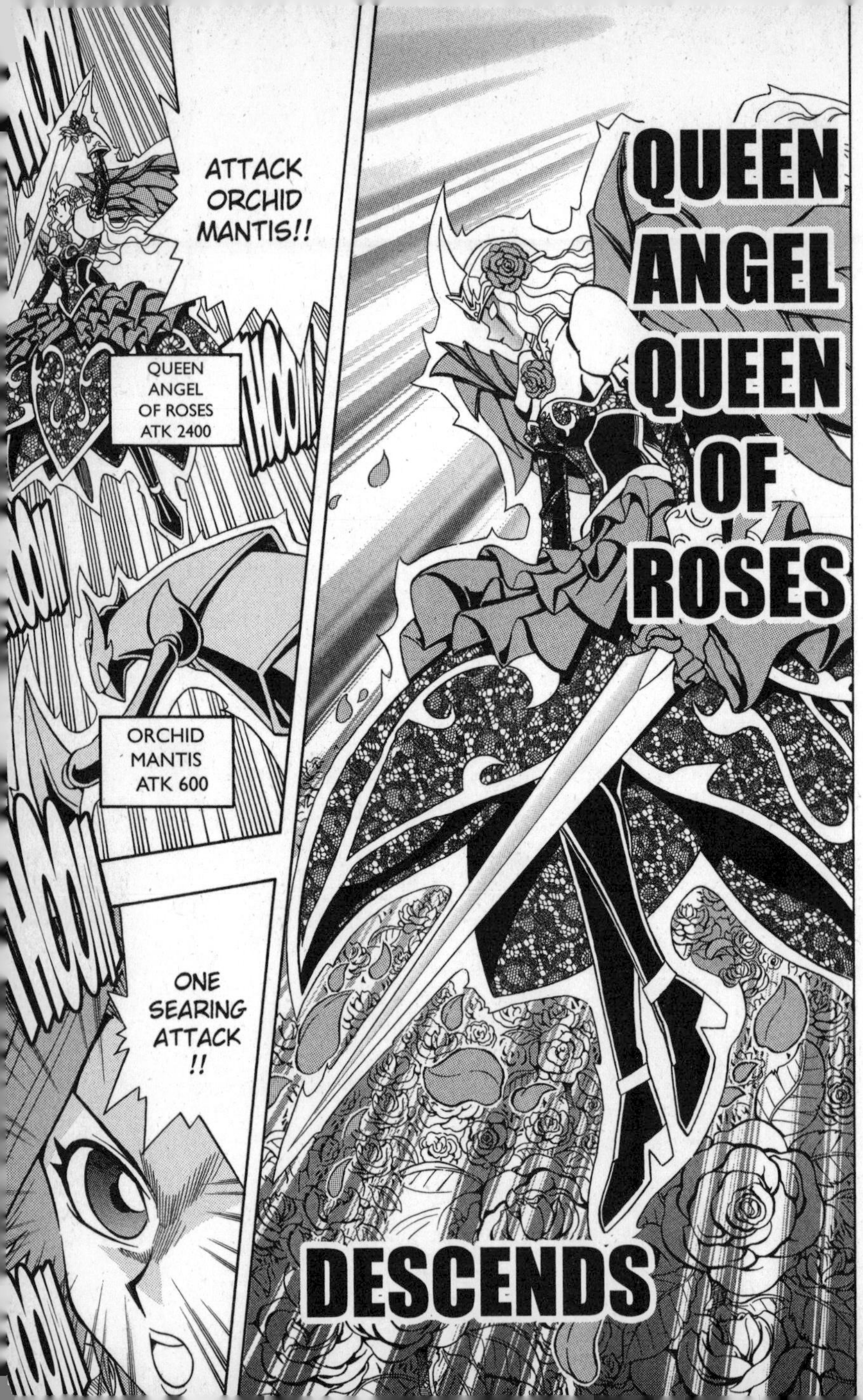
QUEEN ANGEL QUEEN OF ROSES
DESCENDS
ATTACK ORCHID MANTIS!!
QUEEN ANGEL OF ROSES ATK 2400
ORCHID MANTIS ATK 600
ONE SEARING ATTACK !!

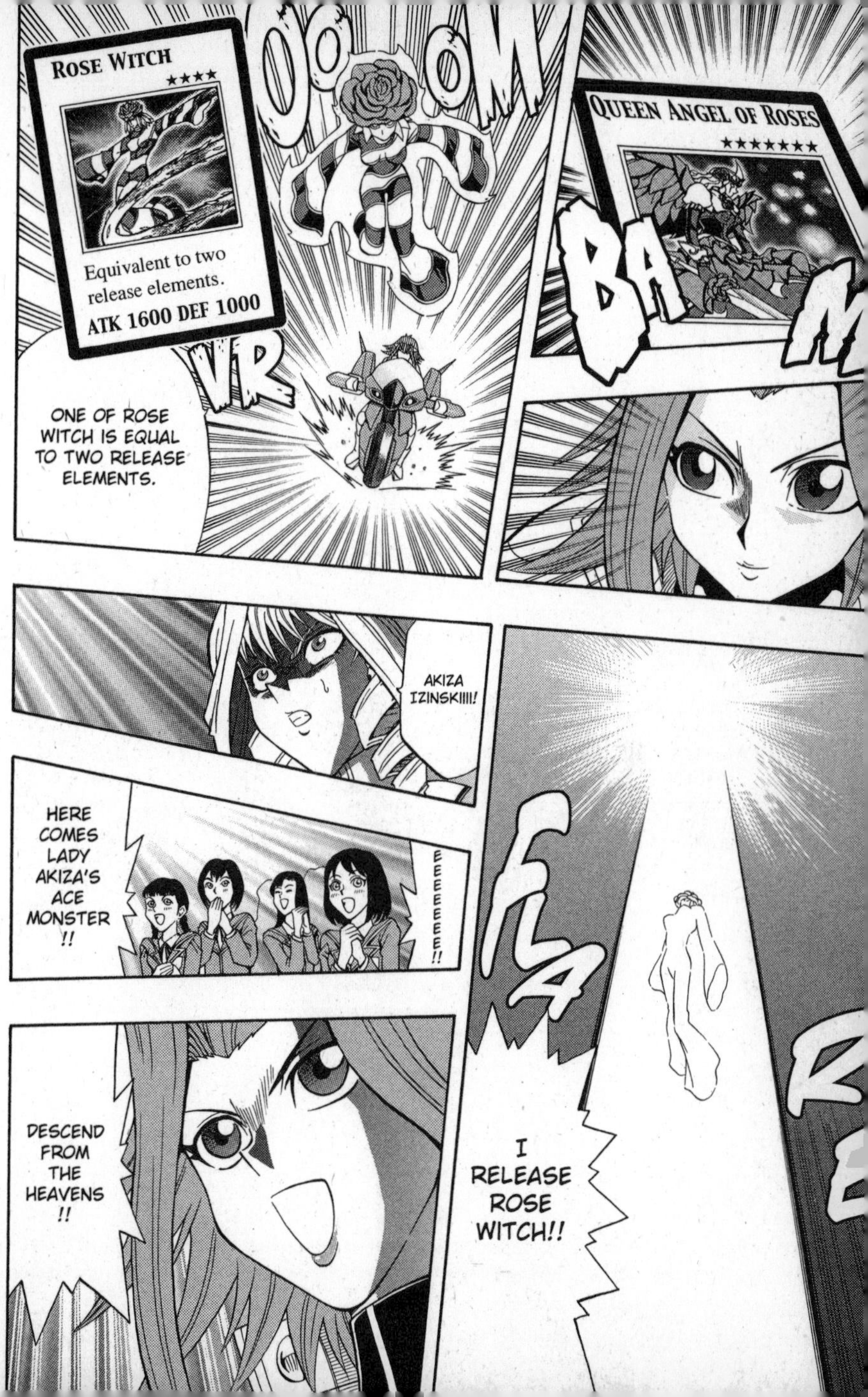
QUEEN ANGEL OF ROSES
★★★★★★★
BAM
ROSE WITCH
★★★★
Equivalent to two release elements.
ATK 1600 DEF 1000
OOOM
VR
ONE OF ROSE WITCH IS EQUAL TO TWO RELEASE ELEMENTS.
FLA
RE
I RELEASE ROSE WITCH!!
AKIZA IZINSKIIII!
HERE COMES LADY AKIZA'S ACE MONSTER!!
EEEEEEEEE!!
DESCEND FROM THE HEAVENS!!

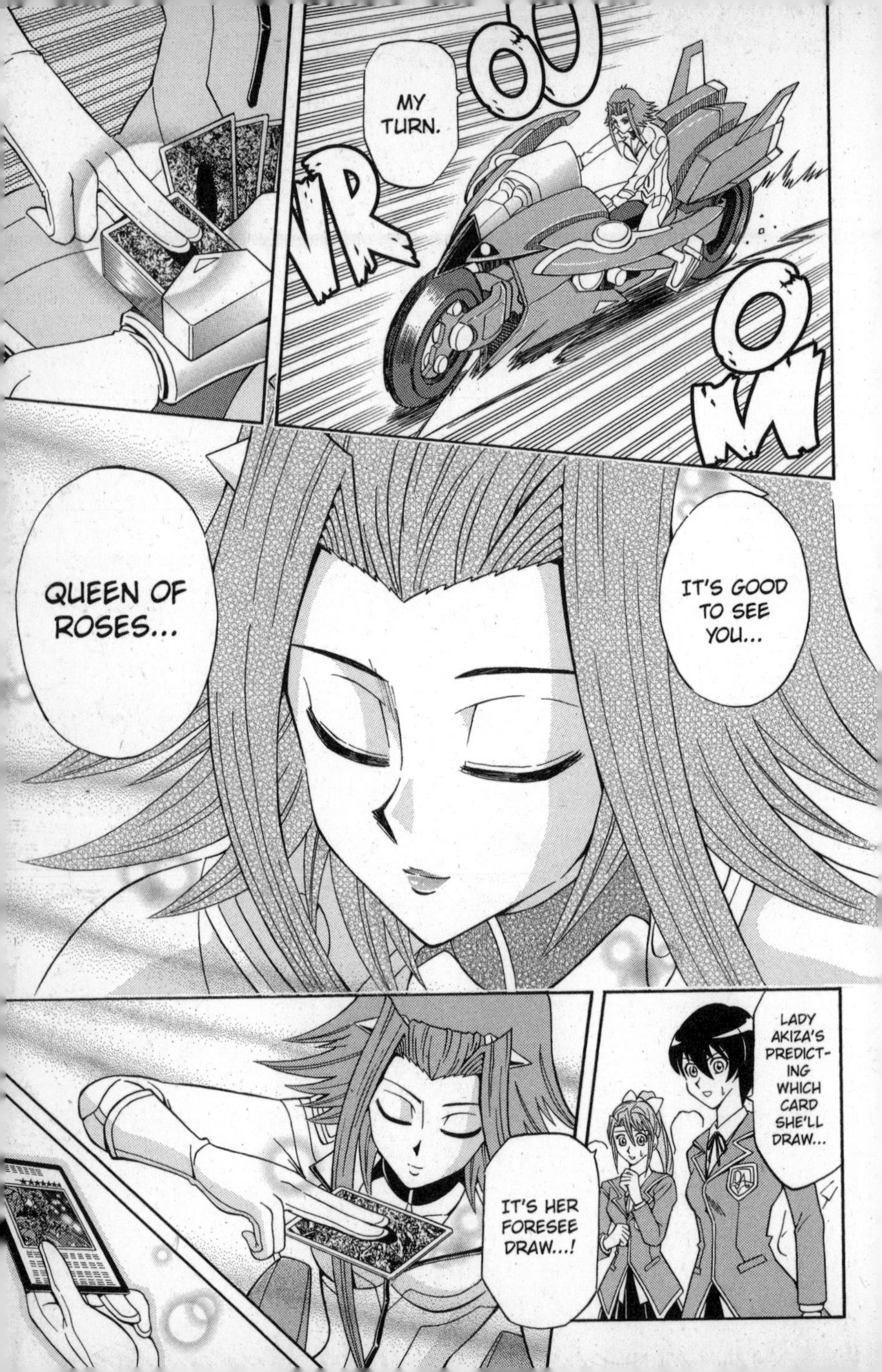
MY TURN.
VROOOM
IT'S GOOD TO SEE YOU...
QUEEN OF ROSES...
LADY AKIZA'S PREDICT-ING WHICH CARD SHE'LL DRAW...
IT'S HER FORESEE DRAW...!

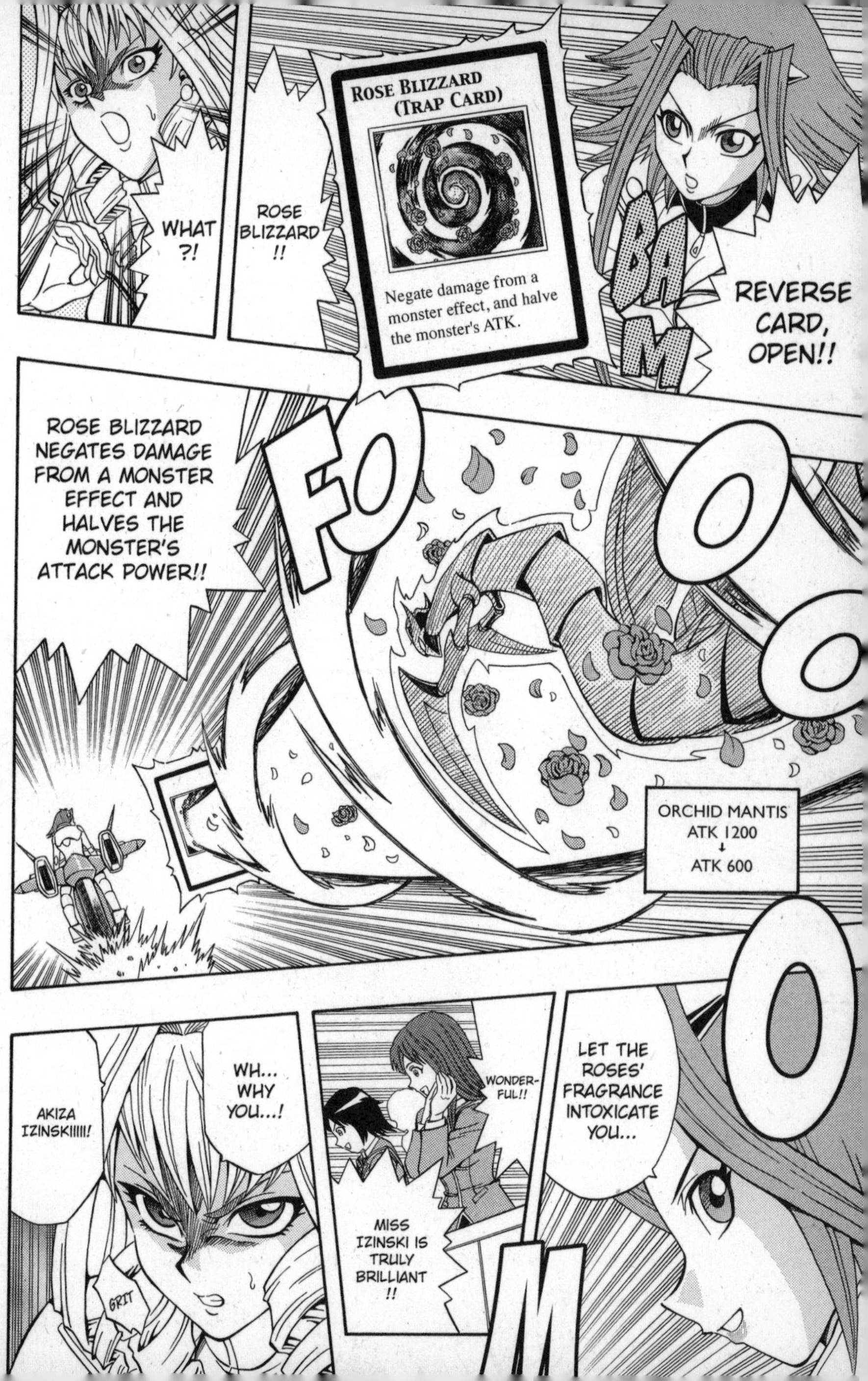
BAM
REVERSE CARD, OPEN!!
ROSE BLIZZARD (TRAP CARD)
Negate damage from a monster effect, and halve the monster's ATK.
ROSE BLIZZARD !!
WHAT ?!
ROSE BLIZZARD NEGATES DAMAGE FROM A MONSTER EFFECT AND HALVES THE MONSTER'S ATTACK POWER!!
FOOOOO
ORCHID MANTIS ATK 1200 ↓ ATK 600
LET THE ROSES' FRAGRANCE INTOXICATE YOU...
M
WONDER-FUL!!
MISS IZINSKI IS TRULY BRILLIANT !!
WH... WHY YOU...!
AKIZA IZINSKIIIII!
GRIT

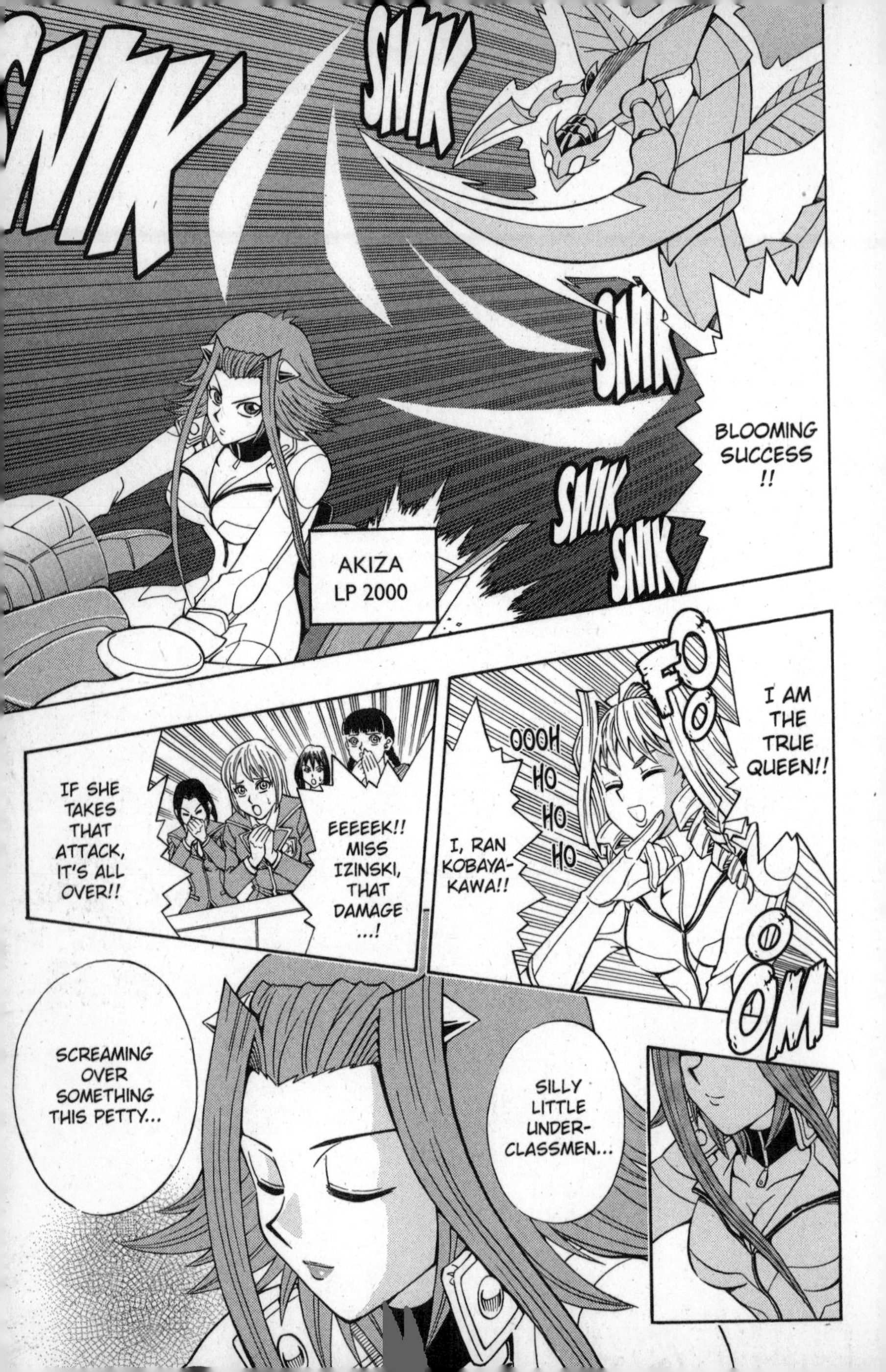
SNIK
SNIK
SNIK
BLOOMING SUCCESS !!
SNIK
SNIK
SNIK
AKIZA LP 2000
FOOOOOM
I AM THE TRUE QUEEN!!
OOOH HO HO HO
I, RAN KOBAYA-KAWA!!
EEEEEK!! MISS IZINSKI, THAT DAMAGE ...!
IF SHE TAKES THAT ATTACK, IT'S ALL OVER!!
SILLY LITTLE UNDER-CLASSMEN...
SCREAMING OVER SOMETHING THIS PETTY...

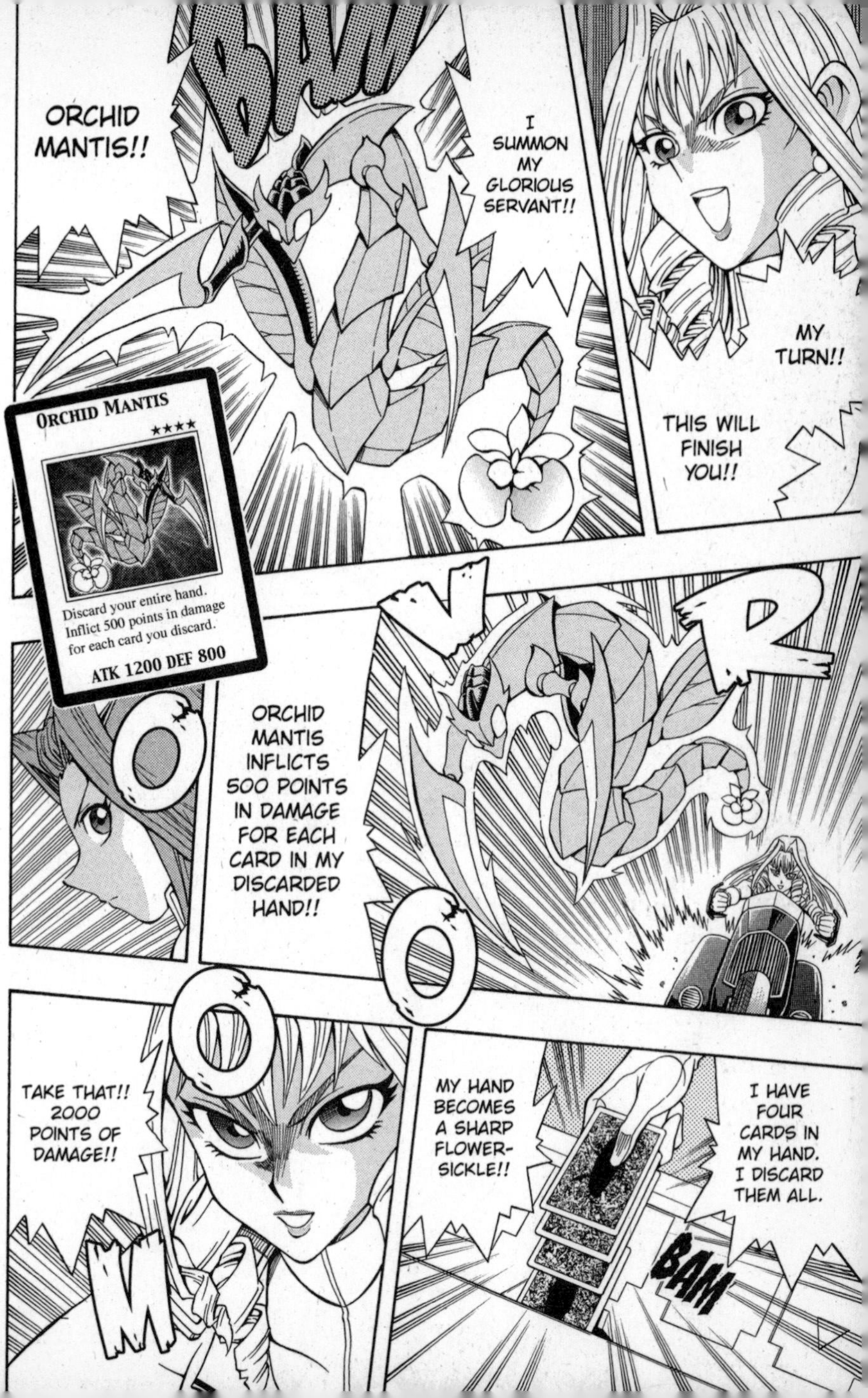
MY TURN!!
THIS WILL FINISH YOU!!
I SUMMON MY GLORIOUS SERVANT!!
ORCHID MANTIS!!
ORCHID MANTIS
★★★★
Discard your entire hand. Inflict 500 points in damage for each card you discard.
ATK 1200 DEF 800
ORCHID MANTIS INFLICTS 500 POINTS IN DAMAGE FOR EACH CARD IN MY DISCARDED HAND!!
I HAVE FOUR CARDS IN MY HAND. I DISCARD THEM ALL.
BAM
MY HAND BECOMES A SHARP FLOWER-SICKLE!!
TAKE THAT!! 2000 POINTS OF DAMAGE!!

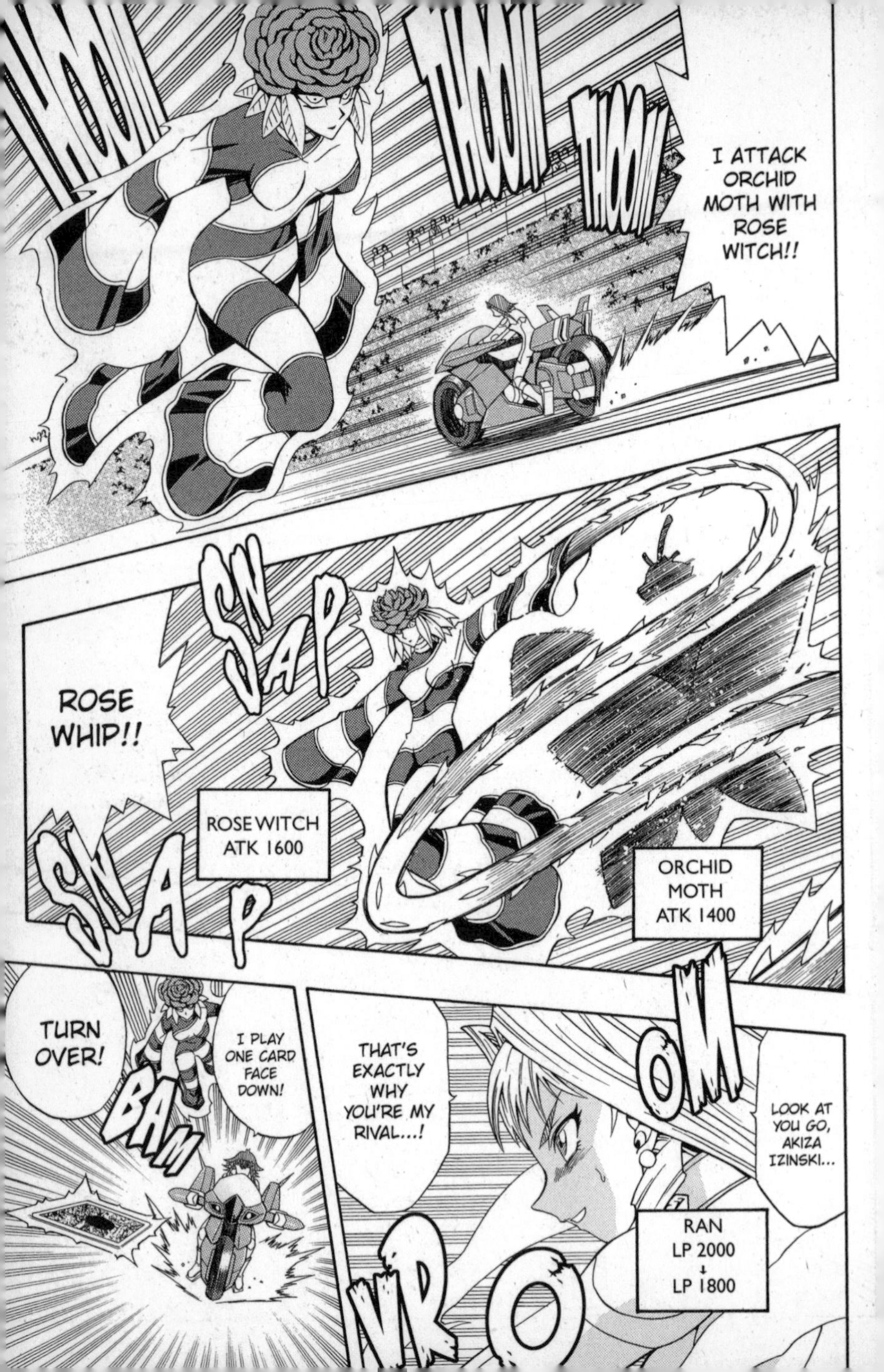
I ATTACK ORCHID MOTH WITH ROSE WITCH!!
THOOM
THOOM
THOOM
SNAP
ROSE WHIP!!
ORCHID MOTH ATK 1400
ROSE WITCH ATK 1600
SNAP
LOOK AT YOU GO, AKIZA IZINSKI...
THAT'S EXACTLY WHY YOU'RE MY RIVAL...!
RAN LP 2000 ↓ LP 1800
VROOM
I PLAY ONE CARD FACE DOWN!
TURN OVER!
BAM

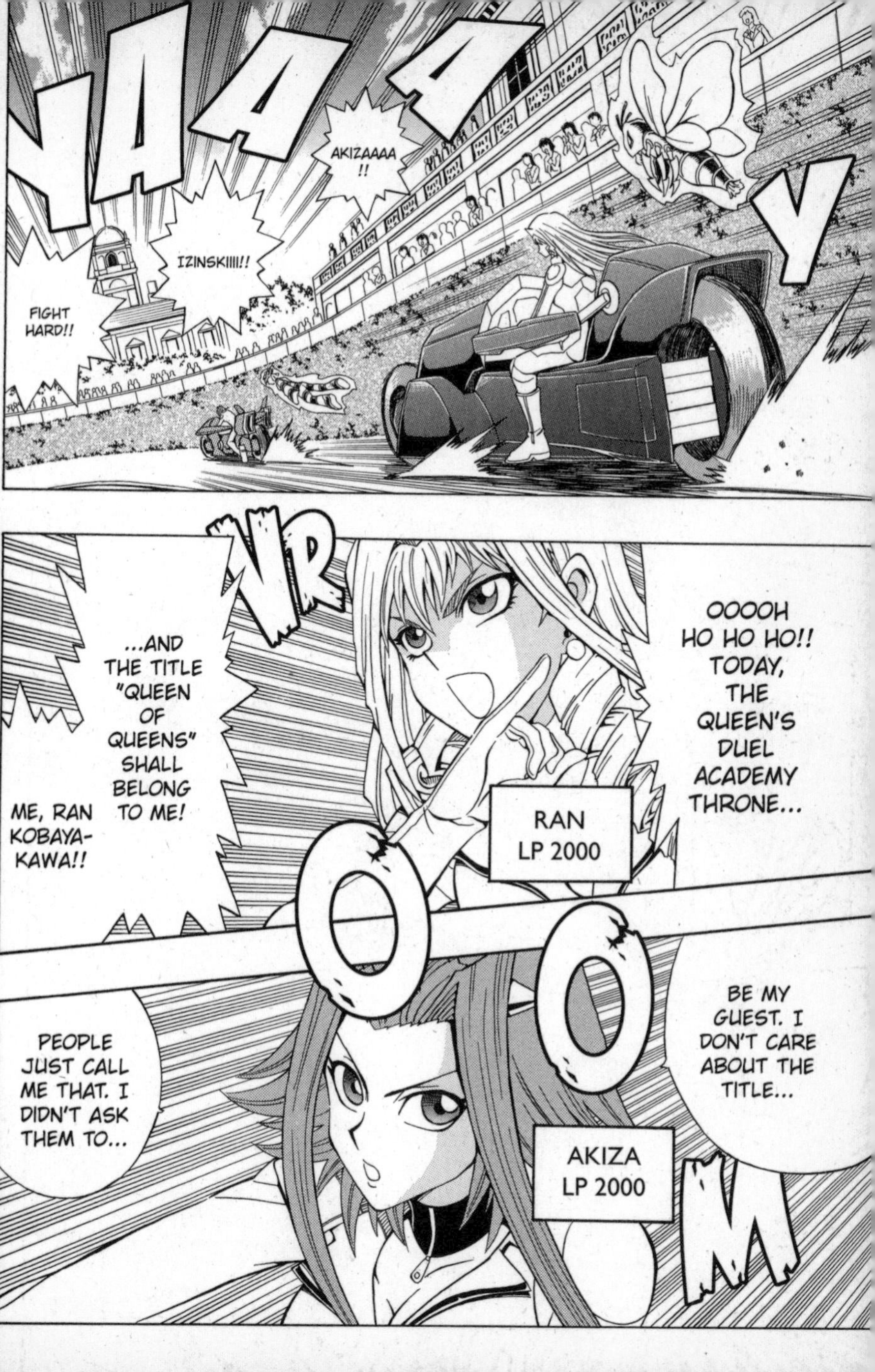
AKIZAAAA!!
IZINSKIIII!!
FIGHT HARD!!
VROOM
OOOOH HO HO HO!! TODAY, THE QUEEN'S DUEL ACADEMY THRONE...
RAN LP 2000
...AND THE TITLE "QUEEN OF QUEENS" SHALL BELONG TO ME!
ME, RAN KOBAYAKAWA!!
BE MY GUEST. I DON'T CARE ABOUT THE TITLE...
AKIZA LP 2000
PEOPLE JUST CALL ME THAT. I DIDN'T ASK THEM TO...

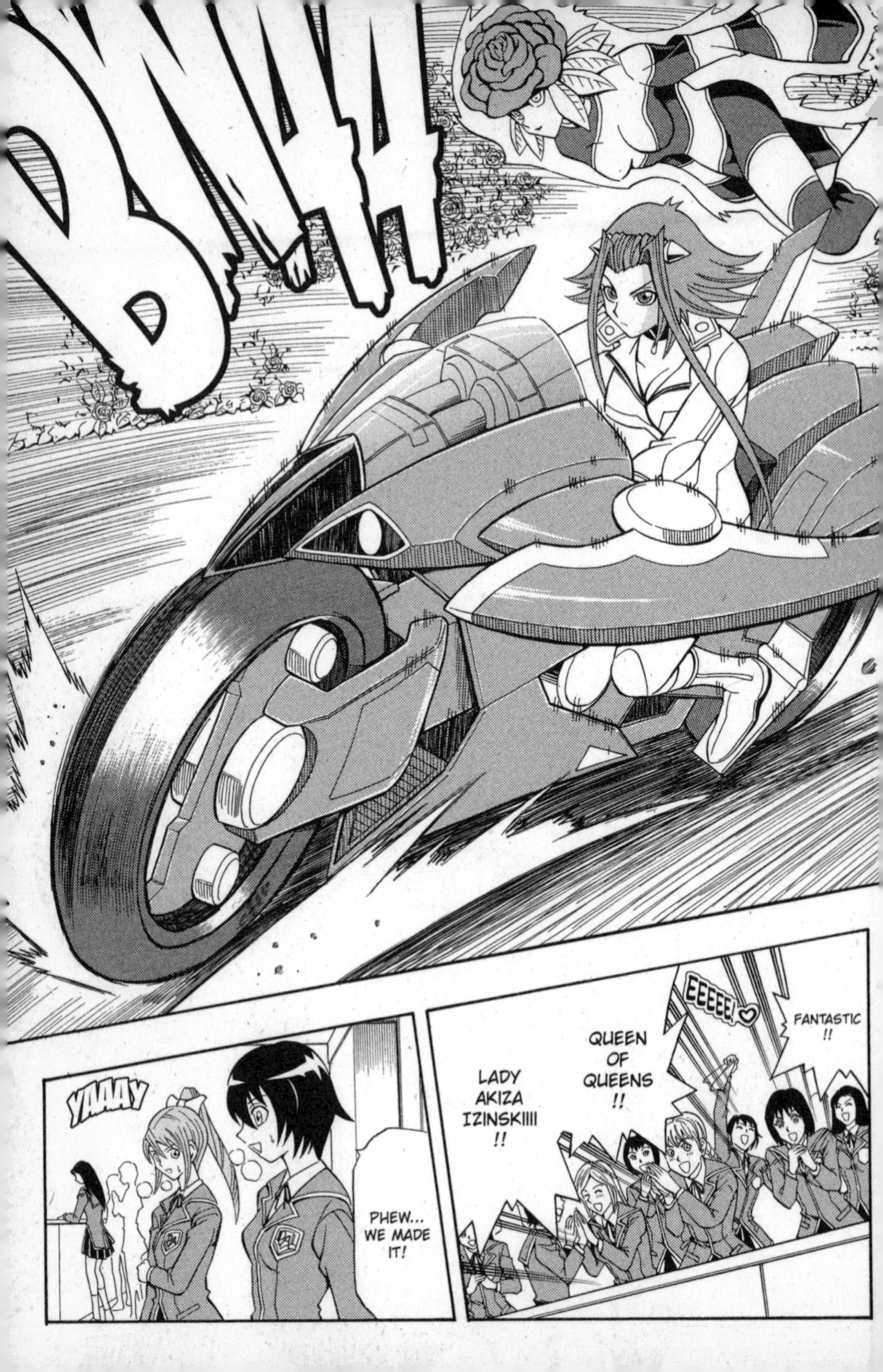
EEEEE! ♥
FANTASTIC !!
QUEEN OF QUEENS !!
LADY AKIZA IZINSKIIII !!
PHEW... WE MADE IT!
YAAAY

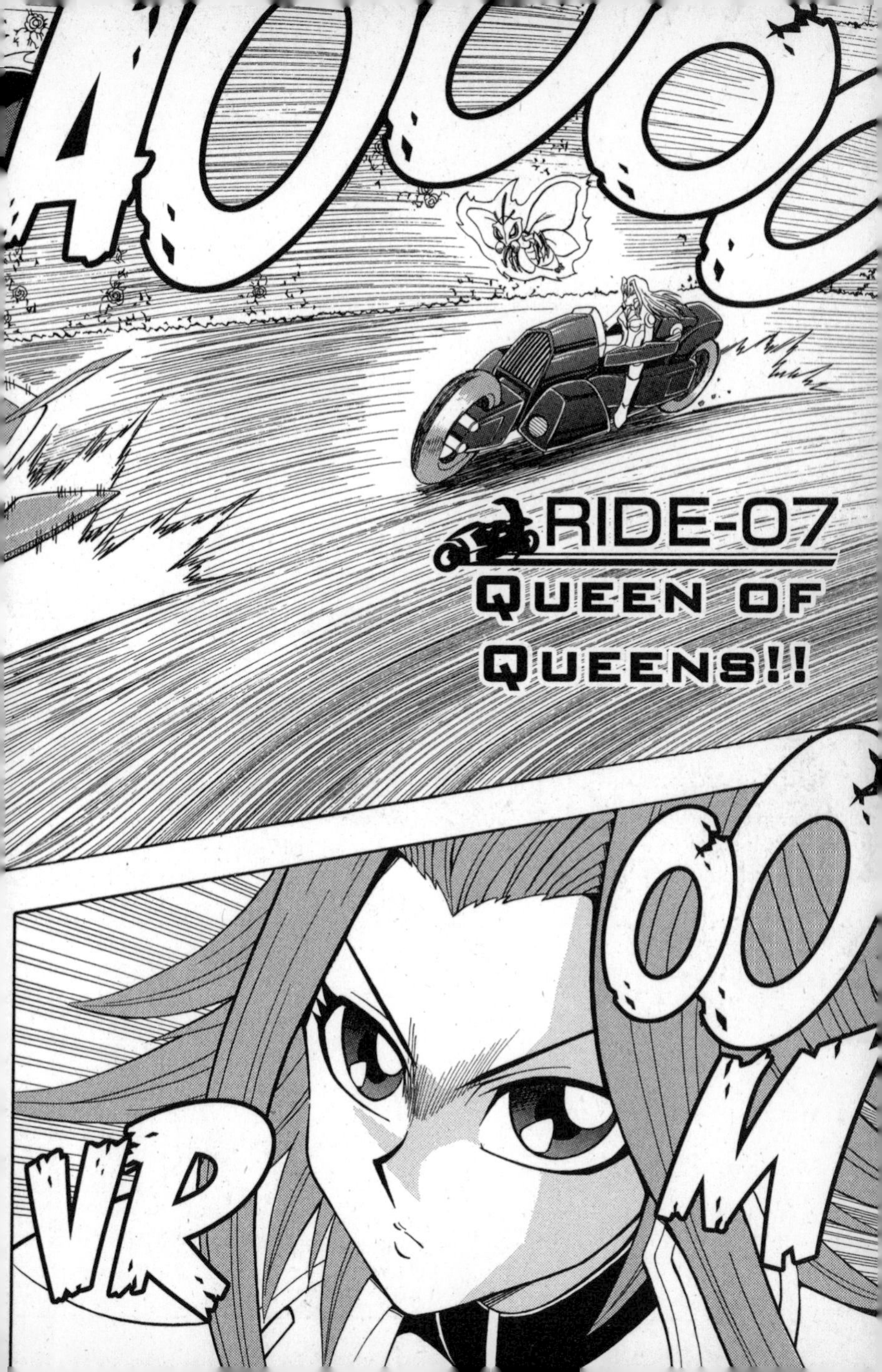
RIDE-07
Queen of Queens!!
VROOM

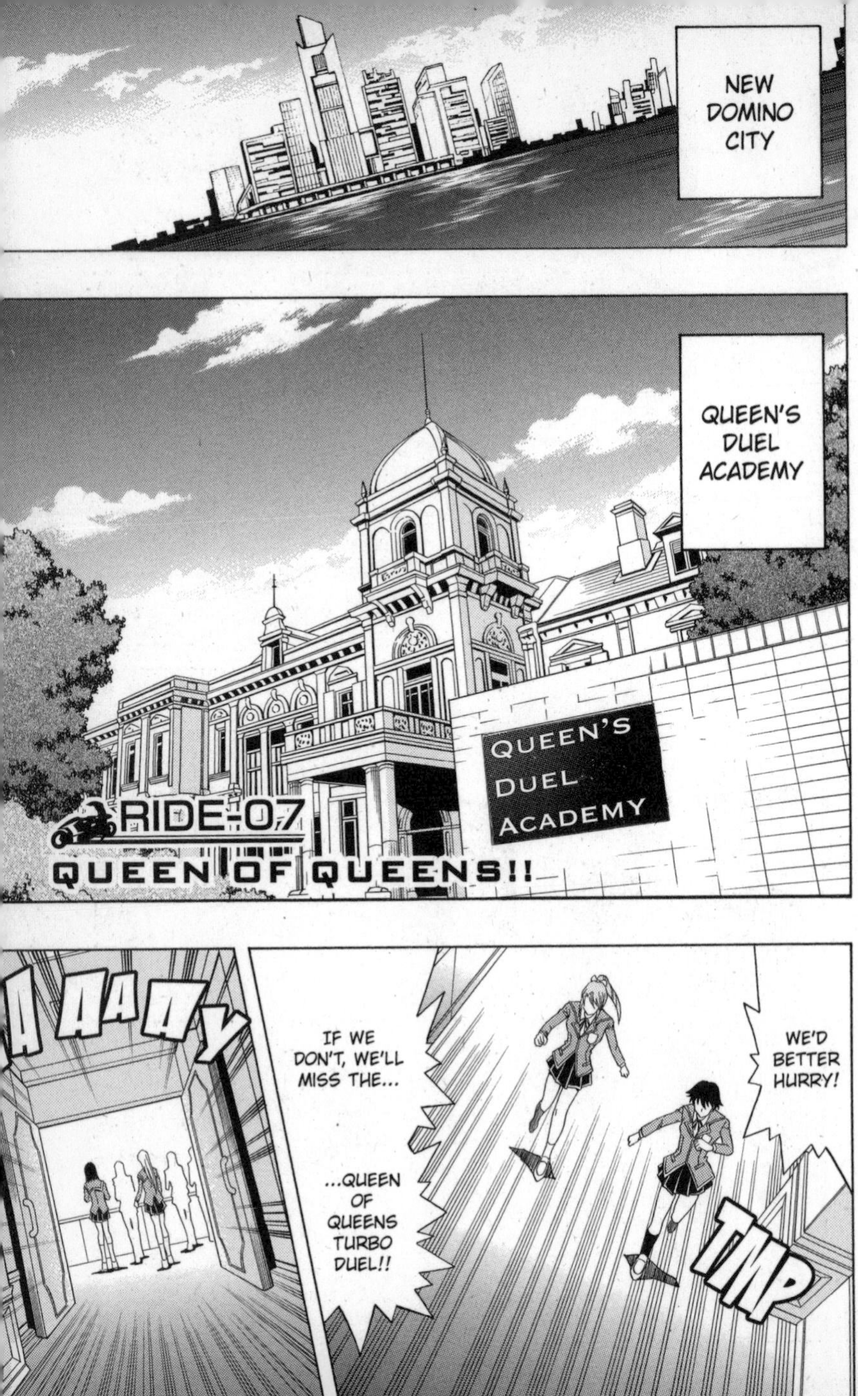
NEW DOMINO CITY
QUEEN'S DUEL ACADEMY
QUEEN'S DUEL ACADEMY
RIDE-07
QUEEN OF QUEENS!!
WE'D BETTER HURRY!
IF WE DON'T, WE'LL MISS THE...
...QUEEN OF QUEENS TURBO DUEL!!
TMP
AAAAY

5D's TRACKS

THE 6TH

BY SATOMASA

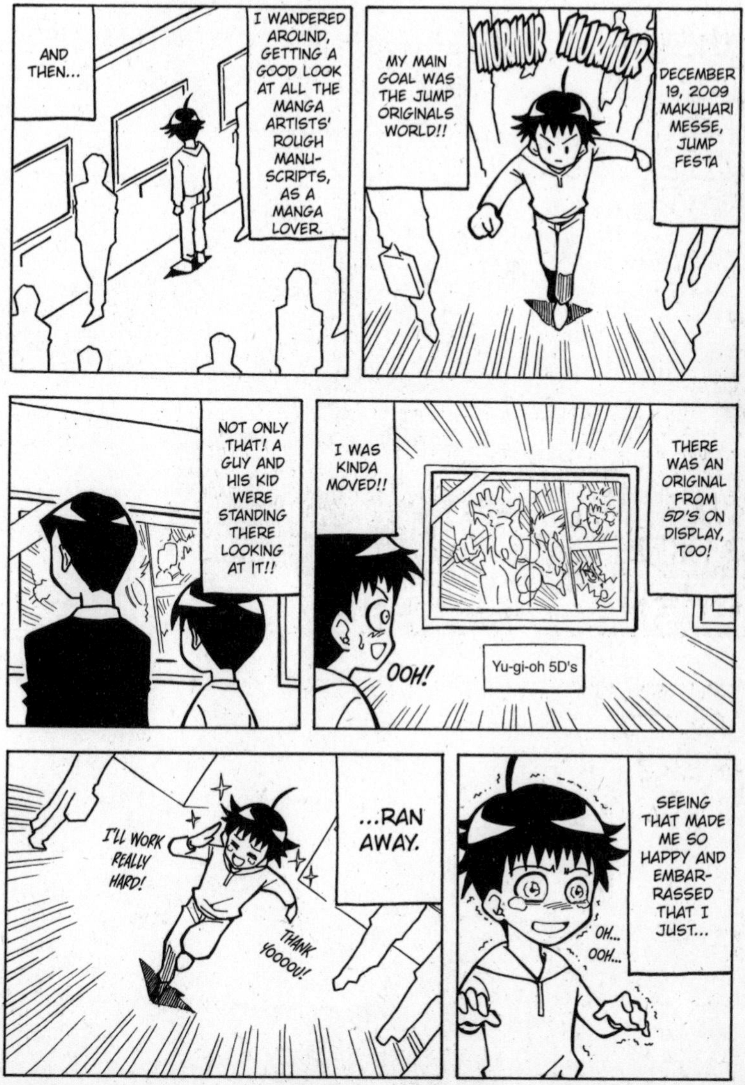
DECEMBER 19, 2009 MAKUHARI MESSE, JUMP FESTA
MURMUR
MURMUR
MY MAIN GOAL WAS THE JUMP ORIGINALS WORLD!!
I WANDERED AROUND, GETTING A GOOD LOOK AT ALL THE MANGA ARTISTS' ROUGH MANU-SCRIPTS, AS A MANGA LOVER.
AND THEN...
THERE WAS AN ORIGINAL FROM 5D'S ON DISPLAY, TOO!
I WAS KINDA MOVED!!
Yu-gi-oh 5D's
OOH!
NOT ONLY THAT! A GUY AND HIS KID WERE STANDING THERE LOOKING AT IT!!
SEEING THAT MADE ME SO HAPPY AND EMBAR-RASSED THAT I JUST...
OH... OOH...
...RAN AWAY.
I'LL WORK REALLY HARD!
THANK YOOOOU!

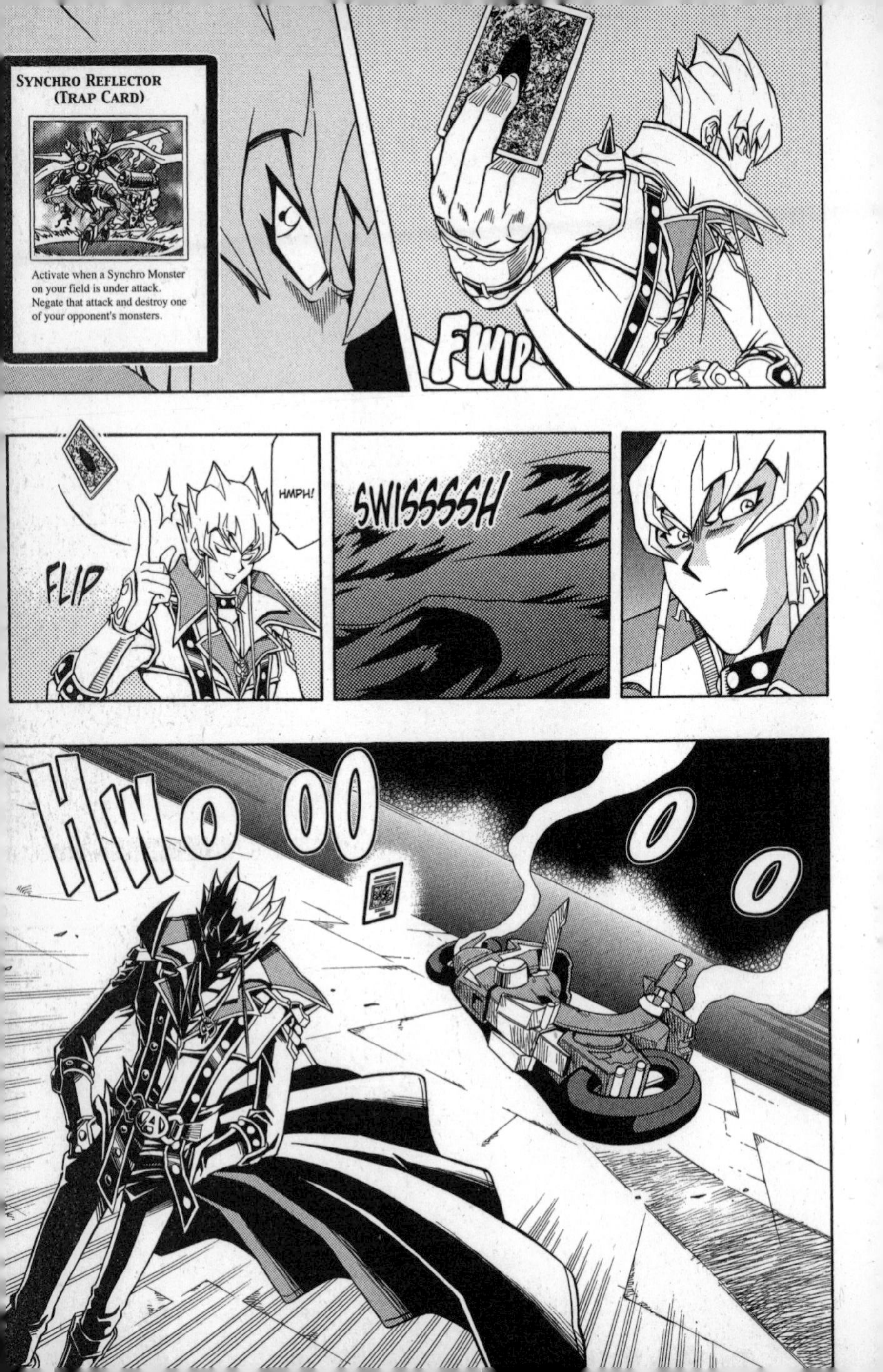
FWIP
SYNCHRO REFLECTOR (TRAP CARD)
Activate when a Synchro Monster on your field is under attack. Negate that attack and destroy one of your opponent's monsters.
SWISSSSH
HMPH!
FLIP
HWOOOOOO

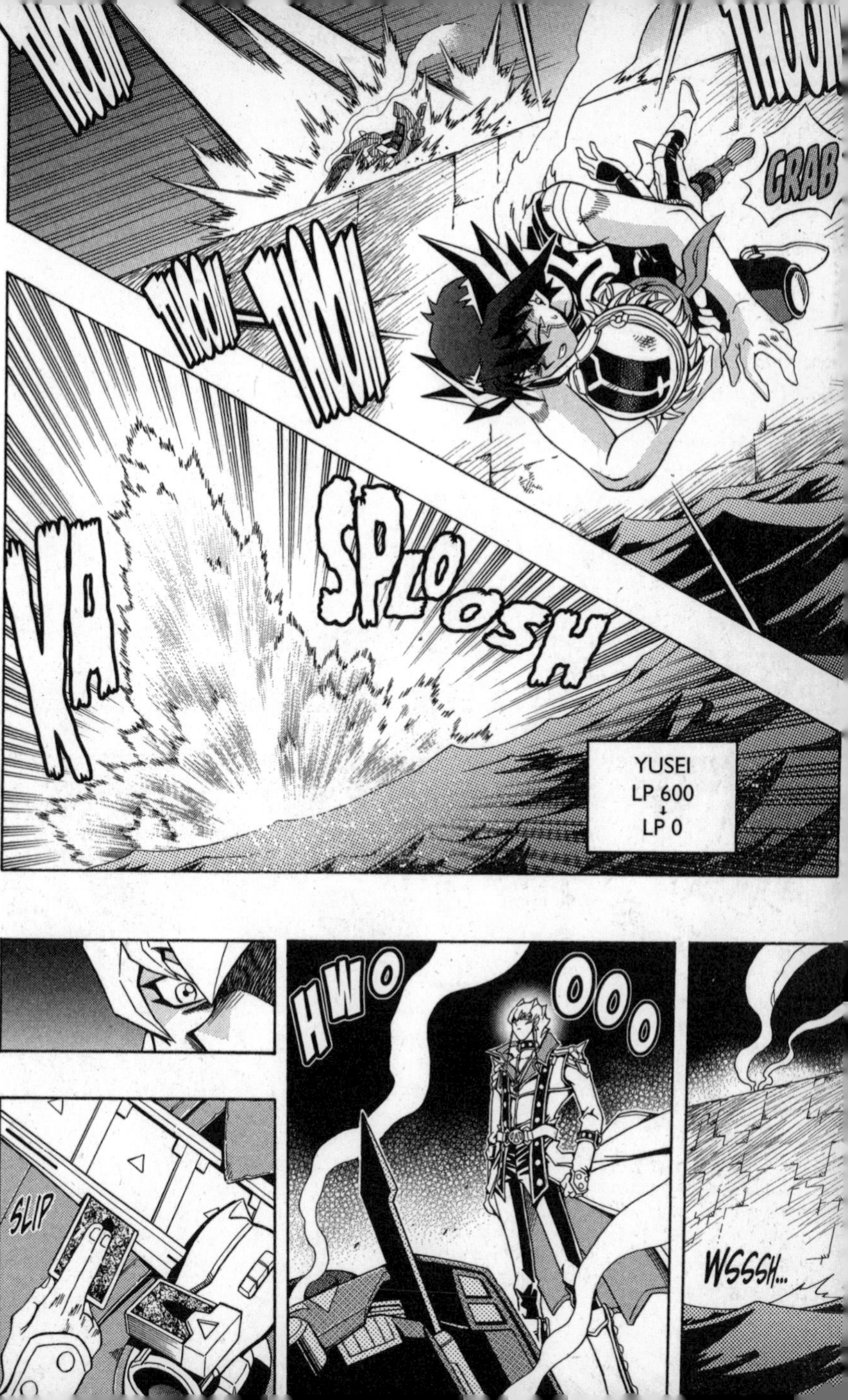
THOOM
GRAB
THOOM
THOOM
THOOM
SPLOOSH
KA
YUSEI
LP 600
↓
LP 0
WSSSH...
HWOOOO
SLIP

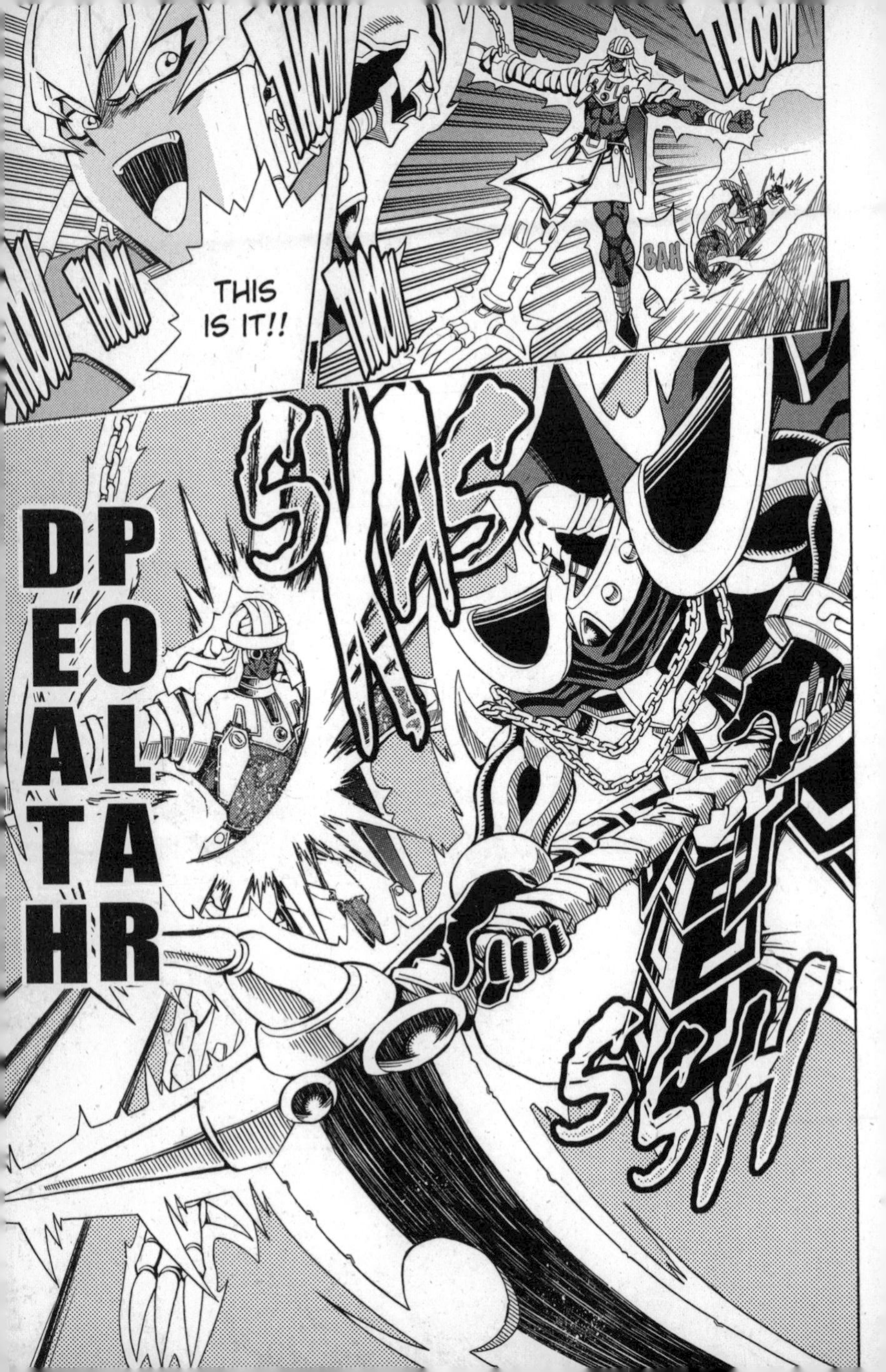
THOOM
BAH
THOOM
THIS IS IT!!
THOOM
THOOM
SWAS
DEATH
POLAR
SSH

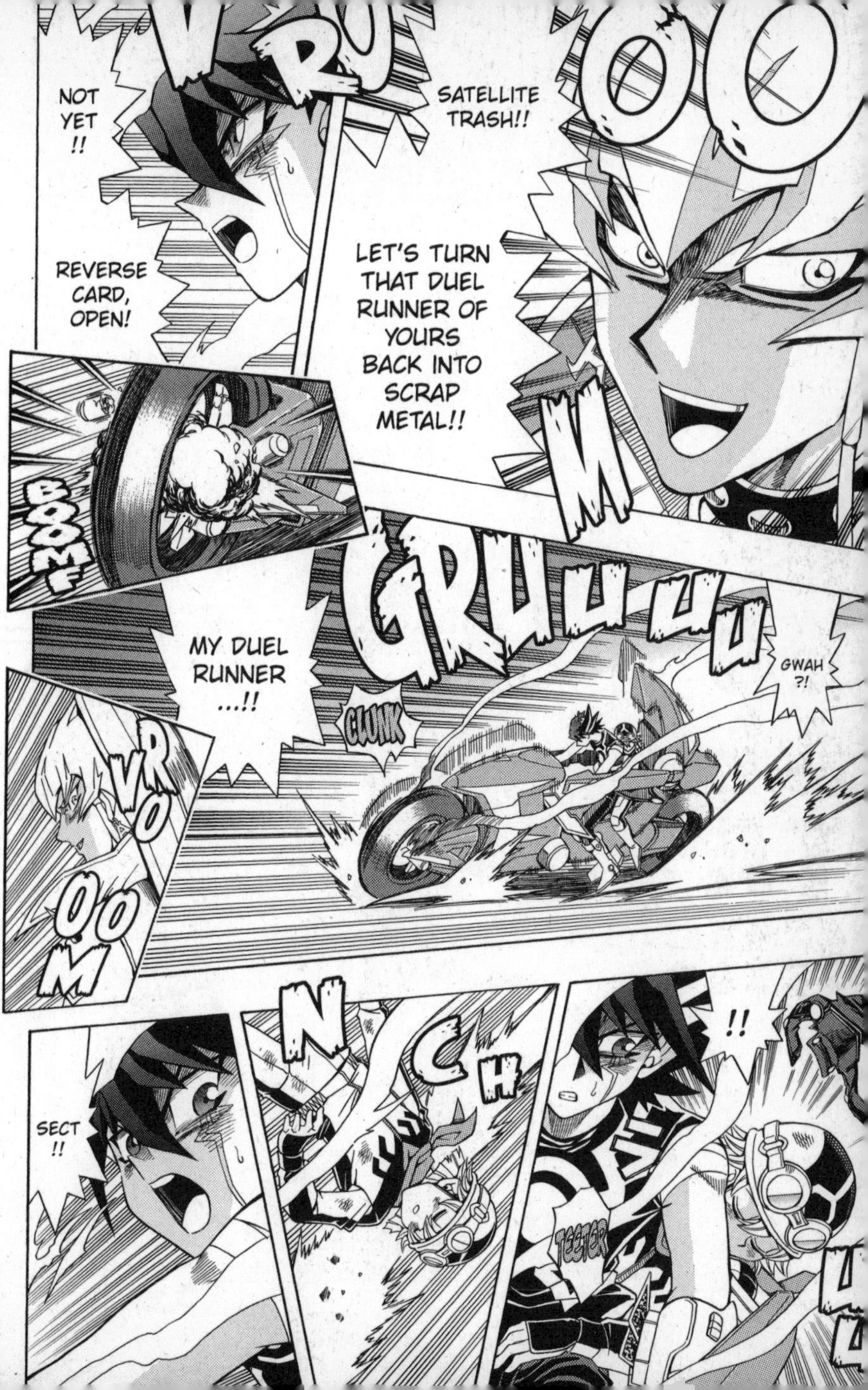
SATELLITE TRASH!!
LET'S TURN THAT DUEL RUNNER OF YOURS BACK INTO SCRAP METAL!!
NOT YET!!
REVERSE CARD, OPEN!
BOOMF
GRUUUU
GWAH?!
CLUNK
MY DUEL RUNNER...!!
VROOOM
!!
TEETER
NCH
SECT!!

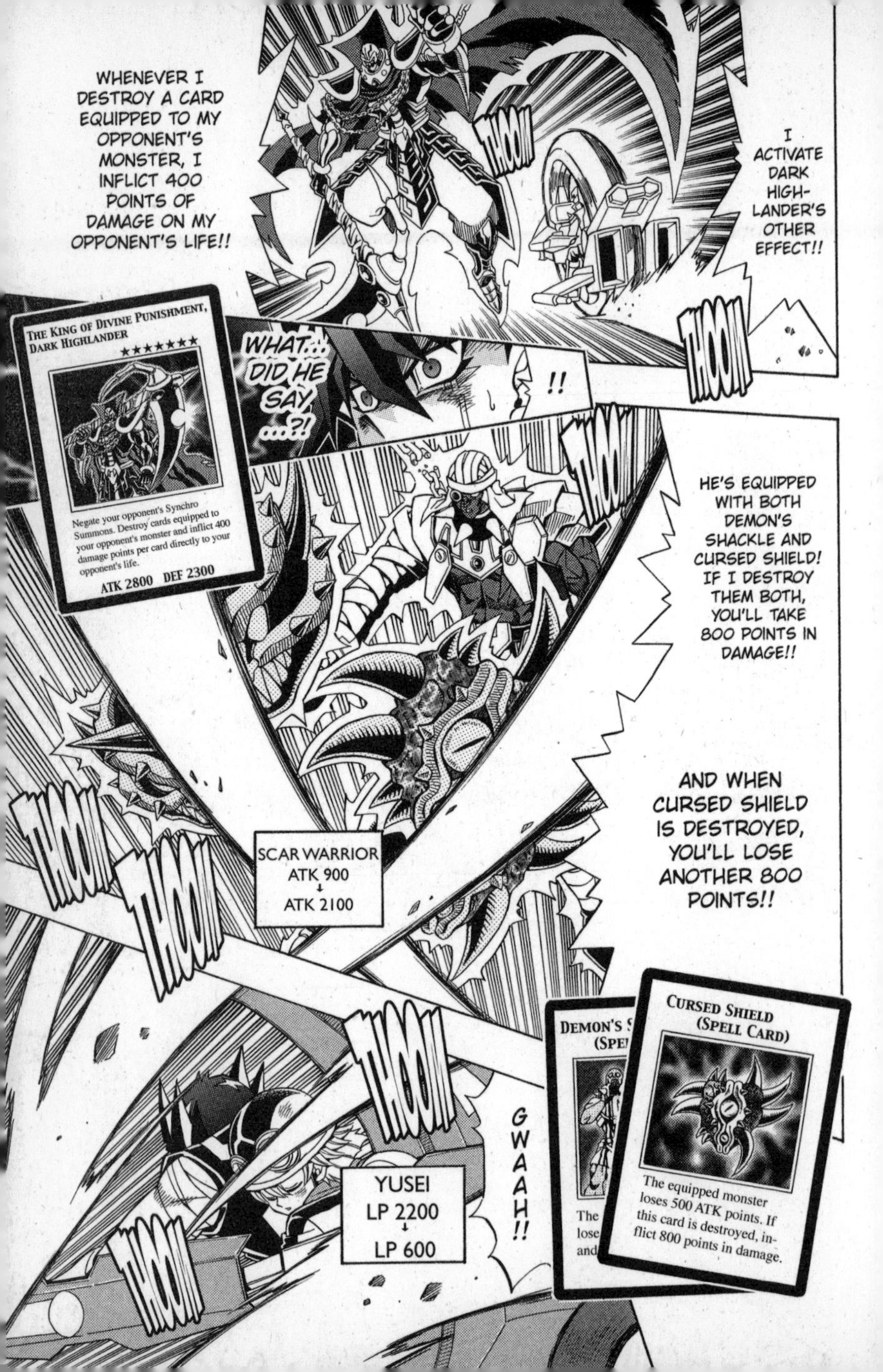
I ACTIVATE DARK HIGH-LANDER'S OTHER EFFECT!!
THOOM
WHENEVER I DESTROY A CARD EQUIPPED TO MY OPPONENT'S MONSTER, I INFLICT 400 POINTS OF DAMAGE ON MY OPPONENT'S LIFE!!
THOOM
The King of Divine Punishment, Dark Highlander
★★★★★★★
Negate your opponent's Synchro Summons. Destroy cards equipped to your opponent's monster and inflict 400 damage points per card directly to your opponent's life.
ATK 2800 DEF 2300
!!
WHAT... DID HE SAY...?!
THOOM
HE'S EQUIPPED WITH BOTH DEMON'S SHACKLE AND CURSED SHIELD! IF I DESTROY THEM BOTH, YOU'LL TAKE 800 POINTS IN DAMAGE!!
AND WHEN CURSED SHIELD IS DESTROYED, YOU'LL LOSE ANOTHER 800 POINTS!!
SCAR WARRIOR ATK 900 ↓ ATK 2100
THOOM
THOOM
Cursed Shield (Spell Card)
The equipped monster loses 500 ATK points. If this card is destroyed, inflict 800 points in damage.
GWAAH!!
THOOM
YUSEI LP 2200 ↓ LP 600
THOOM

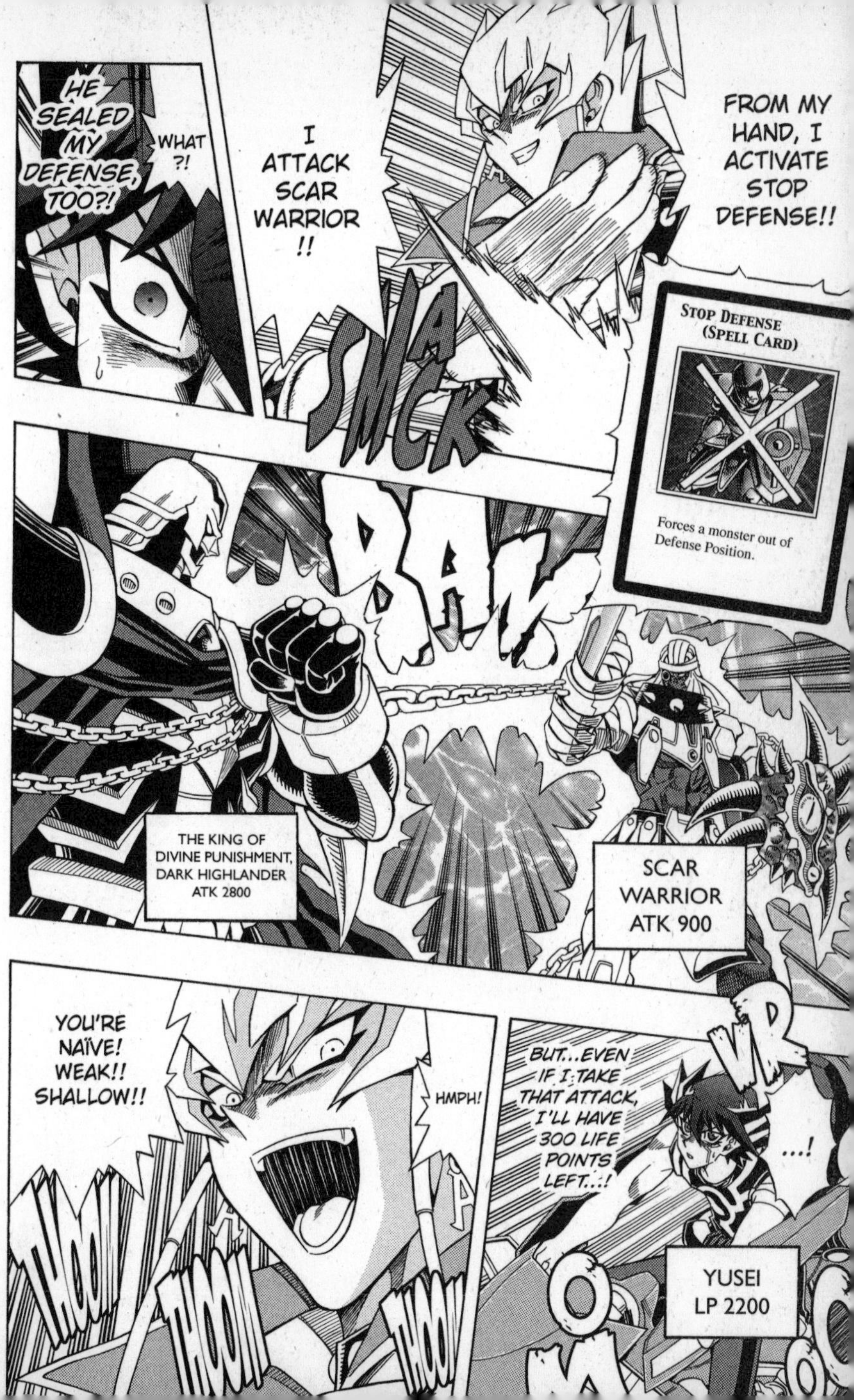
FROM MY HAND, I ACTIVATE STOP DEFENSE!!
STOP DEFENSE (SPELL CARD)
Forces a monster out of Defense Position.
I ATTACK SCAR WARRIOR!!
SMACK
WHAT?!
HE SEALED MY DEFENSE, TOO?!
BAM
SCAR WARRIOR ATK 900
THE KING OF DIVINE PUNISHMENT, DARK HIGHLANDER ATK 2800
...!
BUT...EVEN IF I TAKE THAT ATTACK, I'LL HAVE 300 LIFE POINTS LEFT...!
YUSEI LP 2200
HMPH!
YOU'RE NAÏVE! WEAK!! SHALLOW!!
THOOM
THOOM
THOOM

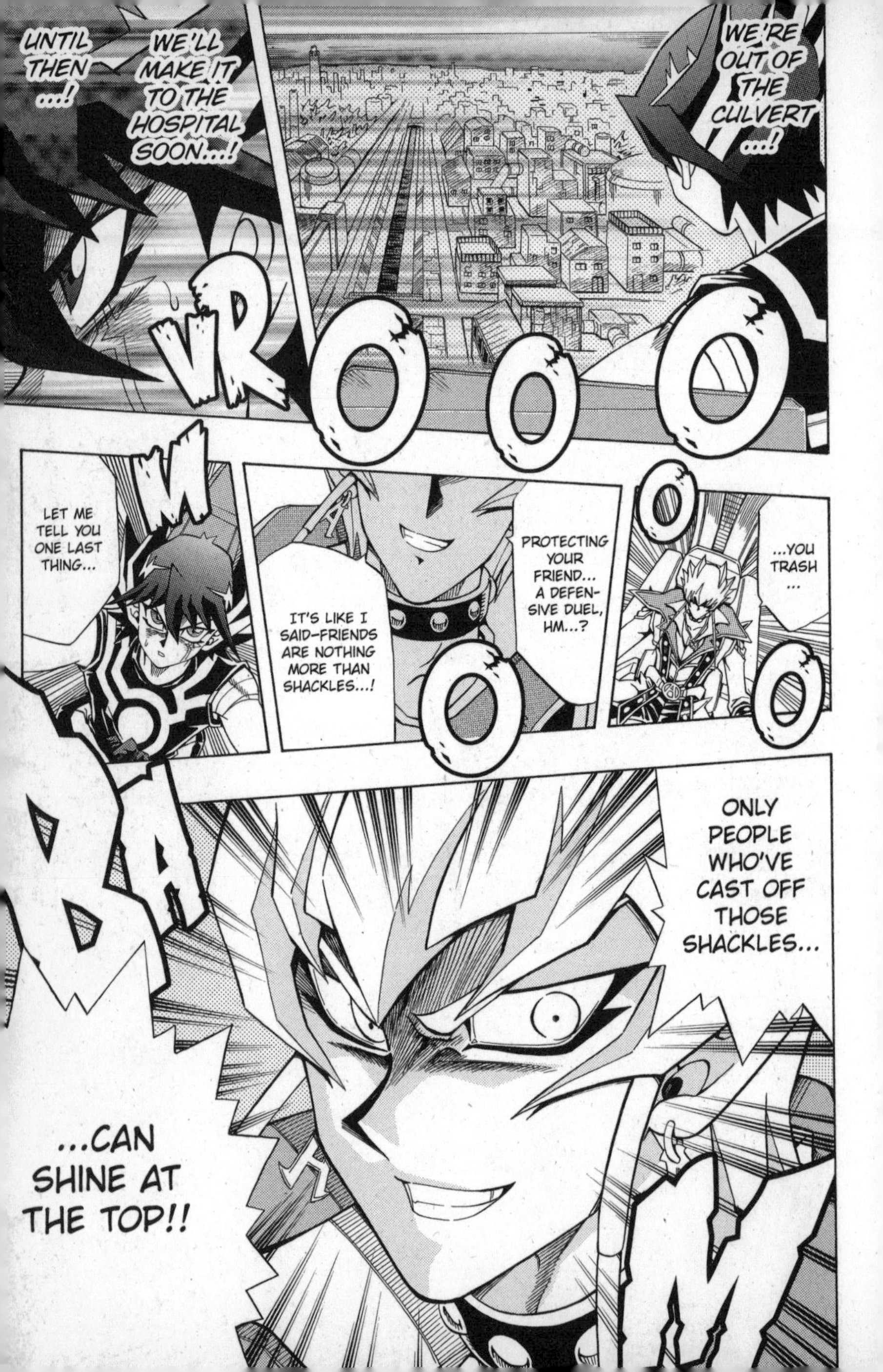
WE'RE OUT OF THE CULVERT...!
WE'LL MAKE IT TO THE HOSPITAL SOON...!
UNTIL THEN...!
VROOOOOOM
...YOU TRASH...
PROTECTING YOUR FRIEND... A DEFEN-SIVE DUEL, HM...?
IT'S LIKE I SAID—FRIENDS ARE NOTHING MORE THAN SHACKLES...!
LET ME TELL YOU ONE LAST THING...
ONLY PEOPLE WHO'VE CAST OFF THOSE SHACKLES...
...CAN SHINE AT THE TOP!!
BAM

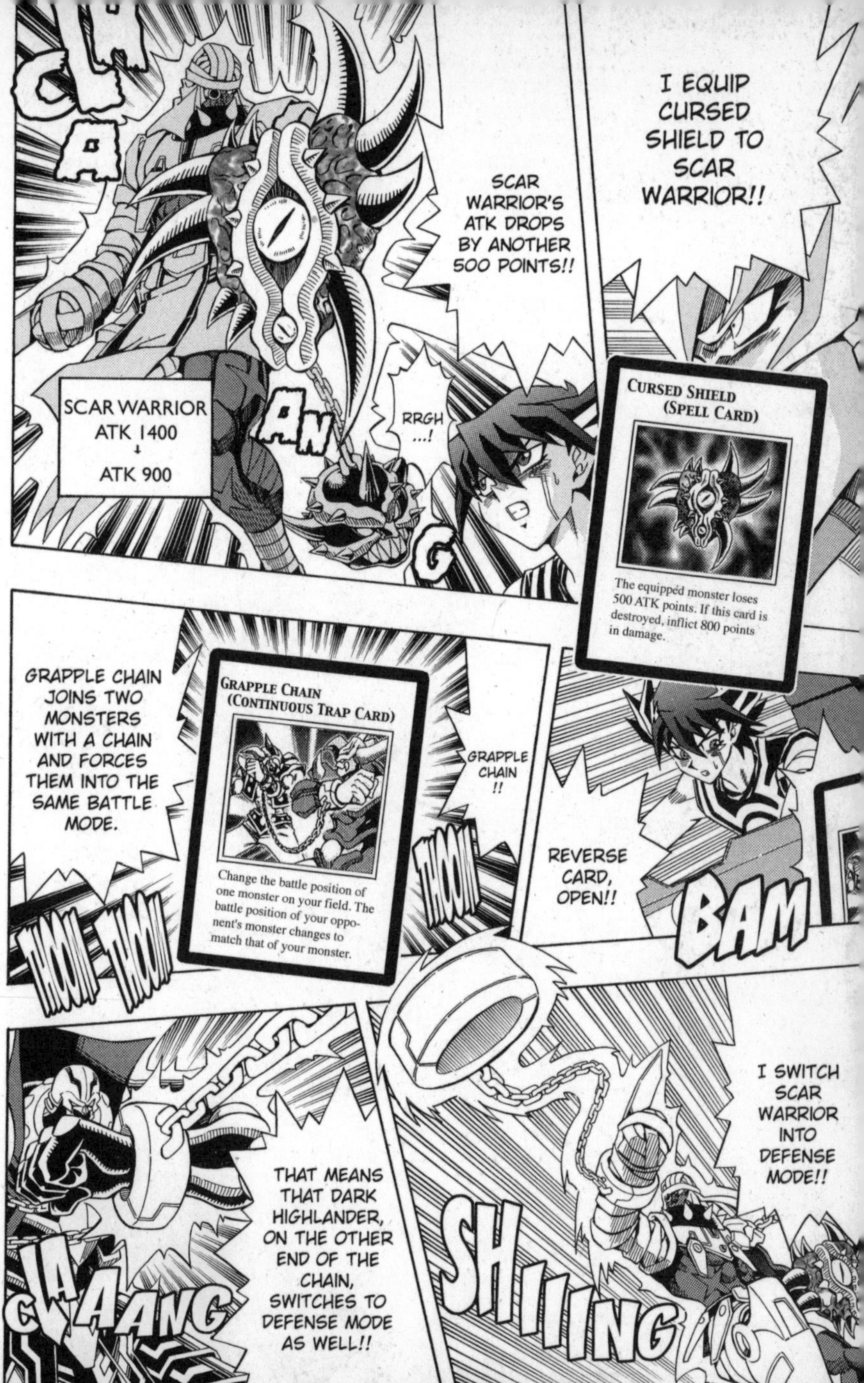
I EQUIP CURSED SHIELD TO SCAR WARRIOR!!
CURSED SHIELD
(SPELL CARD)
The equipped monster loses 500 ATK points. If this card is destroyed, inflict 800 points in damage.
SCAR WARRIOR'S ATK DROPS BY ANOTHER 500 POINTS!!
RRGH ...!
CLAANG
SCAR WARRIOR
ATK 1400
↓
ATK 900
REVERSE CARD, OPEN!!
BAM
GRAPPLE CHAIN !!
THOOM
GRAPPLE CHAIN
(CONTINUOUS TRAP CARD)
Change the battle position of one monster on your field. The battle position of your opponent's monster changes to match that of your monster.
GRAPPLE CHAIN JOINS TWO MONSTERS WITH A CHAIN AND FORCES THEM INTO THE SAME BATTLE MODE.
THOOM THOOM
I SWITCH SCAR WARRIOR INTO DEFENSE MODE!!
SHIIIING
THAT MEANS THAT DARK HIGHLANDER, ON THE OTHER END OF THE CHAIN, SWITCHES TO DEFENSE MODE AS WELL!!
CLAAANG

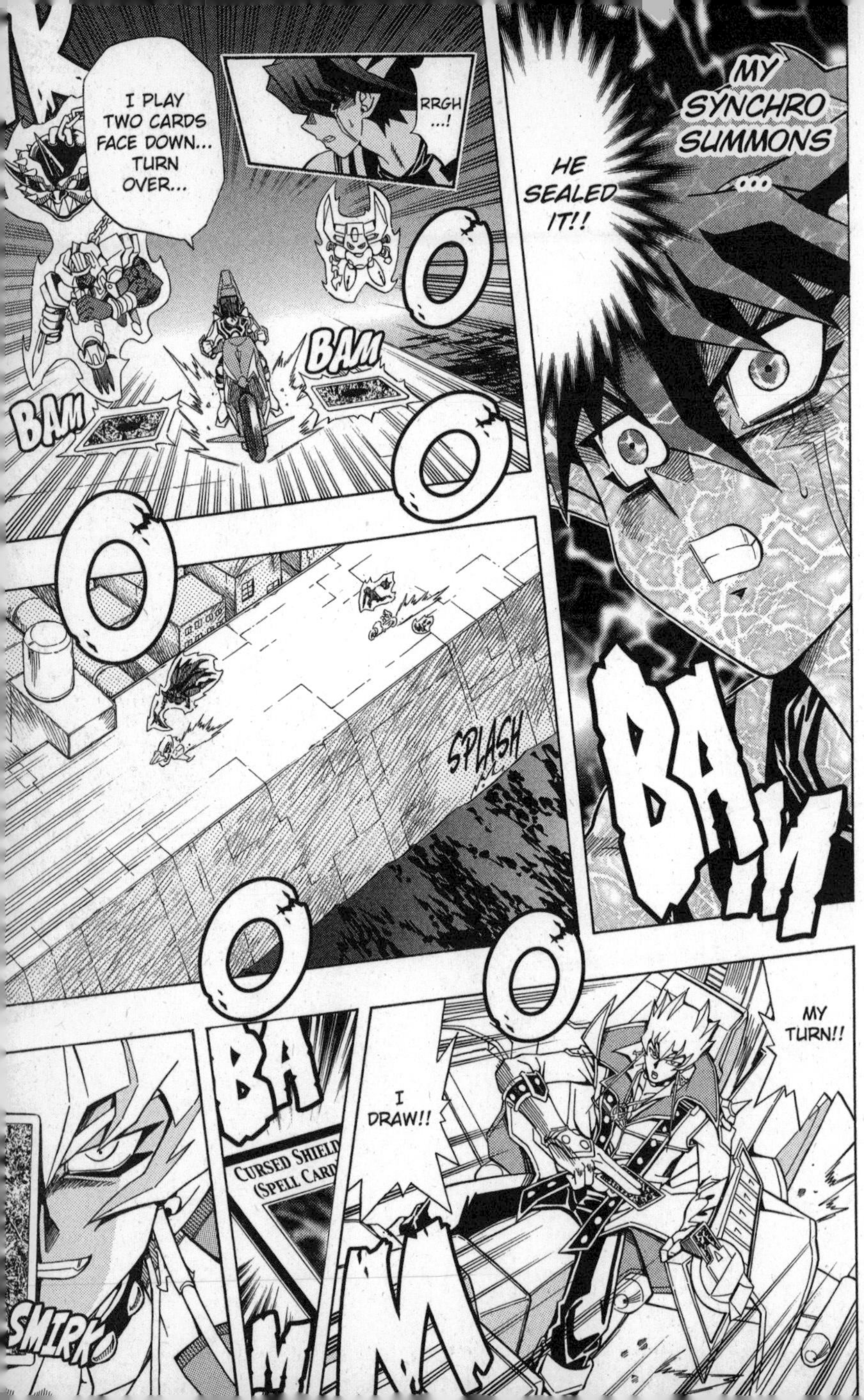
I PLAY TWO CARDS FACE DOWN... TURN OVER...
RRGH ...!
BAM
BAM
SPLASH
MY SYNCHRO SUMMONS ...
HE SEALED IT!!
BAM
MY TURN!!
I DRAW!!
BAM
CURSED SHIELD (SPELL CARD)
SMIRK

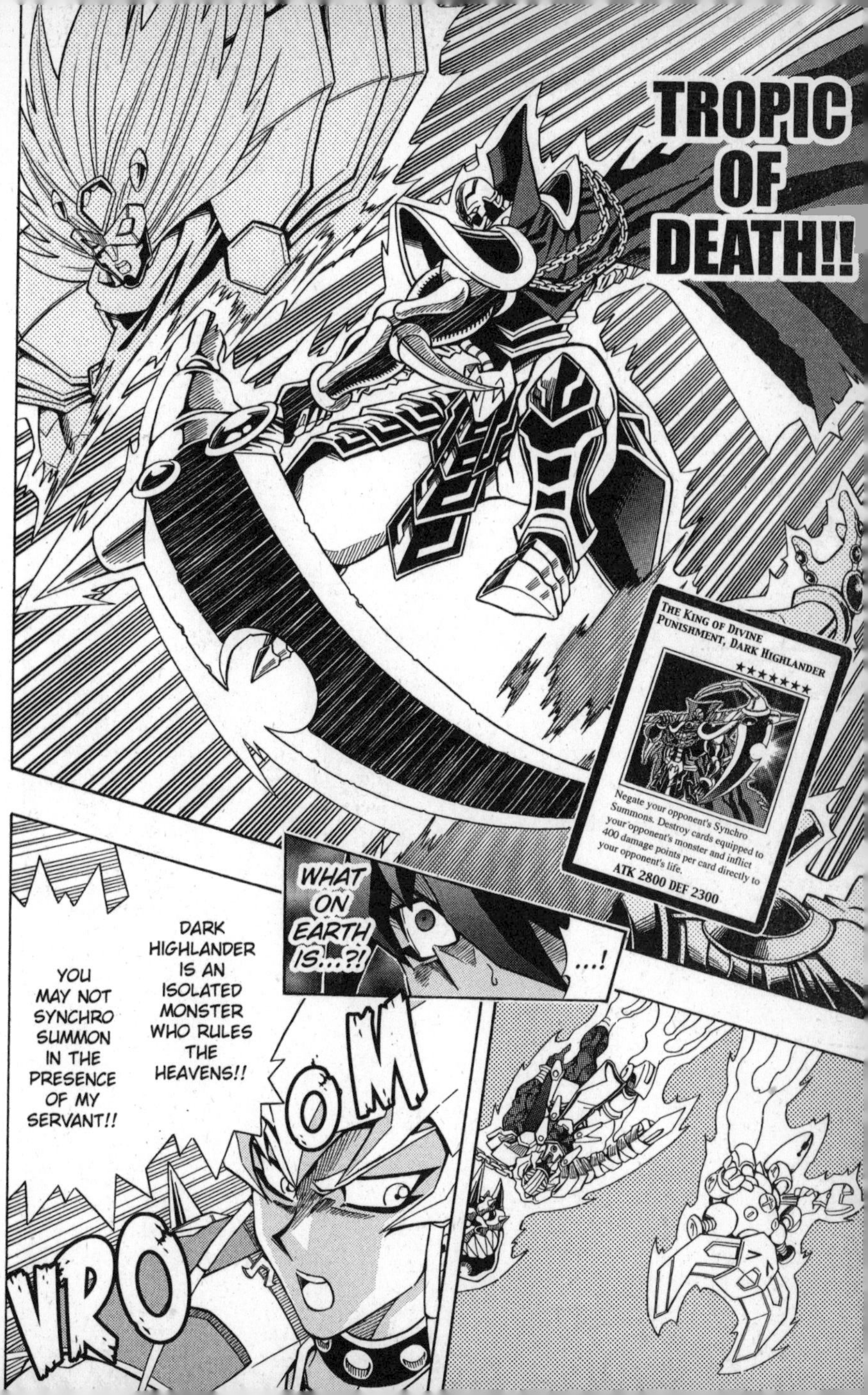
TROPIC OF DEATH!!
THE KING OF DIVINE PUNISHMENT, DARK HIGHLANDER
Negate your opponent's Synchro Summons. Destroy cards equipped to your opponent's monster and inflict 400 damage points per card directly to your opponent's life.
ATK 2800 DEF 2300
WHAT ON EARTH IS...?!
...!
DARK HIGHLANDER IS AN ISOLATED MONSTER WHO RULES THE HEAVENS!!
YOU MAY NOT SYNCHRO SUMMON IN THE PRESENCE OF MY SERVANT!!
VROOM

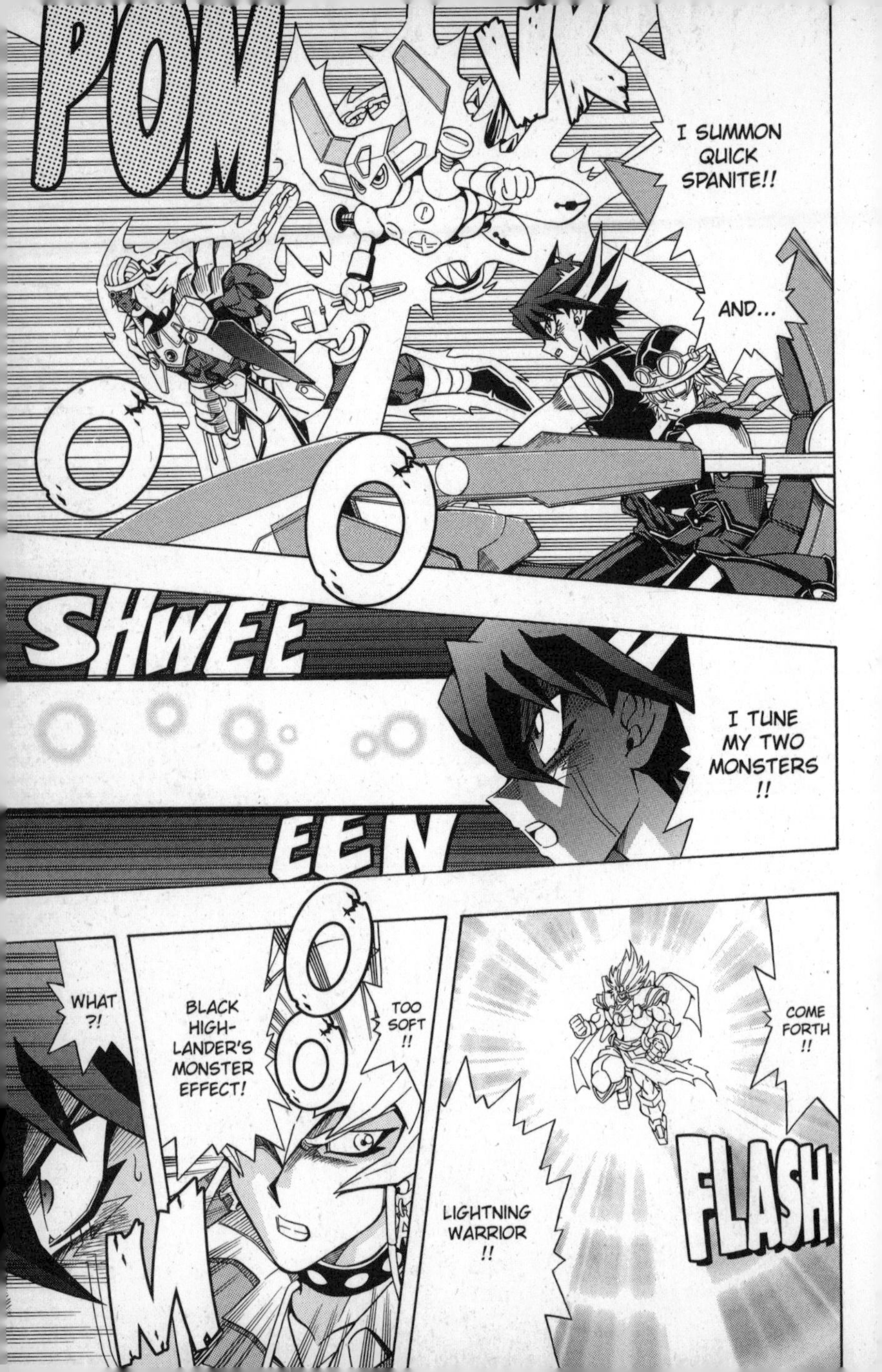
POM
VK
I SUMMON QUICK SPANITE!!
AND...
SHWEE
I TUNE MY TWO MONSTERS !!
EEN
COME FORTH !!
FLASH
LIGHTNING WARRIOR !!
TOO SOFT !!
BLACK HIGH-LANDER'S MONSTER EFFECT!
WHAT ?!
M

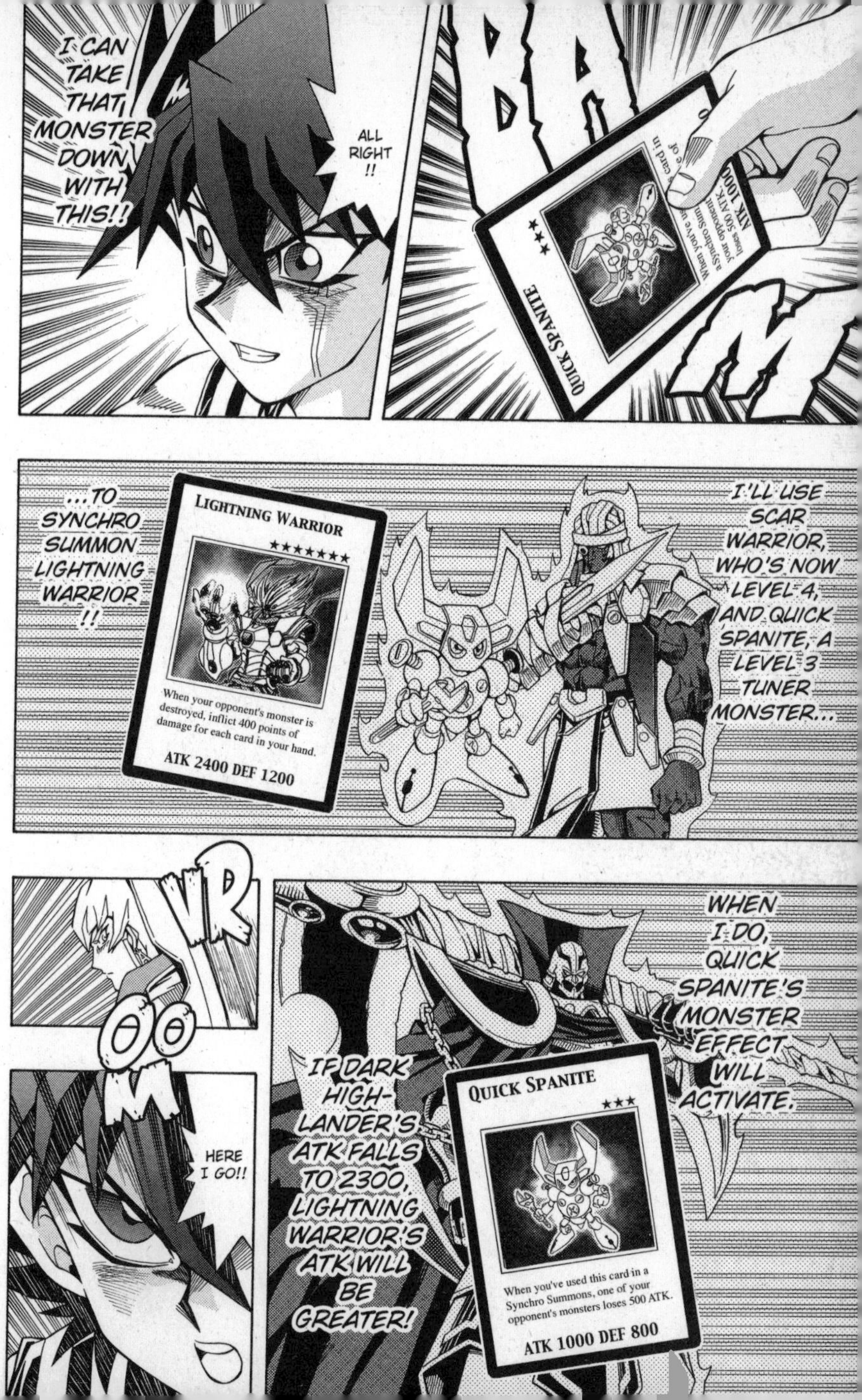
BAM
QUICK SPANITE
ATK 1000
ALL RIGHT !!
I CAN TAKE THAT MONSTER DOWN WITH THIS!!
I'LL USE SCAR WARRIOR, WHO'S NOW LEVEL 4, AND QUICK SPANITE, A LEVEL 3 TUNER MONSTER...
LIGHTNING WARRIOR
When your opponent's monster is destroyed, inflict 400 points of damage for each card in your hand.
ATK 2400 DEF 1200
...TO SYNCHRO SUMMON LIGHTNING WARRIOR !!
WHEN I DO, QUICK SPANITE'S MONSTER EFFECT WILL ACTIVATE.
IF DARK HIGH-LANDER'S ATK FALLS TO 2300, LIGHTNING WARRIOR'S ATK WILL BE GREATER!
QUICK SPANITE
When you've used this card in a Synchro Summons, one of your opponent's monsters loses 500 ATK.
ATK 1000 DEF 800
VR
HERE I GO!!

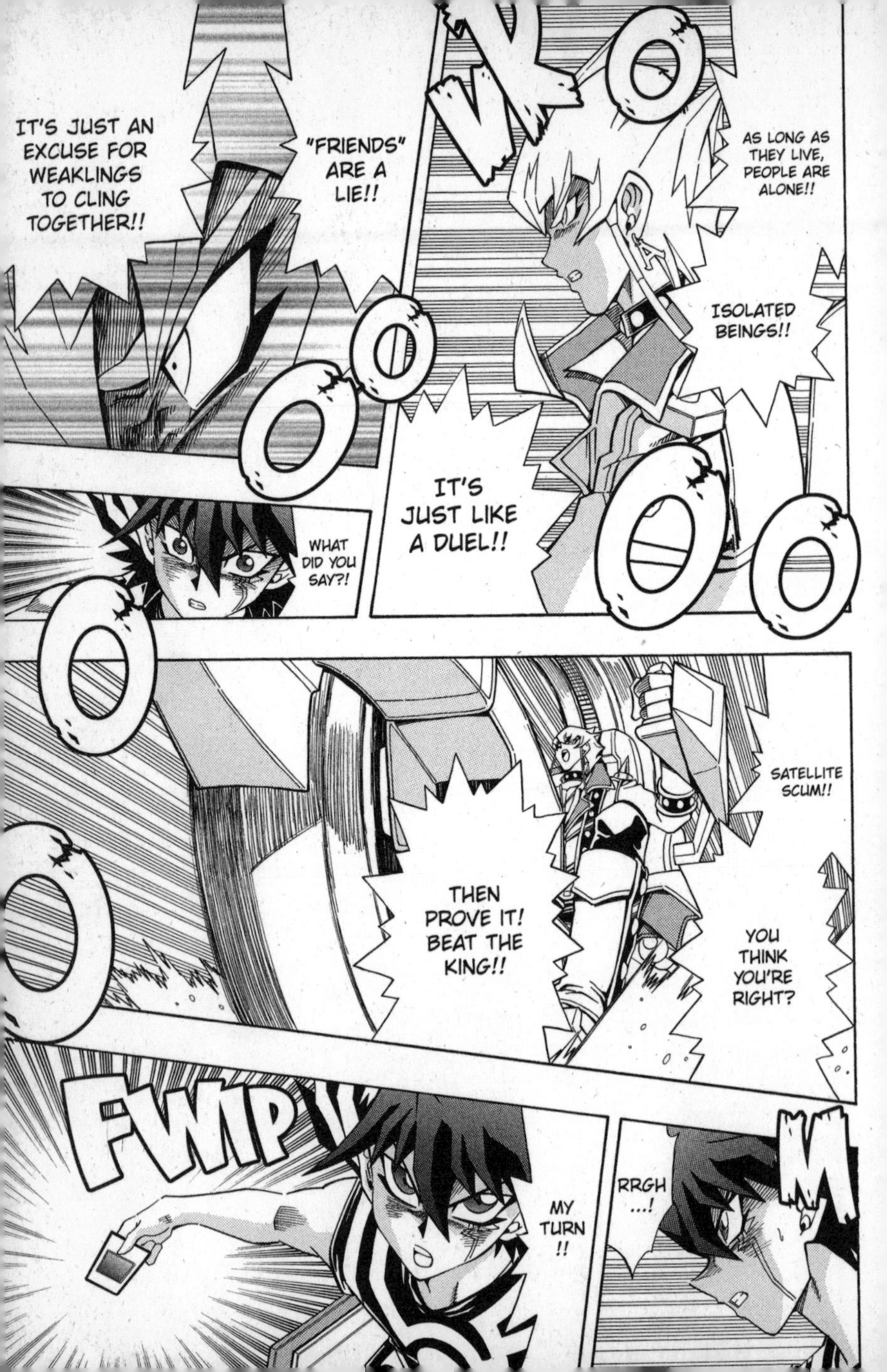
AS LONG AS THEY LIVE, PEOPLE ARE ALONE!!
ISOLATED BEINGS!!
IT'S JUST LIKE A DUEL!!
"FRIENDS" ARE A LIE!!
IT'S JUST AN EXCUSE FOR WEAKLINGS TO CLING TOGETHER!!
WHAT DID YOU SAY?!
SATELLITE SCUM!!
YOU THINK YOU'RE RIGHT?
THEN PROVE IT! BEAT THE KING!!
RRGH ...!
FWMP
MY TURN !!

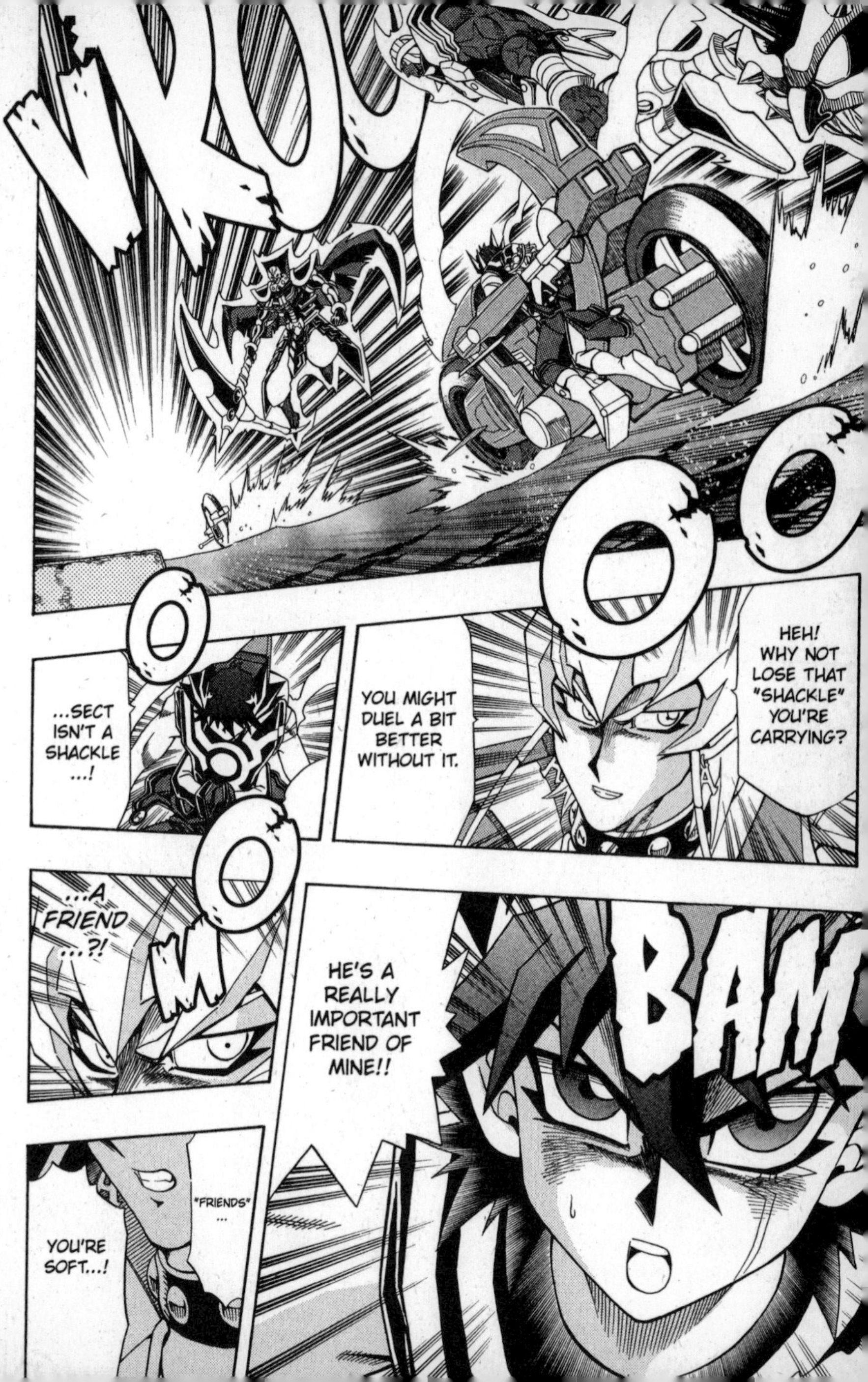
VROOOOM
HEH! WHY NOT LOSE THAT "SHACKLE" YOU'RE CARRYING?
YOU MIGHT DUEL A BIT BETTER WITHOUT IT.
...SECT ISN'T A SHACKLE ...!
BAM
HE'S A REALLY IMPORTANT FRIEND OF MINE!!
...A FRIEND ...?!
"FRIENDS" ...
YOU'RE SOFT...!

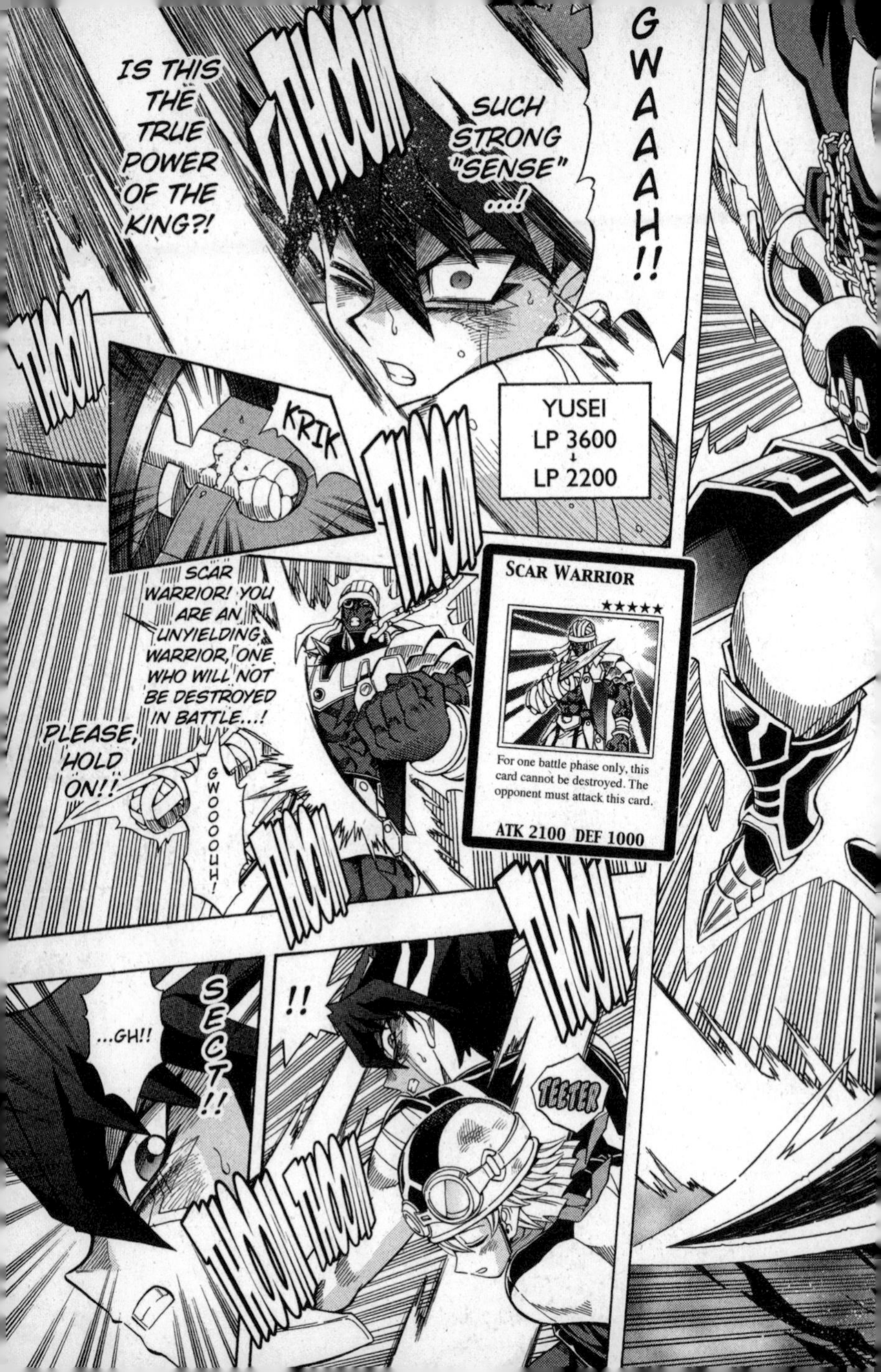
GWAAAAH!!
SUCH STRONG "SENSE" ...!
THOOM
IS THIS THE TRUE POWER OF THE KING?!
THOOM
YUSEI
LP 3600
LP 2200
THOOM
KRIK
SCAR WARRIOR
For one battle phase only, this card cannot be destroyed. The opponent must attack this card.
ATK 2100 DEF 1000
SCAR WARRIOR! YOU ARE AN UNYIELDING WARRIOR, ONE WHO WILL NOT BE DESTROYED IN BATTLE...!
GWOOOOUH!
PLEASE, HOLD ON!!
THOOM
THOOM
THOOM
TEETER
!!
SECT!!
...GH!!
THOOM THOOM

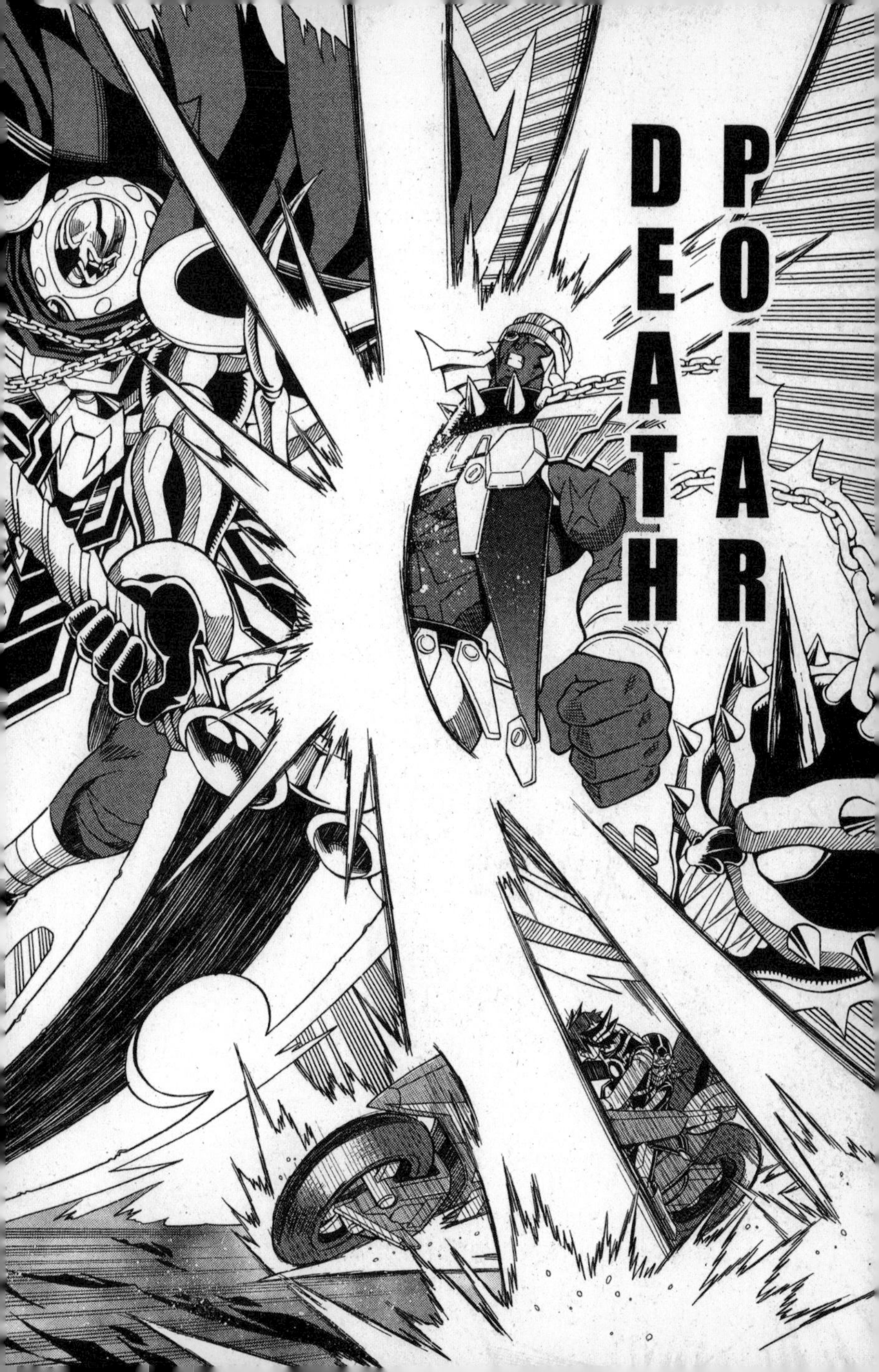
POLAR
DEATH

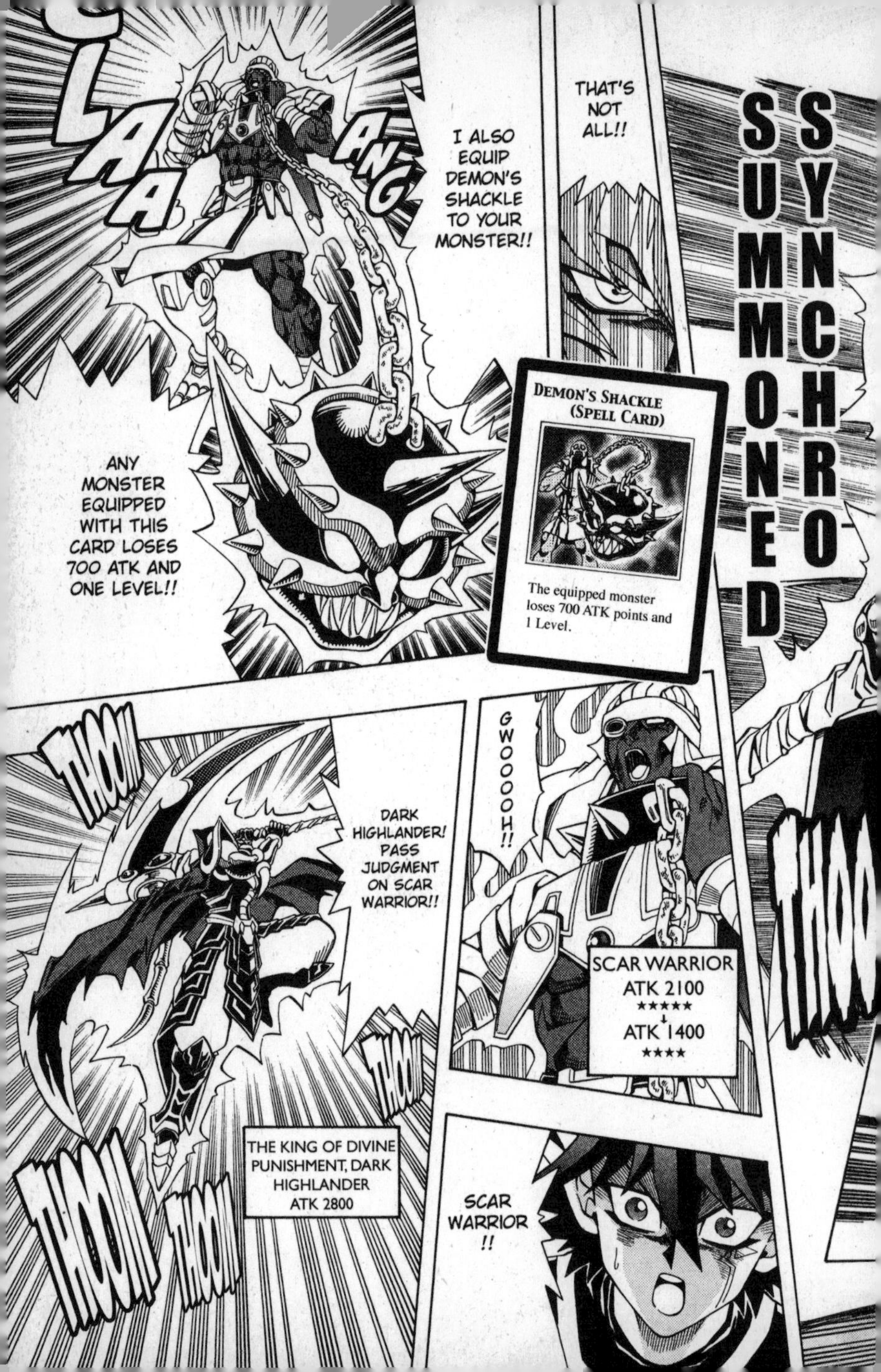
SYNCHRO
SUMMONED
THAT'S NOT ALL!!
I ALSO EQUIP DEMON'S SHACKLE TO YOUR MONSTER!!
CLAAANG
DEMON'S SHACKLE (SPELL CARD)
The equipped monster loses 700 ATK points and 1 Level.
ANY MONSTER EQUIPPED WITH THIS CARD LOSES 700 ATK AND ONE LEVEL!!
THOOM
GWOOOOOH!!
SCAR WARRIOR
ATK 2100
★★★★★
↓
ATK 1400
★★★★
SCAR WARRIOR!!
THOOM
DARK HIGHLANDER! PASS JUDGMENT ON SCAR WARRIOR!!
THOOM
THE KING OF DIVINE PUNISHMENT, DARK HIGHLANDER
ATK 2800
THOOM
THOOM

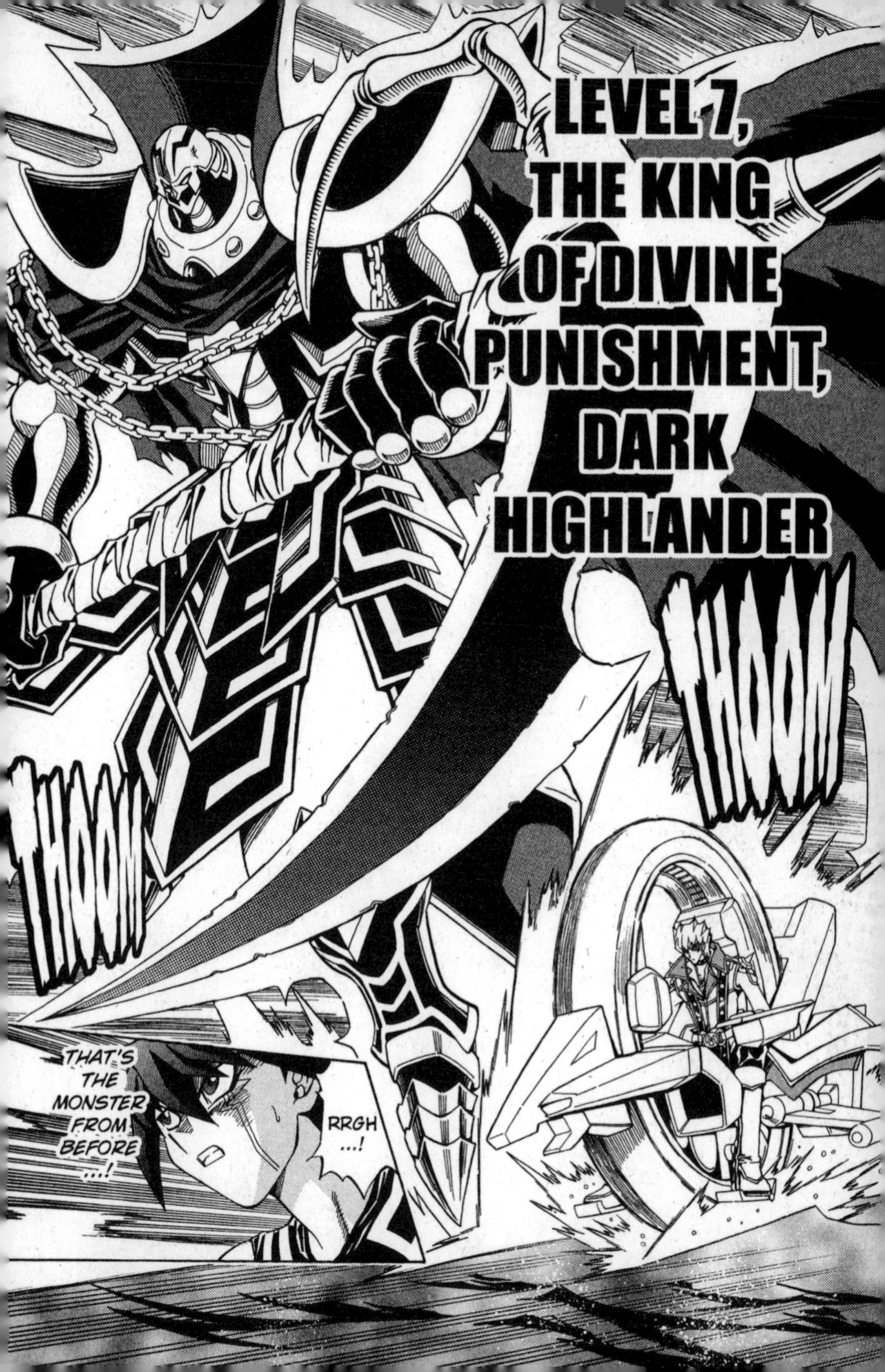
LEVEL 7, THE KING OF DIVINE PUNISHMENT, DARK HIGHLANDER
THOOM
THOOM
RRGH ...!
THAT'S THE MONSTER FROM BEFORE ...!

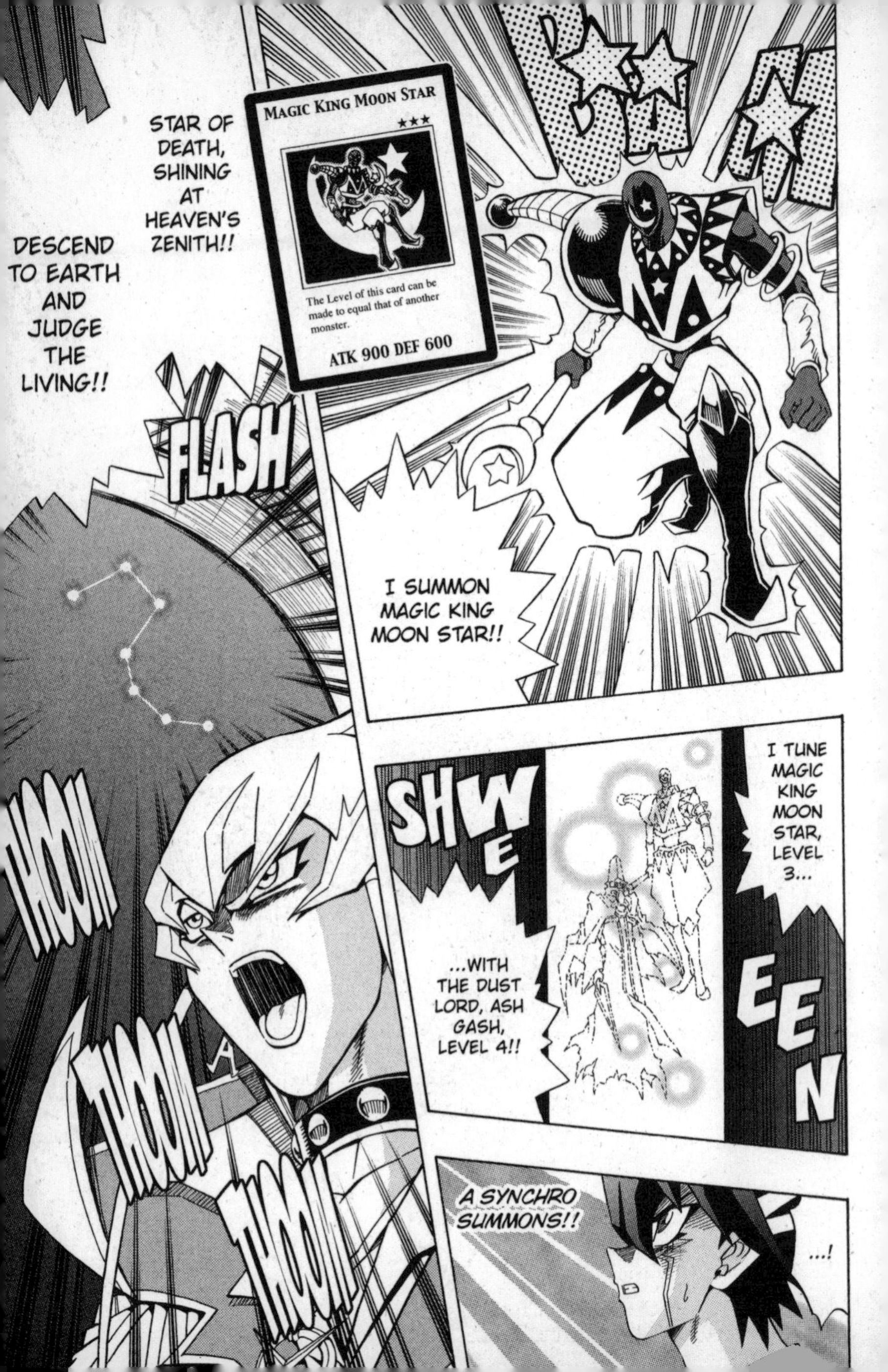

MAGIC KING MOON STAR
The Level of this card can be made to equal that of another monster.
ATK 900 DEF 600
I SUMMON MAGIC KING MOON STAR!!
I TUNE MAGIC KING MOON STAR, LEVEL 3...
SHWEEEN
...WITH THE DUST LORD, ASH GASH, LEVEL 4!!
A SYNCHRO SUMMONS!!
...!
STAR OF DEATH, SHINING AT HEAVEN'S ZENITH!!
DESCEND TO EARTH AND JUDGE THE LIVING!!
FLASH
THOOM
THOOM
THOOM

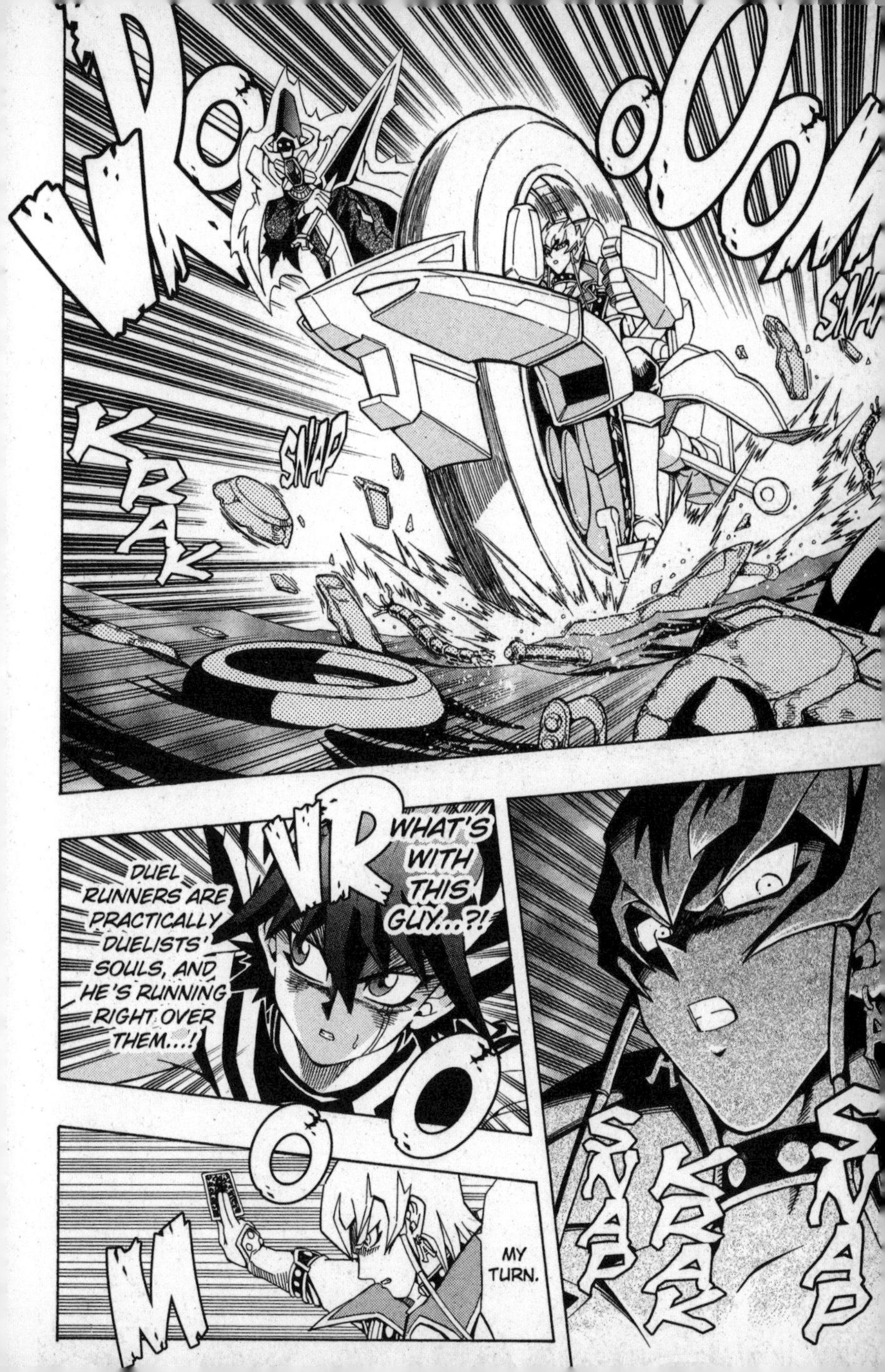
VROOOOM
SNAP
SNAP
KRAK
SNAP
SKRAK
SNAP
VROOOM
WHAT'S WITH THIS GUY...?!
DUEL RUNNERS ARE PRACTICALLY DUELISTS' SOULS, AND HE'S RUNNING RIGHT OVER THEM...!
MY TURN.

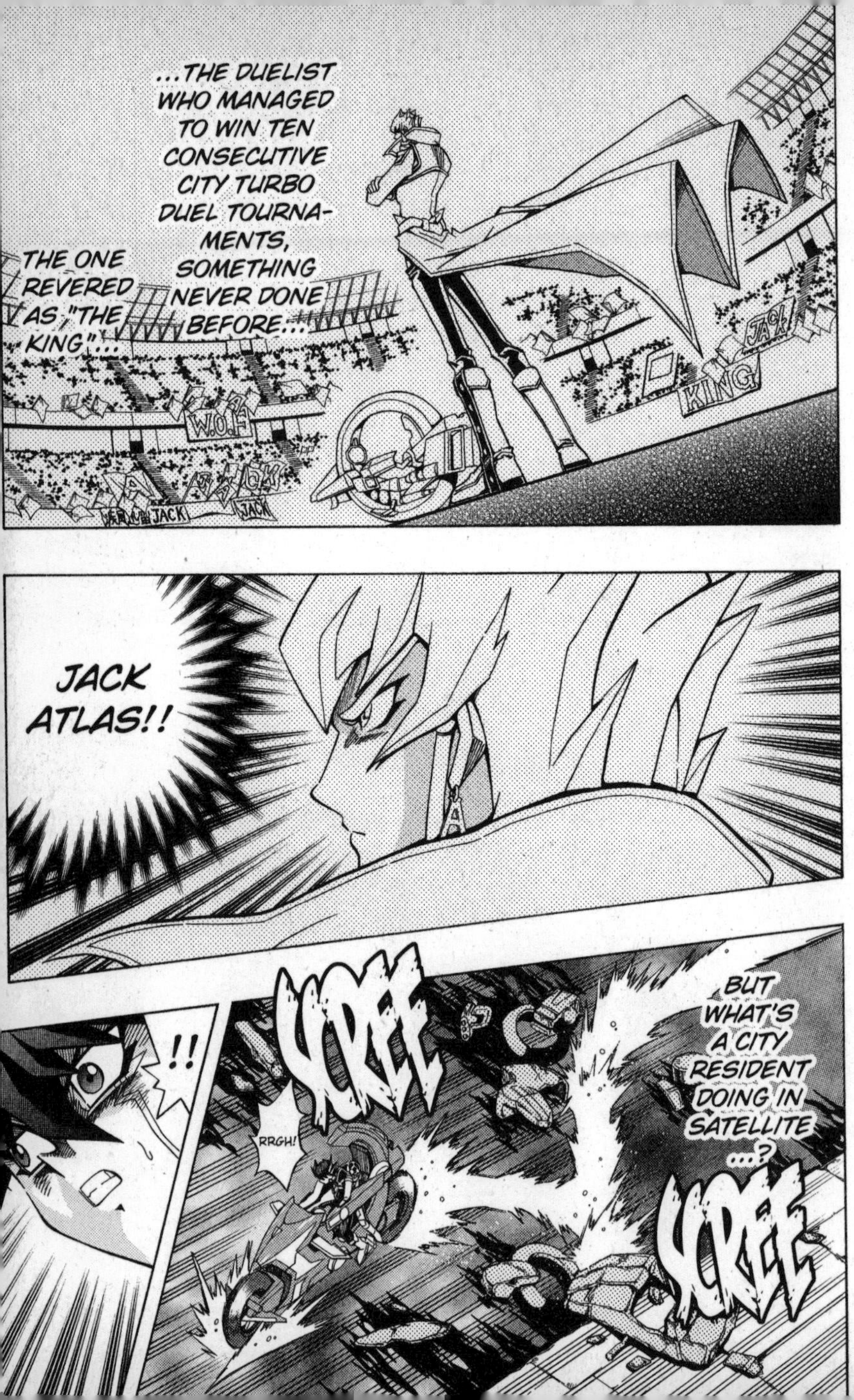
...THE DUELIST WHO MANAGED TO WIN TEN CONSECUTIVE CITY TURBO DUEL TOURNAMENTS, SOMETHING NEVER DONE BEFORE...
THE ONE REVERED AS "THE KING"...
KING
JACK
JACK
W.O.F
JACK ATLAS!!
BUT WHAT'S A CITY RESIDENT DOING IN SATELLITE ...?
RRGH!
!!

RIDE-06

"SHACKLE"...!!

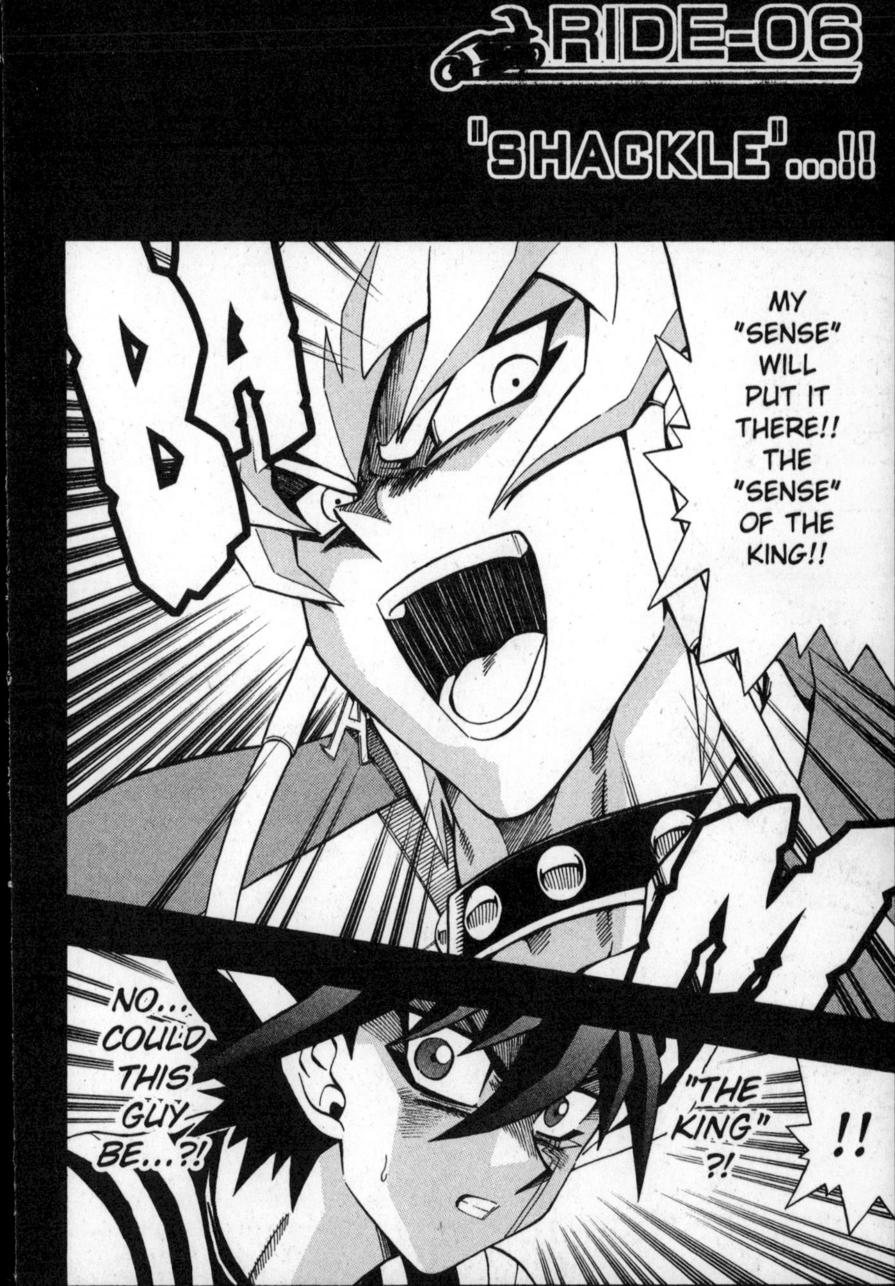

MY "SENSE" WILL PUT IT THERE!! THE "SENSE" OF THE KING!!
BA
M
!!
"THE KING" ?!
NO... COULD THIS GUY BE...?!

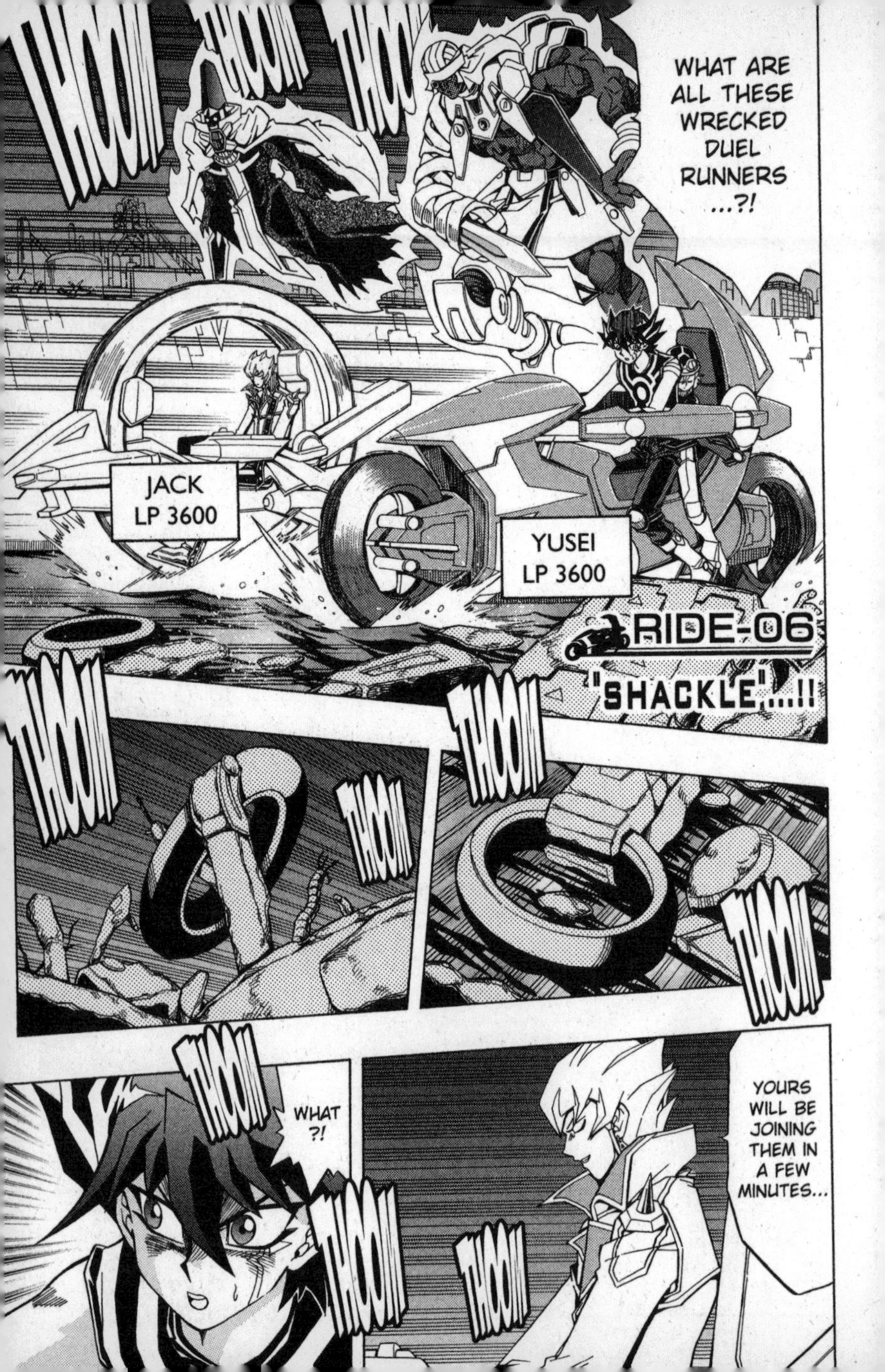
WHAT ARE ALL THESE WRECKED DUEL RUNNERS ...?!
THOOM
THOOM
THOOM
YUSEI LP 3600
JACK LP 3600
RIDE-06
"SHACKLE"...!!
THOOM
THOOM
THOOM
THOOM
YOURS WILL BE JOINING THEM IN A FEW MINUTES...
THOOM
WHAT ?!
THOOM
THOOM

5D's TRACKS

THE 5TH

BY SATOMASA

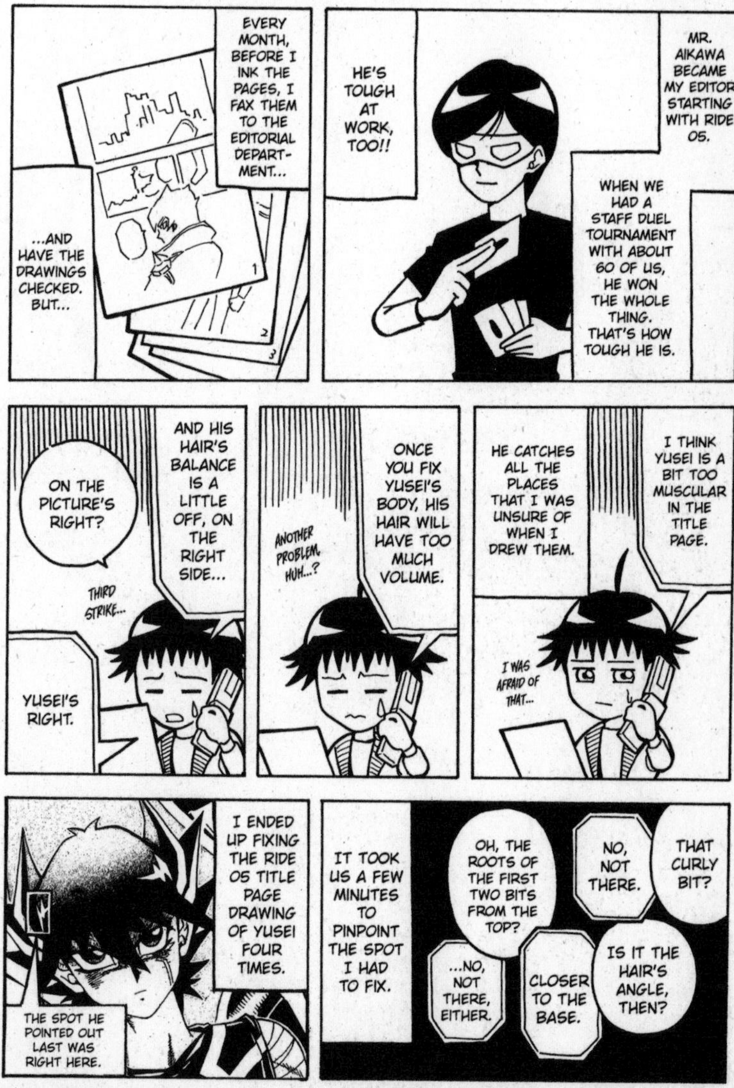

MR. AIKAWA BECAME MY EDITOR STARTING WITH RIDE 05.
WHEN WE HAD A STAFF DUEL TOURNAMENT WITH ABOUT 60 OF US, HE WON THE WHOLE THING. THAT'S HOW TOUGH HE IS.
HE'S TOUGH AT WORK, TOO!!
EVERY MONTH, BEFORE I INK THE PAGES, I FAX THEM TO THE EDITORIAL DEPARTMENT...
...AND HAVE THE DRAWINGS CHECKED. BUT...
I THINK YUSEI IS A BIT TOO MUSCULAR IN THE TITLE PAGE.
HE CATCHES ALL THE PLACES THAT I WAS UNSURE OF WHEN I DREW THEM.
I WAS AFRAID OF THAT...
ONCE YOU FIX YUSEI'S BODY, HIS HAIR WILL HAVE TOO MUCH VOLUME.
ANOTHER PROBLEM, HUH...?
AND HIS HAIR'S BALANCE IS A LITTLE OFF, ON THE RIGHT SIDE...
ON THE PICTURE'S RIGHT?
THIRD STRIKE...
YUSEI'S RIGHT.
THAT CURLY BIT?
NO, NOT THERE.
OH, THE ROOTS OF THE FIRST TWO BITS FROM THE TOP?
IS IT THE HAIR'S ANGLE, THEN?
CLOSER TO THE BASE.
...NO, NOT THERE, EITHER.
IT TOOK US A FEW MINUTES TO PINPOINT THE SPOT I HAD TO FIX.
I ENDED UP FIXING THE RIDE 05 TITLE PAGE DRAWING OF YUSEI FOUR TIMES.
THE SPOT HE POINTED OUT LAST WAS RIGHT HERE.

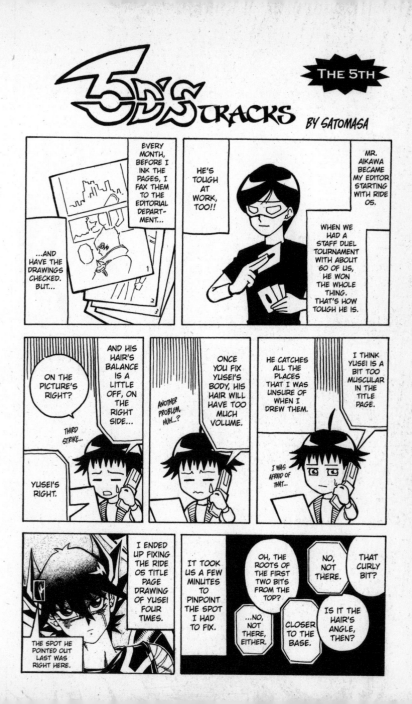

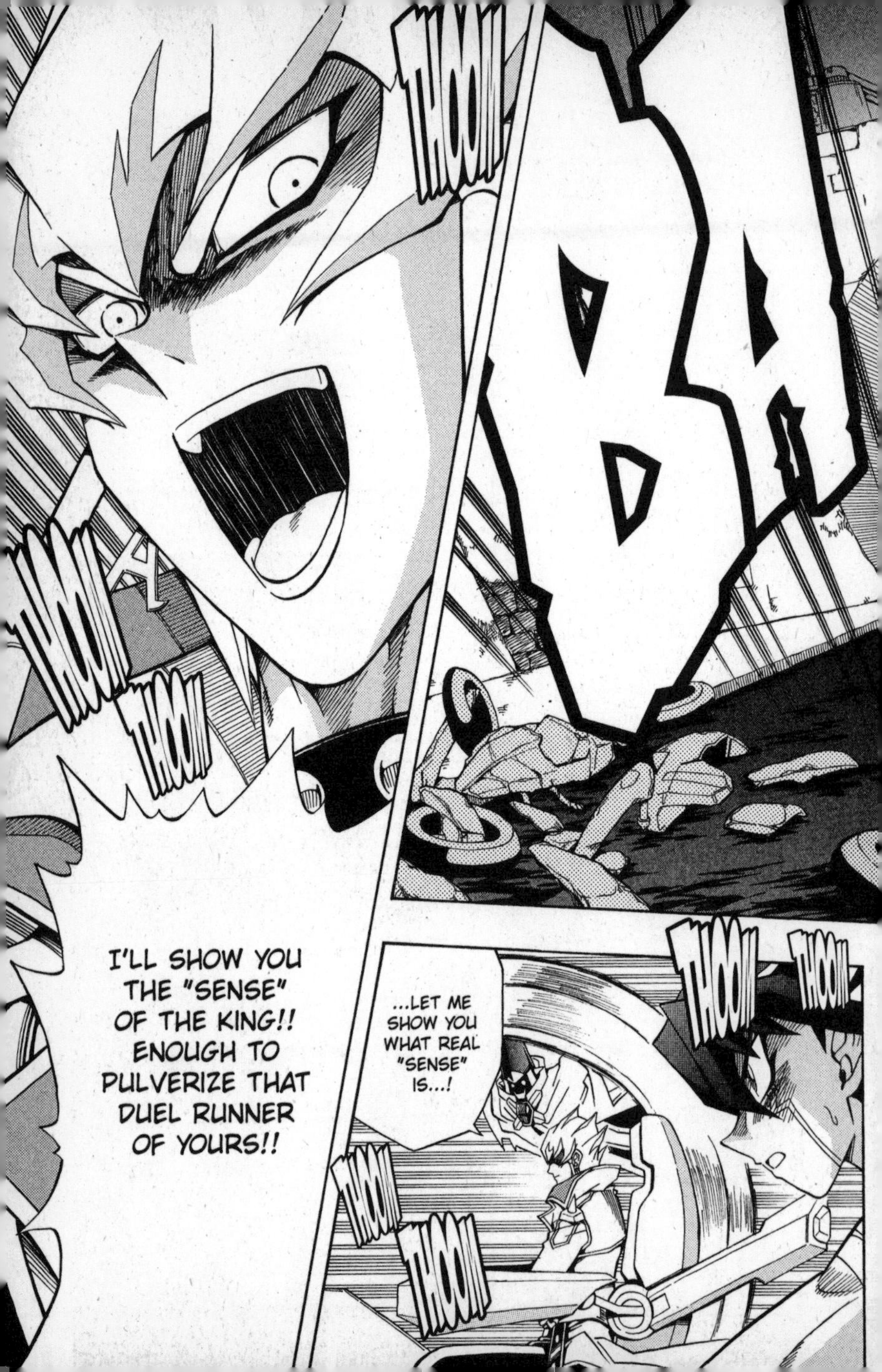
THOOM
THOOM
THOOM
I'LL SHOW YOU THE "SENSE" OF THE KING!! ENOUGH TO PULVERIZE THAT DUEL RUNNER OF YOURS!!
THOOM
THOOM
...LET ME SHOW YOU WHAT REAL "SENSE" IS...!
THOOM
THOOM

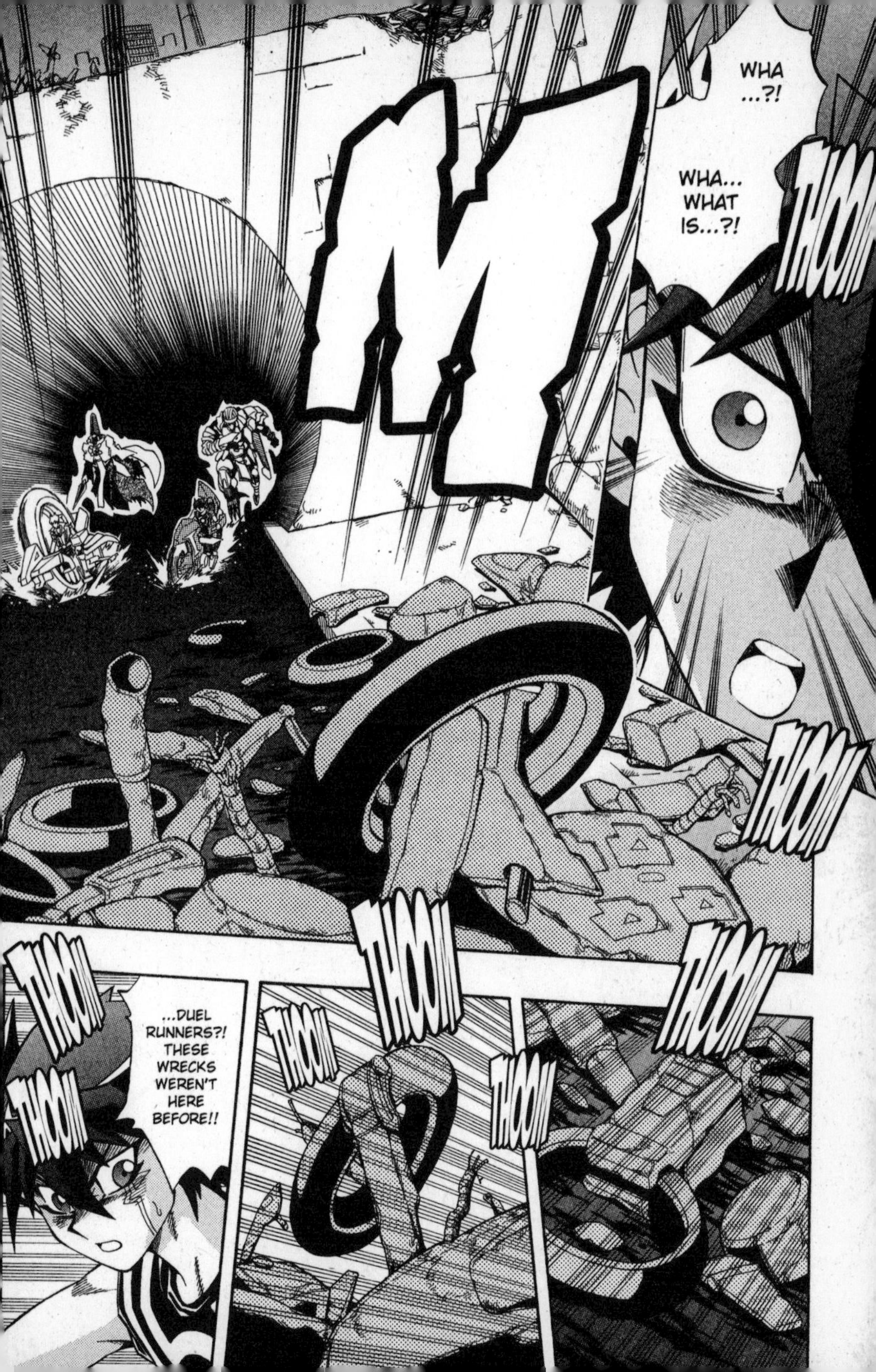
WHA ...?!
WHA... WHAT IS...?!
M
THOOM
THOOM
THOOM
THOOM
THOOM
THOOM
THOOM
THOOM
...DUEL RUNNERS?! THESE WRECKS WEREN'T HERE BEFORE!!

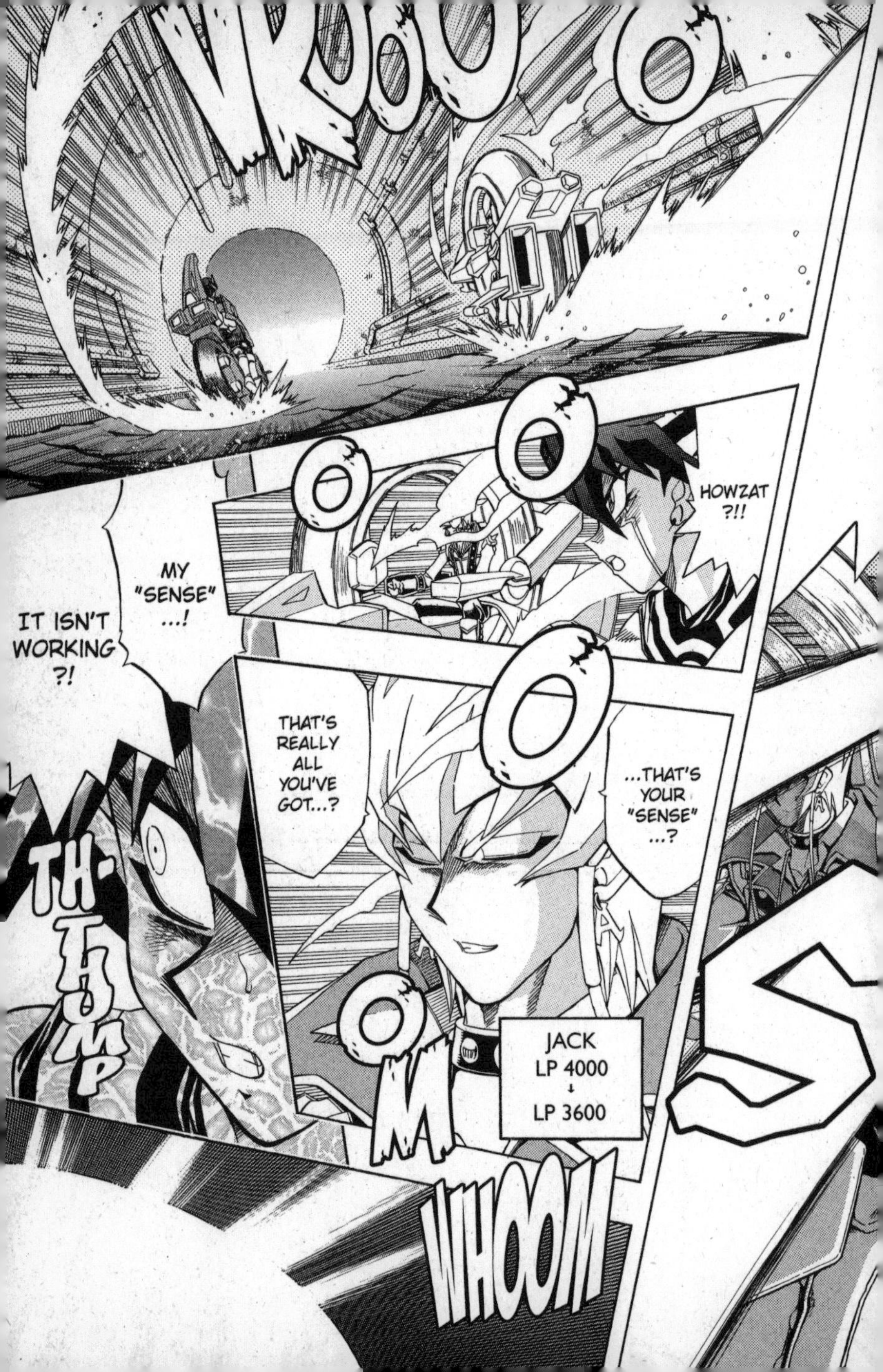
HOWZAT ?!!
MY "SENSE" ...!
IT ISN'T WORKING ?!
...THAT'S YOUR "SENSE" ...?
THAT'S REALLY ALL YOU'VE GOT...?
JACK LP 4000 ↓ LP 3600
TH-THUMP
WHOOM

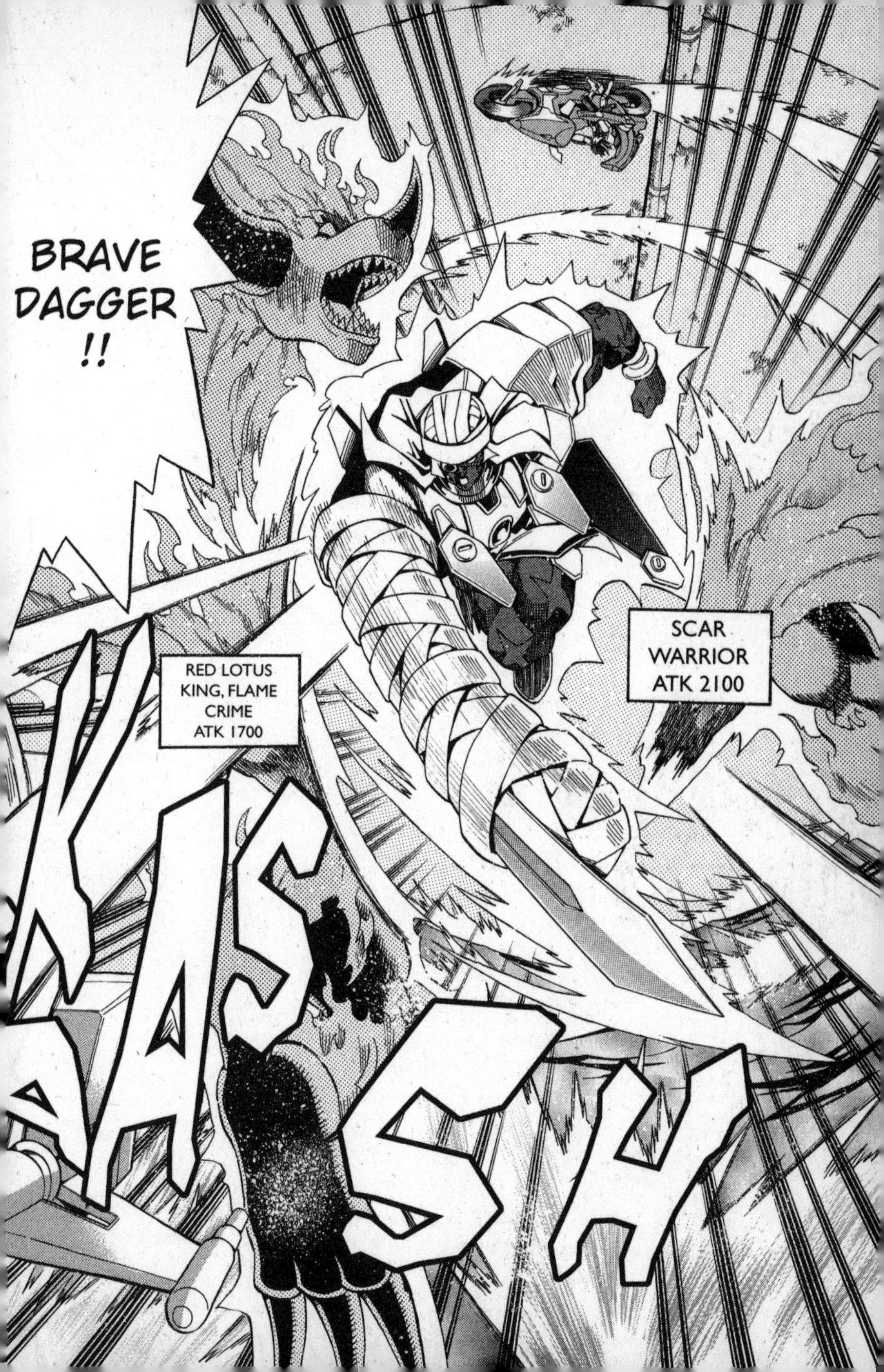
BRAVE DAGGER !!
SCAR WARRIOR ATK 2100
RED LOTUS KING, FLAME CRIME ATK 1700
KASSSH

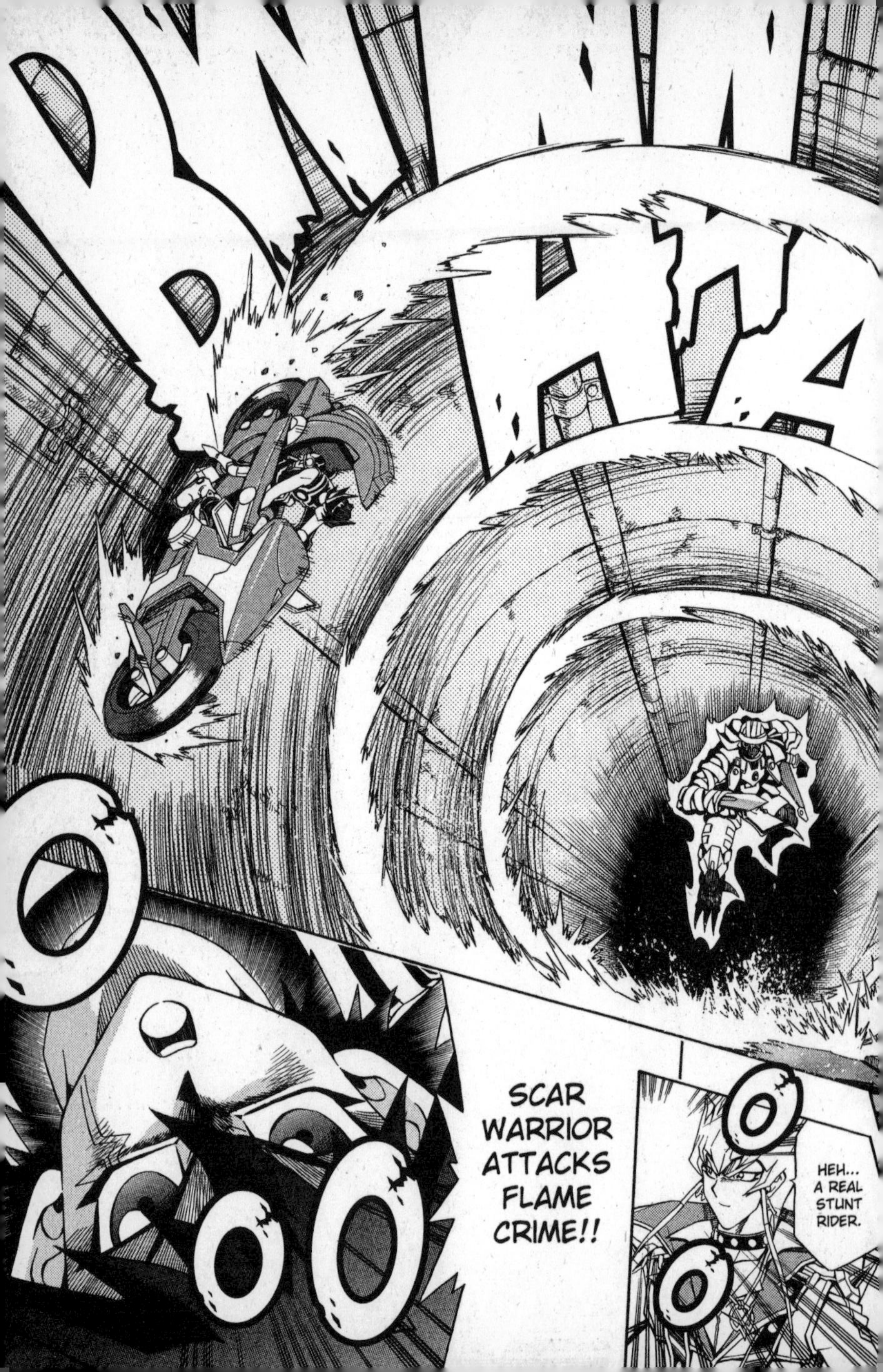

HEH... A REAL STUNT RIDER.
SCAR WARRIOR ATTACKS FLAME CRIME!!

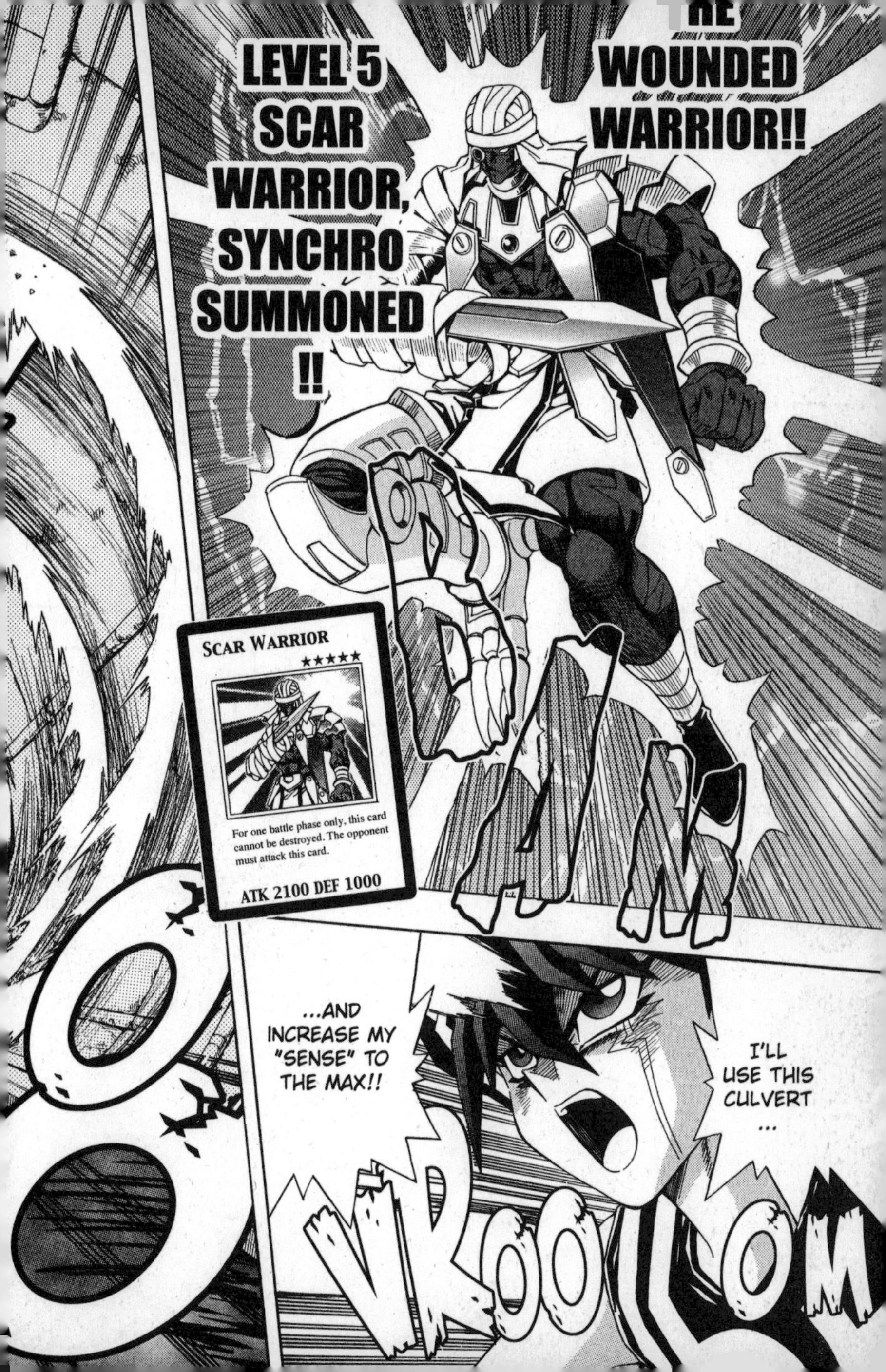
HE WOUNDED WARRIOR!!
LEVEL 5 SCAR WARRIOR, SYNCHRO SUMMONED!!
SCAR WARRIOR
For one battle phase only, this card cannot be destroyed. The opponent must attack this card.
ATK 2100 DEF 1000
I'LL USE THIS CULVERT...
...AND INCREASE MY "SENSE" TO THE MAX!!
VROOOOM

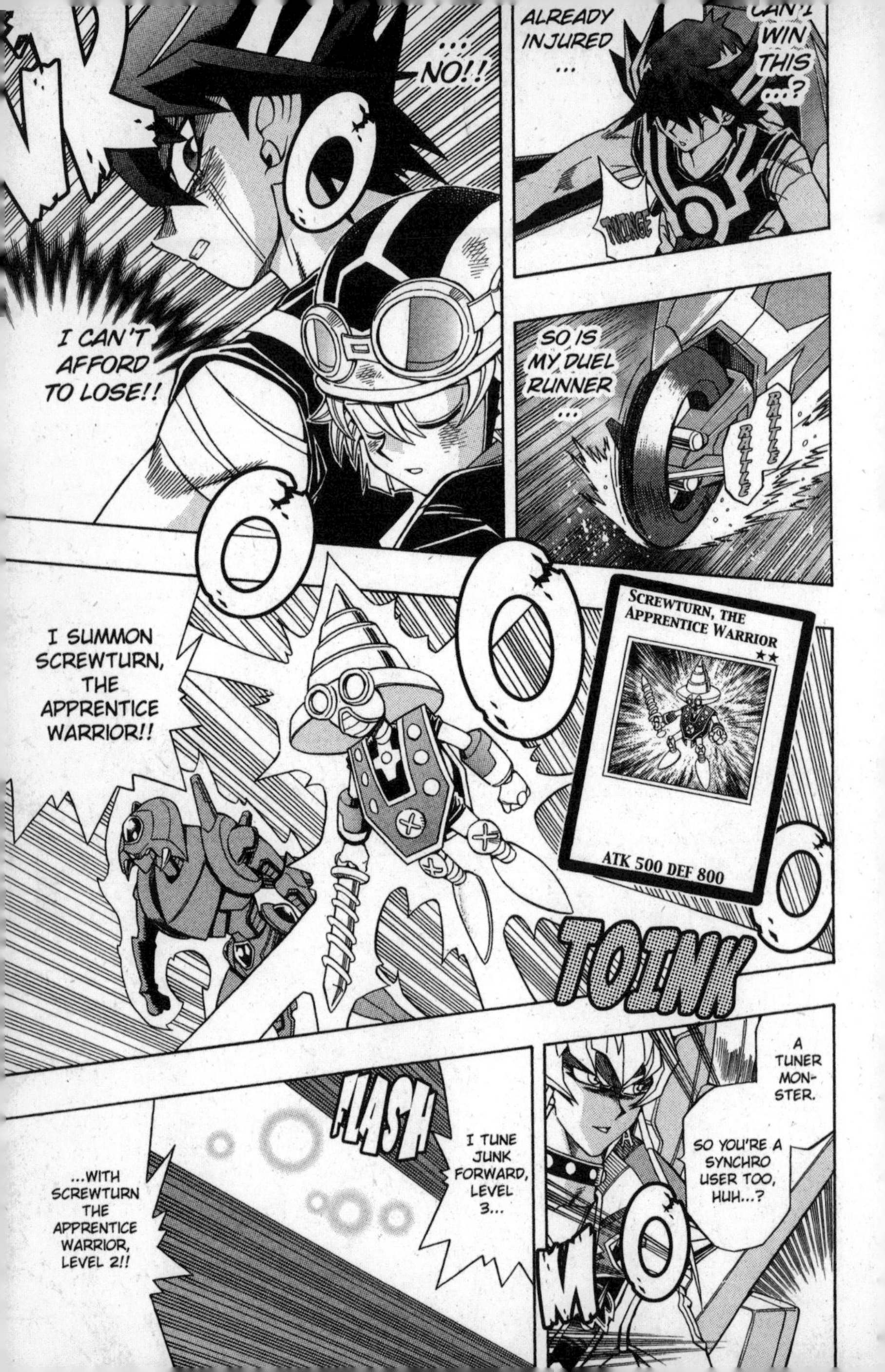
CAN'T WIN THIS ...?
ALREADY INJURED ...
TWINGE
SO IS MY DUEL RUNNER ...
RATTLE RATTLE
... NO!!
I CAN'T AFFORD TO LOSE!!
SCREWTURN, THE APPRENTICE WARRIOR
ATK 500 DEF 800
TOINK
I SUMMON SCREWTURN, THE APPRENTICE WARRIOR!!
A TUNER MONSTER.
SO YOU'RE A SYNCHRO USER TOO, HUH...?
FLASH
I TUNE JUNK FORWARD, LEVEL 3...
...WITH SCREWTURN THE APPRENTICE WARRIOR, LEVEL 2!!

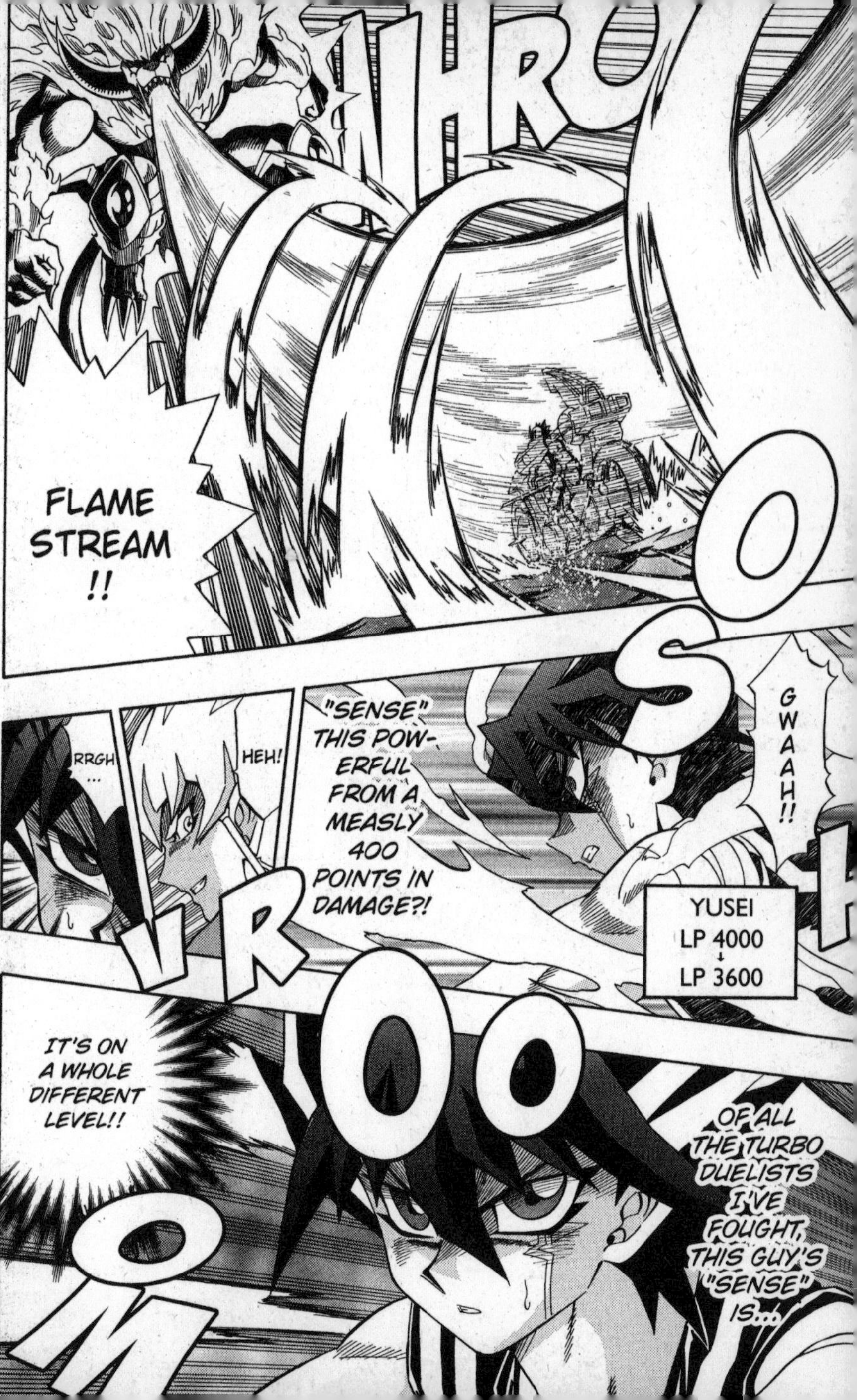
WHROOSH
FLAME STREAM!!
GWAAAH!!
YUSEI
LP 4000
↓
LP 3600
"SENSE" THIS POW-ERFUL FROM A MEASLY 400 POINTS IN DAMAGE?!
HEH!
RRGH ...
VROOOM
OF ALL THE TURBO DUELISTS I'VE FOUGHT, THIS GUY'S "SENSE" IS...
IT'S ON A WHOLE DIFFERENT LEVEL!!

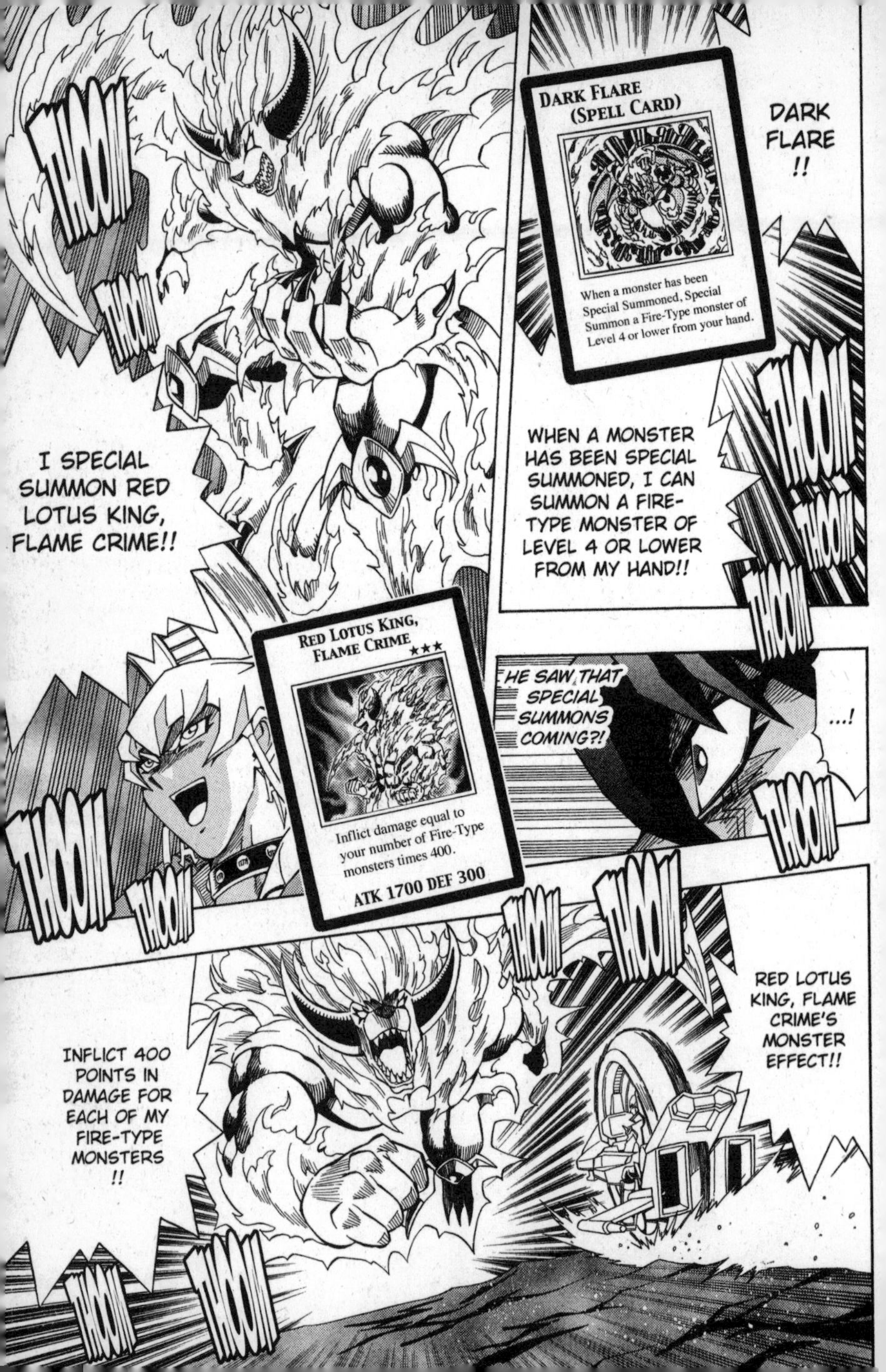
DARK FLARE!!
DARK FLARE (SPELL CARD)
When a monster has been Special Summoned, Special Summon a Fire-Type monster of Level 4 or lower from your hand.
WHEN A MONSTER HAS BEEN SPECIAL SUMMONED, I CAN SUMMON A FIRE-TYPE MONSTER OF LEVEL 4 OR LOWER FROM MY HAND!!
THOOM
THOOM
THOOM
THOOM
THOOM
I SPECIAL SUMMON RED LOTUS KING, FLAME CRIME!!
...!
HE SAW THAT SPECIAL SUMMONS COMING?!
THOOM
RED LOTUS KING, FLAME CRIME ★★★
Inflict damage equal to your number of Fire-Type monsters times 400.
ATK 1700 DEF 300
THOOM
THOOM
THOOM
THOOM
RED LOTUS KING, FLAME CRIME'S MONSTER EFFECT!!
INFLICT 400 POINTS IN DAMAGE FOR EACH OF MY FIRE-TYPE MONSTERS!!
THOOM
THOOM

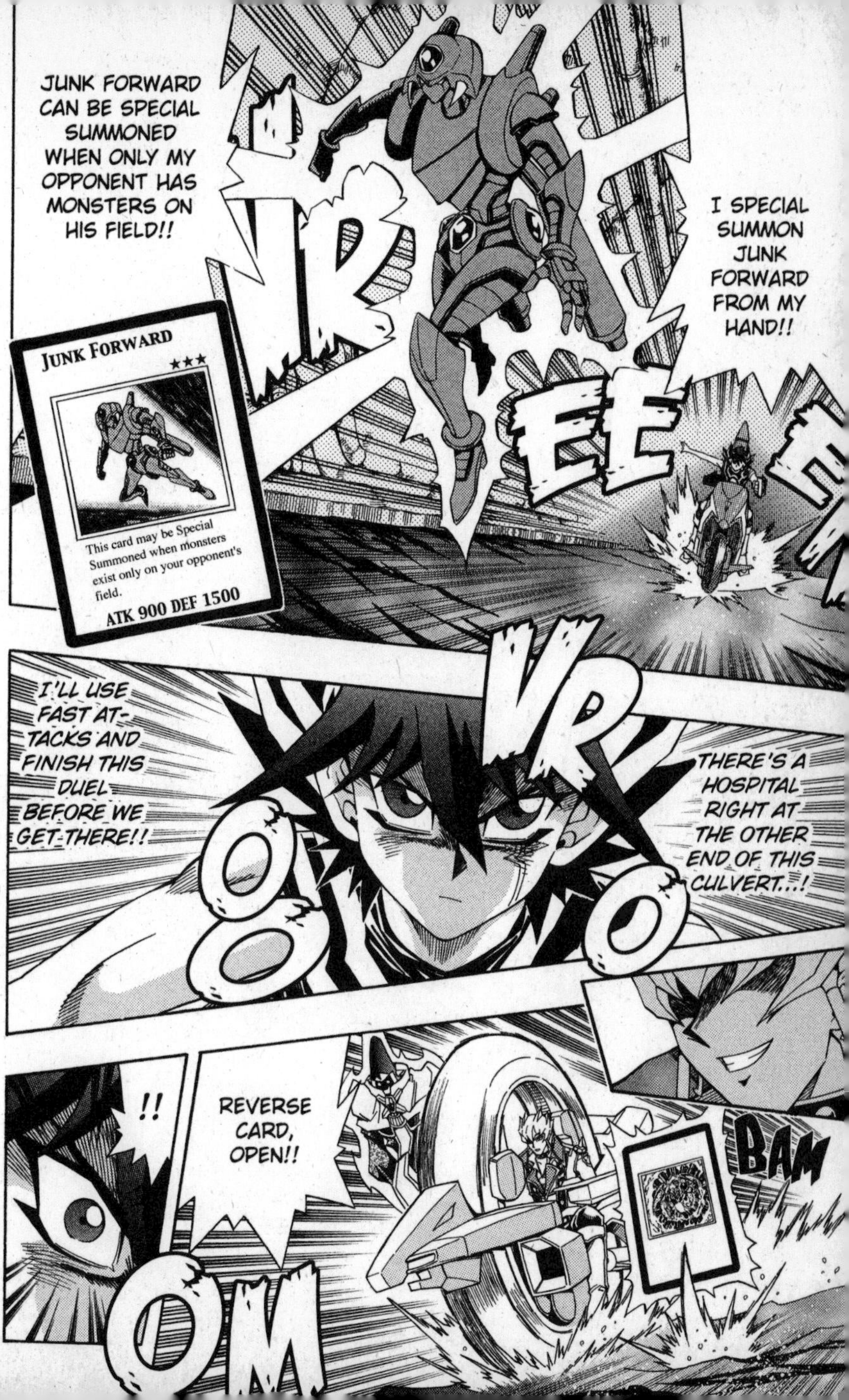
I SPECIAL SUMMON JUNK FORWARD FROM MY HAND!!
JUNK FORWARD CAN BE SPECIAL SUMMONED WHEN ONLY MY OPPONENT HAS MONSTERS ON HIS FIELD!!
JUNK FORWARD ★★★
This card may be Special Summoned when monsters exist only on your opponent's field.
ATK 900 DEF 1500
THERE'S A HOSPITAL RIGHT AT THE OTHER END OF THIS CULVERT...!
I'LL USE FAST AT-TACKS AND FINISH THIS DUEL BEFORE WE GET THERE!!
REVERSE CARD, OPEN!!
BAM
!!

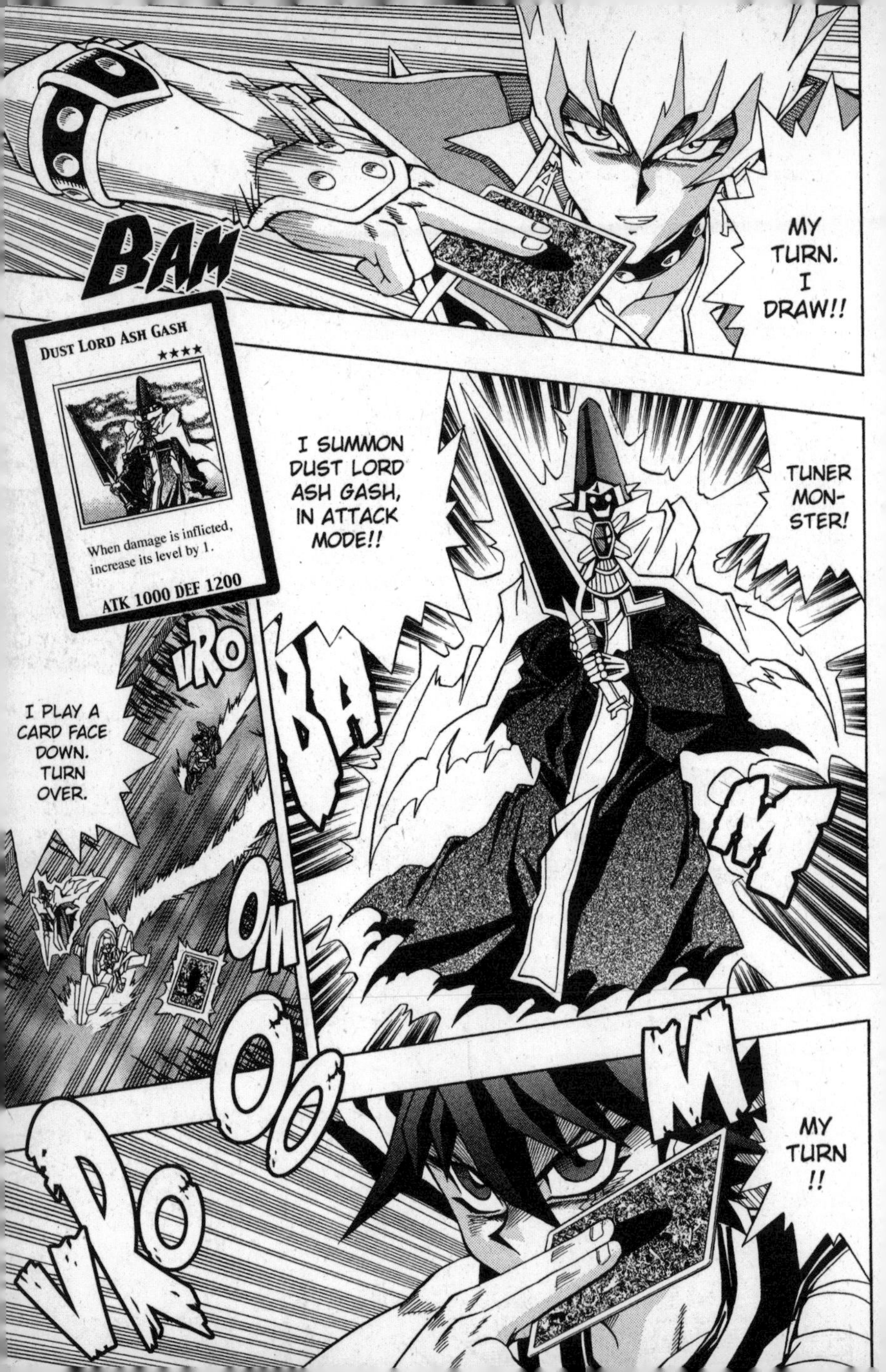
MY TURN. I DRAW!!
BAM
TUNER MONSTER!
I SUMMON DUST LORD ASH GASH, IN ATTACK MODE!!
DUST LORD ASH GASH
★★★★
When damage is inflicted, increase its level by 1.
ATK 1000 DEF 1200
BAM
I PLAY A CARD FACE DOWN. TURN OVER.
VROOM
MY TURN!!
VROOOOM

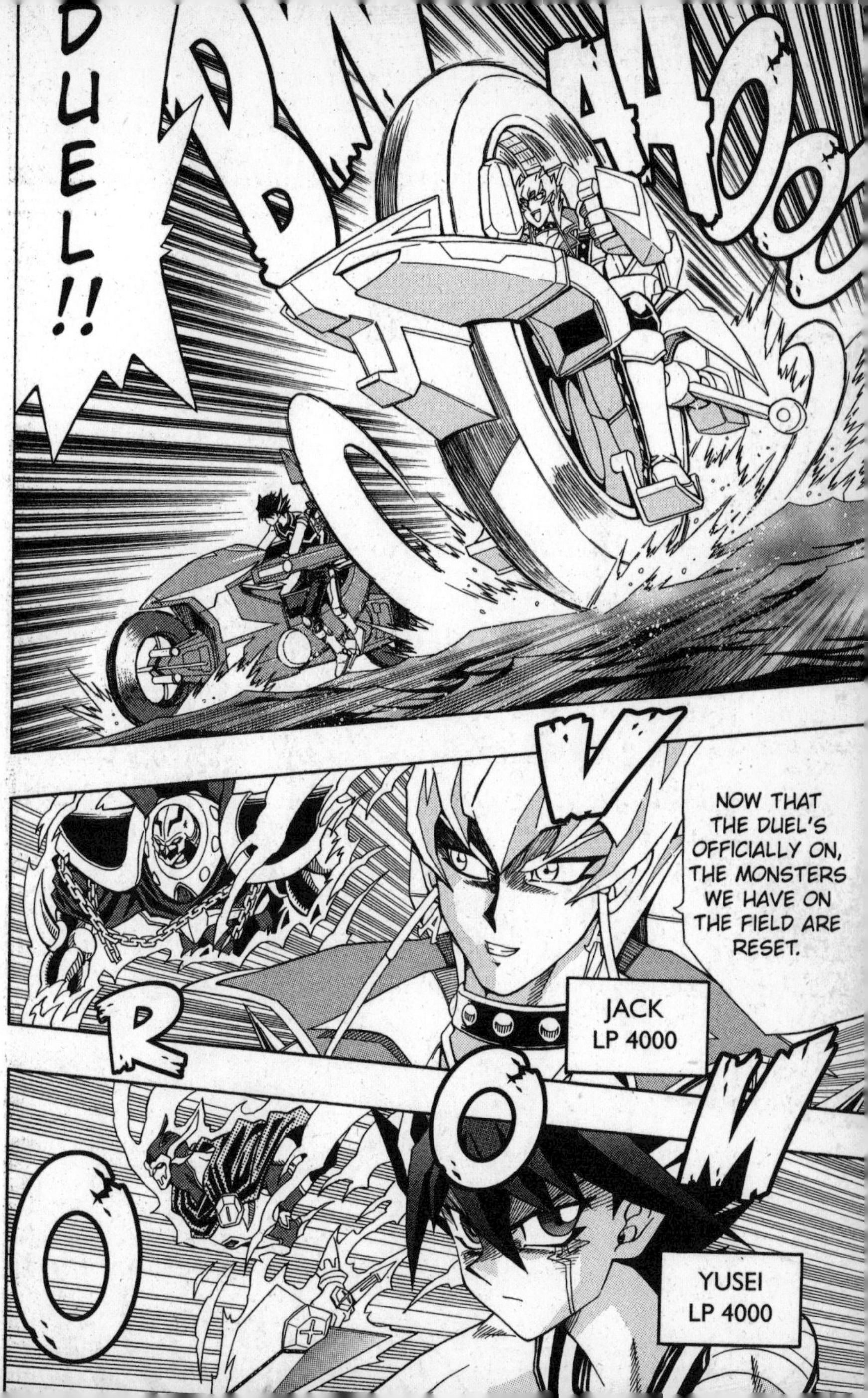
DUEL!!
NOW THAT THE DUEL'S OFFICIALLY ON, THE MONSTERS WE HAVE ON THE FIELD ARE RESET.
JACK LP 4000
YUSEI LP 4000

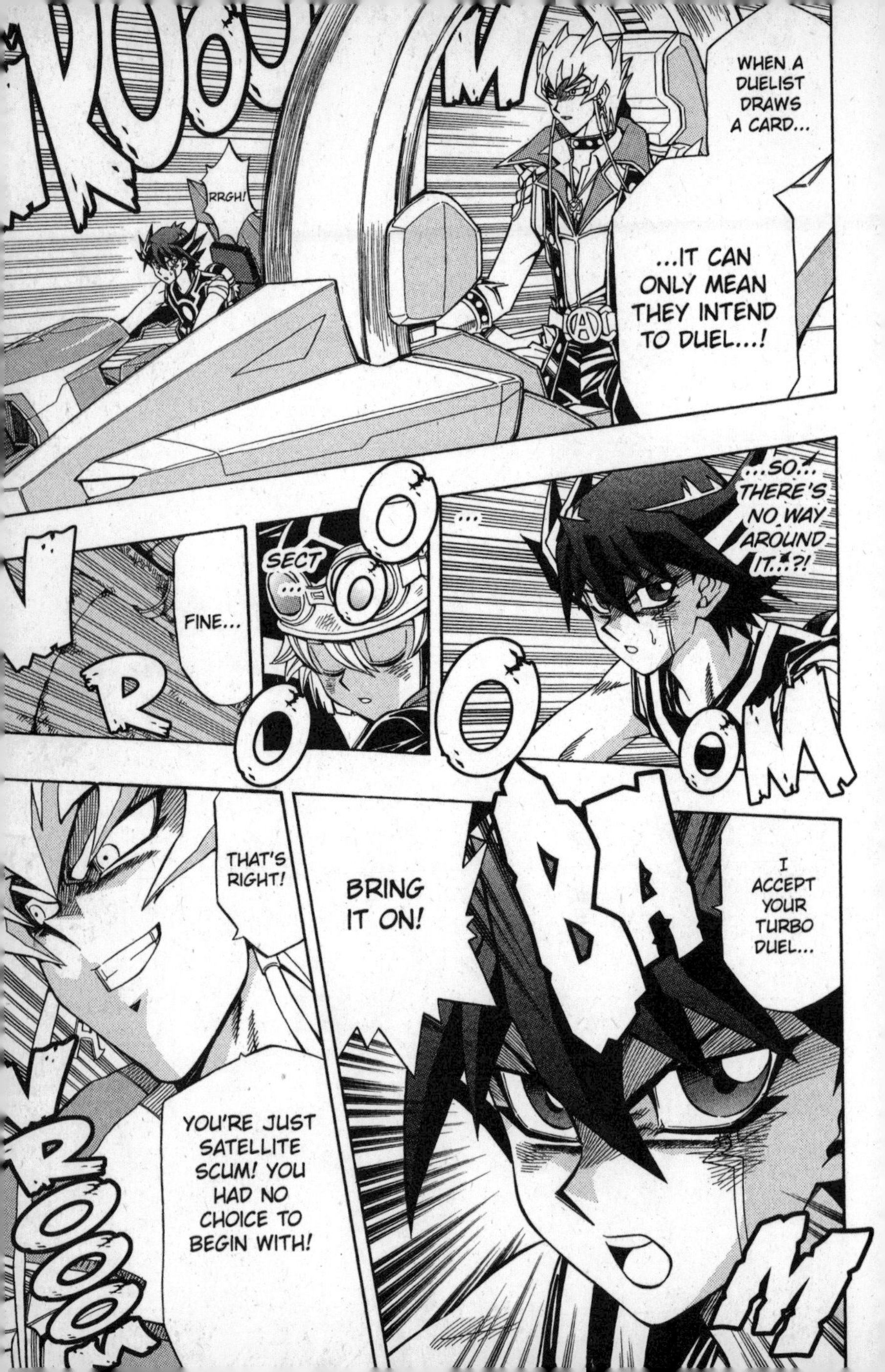
WHEN A DUELIST DRAWS A CARD...
...IT CAN ONLY MEAN THEY INTEND TO DUEL...!
RRGH!
...SO... THERE'S NO WAY AROUND IT...?!
...
SECT ...
FINE...
I ACCEPT YOUR TURBO DUEL...
BRING IT ON!
THAT'S RIGHT!
YOU'RE JUST SATELLITE SCUM! YOU HAD NO CHOICE TO BEGIN WITH!

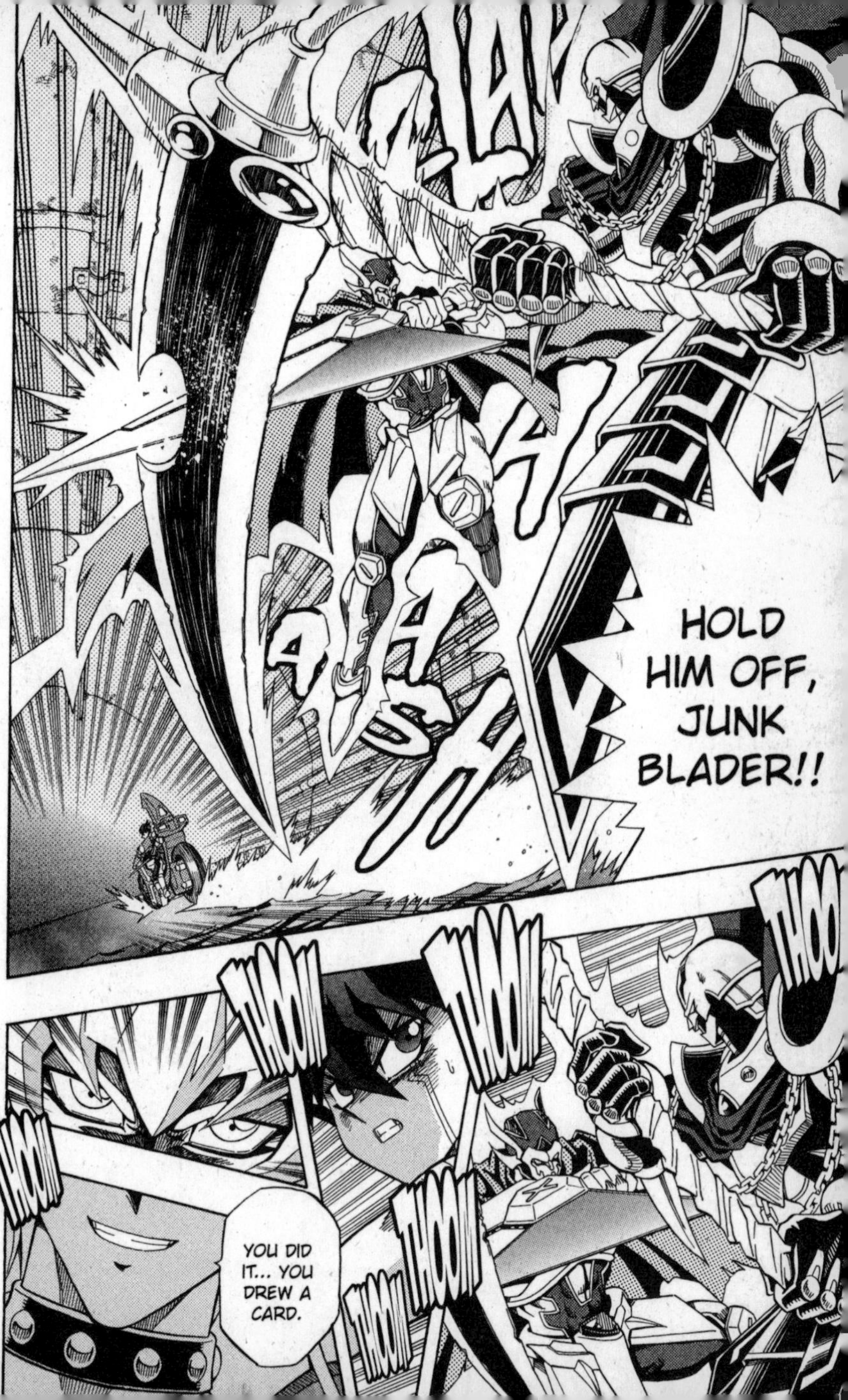
HOLD HIM OFF, JUNK BLADER!!
THOOM
THOOM
THOOM
THOOM
THOOM
THOOM
THOOM
YOU DID IT... YOU DREW A CARD.

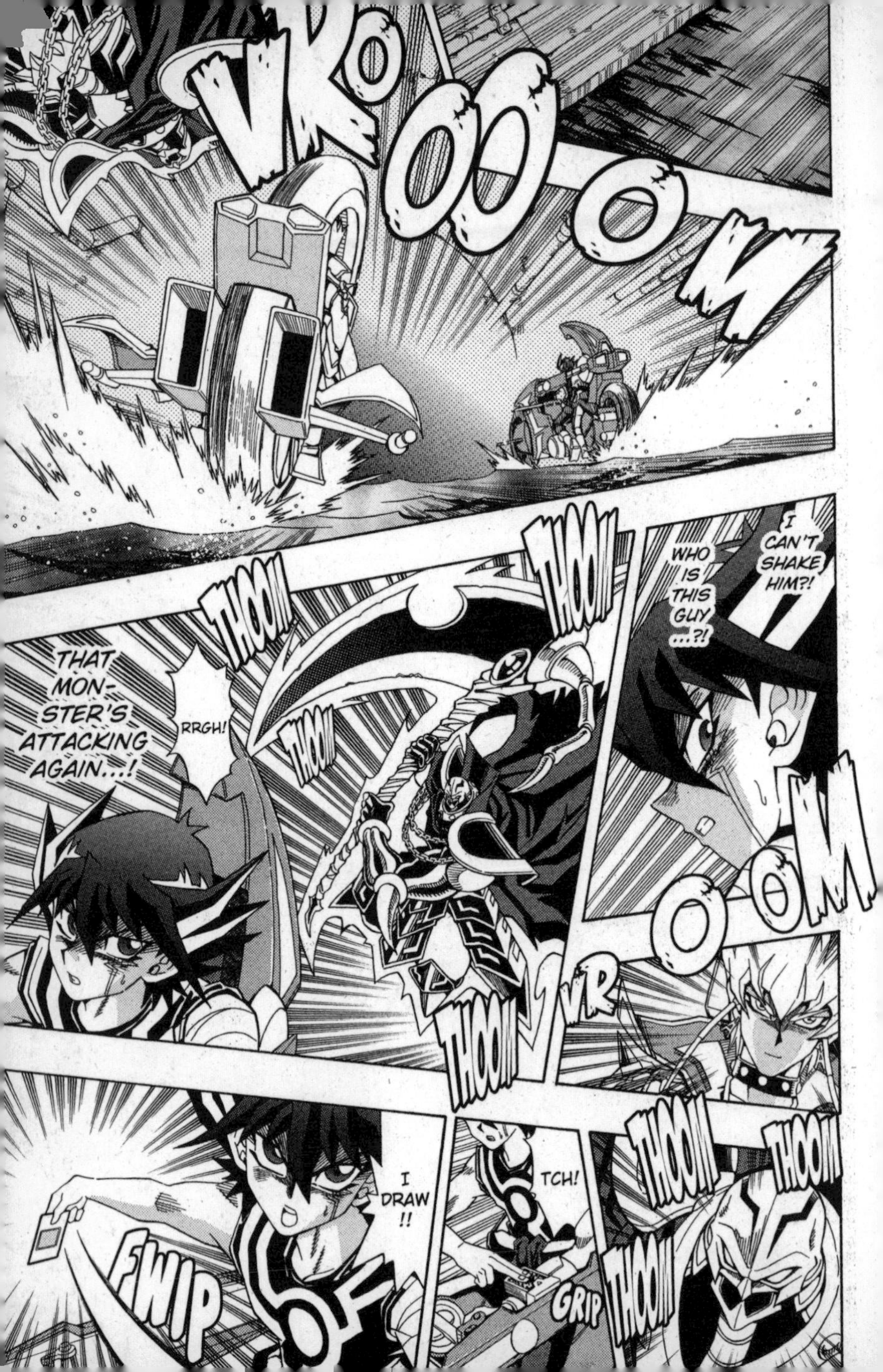
VROOOOOM
I CAN'T SHAKE HIM?!
WHO IS THIS GUY...?!
THOOM
VROOOM
THOOM
THOOM
THAT MON-STER'S ATTACKING AGAIN...!
RRGH!
THOOM
VR
THOOM
THOOM
TCH!
THOOM
GRIP
I DRAW!!
FWIP

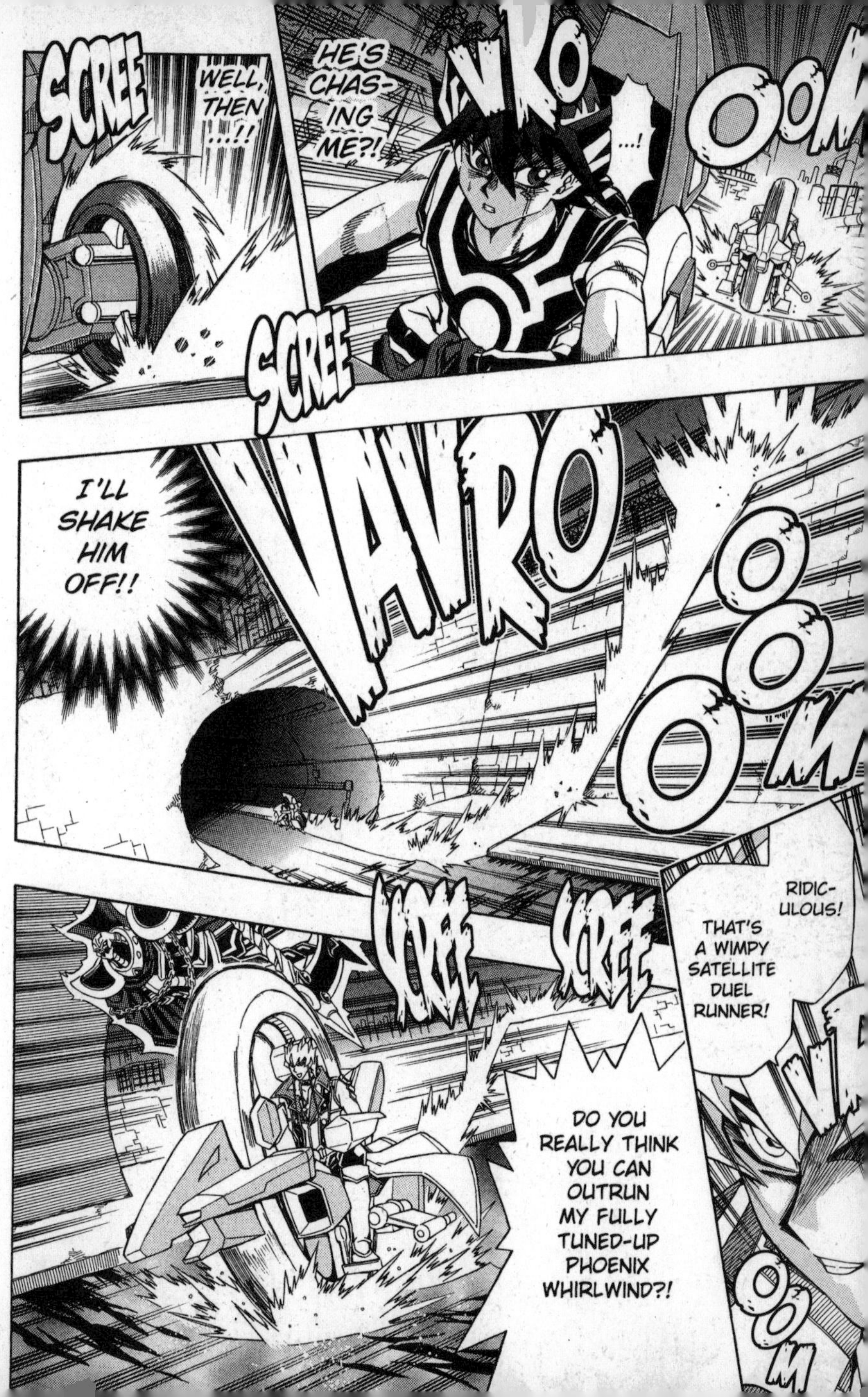
HE'S CHAS-ING ME?!
...!
SCREE
SCREE
WELL, THEN ...!!
I'LL SHAKE HIM OFF!!
RIDIC-ULOUS!
THAT'S A WIMPY SATELLITE DUEL RUNNER!
DO YOU REALLY THINK YOU CAN OUTRUN MY FULLY TUNED-UP PHOENIX WHIRLWIND?!

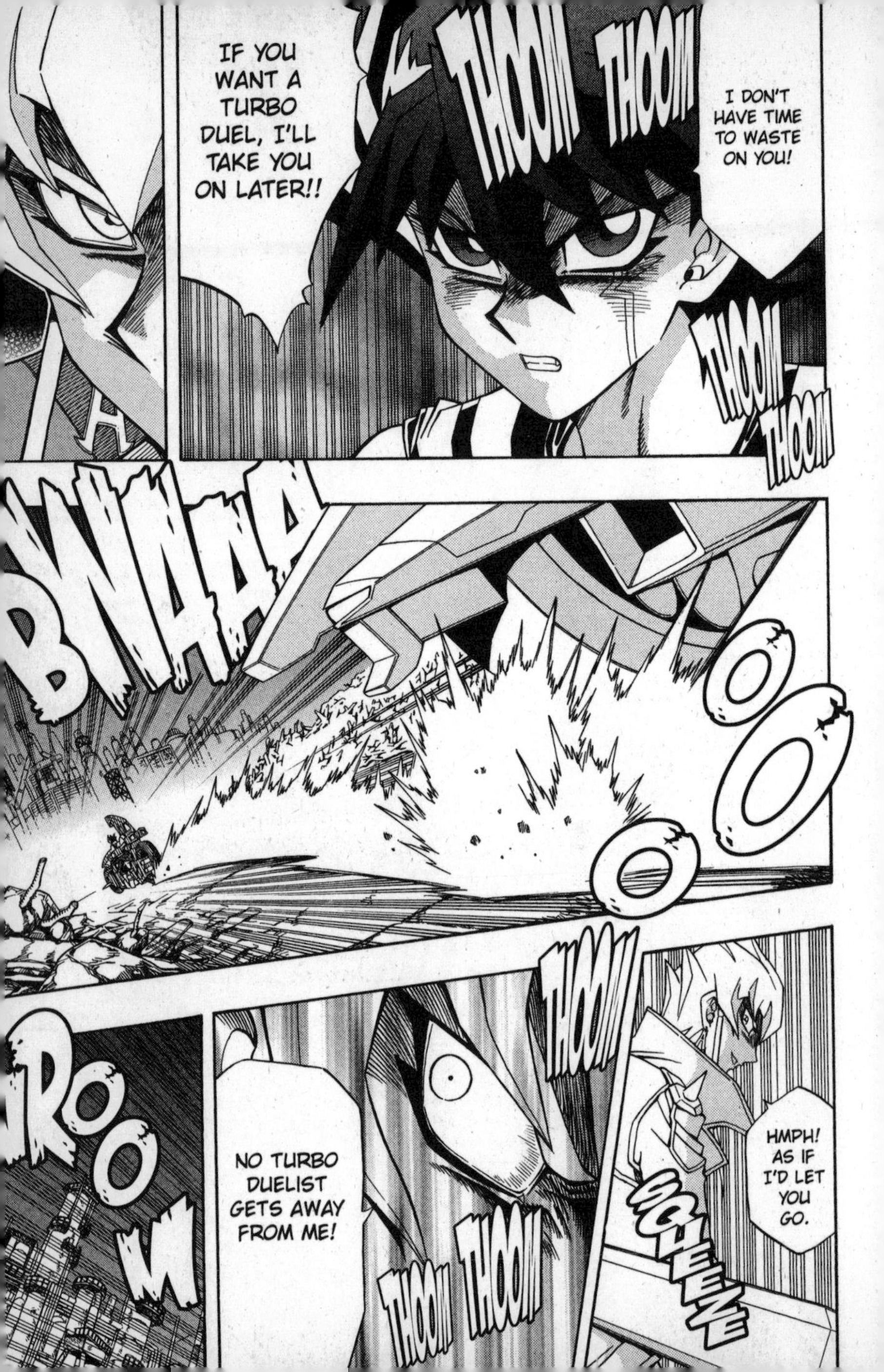
THOOM THOOM
IF YOU WANT A TURBO DUEL, I'LL TAKE YOU ON LATER!!
I DON'T HAVE TIME TO WASTE ON YOU!
THOOM THOOM
BWAAA
OOOO
THOOM
HMPH! AS IF I'D LET YOU GO.
NO TURBO DUELIST GETS AWAY FROM ME!
THOOM THOOM
ROOOM

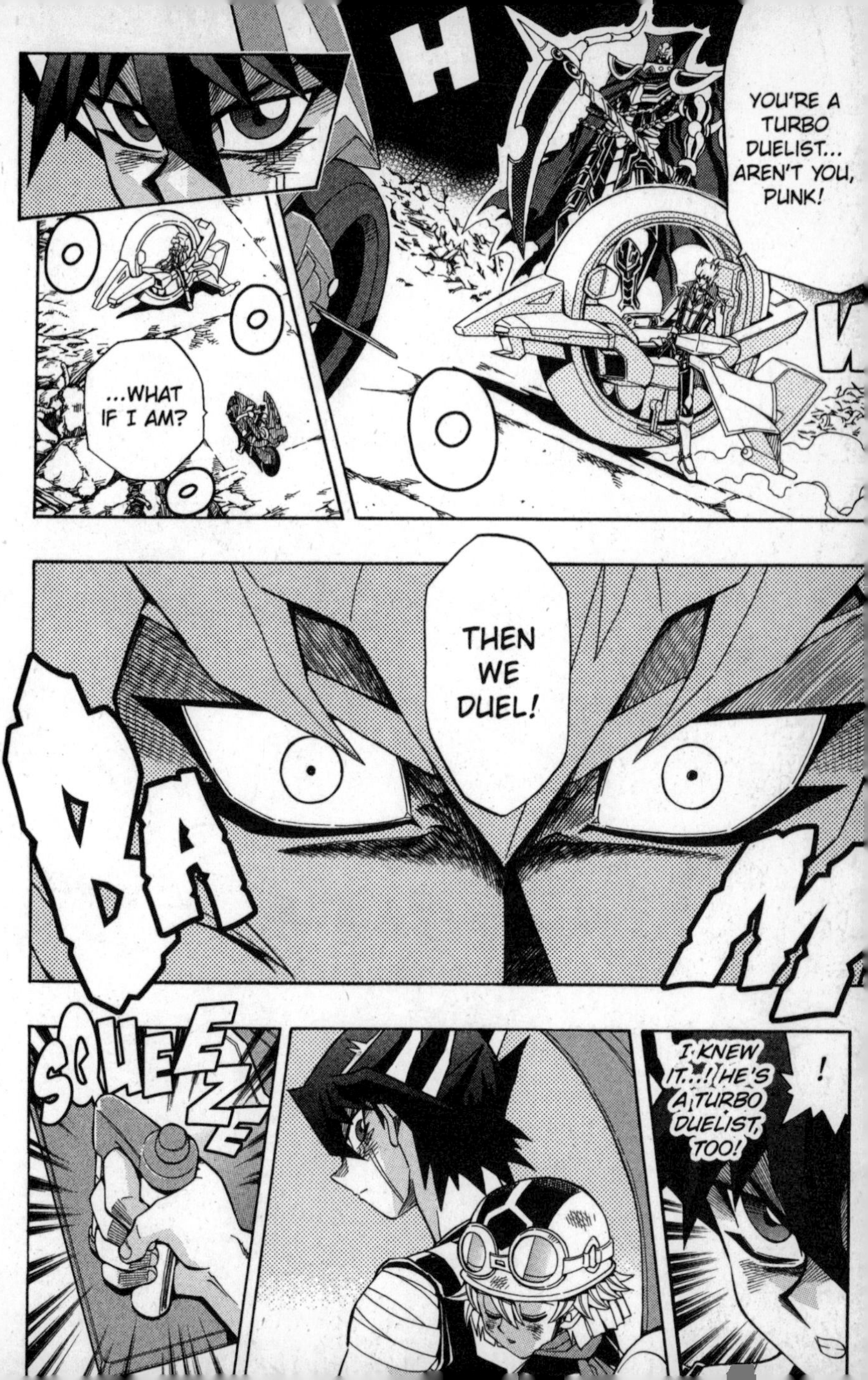
YOU'RE A TURBO DUELIST... AREN'T YOU, PUNK!
...WHAT IF I AM?
THEN WE DUEL!
BAM
!
I KNEW IT...! HE'S A TURBO DUELIST, TOO!
SQUEEZE

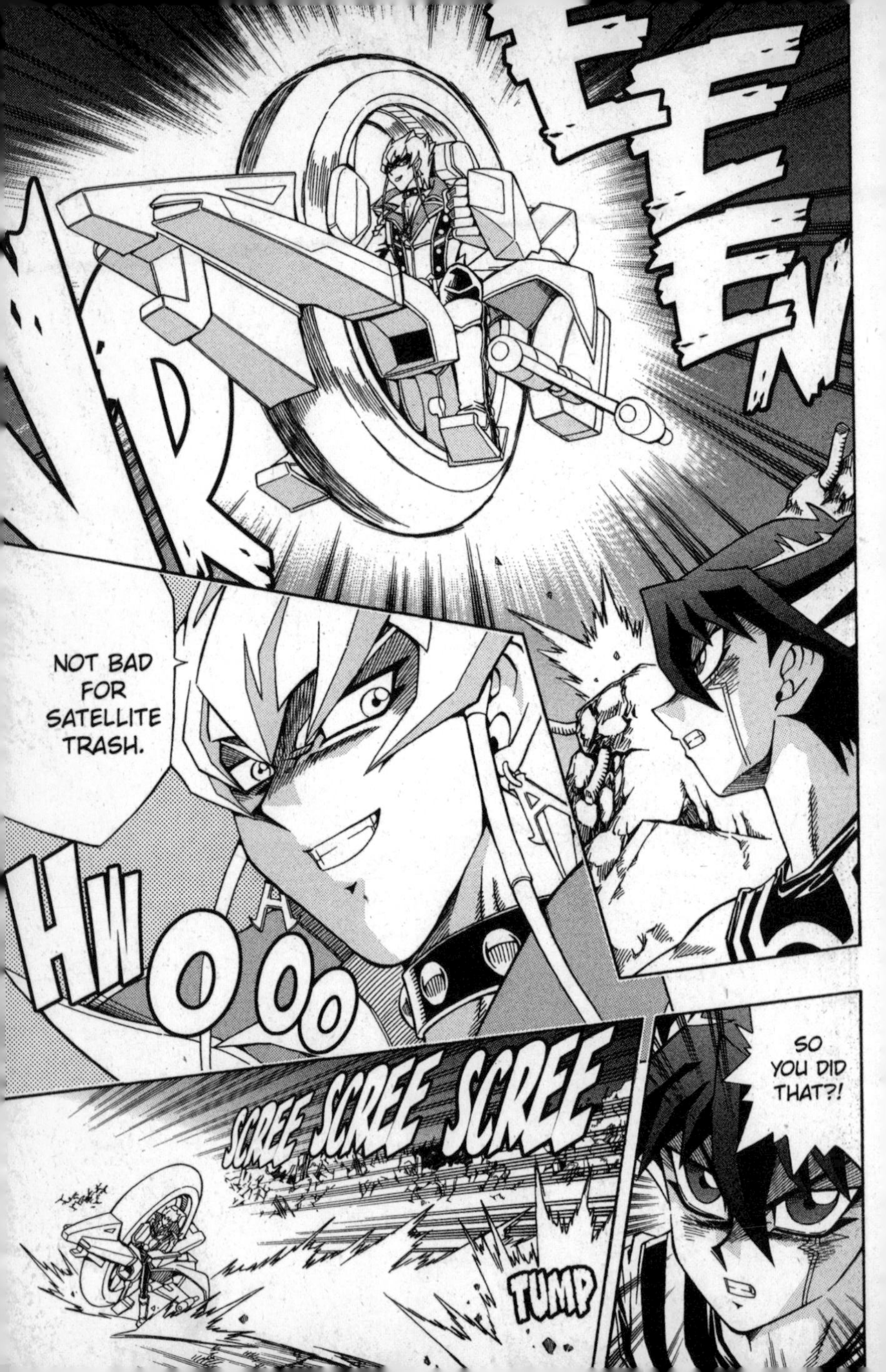

EEEN
VRROOM
NOT BAD FOR SATELLITE TRASH.
HWOOOO
SO YOU DID THAT?!
SCREE SCREE SCREE
TUMP

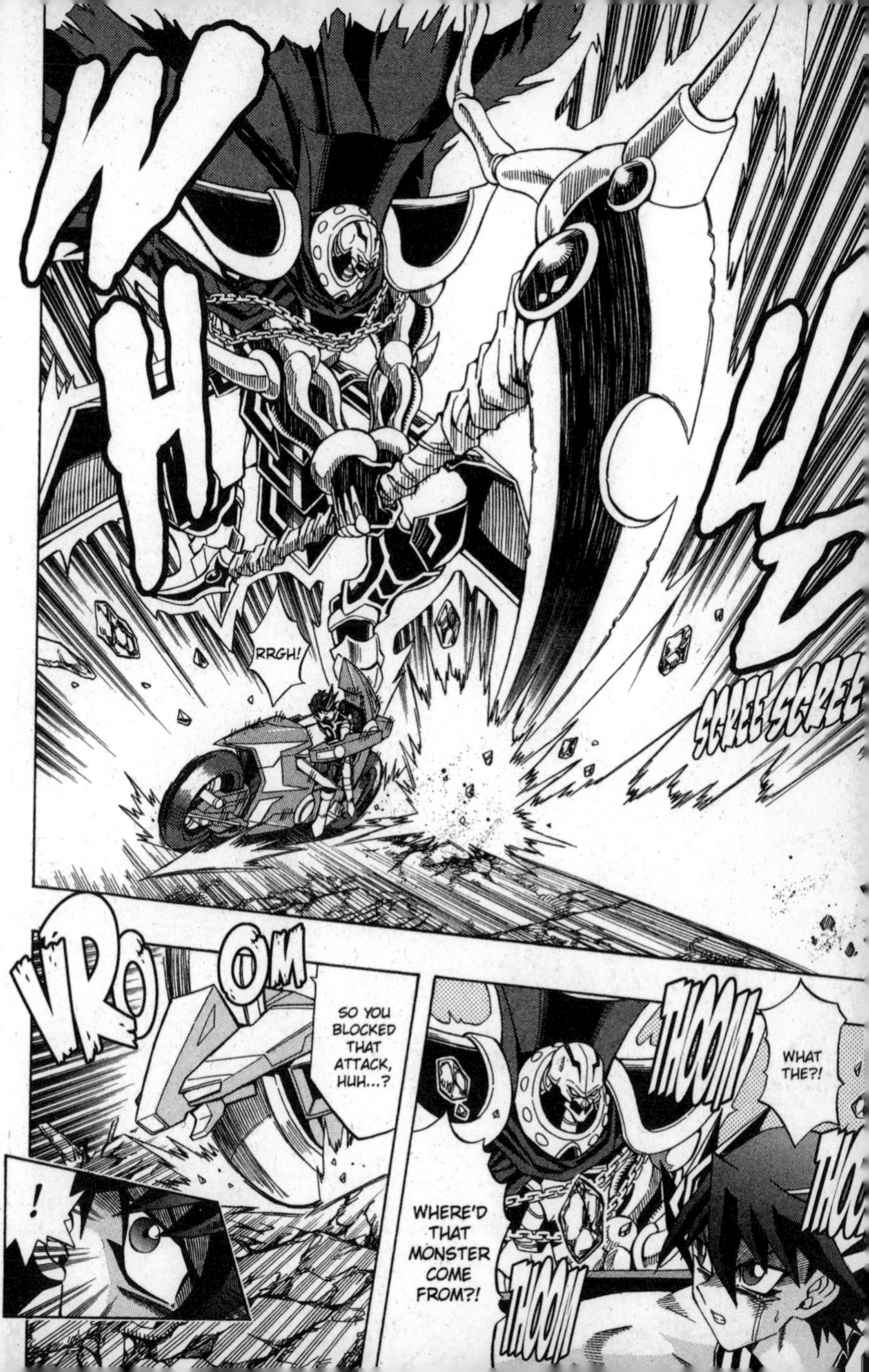
RRGH!
SCREE SCREE
THOOM
WHAT THE?!
WHERE'D THAT MONSTER COME FROM?!
THOOM
VROOM
SO YOU BLOCKED THAT ATTACK, HUH...?
!

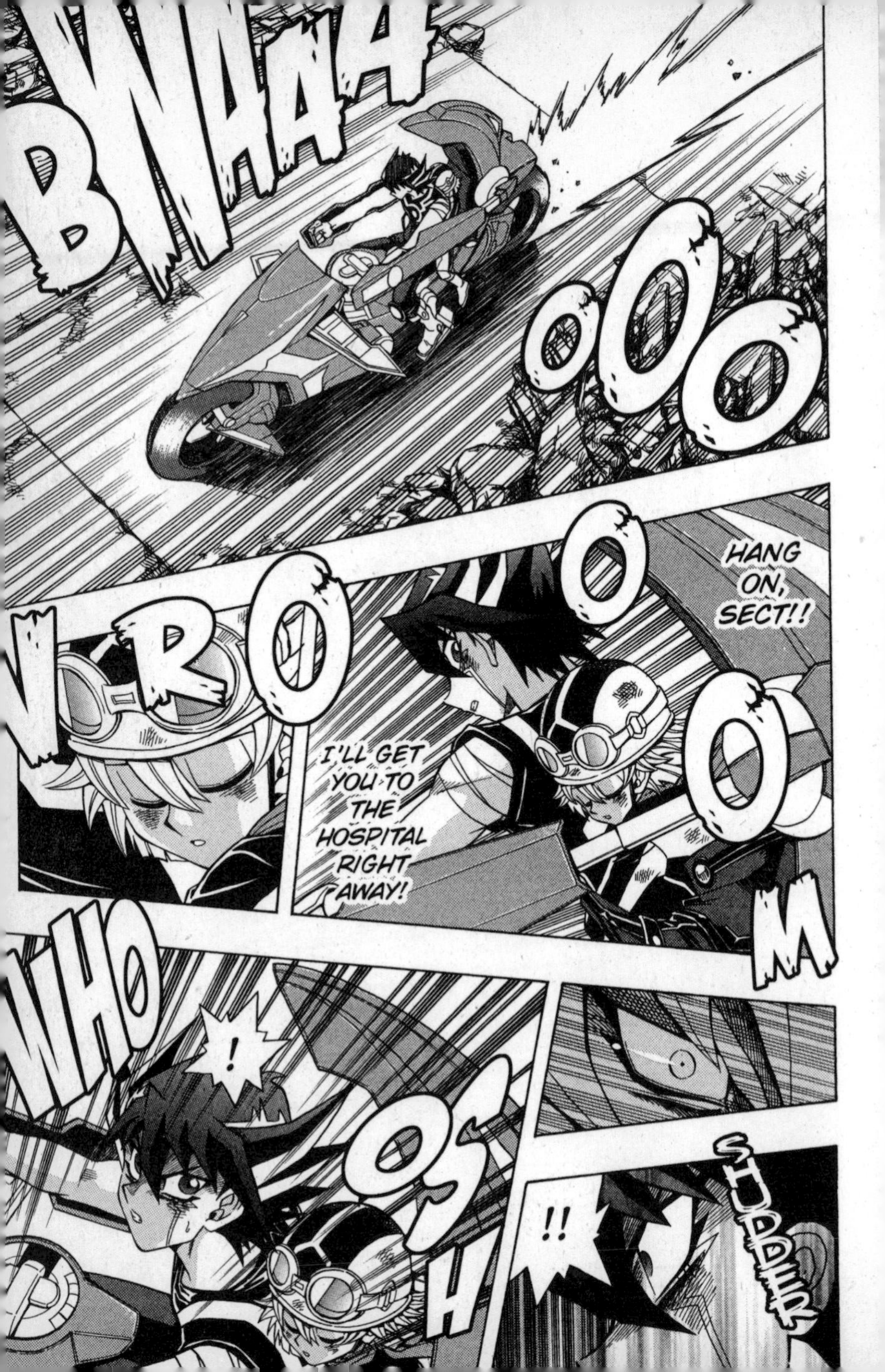
BWAA
OOO
VROOOOOM
HANG ON, SECT!!
I'LL GET YOU TO THE HOSPITAL RIGHT AWAY!
WHOOSH
!
!!
SHUDDER

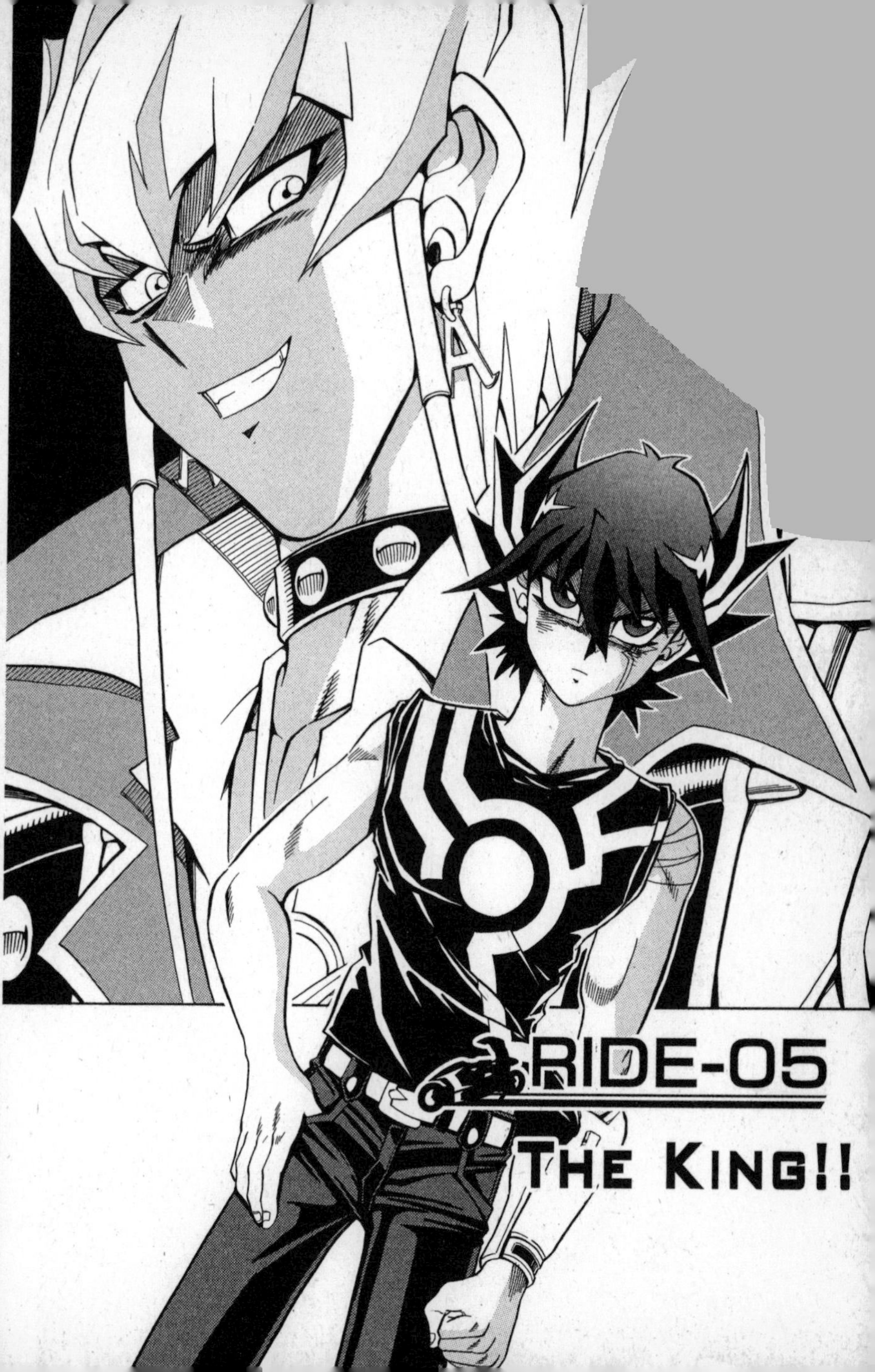
RIDE-05
THE KING!!

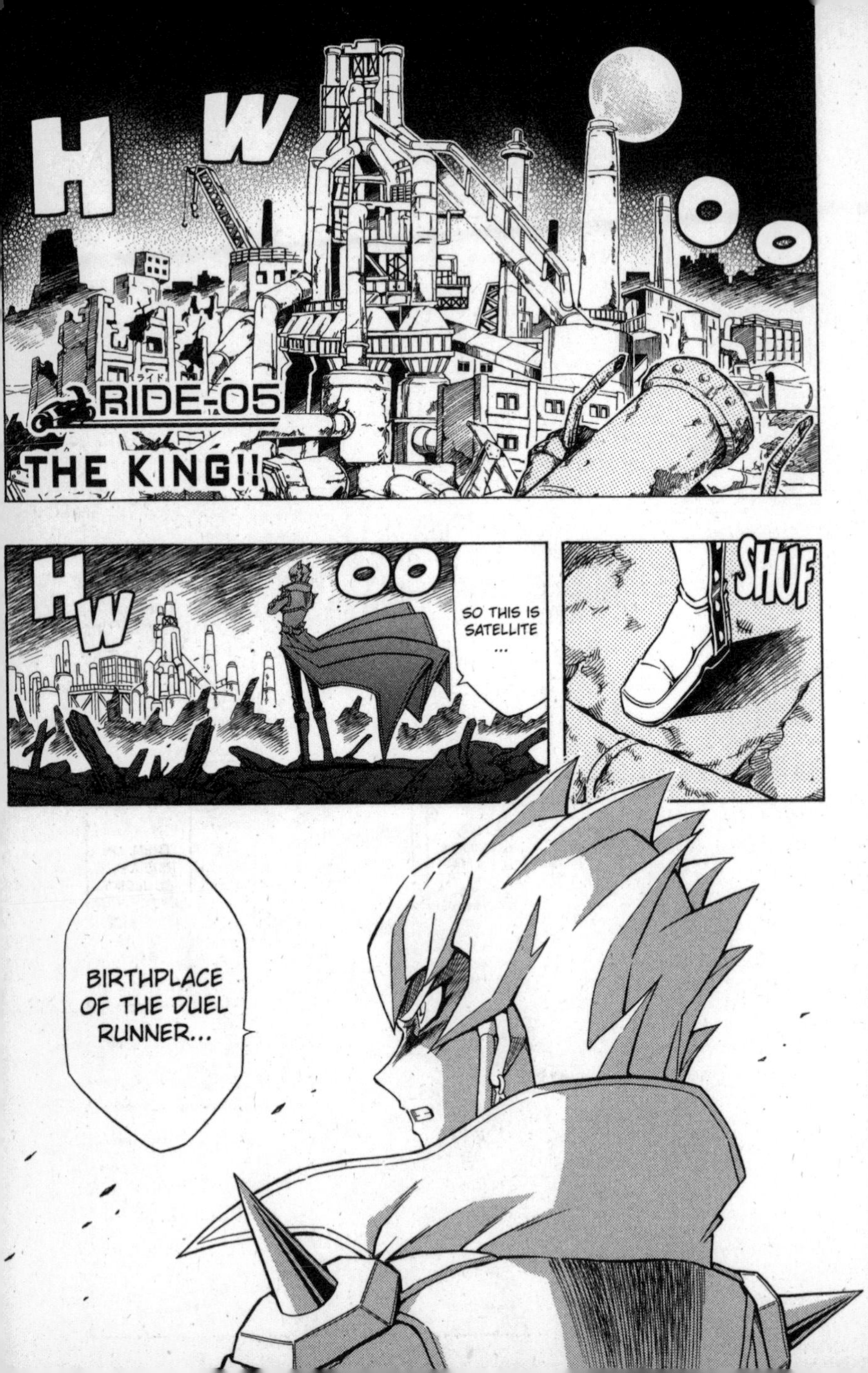
HWOO
ライド
RIDE-05
THE KING!!
SHUF
HWOO
SO THIS IS SATELLITE...
BIRTHPLACE OF THE DUEL RUNNER...

5D's TRACKS BY SATOMASA

THE 4TH

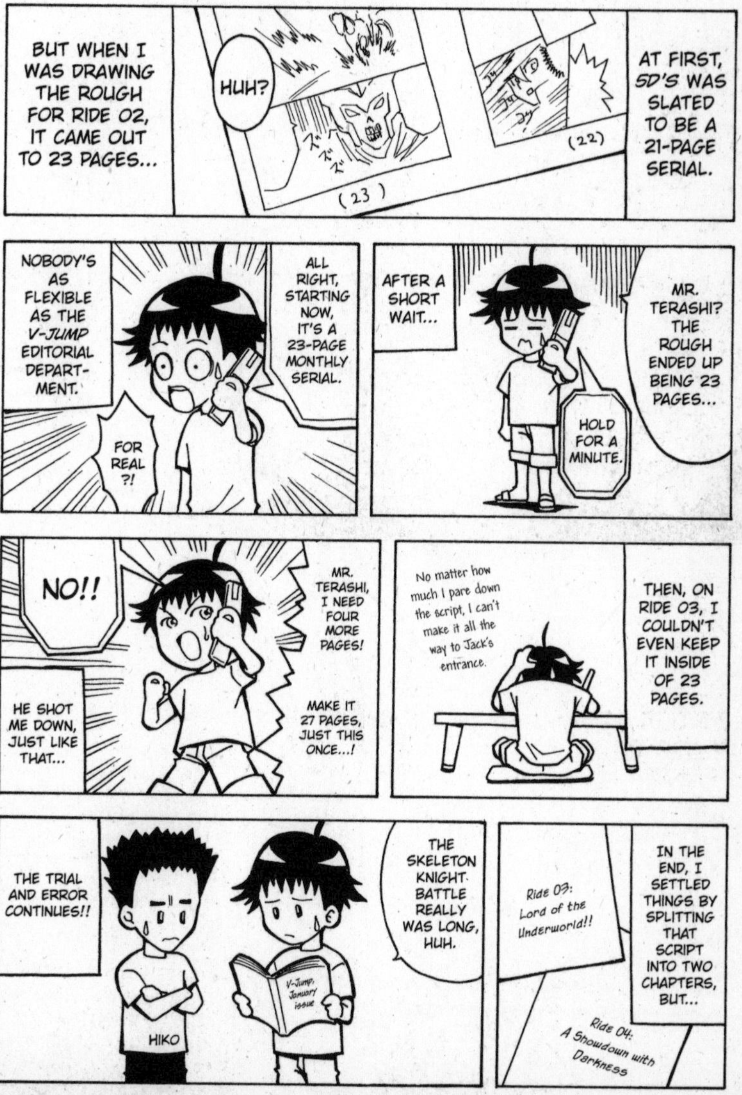
AT FIRST, 5D'S WAS SLATED TO BE A 21-PAGE SERIAL.
(22)
HUH?
(23)
BUT WHEN I WAS DRAWING THE ROUGH FOR RIDE 02, IT CAME OUT TO 23 PAGES...
MR. TERASHI? THE ROUGH ENDED UP BEING 23 PAGES...
HOLD FOR A MINUTE.
AFTER A SHORT WAIT...
ALL RIGHT, STARTING NOW, IT'S A 23-PAGE MONTHLY SERIAL.
NOBODY'S AS FLEXIBLE AS THE V-JUMP EDITORIAL DEPARTMENT.
FOR REAL?!
THEN, ON RIDE 03, I COULDN'T EVEN KEEP IT INSIDE OF 23 PAGES.
No matter how much I pare down the script, I can't make it all the way to Jack's entrance.
MR. TERASHI, I NEED FOUR MORE PAGES!
MAKE IT 27 PAGES, JUST THIS ONCE...!
NO!!
HE SHOT ME DOWN, JUST LIKE THAT...
IN THE END, I SETTLED THINGS BY SPLITTING THAT SCRIPT INTO TWO CHAPTERS, BUT...
Ride 03: Lord of the Underworld!!
Ride 04: A Showdown with Darkness
THE SKELETON KNIGHT BATTLE REALLY WAS LONG, HUH.
V-Jump, January issue
THE TRIAL AND ERROR CONTINUES!!
HIKO

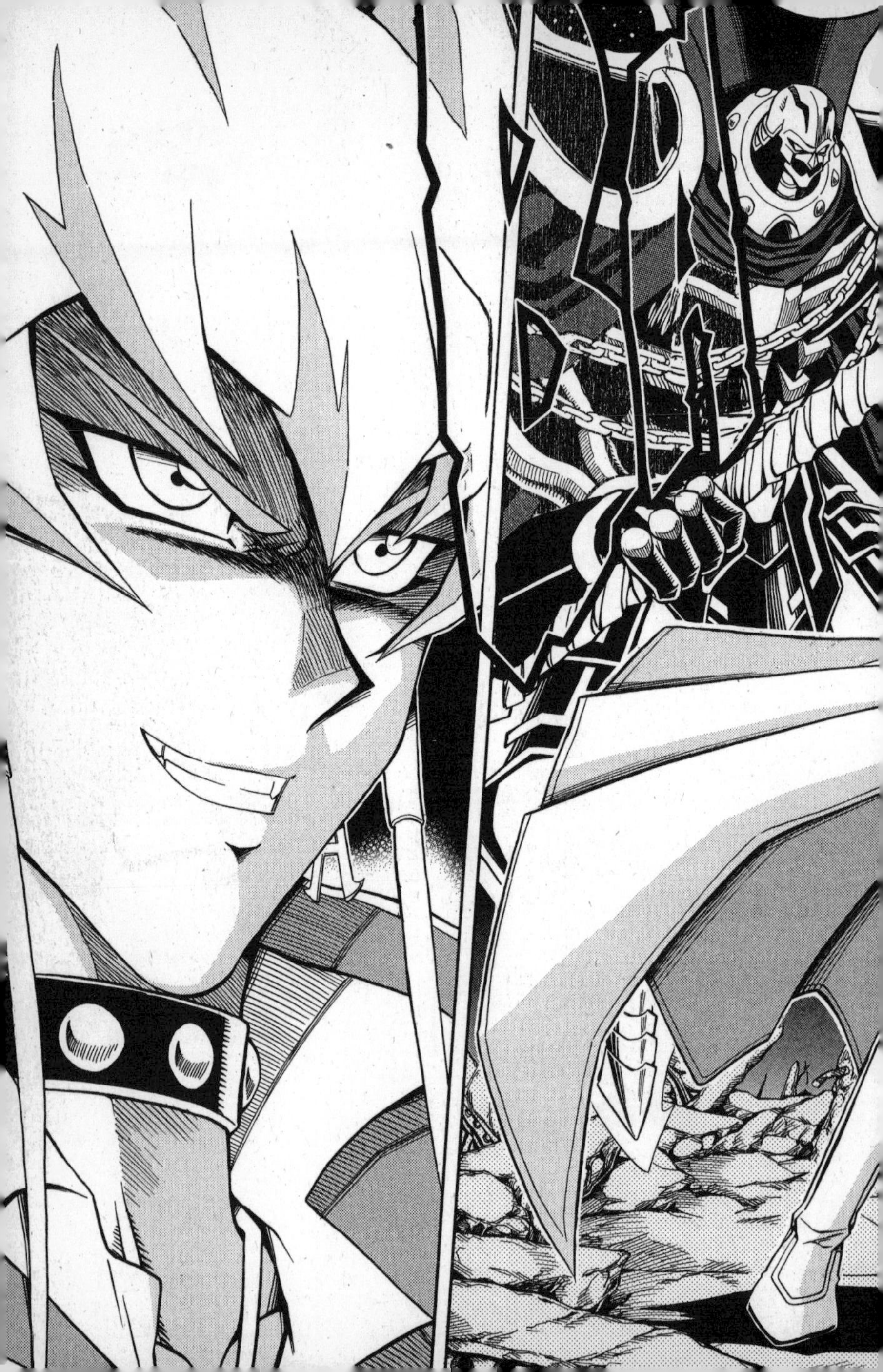

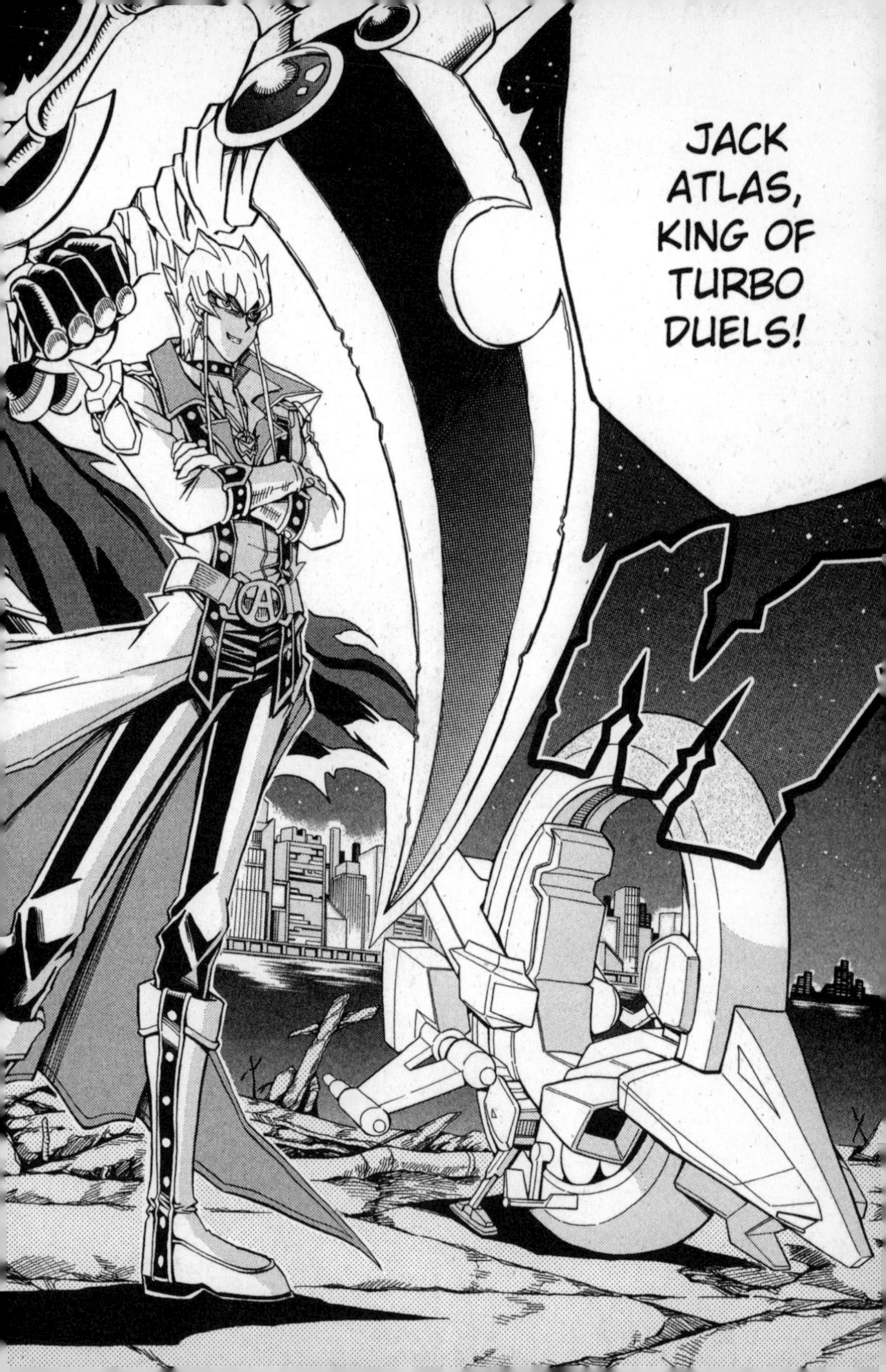
JACK ATLAS, KING OF TURBO DUELS!

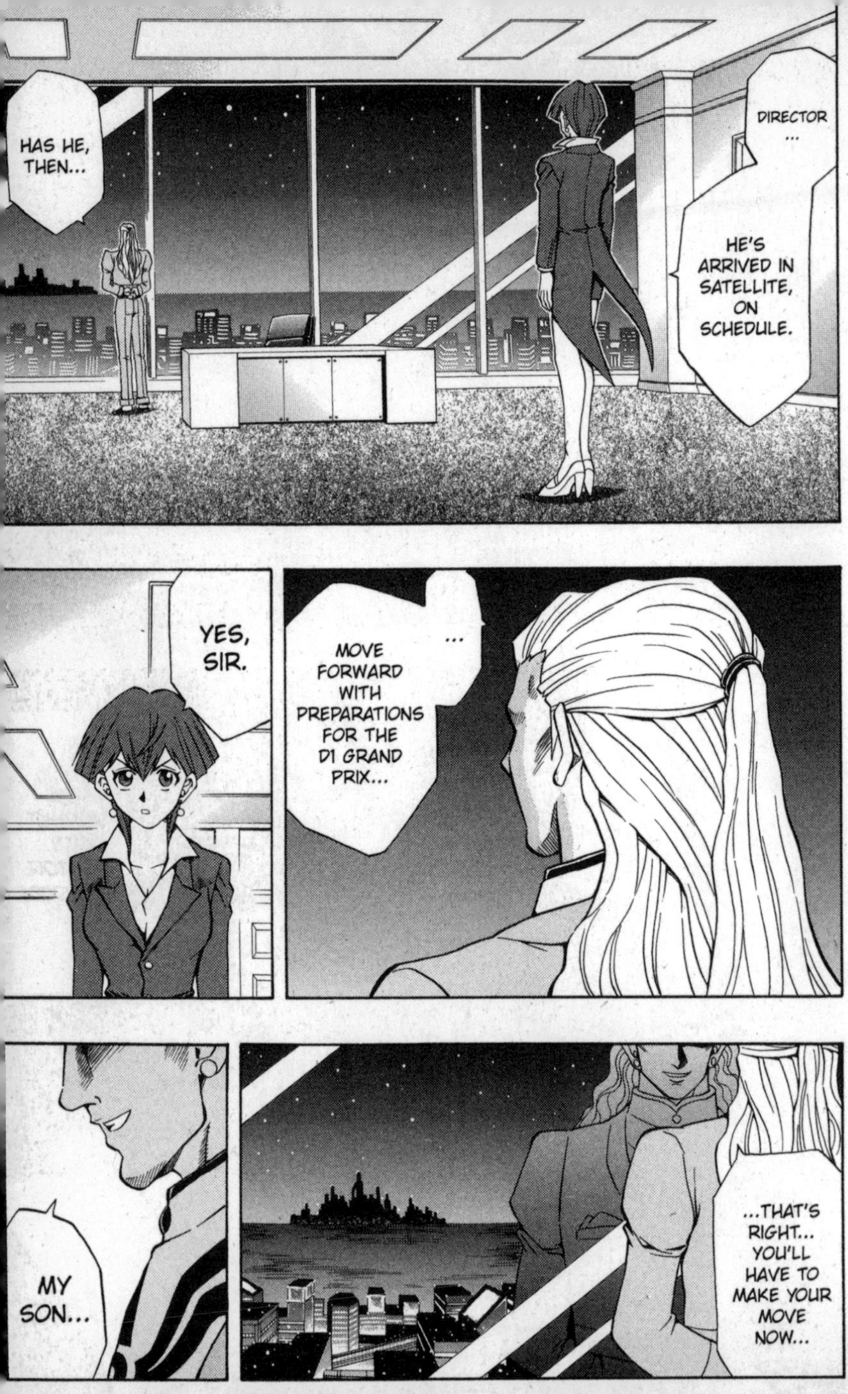
DIRECTOR ...
HE'S ARRIVED IN SATELLITE, ON SCHEDULE.
HAS HE, THEN...
...
MOVE FORWARD WITH PREPARATIONS FOR THE D1 GRAND PRIX...
YES, SIR.
...THAT'S RIGHT... YOU'LL HAVE TO MAKE YOUR MOVE NOW...
MY SON...

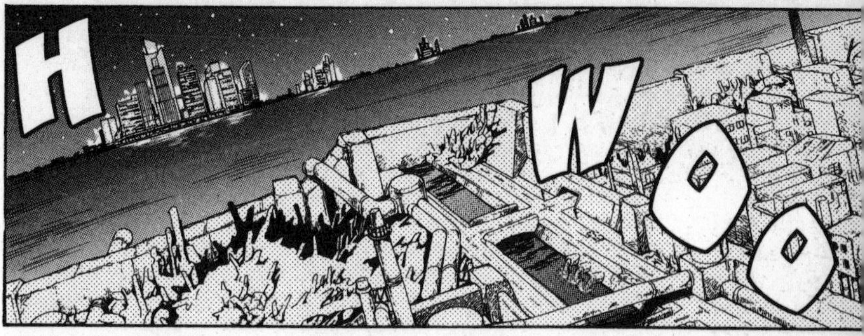
HWOOO

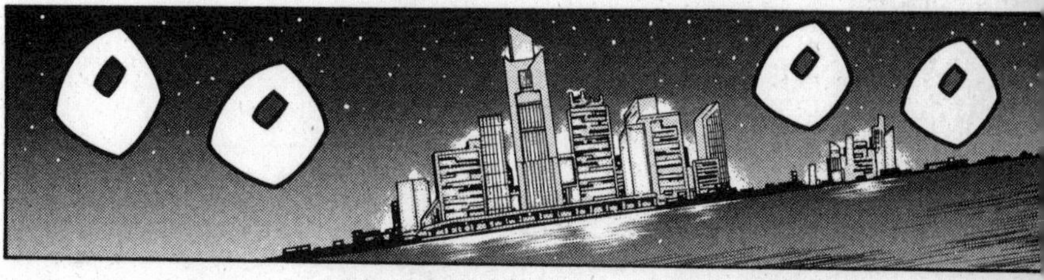
OOOO

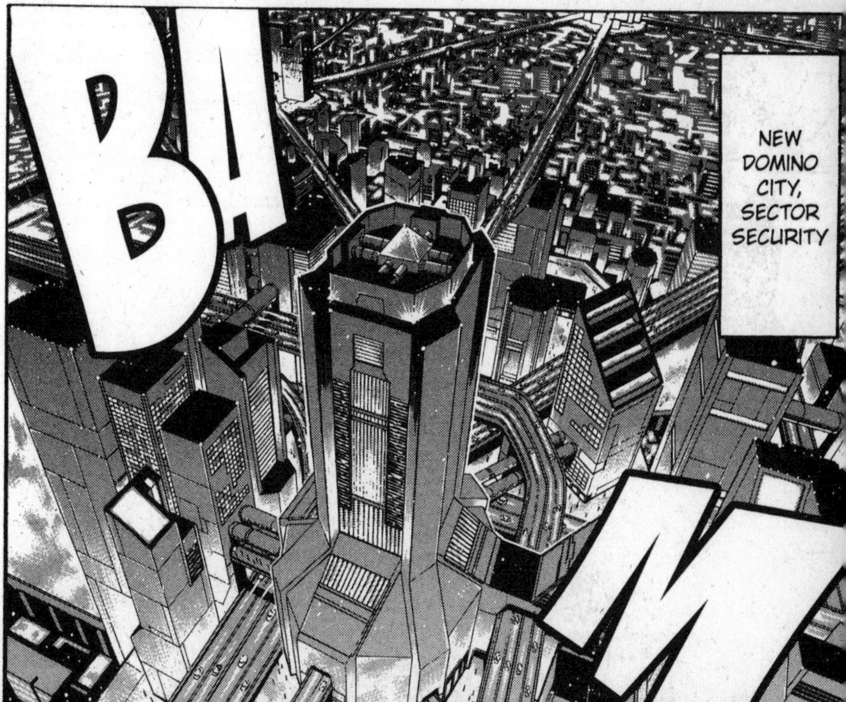
NEW DOMINO CITY, SECTOR SECURITY
BAM

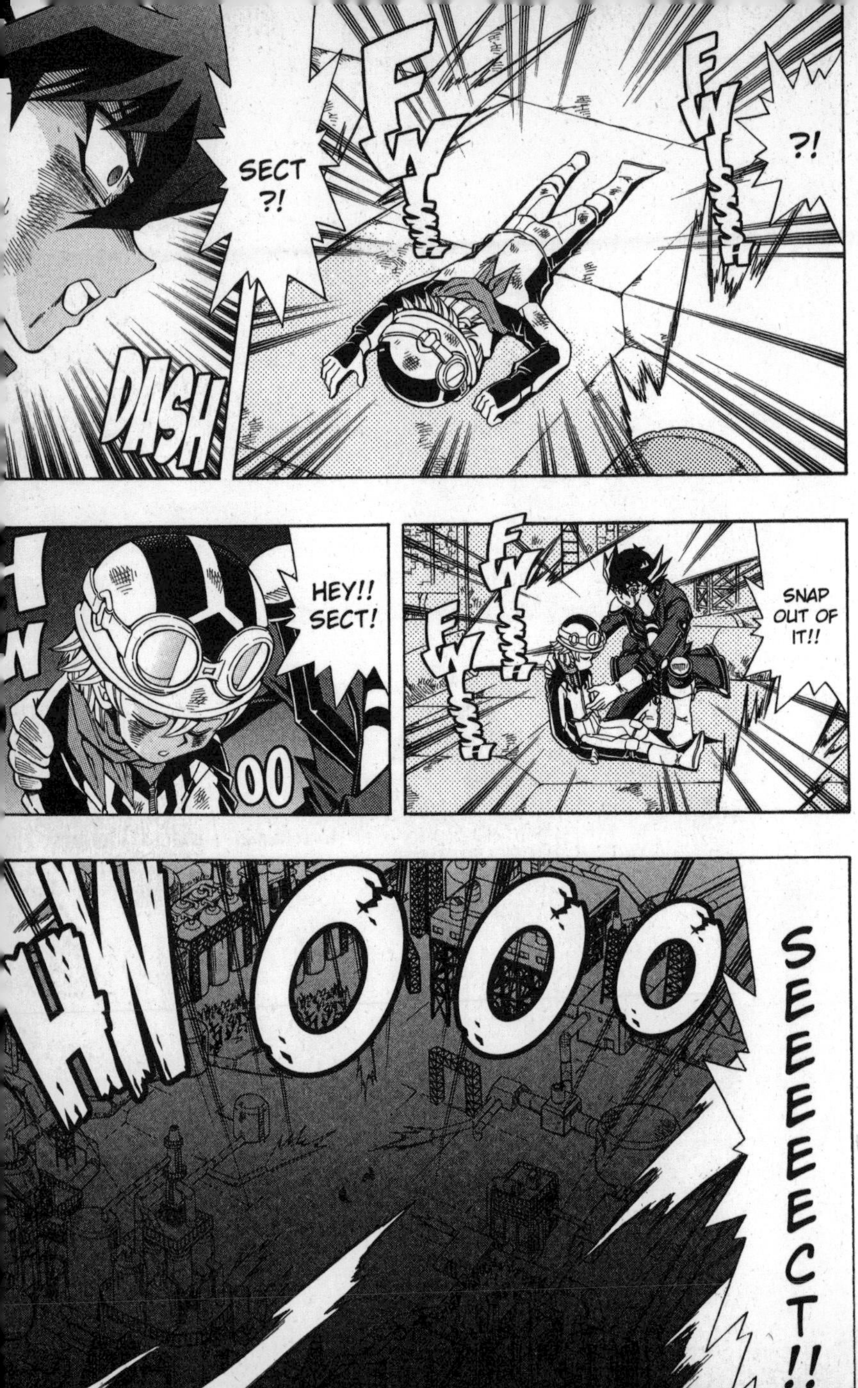
?!
FWISSH
SECT ?!
DASH
SNAP OUT OF IT!!
HEY!! SECT!
SEEEEECT!!

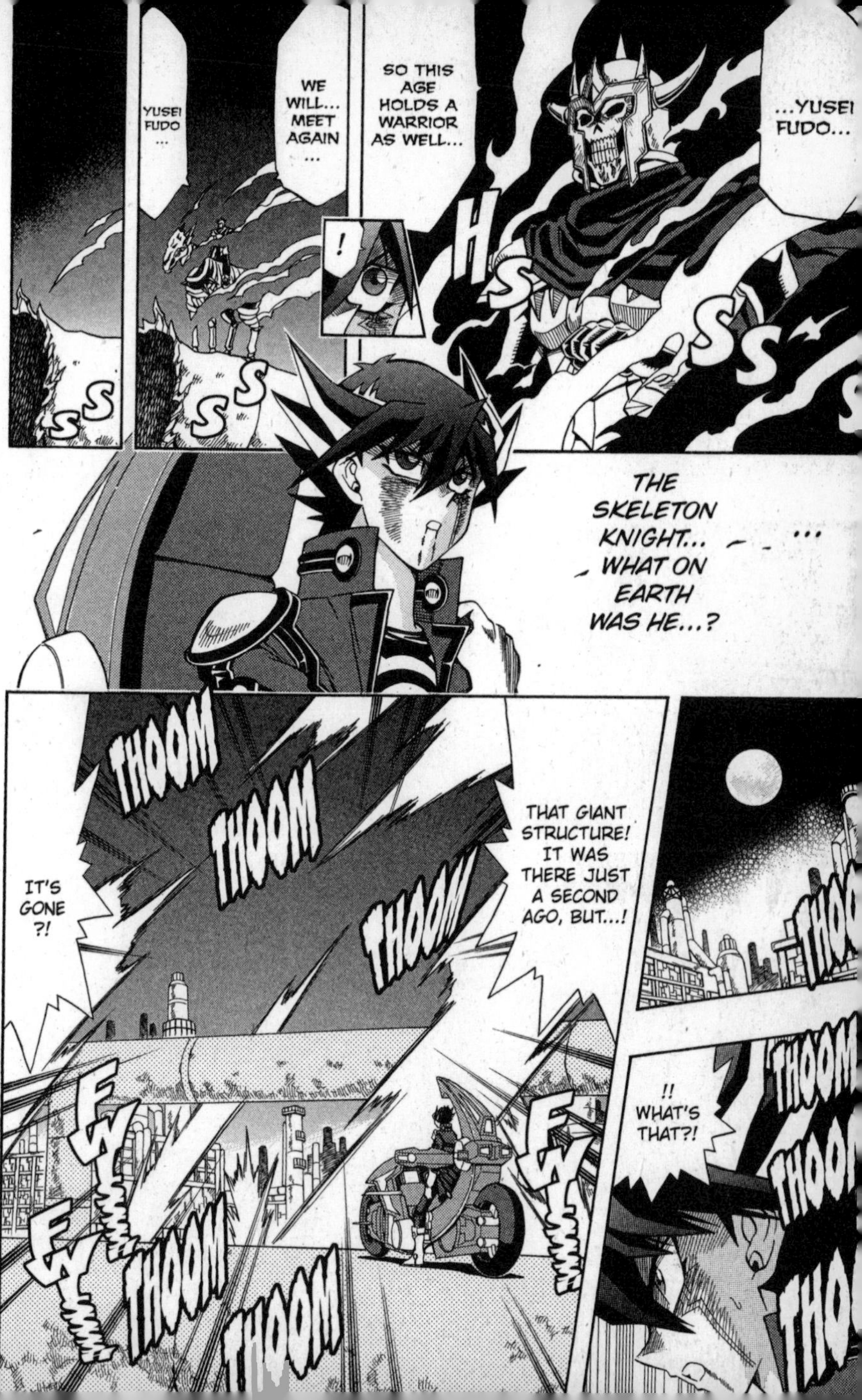
...YUSEI FUDO...
SO THIS AGE HOLDS A WARRIOR AS WELL...
!
HSSSS
WE WILL... MEET AGAIN ...
SSS
YUSEI FUDO ...
SS
...
THE SKELETON KNIGHT... WHAT ON EARTH WAS HE...?
THOOM
!! WHAT'S THAT?!
THOOM
THOOM
THOOM
THOOM
THOOM
THOOM
THAT GIANT STRUCTURE! IT WAS THERE JUST A SECOND AGO, BUT...!
IT'S GONE ?!
THOOM
THOOM

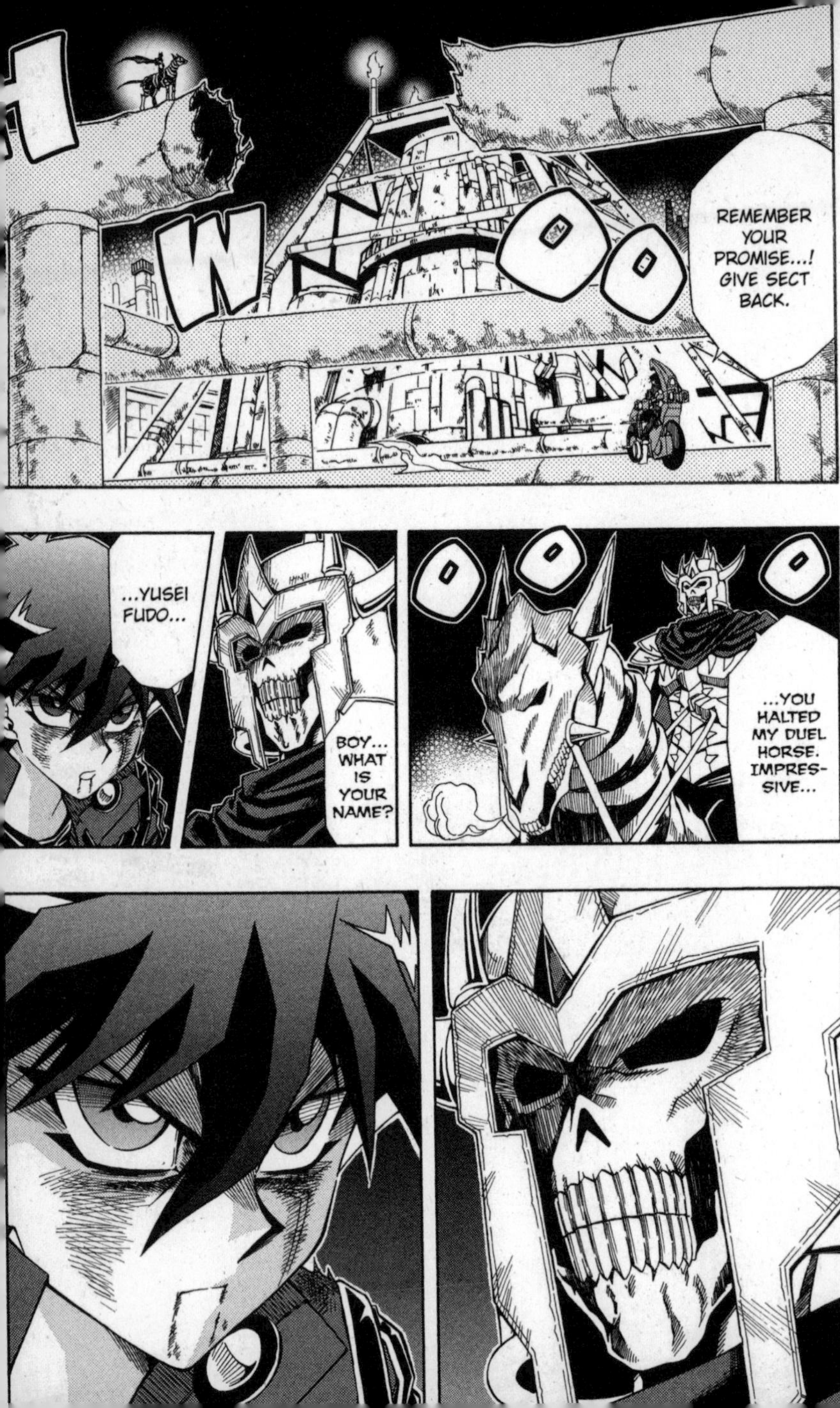
HWOOO
REMEMBER YOUR PROMISE...! GIVE SECT BACK.
OOOO
...YOU HALTED MY DUEL HORSE. IMPRESSIVE...
BOY... WHAT IS YOUR NAME?
...YUSEI FUDO...

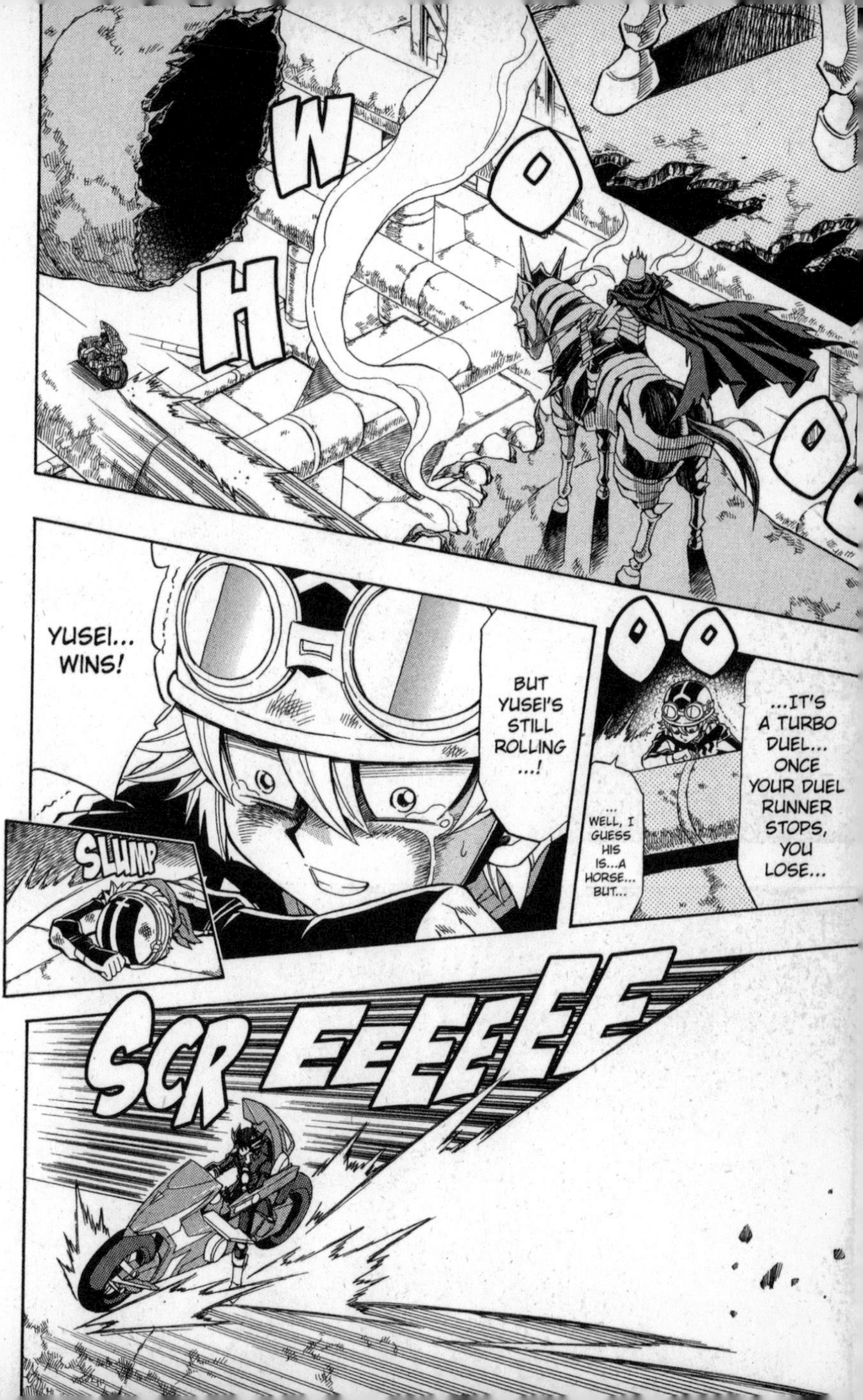
WHOOOO
OO
...IT'S A TURBO DUEL... ONCE YOUR DUEL RUNNER STOPS, YOU LOSE...
...WELL, I GUESS HIS IS...A HORSE... BUT...
BUT YUSEI'S STILL ROLLING ...!
YUSEI... WINS!
SLUMP
SCREEEEEE

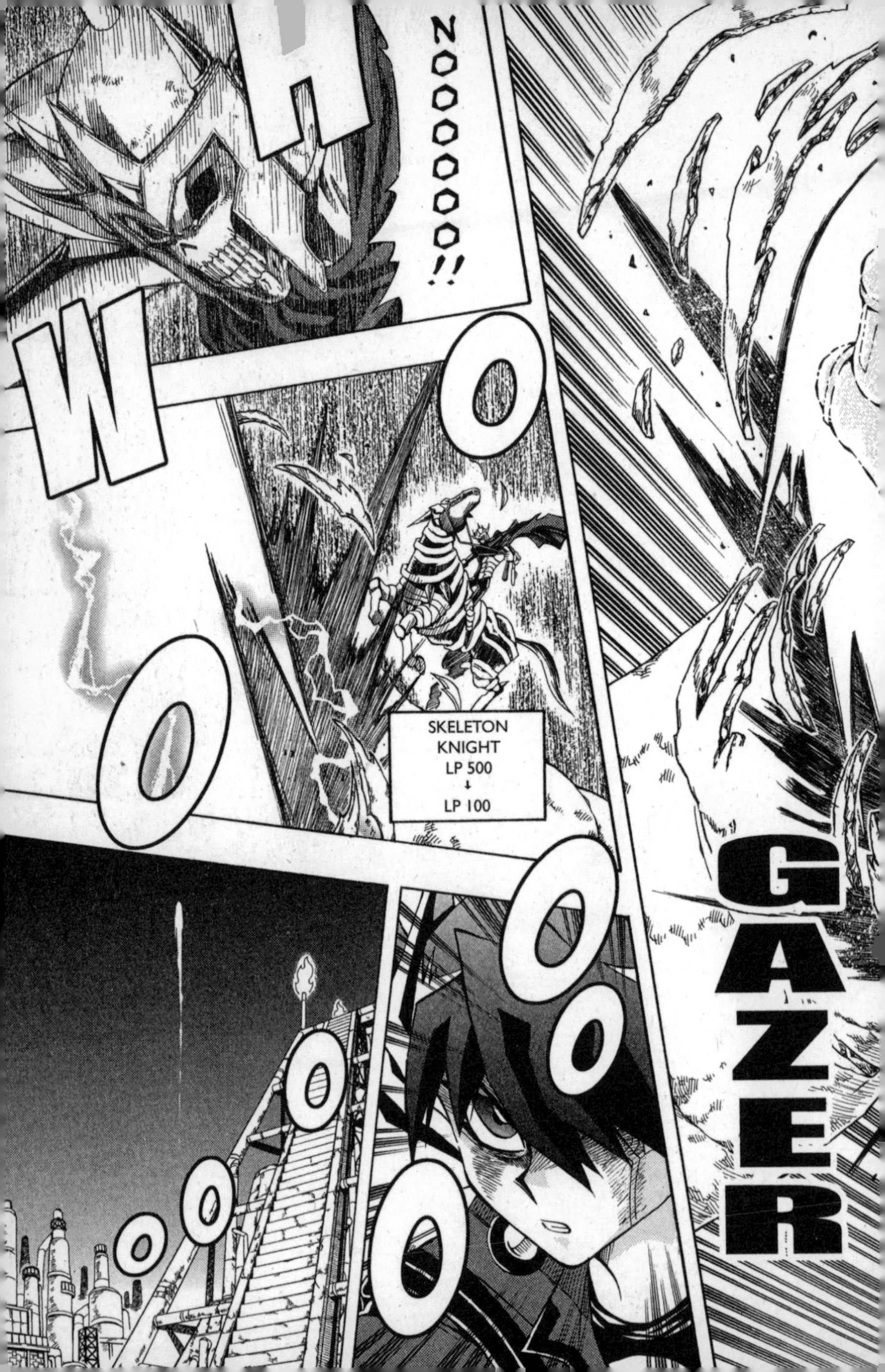
GAZER
NOOOOOOOO!!
WHOOOOOOOOOO
SKELETON KNIGHT
LP 500
↓
LP 100

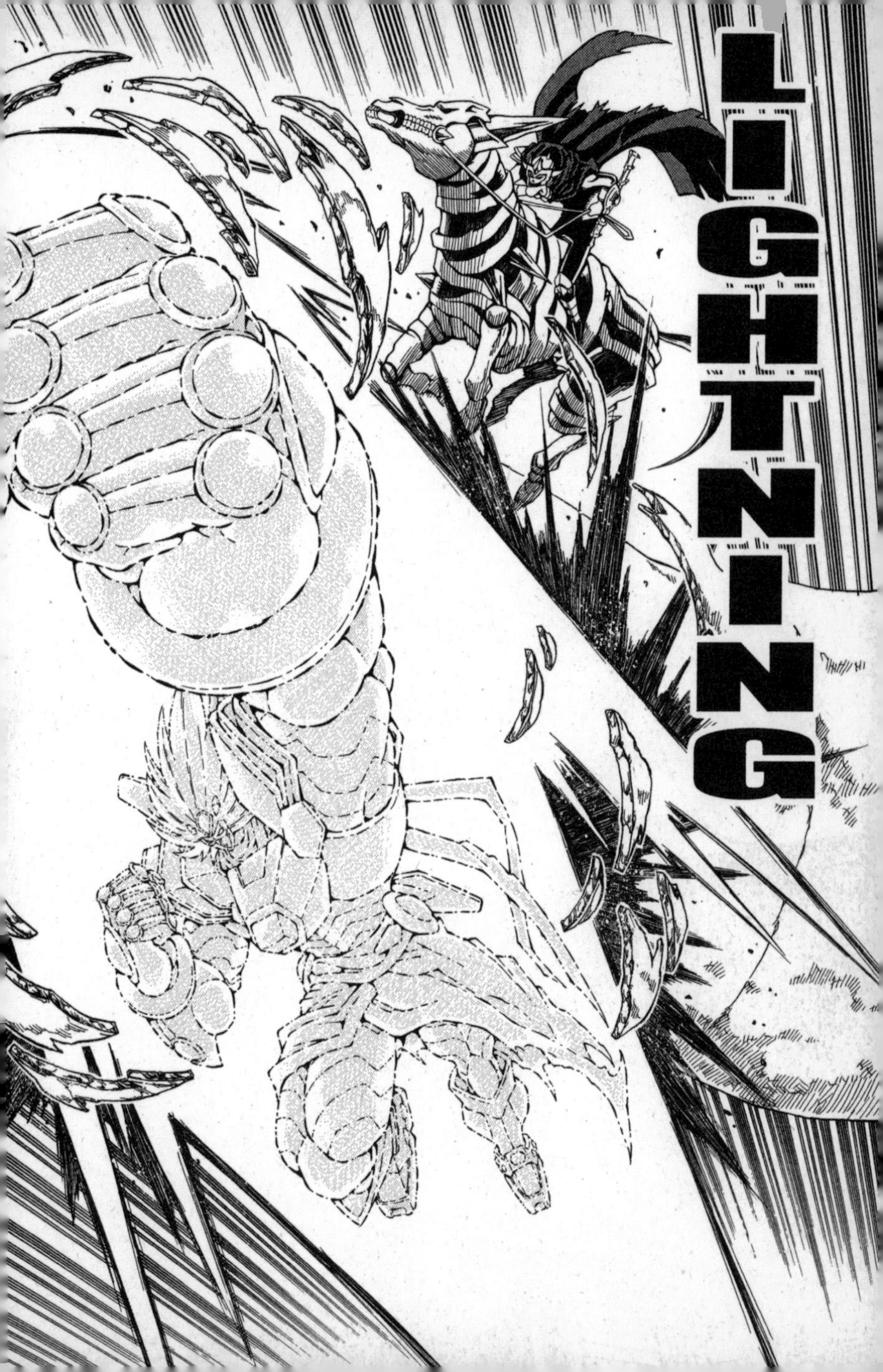
LIGHTNING

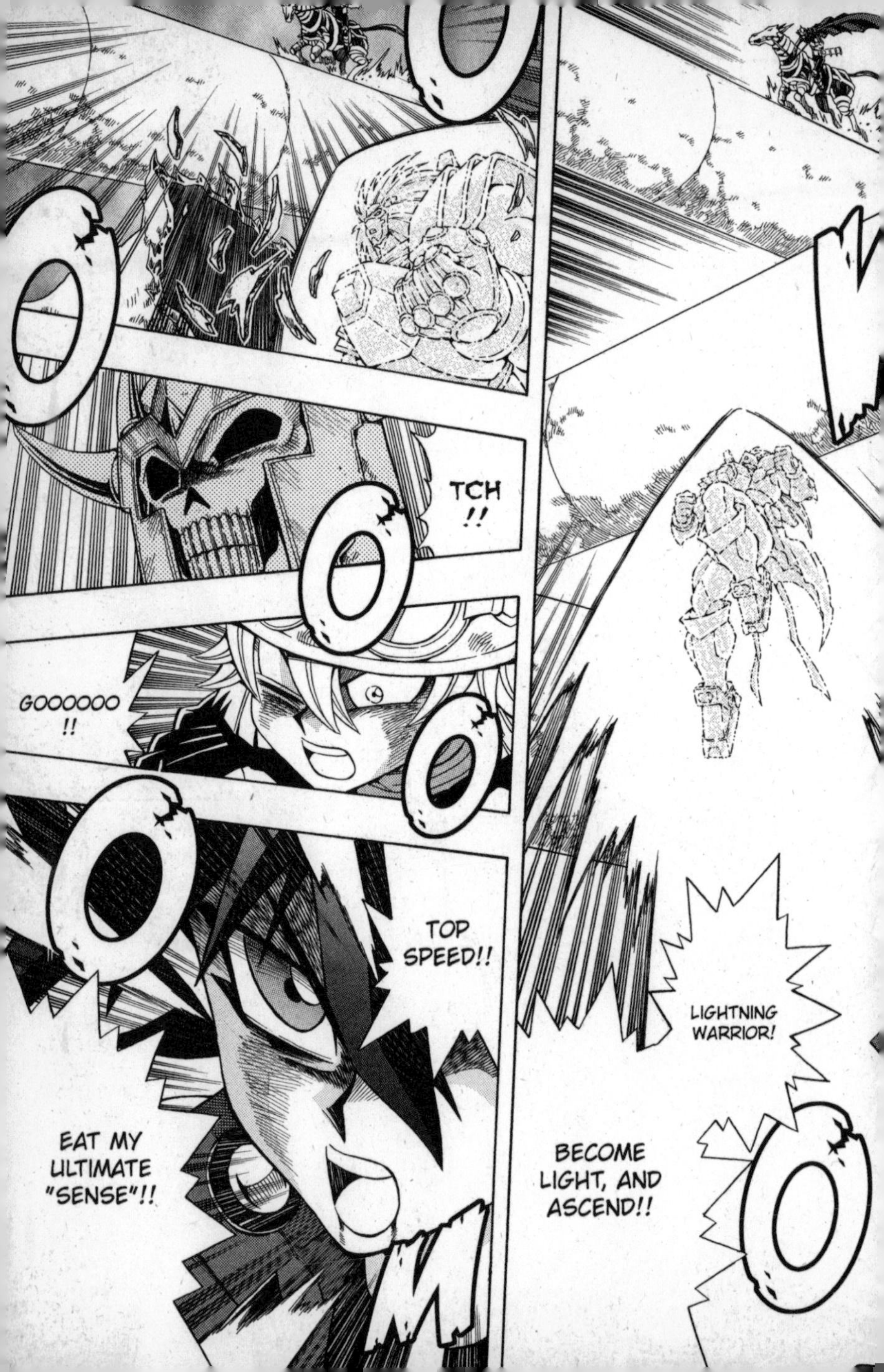
LIGHTNING WARRIOR!
BECOME LIGHT, AND ASCEND!!
TCH!!
GOOOOOO!!
TOP SPEED!!
EAT MY ULTIMATE "SENSE"!!

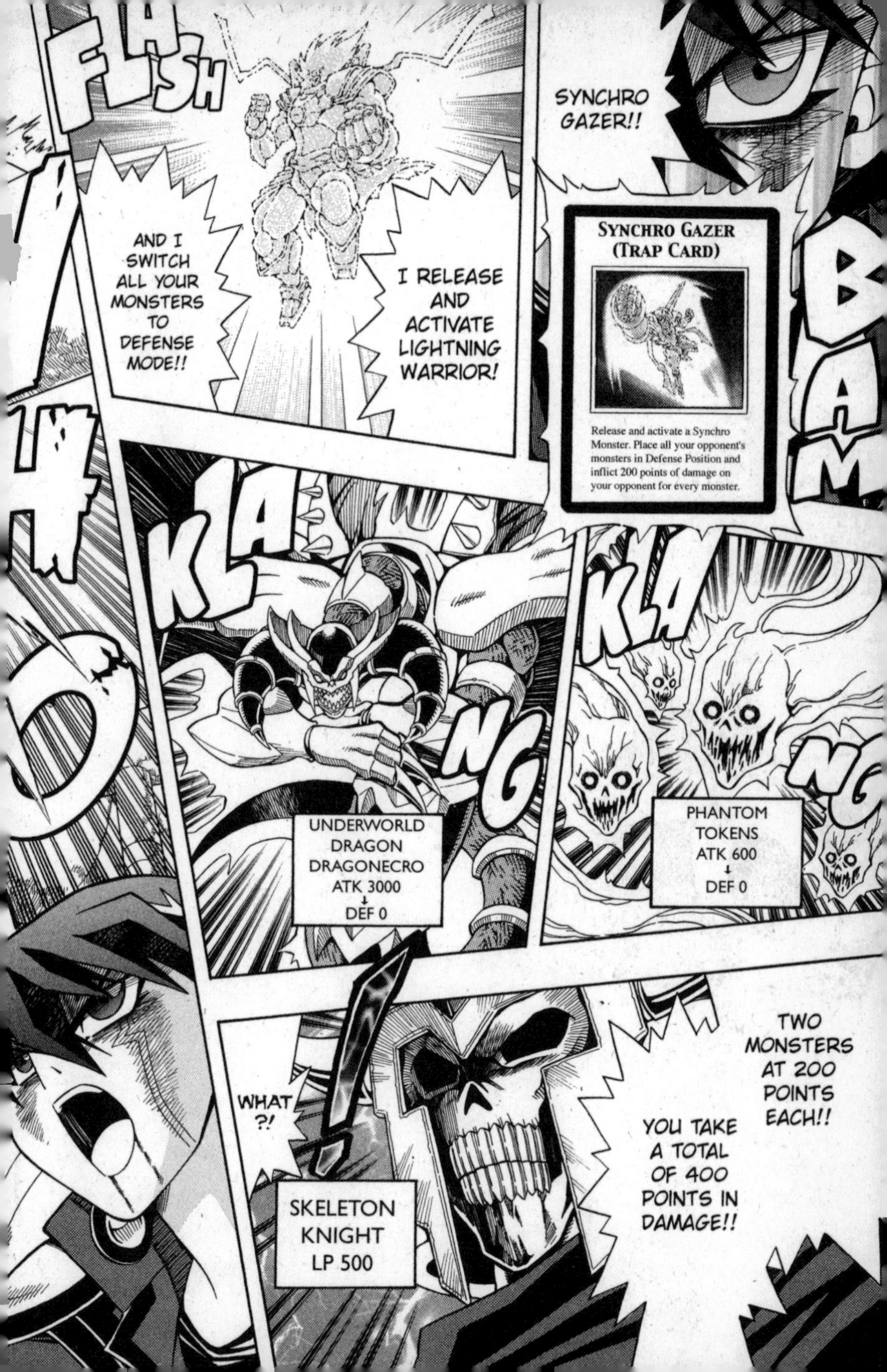
SYNCHRO GAZER!!
BAM
SYNCHRO GAZER
(TRAP CARD)
Release and activate a Synchro Monster. Place all your opponent's monsters in Defense Position and inflict 200 points of damage on your opponent for every monster.
FLASH
I RELEASE AND ACTIVATE LIGHTNING WARRIOR!
AND I SWITCH ALL YOUR MONSTERS TO DEFENSE MODE!!
KLANG
PHANTOM TOKENS ATK 600 ↓ DEF 0
KLANG
UNDERWORLD DRAGON DRAGONECRO ATK 3000 ↓ DEF 0
TWO MONSTERS AT 200 POINTS EACH!!
YOU TAKE A TOTAL OF 400 POINTS IN DAMAGE!!
WHAT?!
SKELETON KNIGHT LP 500

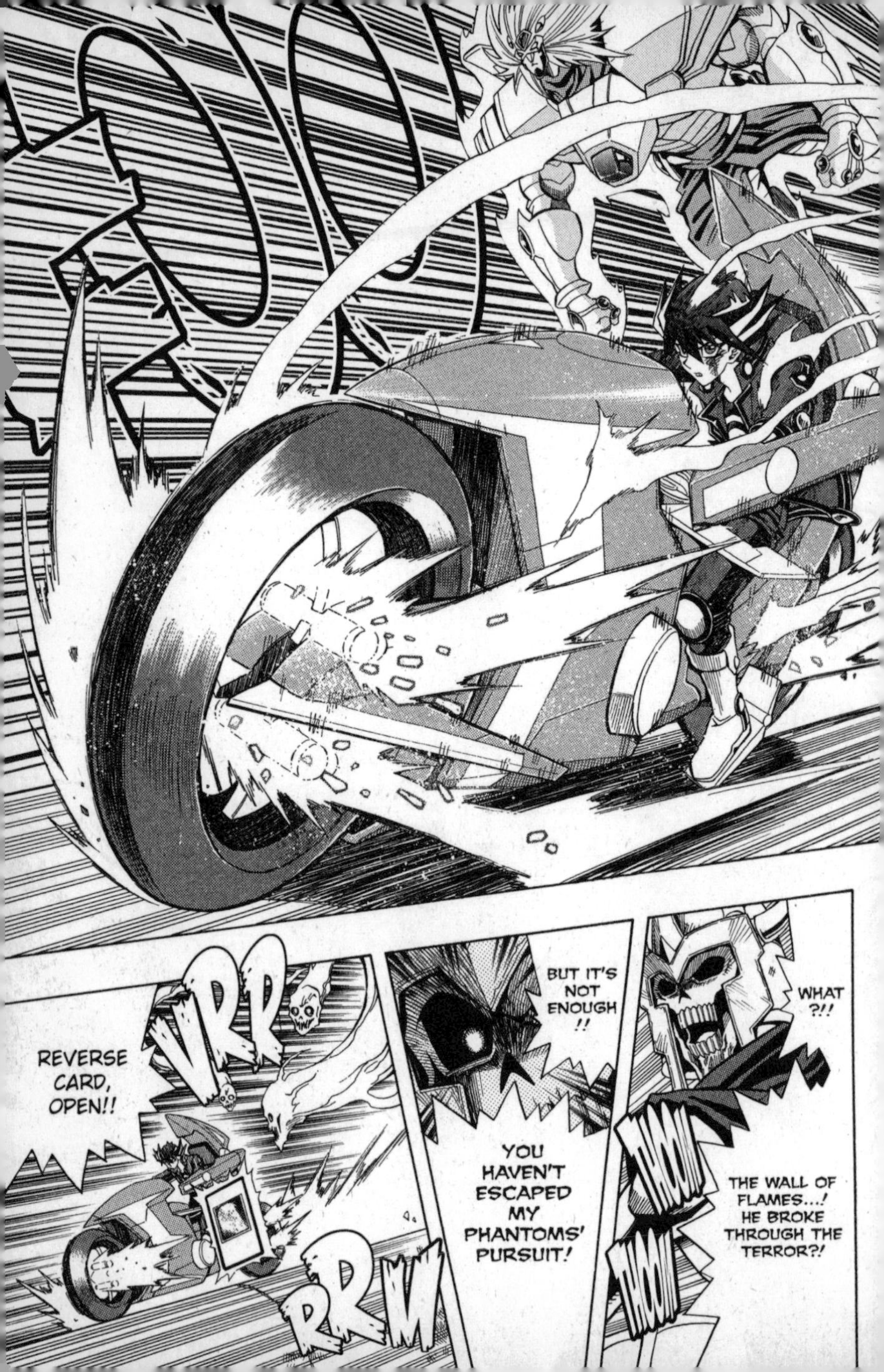
WHAT?!!
THE WALL OF FLAMES...! HE BROKE THROUGH THE TERROR?!
BUT IT'S NOT ENOUGH!!
YOU HAVEN'T ESCAPED MY PHANTOMS' PURSUIT!
REVERSE CARD, OPEN!!

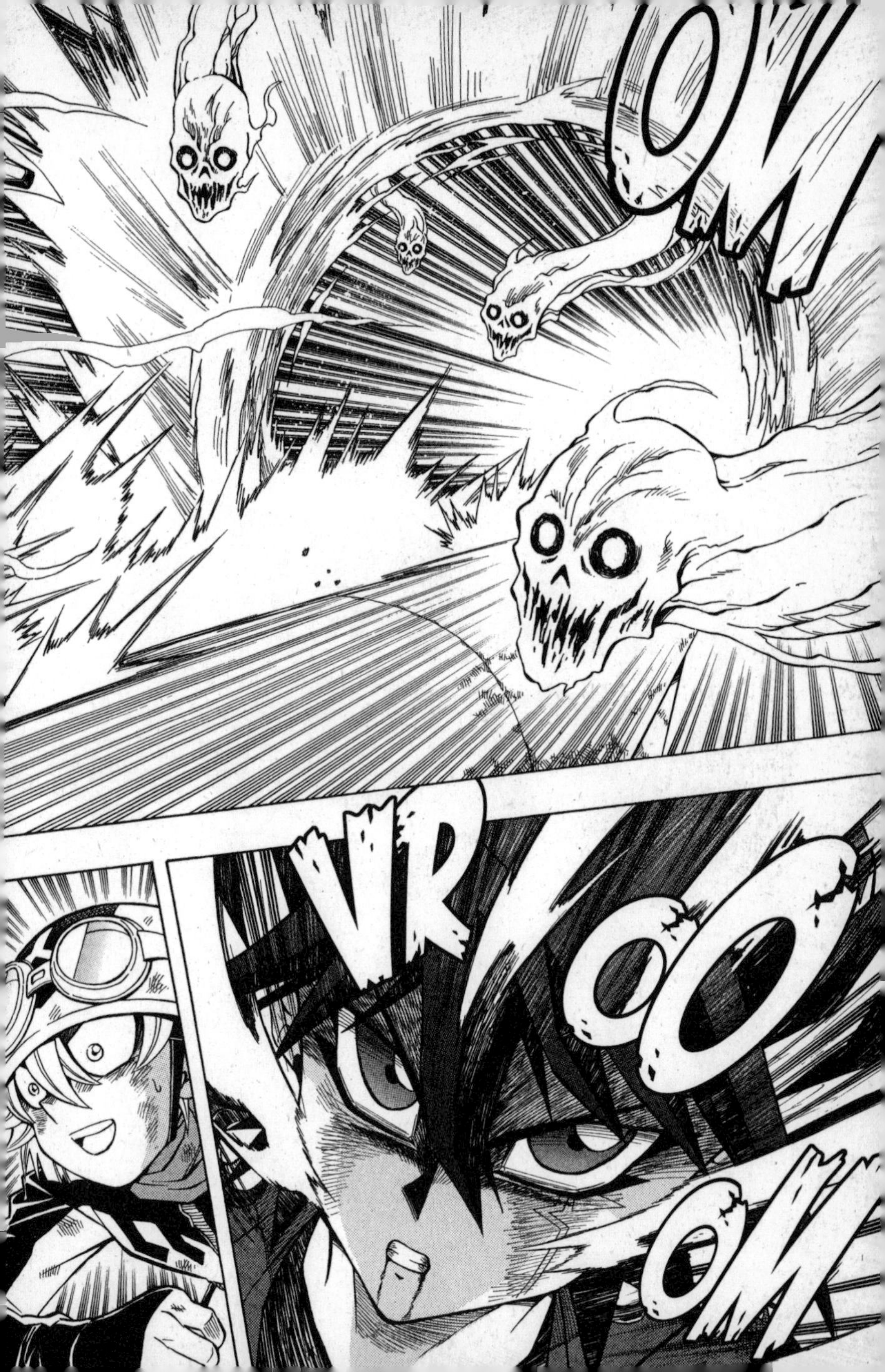
VROOOM

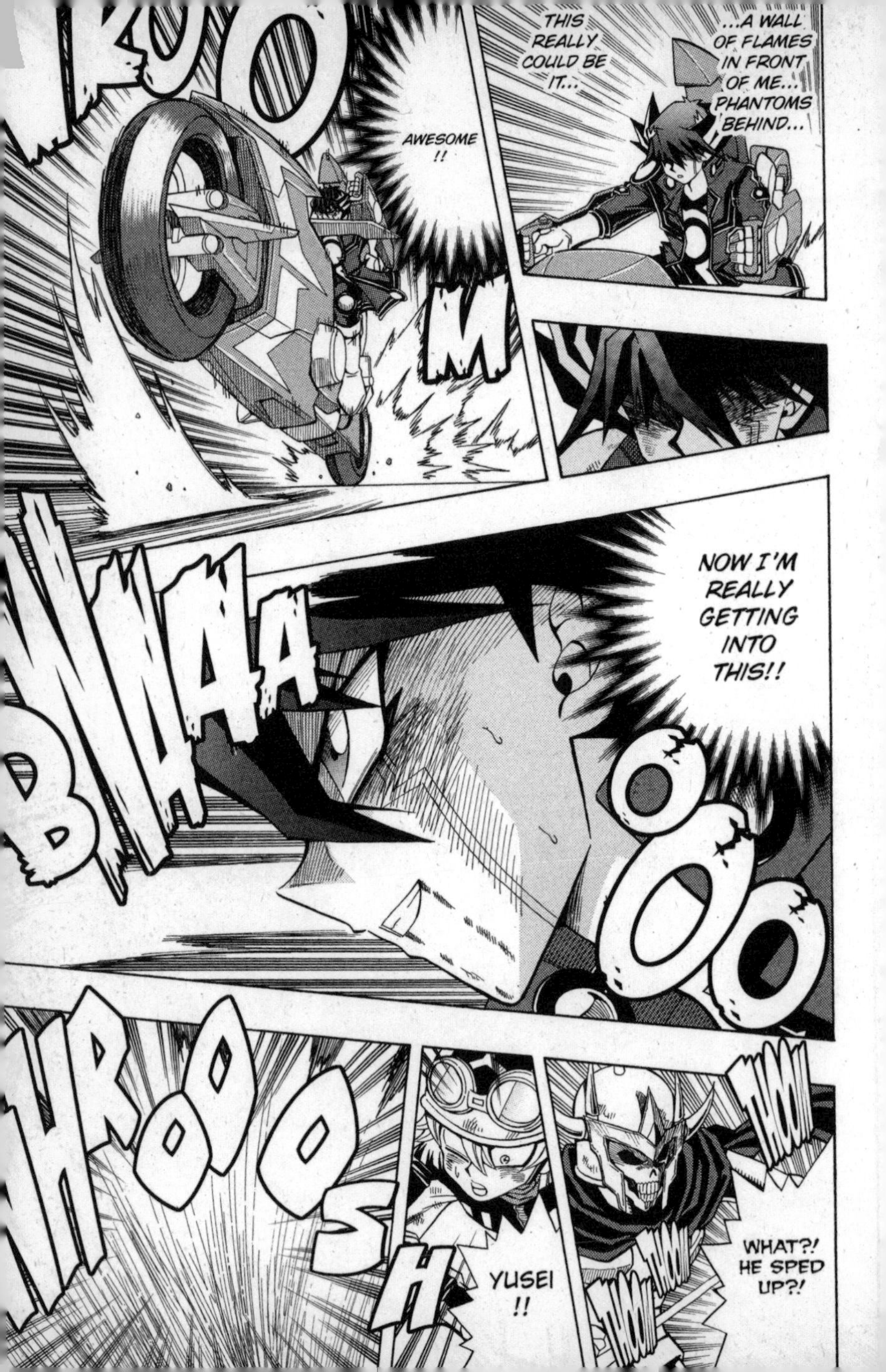
THIS REALLY COULD BE IT...
...A WALL OF FLAMES IN FRONT OF ME... PHANTOMS BEHIND...
ROOOM
AWESOME!!
NOW I'M REALLY GETTING INTO THIS!!
BWAAOOO
WHAT?! HE SPED UP?!
THOOM
THOOM THOOM THOOM THOOM
YUSEI!!
ROOOSH

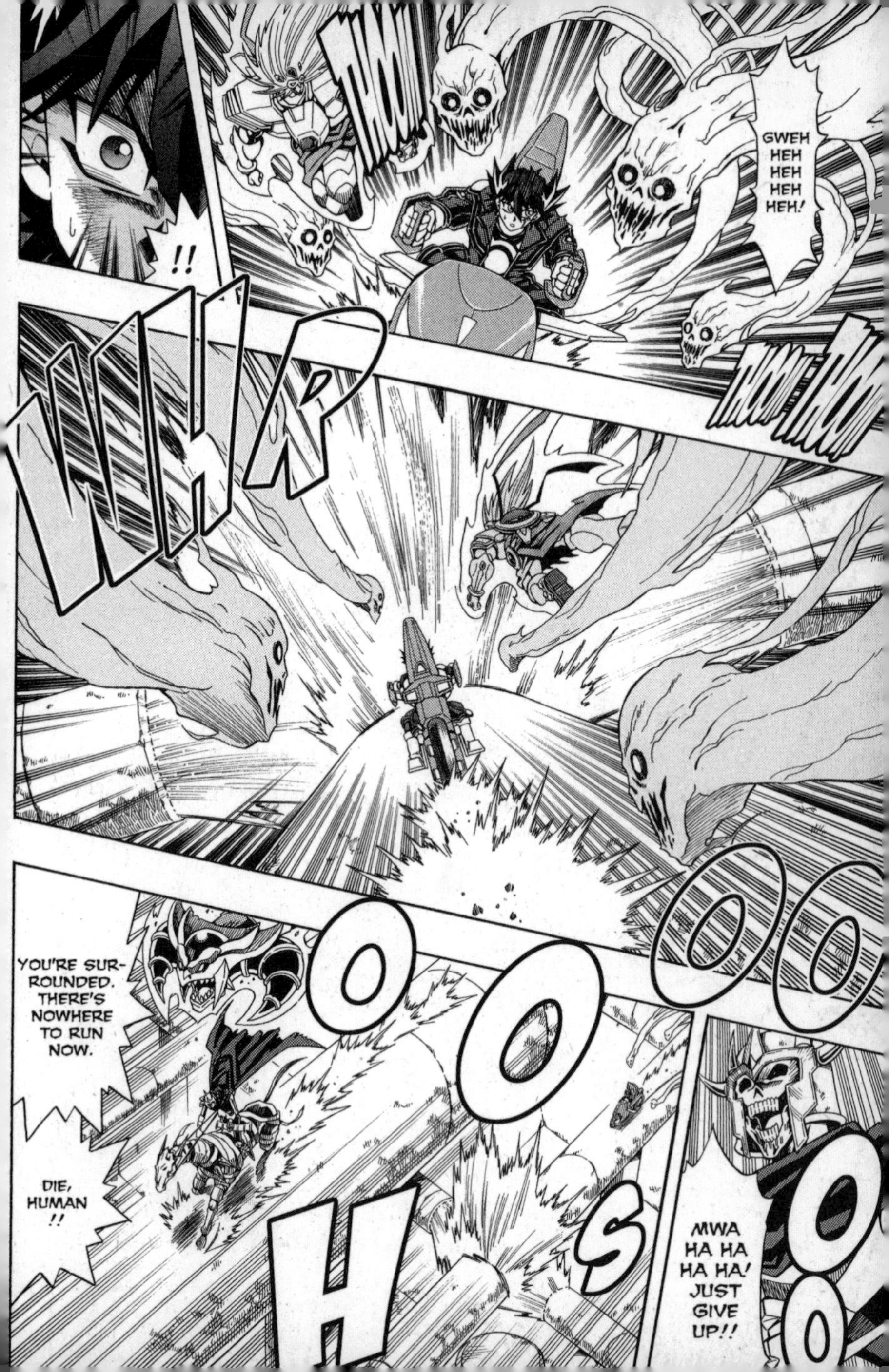
GWEH HEH HEH HEH HEH!
THOOM
!!
THOOM THOOM
WHAP
OOOOOO
MWA HA HA HA HA! JUST GIVE UP!!
YOU'RE SURROUNDED. THERE'S NOWHERE TO RUN NOW.
DIE, HUMAN!!
HSS

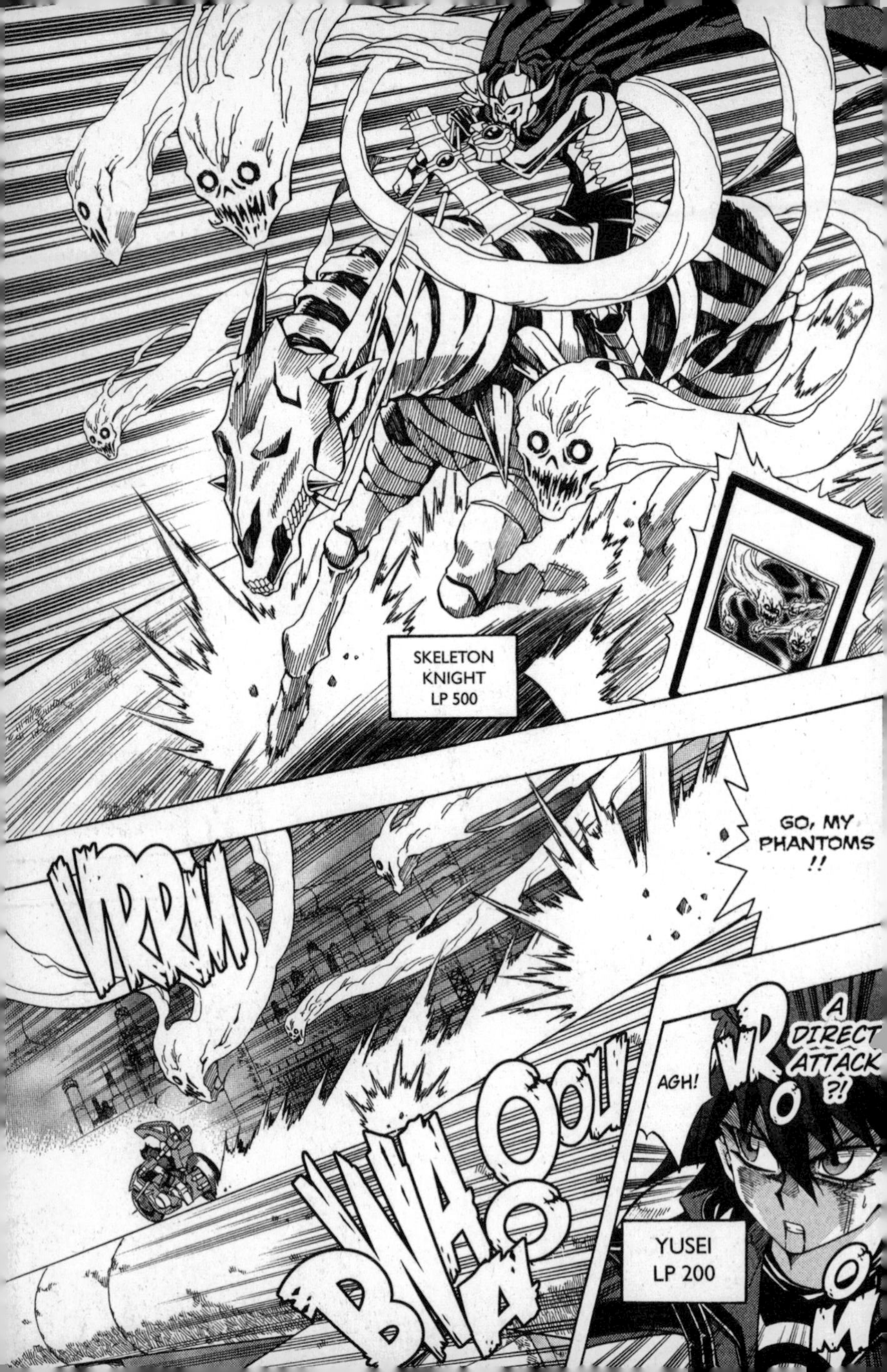
SKELETON KNIGHT LP 500
GO, MY PHANTOMS !!
VRRM
A DIRECT ATTACK ?!
VROOO
AGH!
YUSEI LP 200
BWAOOOU

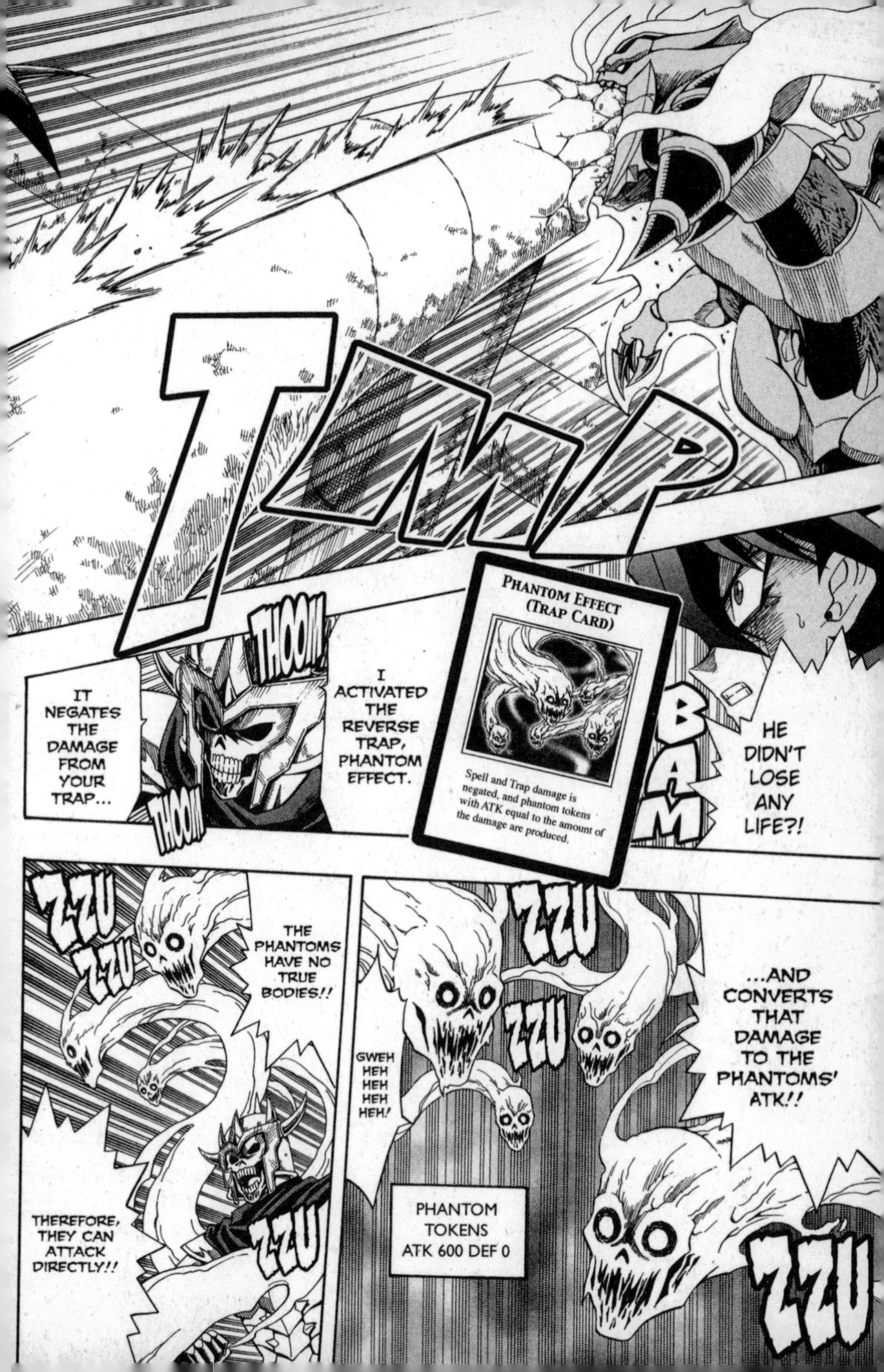

TMP
HE DIDN'T LOSE ANY LIFE?!
BAM
PHANTOM EFFECT (TRAP CARD)
Spell and Trap damage is negated, and phantom tokens with ATK equal to the amount of the damage are produced.
I ACTIVATED THE REVERSE TRAP, PHANTOM EFFECT.
THOOM
IT NEGATES THE DAMAGE FROM YOUR TRAP...
THOOM
ZZU
...AND CONVERTS THAT DAMAGE TO THE PHANTOMS' ATK!!
ZZU
GWEH HEH HEH HEH HEH!
PHANTOM TOKENS ATK 600 DEF 0
ZZU
Z-ZU
ZZU
THE PHANTOMS HAVE NO TRUE BODIES!!
THEREFORE, THEY CAN ATTACK DIRECTLY!!
ZZU

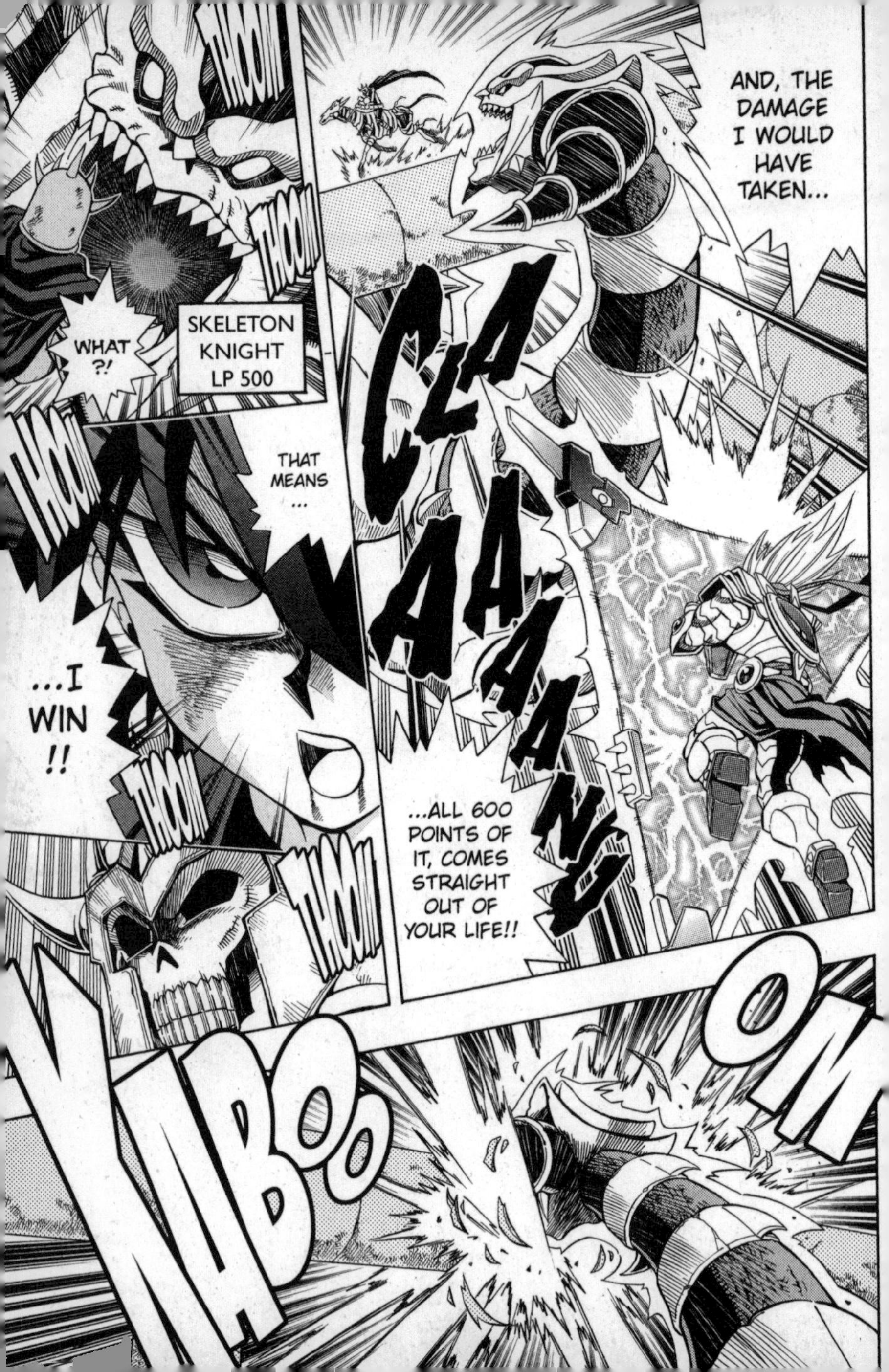
AND, THE DAMAGE I WOULD HAVE TAKEN...
CLAAAANG
...ALL 600 POINTS OF IT, COMES STRAIGHT OUT OF YOUR LIFE!!
THOOM
THOOM
WHAT ?!
SKELETON KNIGHT LP 500
THOOM
THAT MEANS ...
...I WIN !!
THOOM
THOOM
WHABOOOOM

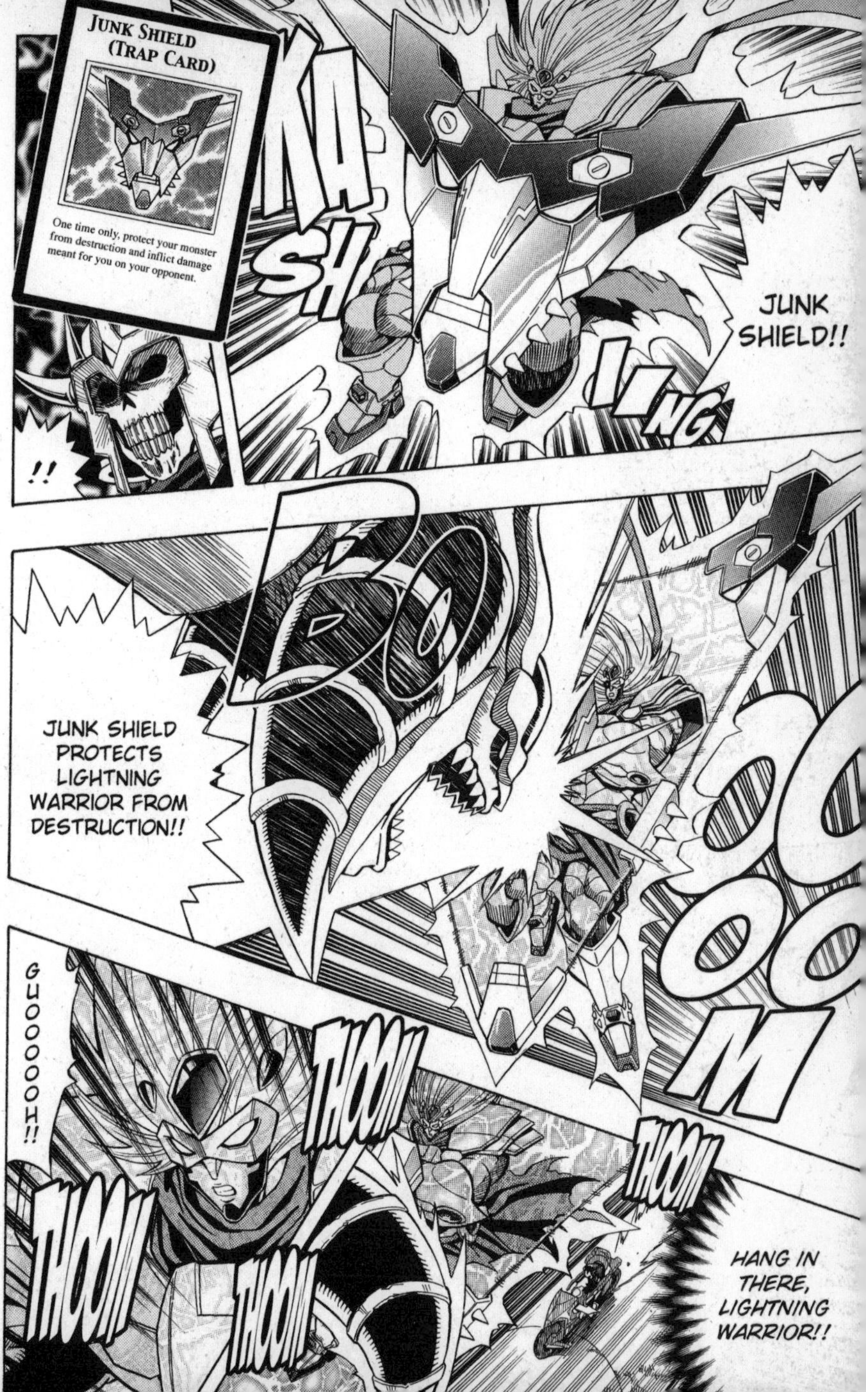
KASH
I NG
JUNK SHIELD!!
JUNK SHIELD (TRAP CARD)
One time only, protect your monster from destruction and inflict damage meant for you on your opponent.
!!
DOOOOM
JUNK SHIELD PROTECTS LIGHTNING WARRIOR FROM DESTRUCTION!!
THOOM
HANG IN THERE, LIGHTNING WARRIOR!!
THOOM
GUOOOOOOH!!
THOOM
THOOM

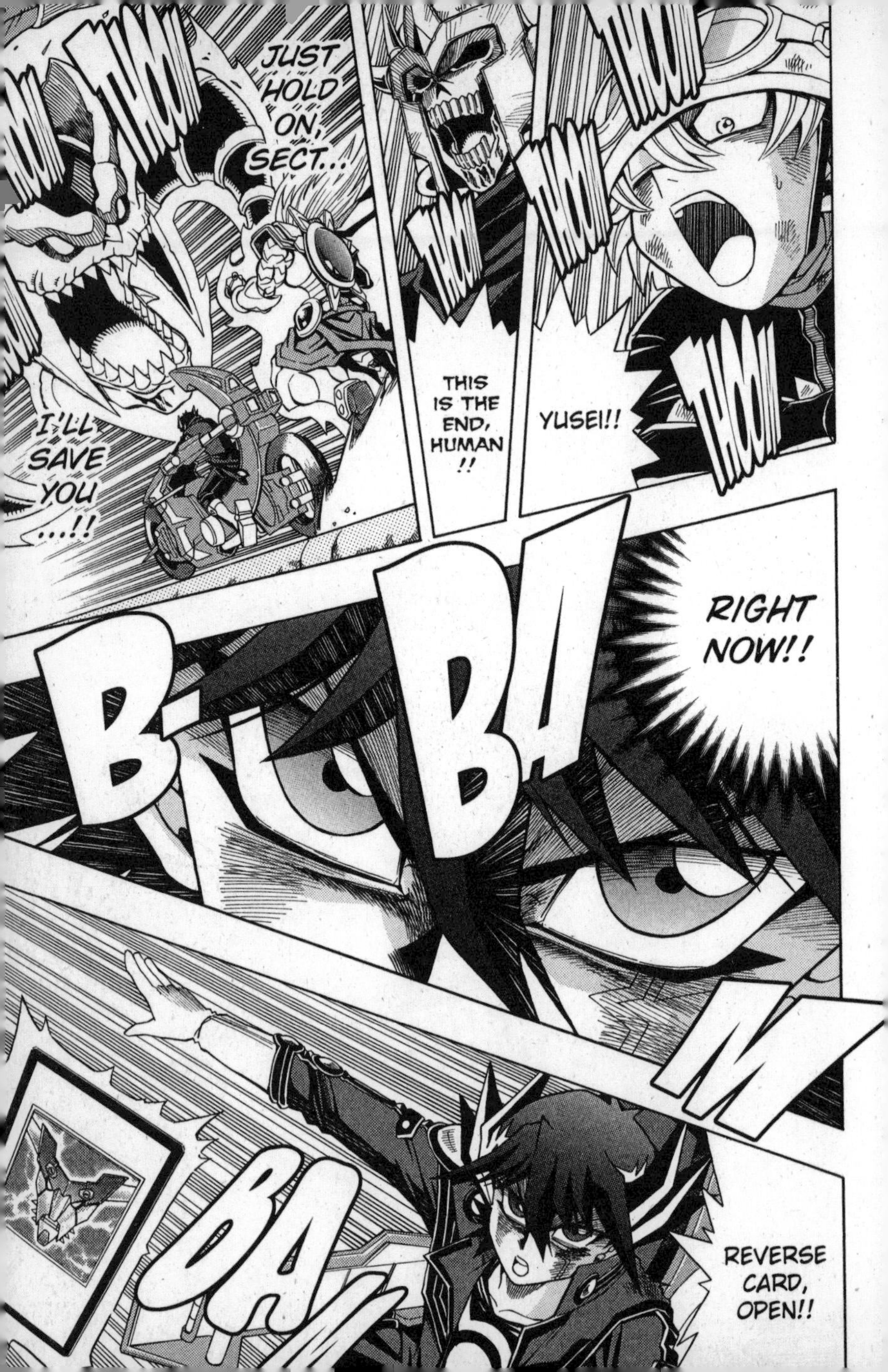
THOOM
YUSEI!!
THIS IS THE END, HUMAN!!
JUST HOLD ON, SECT...
I'LL SAVE YOU...!!
B-BA-M
RIGHT NOW!!
REVERSE CARD, OPEN!!

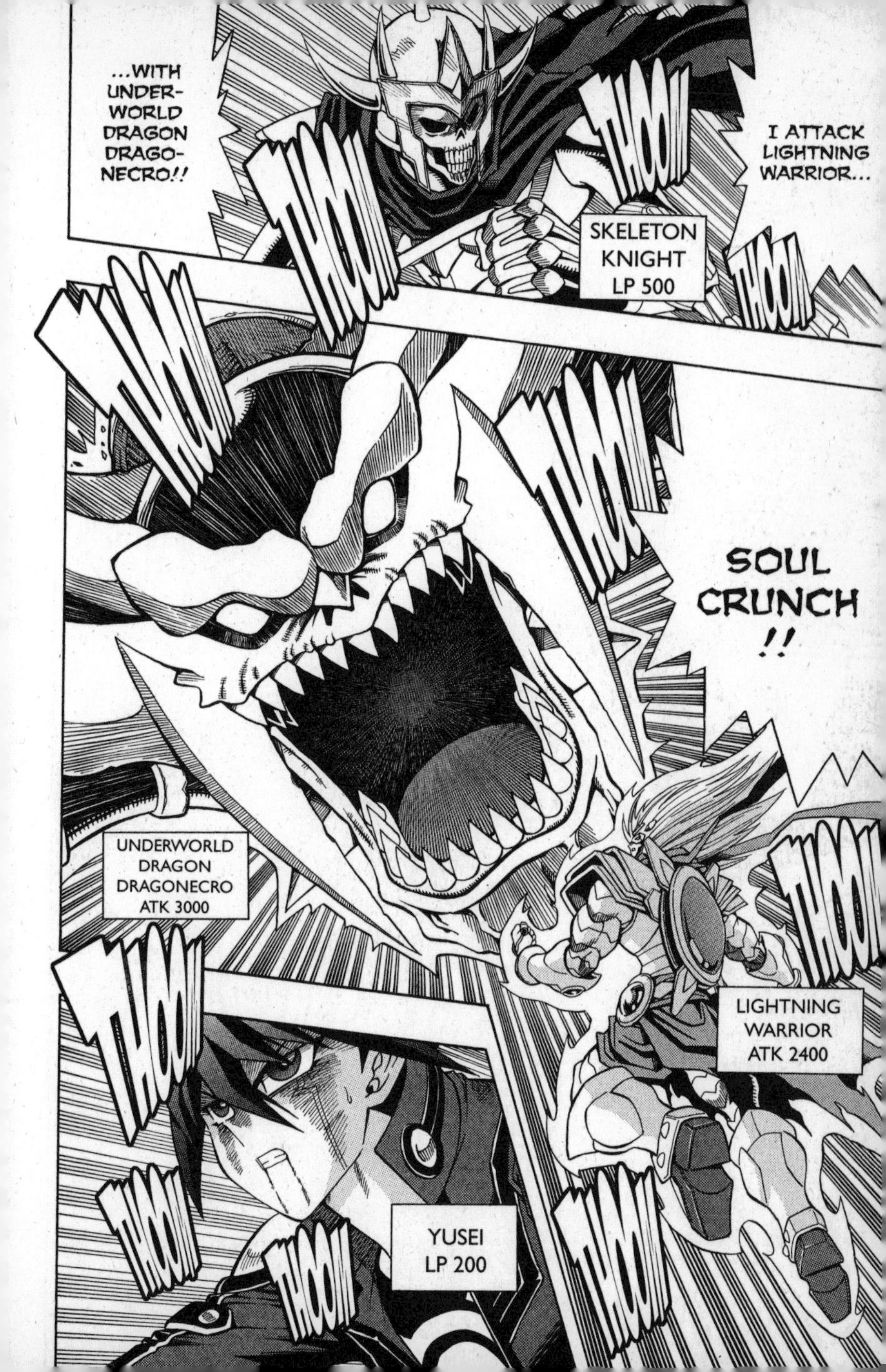

I ATTACK LIGHTNING WARRIOR...
...WITH UNDER-WORLD DRAGON DRAGO-NECRO!!
THOOM
THOOM
SKELETON KNIGHT LP 500
THOOM
THOOM
THOOM
SOUL CRUNCH!!
UNDERWORLD DRAGON DRAGONECRO ATK 3000
THOOM
LIGHTNING WARRIOR ATK 2400
THOOM
THOOM
YUSEI LP 200
THOOM
THOOM

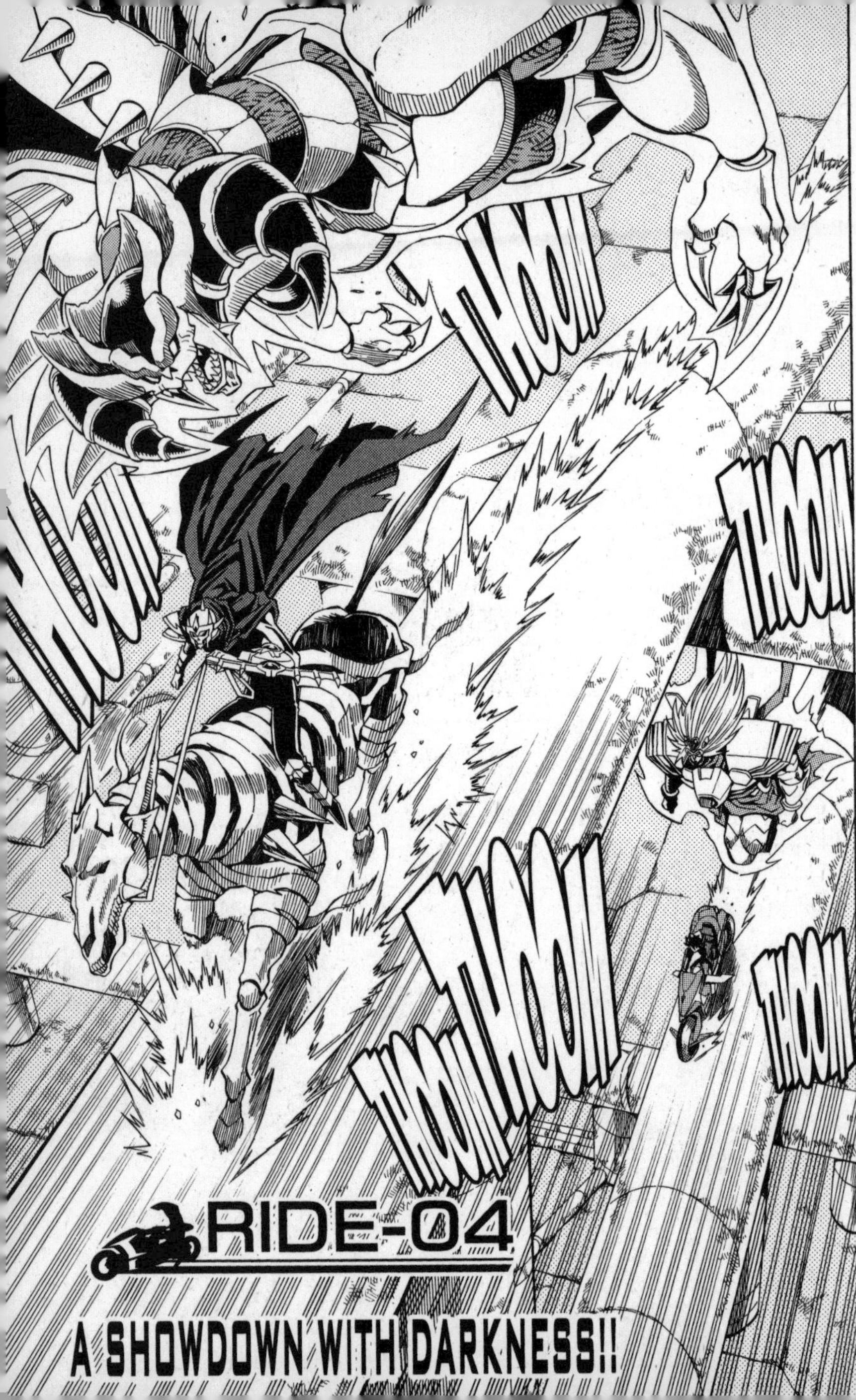
THOOM
THOOM
THOOM
THOOM
THOOM
THOOM
THOOM

RIDE-04
A SHOWDOWN WITH DARKNESS!!

5D's TRACKS

THE 3RD

BY SATOMASA

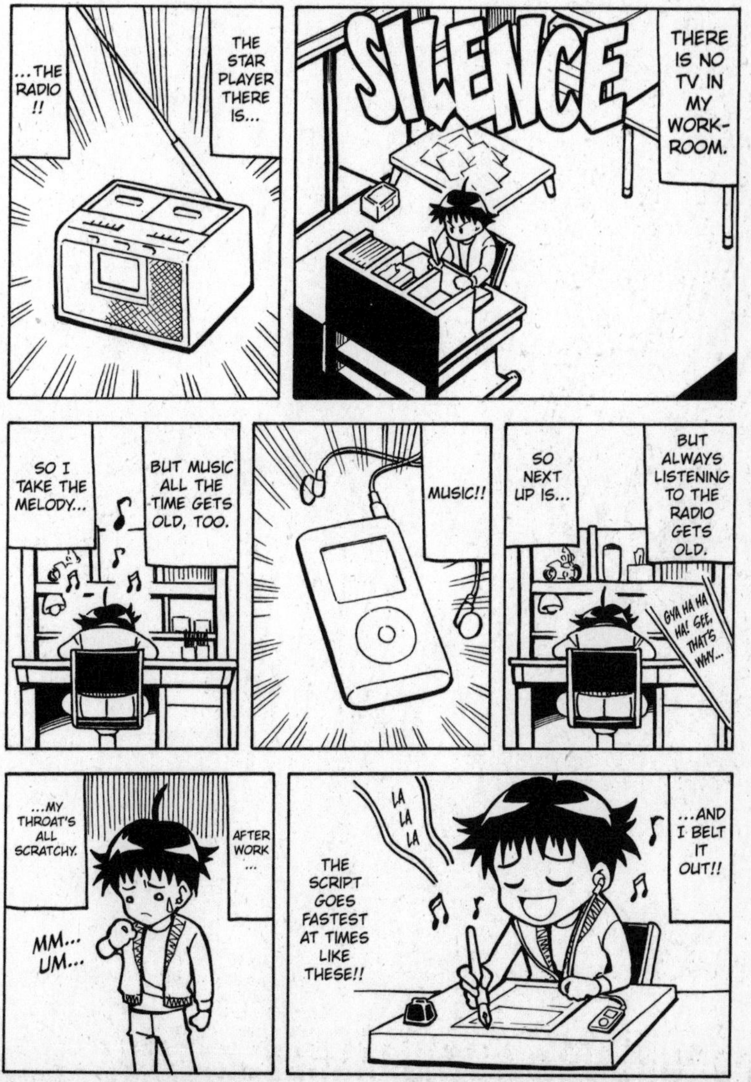
THERE IS NO TV IN MY WORK-ROOM.
SILENCE
THE STAR PLAYER THERE IS...
...THE RADIO!!
BUT ALWAYS LISTENING TO THE RADIO GETS OLD.
SO NEXT UP IS...
GYA HA HA HA! SEE, THAT'S WHY...
MUSIC!!
BUT MUSIC ALL THE TIME GETS OLD, TOO.
SO I TAKE THE MELODY...
...AND I BELT IT OUT!!
LA LA LA
THE SCRIPT GOES FASTEST AT TIMES LIKE THESE!!
AFTER WORK...
...MY THROAT'S ALL SCRATCHY.
MM... UM...

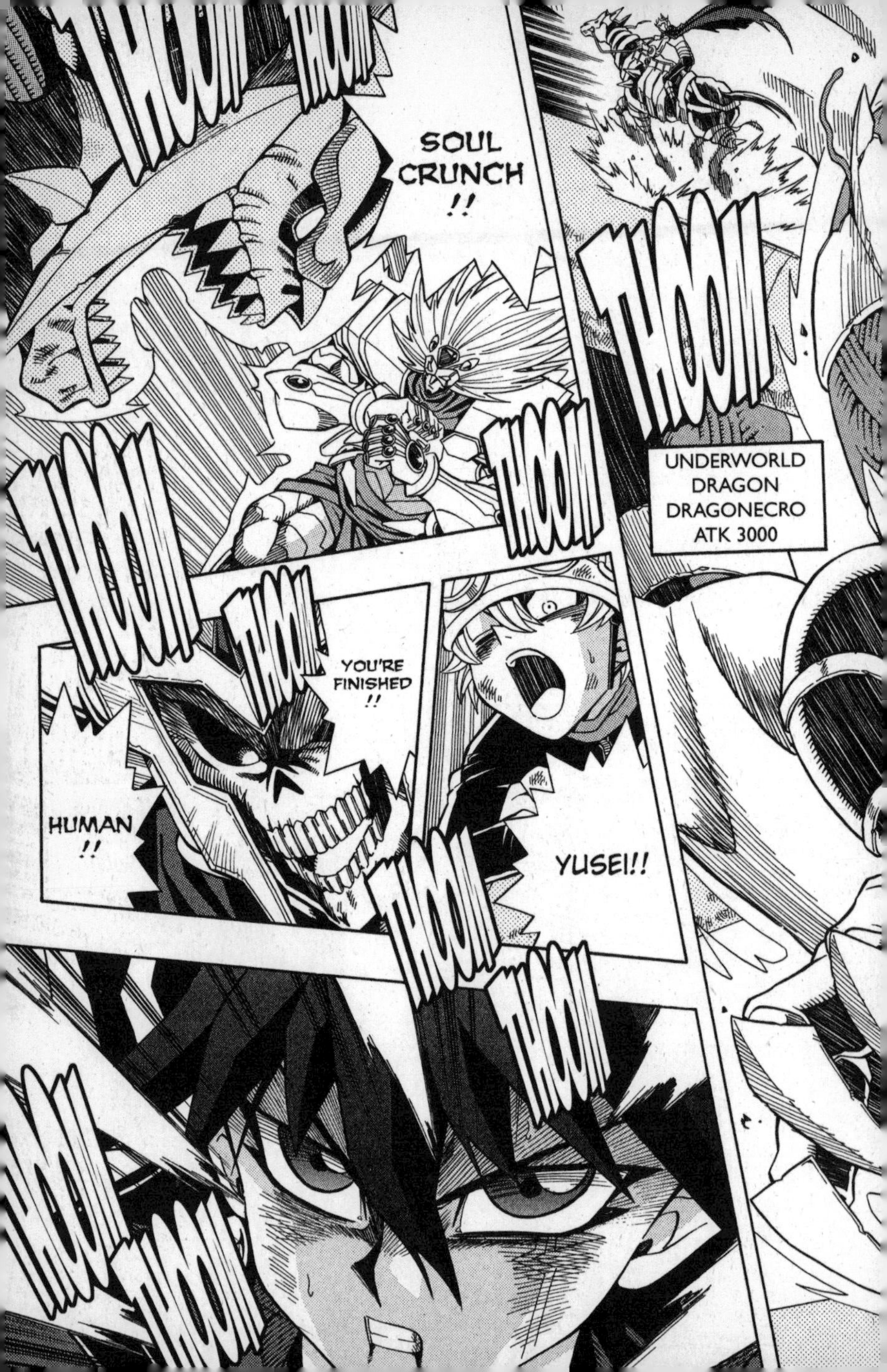
THOOM
UNDERWORLD DRAGON DRAGONECRO ATK 3000
THOOM
THOOM
SOUL CRUNCH !!
THOOM
THOOM
YUSEI!!
THOOM
YOU'RE FINISHED !!
HUMAN !!
THOOM
THOOM
THOOM
THOOM

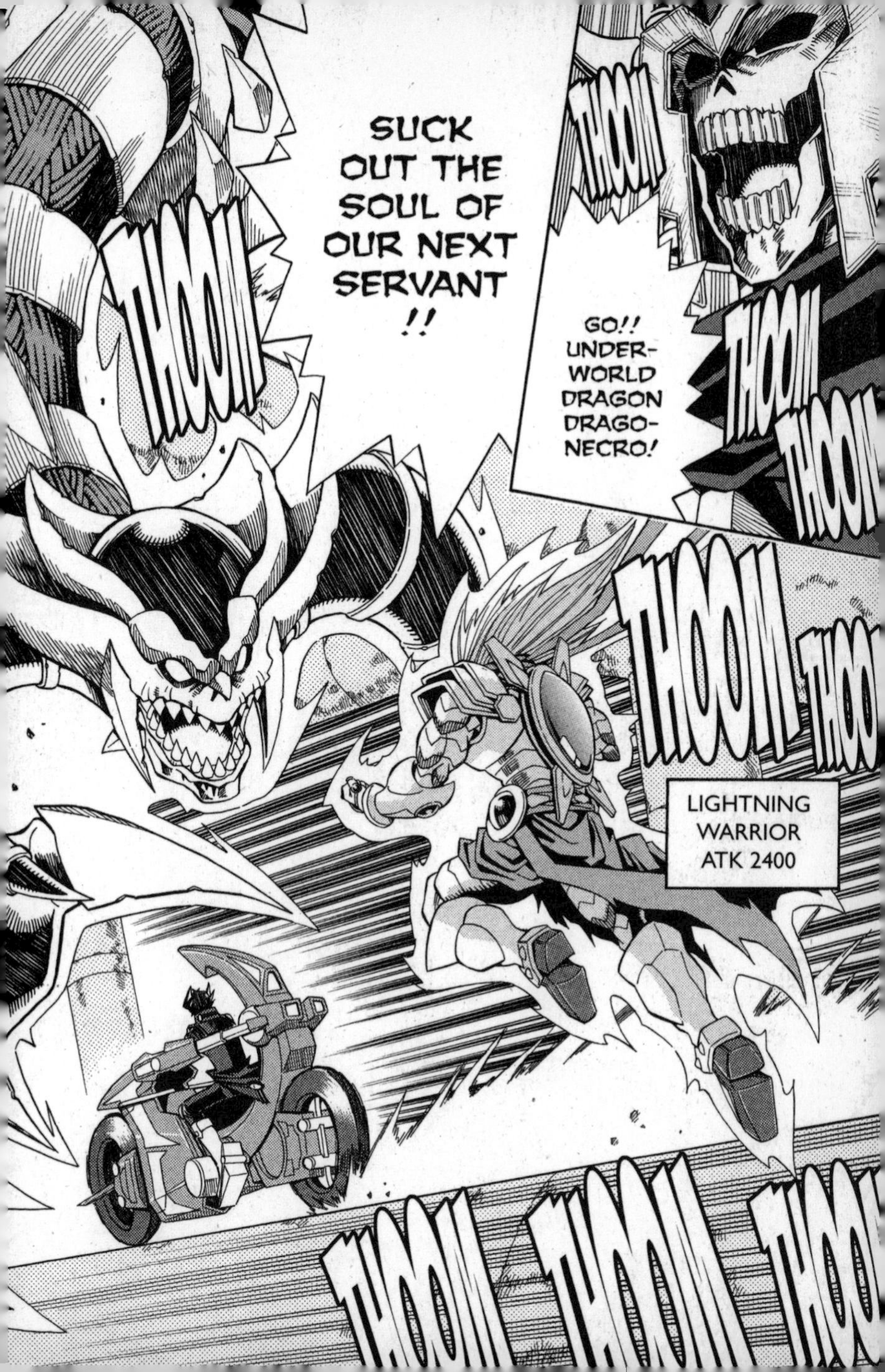
THOOM
GO!! UNDER-WORLD DRAGON DRAGO-NECRO!
THOOM
THOOM
SUCK OUT THE SOUL OF OUR NEXT SERVANT !!
THOOM
THOO
THOOM
LIGHTNING WARRIOR ATK 2400
THOO
THOOM
THOOM

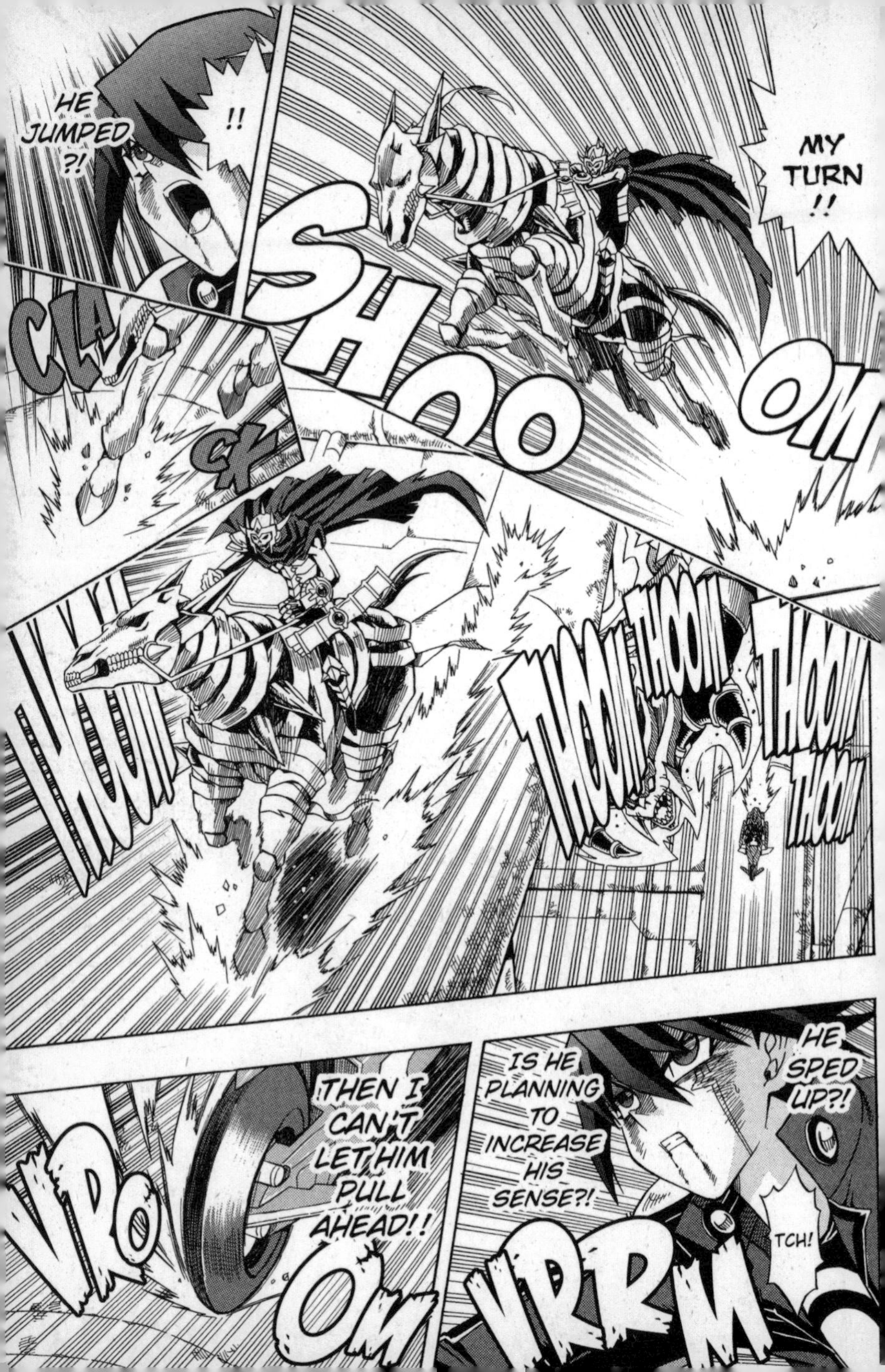
MY TURN!!
SHOOOOM
!!
HE JUMPED?!
CLACK
THOOM THOOM THOOM THOOM
WHOOM
HE SPED UP?!
TCH!
IS HE PLANNING TO INCREASE HIS SENSE?!
VRRM
THEN I CAN'T LET HIM PULL AHEAD!!
VROOM

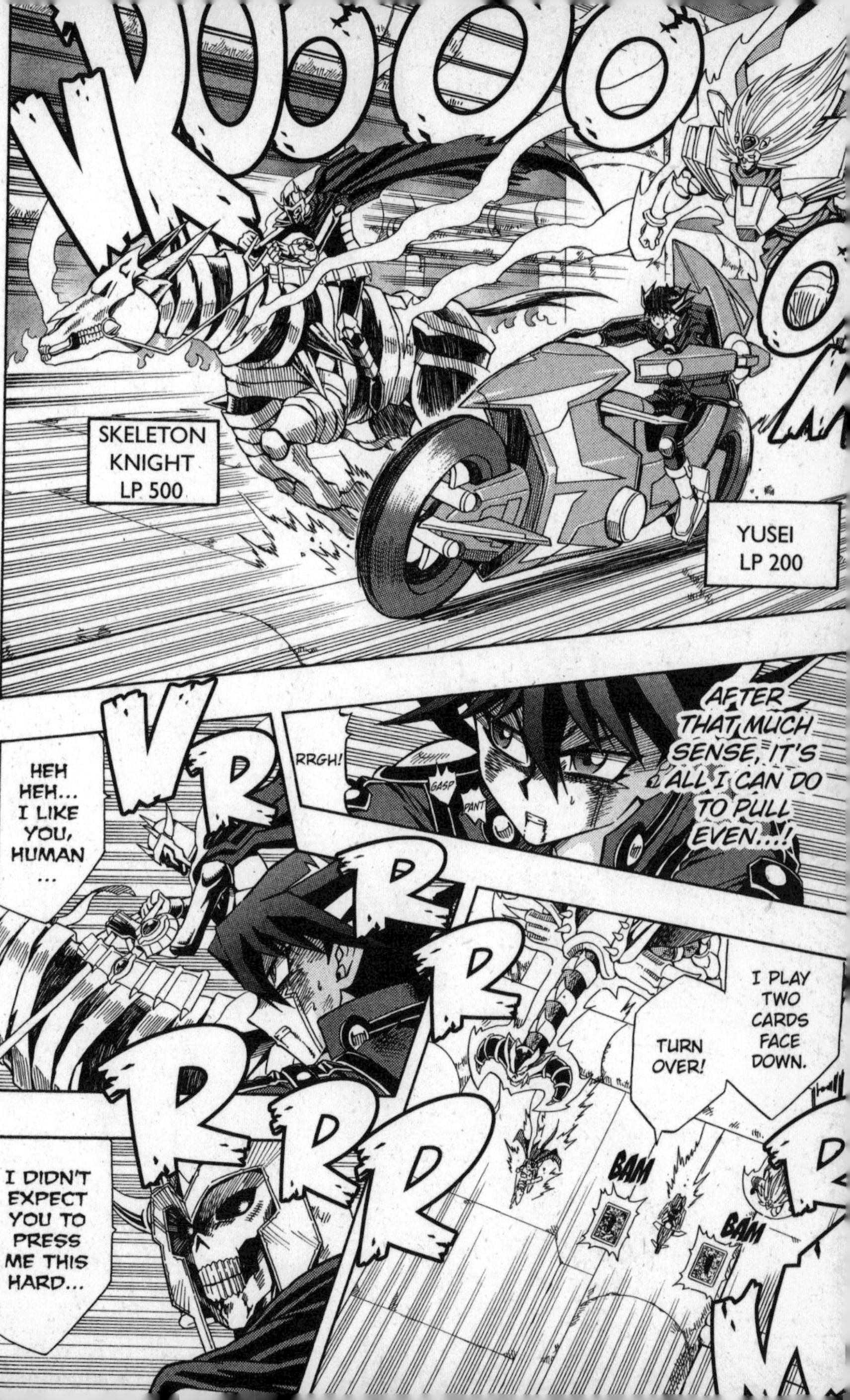VOOOOOOM
YUSEI
LP 200
SKELETON
KNIGHT
LP 500
AFTER THAT MUCH SENSE, IT'S ALL I CAN DO TO PULL EVEN...!
GASP
PANT
RRGH!
HEH HEH... I LIKE YOU, HUMAN...
VRRRRRR
I PLAY TWO CARDS FACE DOWN.
TURN OVER!
BAM
BAM
I DIDN'T EXPECT YOU TO PRESS ME THIS HARD...

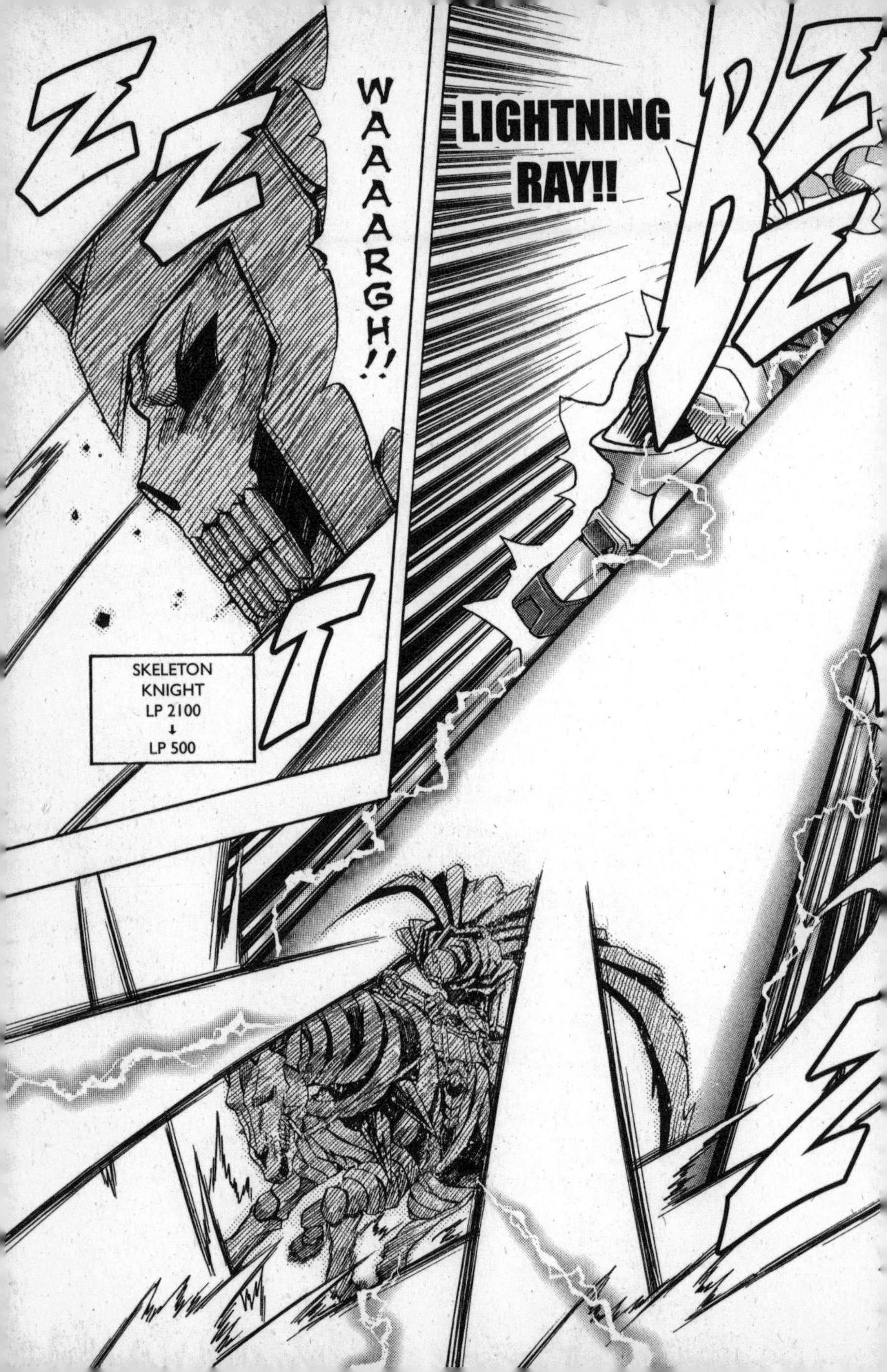
LIGHTNING RAY!!
WAAAAARGH!!
SKELETON KNIGHT LP 2100 ↓ LP 500

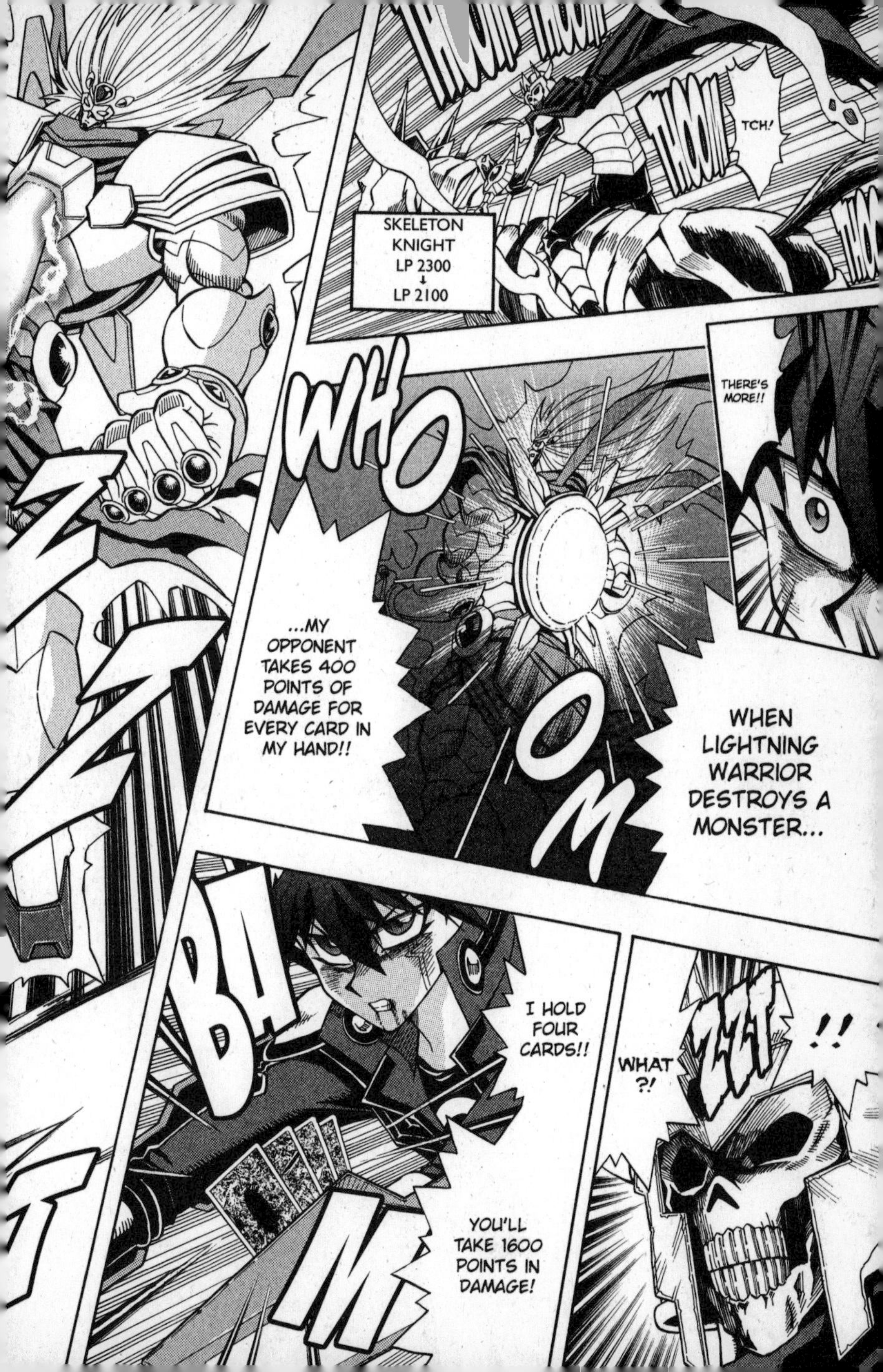
THOOM THOOM
THOOM
TCH!
SKELETON KNIGHT LP 2300 ↓ LP 2100
THERE'S MORE!!
WHOOM
WHEN LIGHTNING WARRIOR DESTROYS A MONSTER...
...MY OPPONENT TAKES 400 POINTS OF DAMAGE FOR EVERY CARD IN MY HAND!!
ZZT
!!
WHAT?!
BAM
I HOLD FOUR CARDS!!
YOU'LL TAKE 1600 POINTS IN DAMAGE!

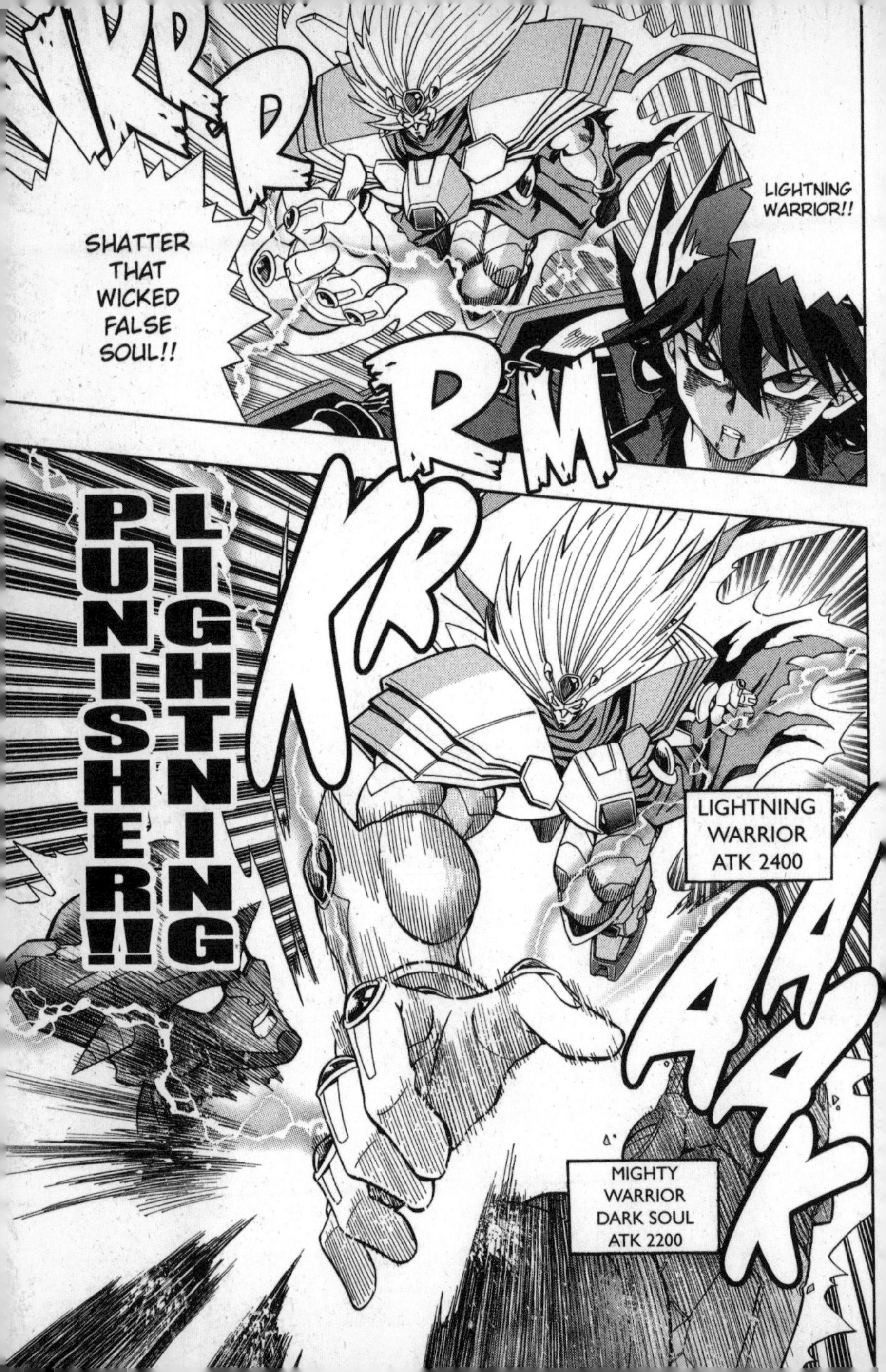
LIGHTNING WARRIOR!!
SHATTER THAT WICKED FALSE SOUL!!
LIGHTNING PUNISHER!!
LIGHTNING WARRIOR ATK 2400
MIGHTY WARRIOR DARK SOUL ATK 2200

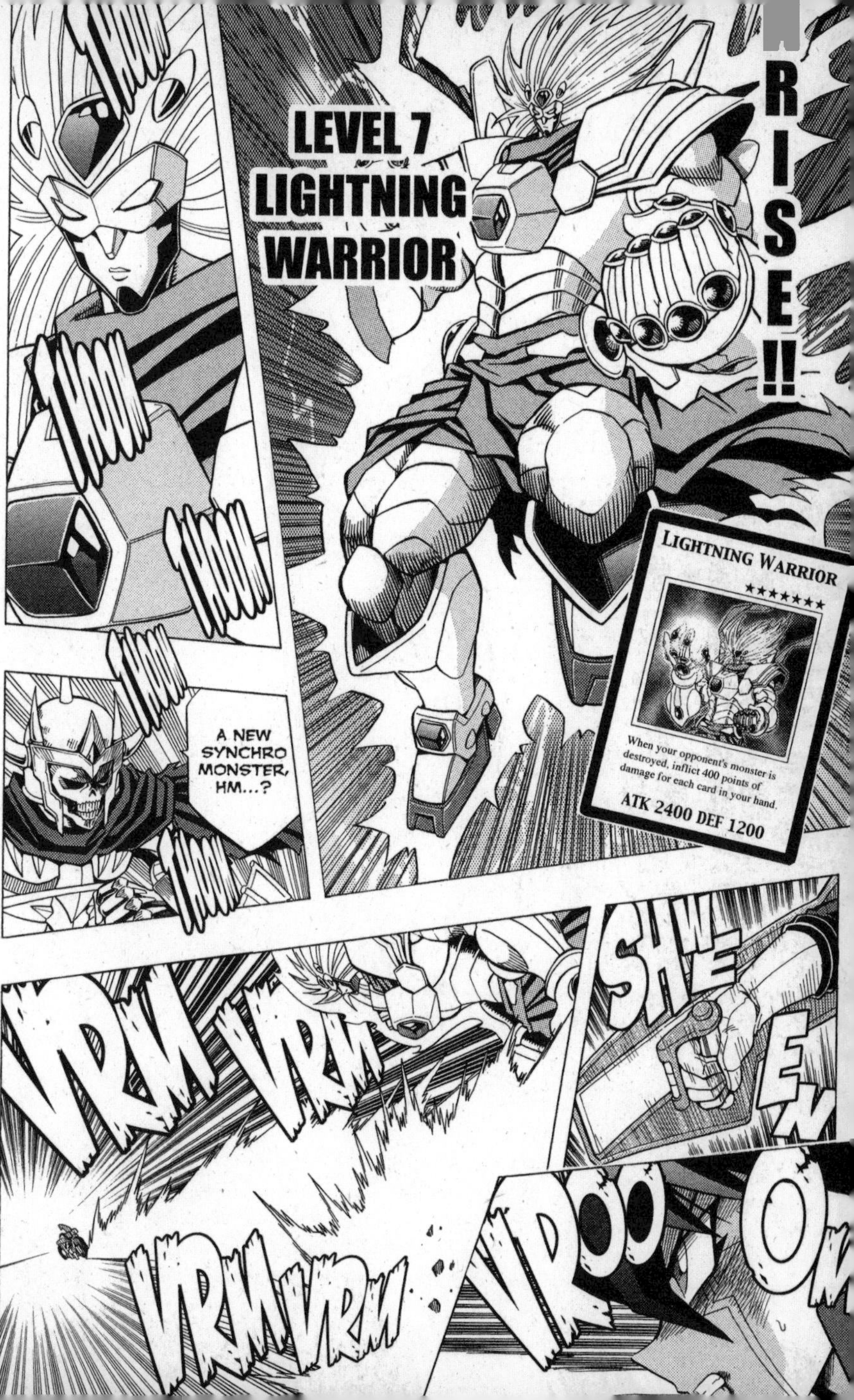
RISE!!
LEVEL 7 LIGHTNING WARRIOR
LIGHTNING WARRIOR
★★★★★★★
When your opponent's monster is destroyed, inflict 400 points of damage for each card in your hand.
ATK 2400 DEF 1200
A NEW SYNCHRO MONSTER, HM...?
SHWEEN
VRM VRM
VRM VRM
VROOOM

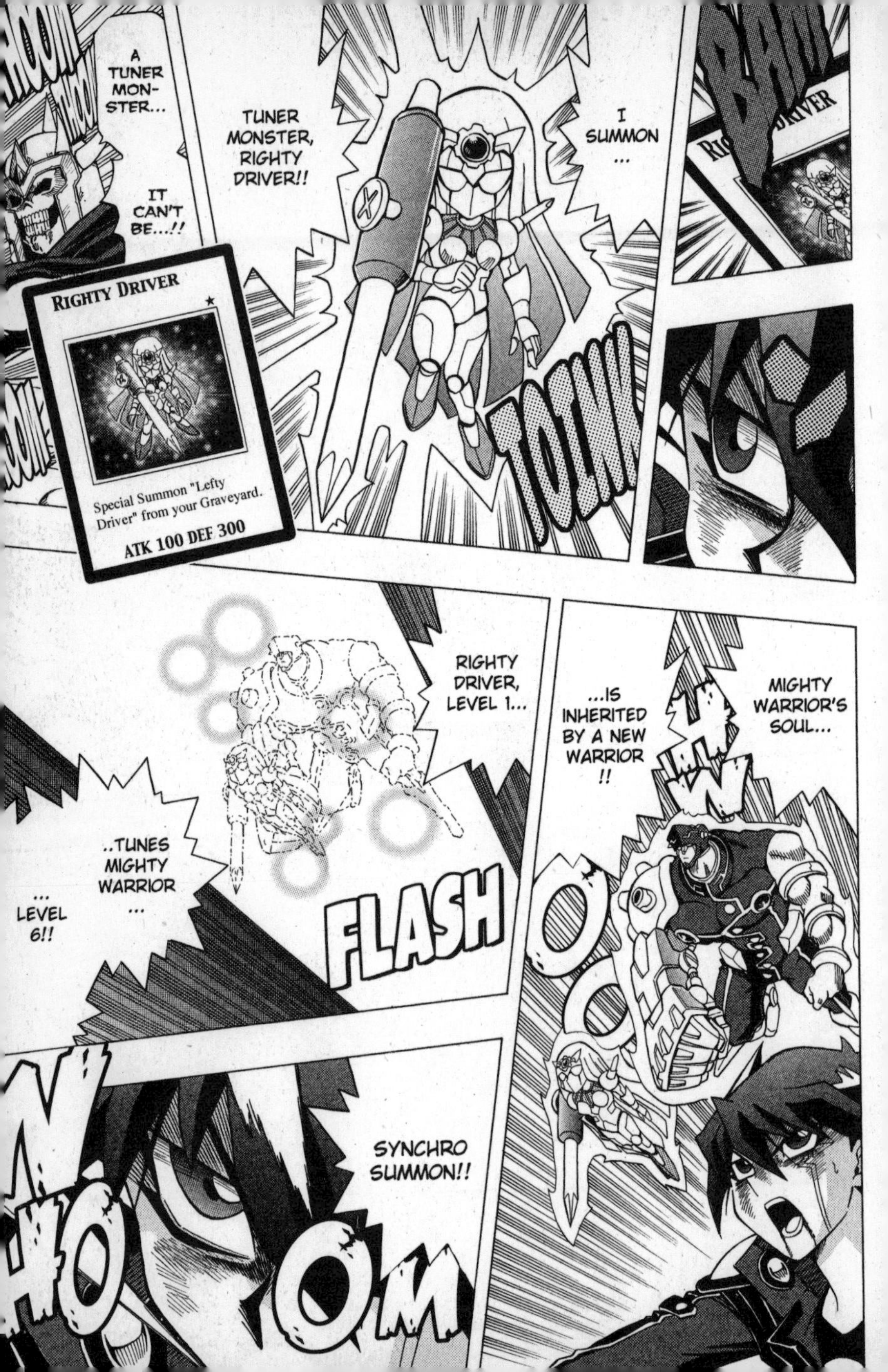
BAM
I SUMMON ...
TUNER MONSTER, RIGHTY DRIVER!!
TOINK
A TUNER MONSTER...
IT CAN'T BE...!!
RIGHTY DRIVER
Special Summon "Lefty Driver" from your Graveyard.
ATK 100 DEF 300
MIGHTY WARRIOR'S SOUL...
...IS INHERITED BY A NEW WARRIOR !!
RIGHTY DRIVER, LEVEL 1...
..TUNES MIGHTY WARRIOR ...
... LEVEL 6!!
FLASH
SYNCHRO SUMMON!!
WHOOM

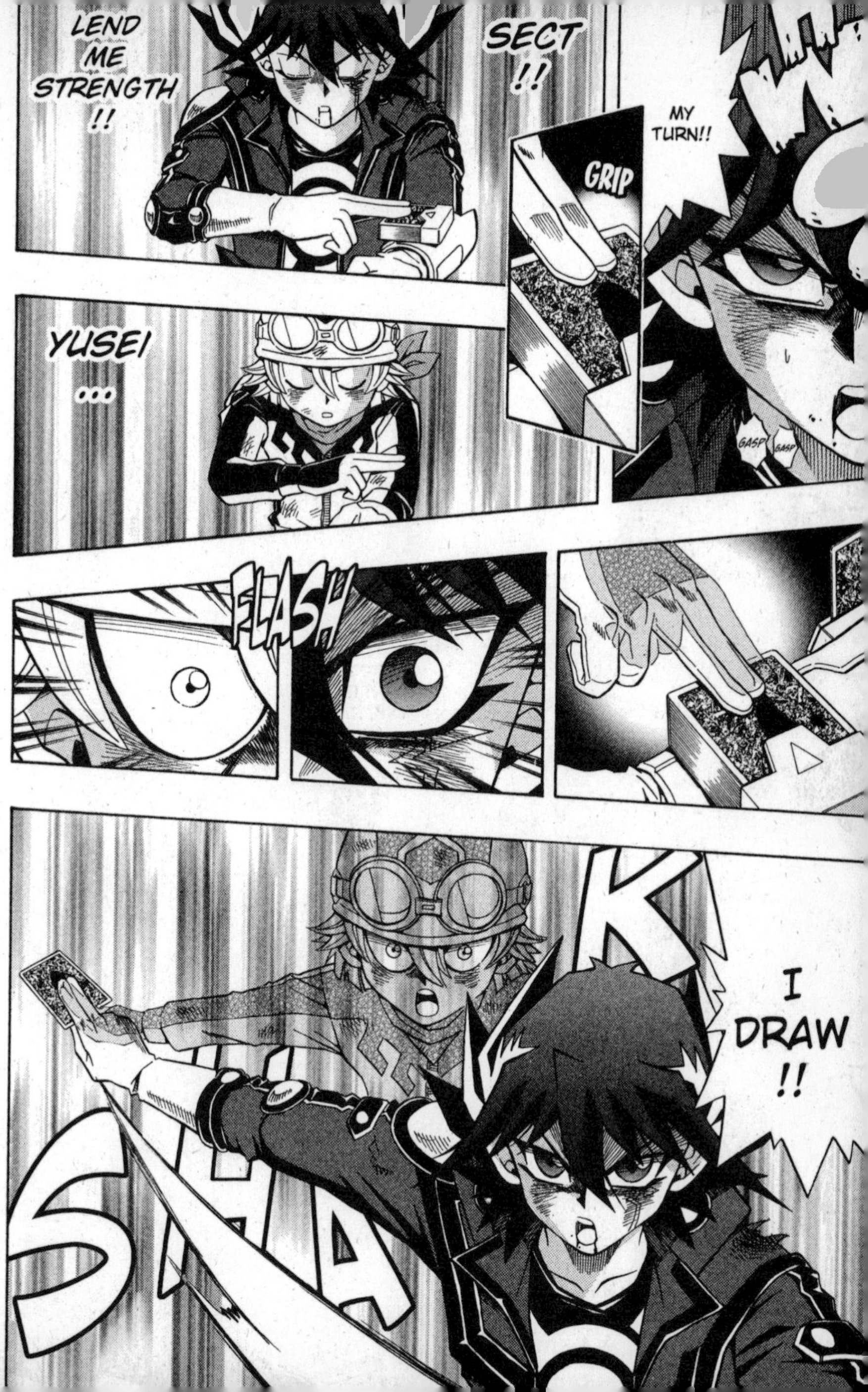
MY TURN!!
GRIP
GASP
GASP
SECT!!
LEND ME STRENGTH!!
YUSEI...
FLASH
I DRAW!!
SHAK

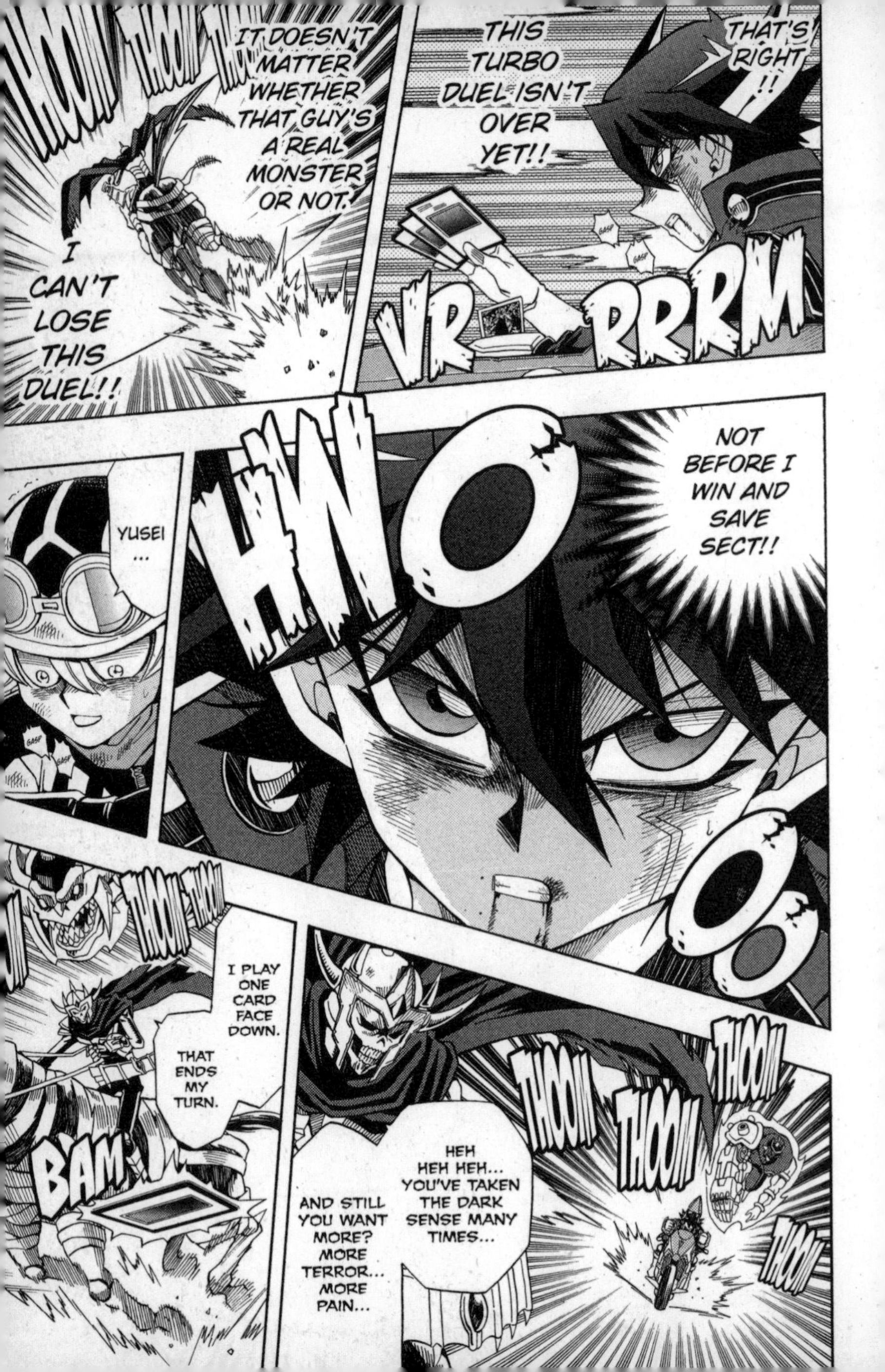
THIS TURBO DUEL ISN'T OVER YET!!
THAT'S RIGHT!!
GASP
GASP
VRRRRM
THOOM THOOM
IT DOESN'T MATTER WHETHER THAT GUY'S A REAL MONSTER OR NOT.
I CAN'T LOSE THIS DUEL!!
NOT BEFORE I WIN AND SAVE SECT!!
HWOOO
YUSEI ...
GASP
GASP
THOOM THOOM THOOM
HEH HEH HEH... YOU'VE TAKEN THE DARK SENSE MANY TIMES...
AND STILL YOU WANT MORE? MORE TERROR... MORE PAIN...
THOOM THOOM
I PLAY ONE CARD FACE DOWN.
THAT ENDS MY TURN.
BAM

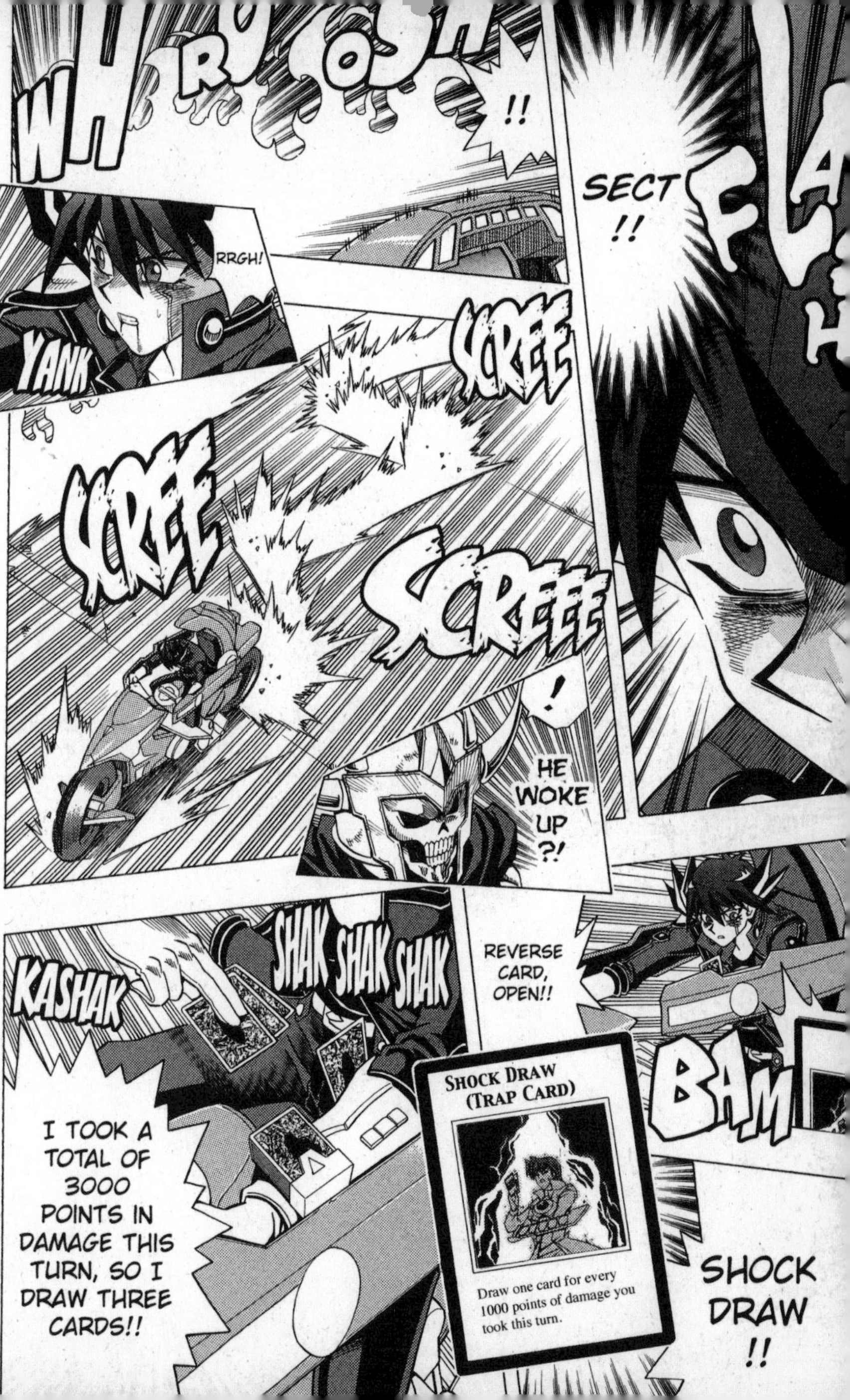
SECT !!
FLASH
WHROOSH !!
RRGH!
YANK
SCREE
SCREE
SCREEE !
HE WOKE UP ?!
REVERSE CARD, OPEN!!
BAM
Shock Draw (Trap Card)
Draw one card for every 1000 points of damage you took this turn.
SHOCK DRAW !!
SHAK SHAK SHAK
KASHAK
I TOOK A TOTAL OF 3000 POINTS IN DAMAGE THIS TURN, SO I DRAW THREE CARDS!!

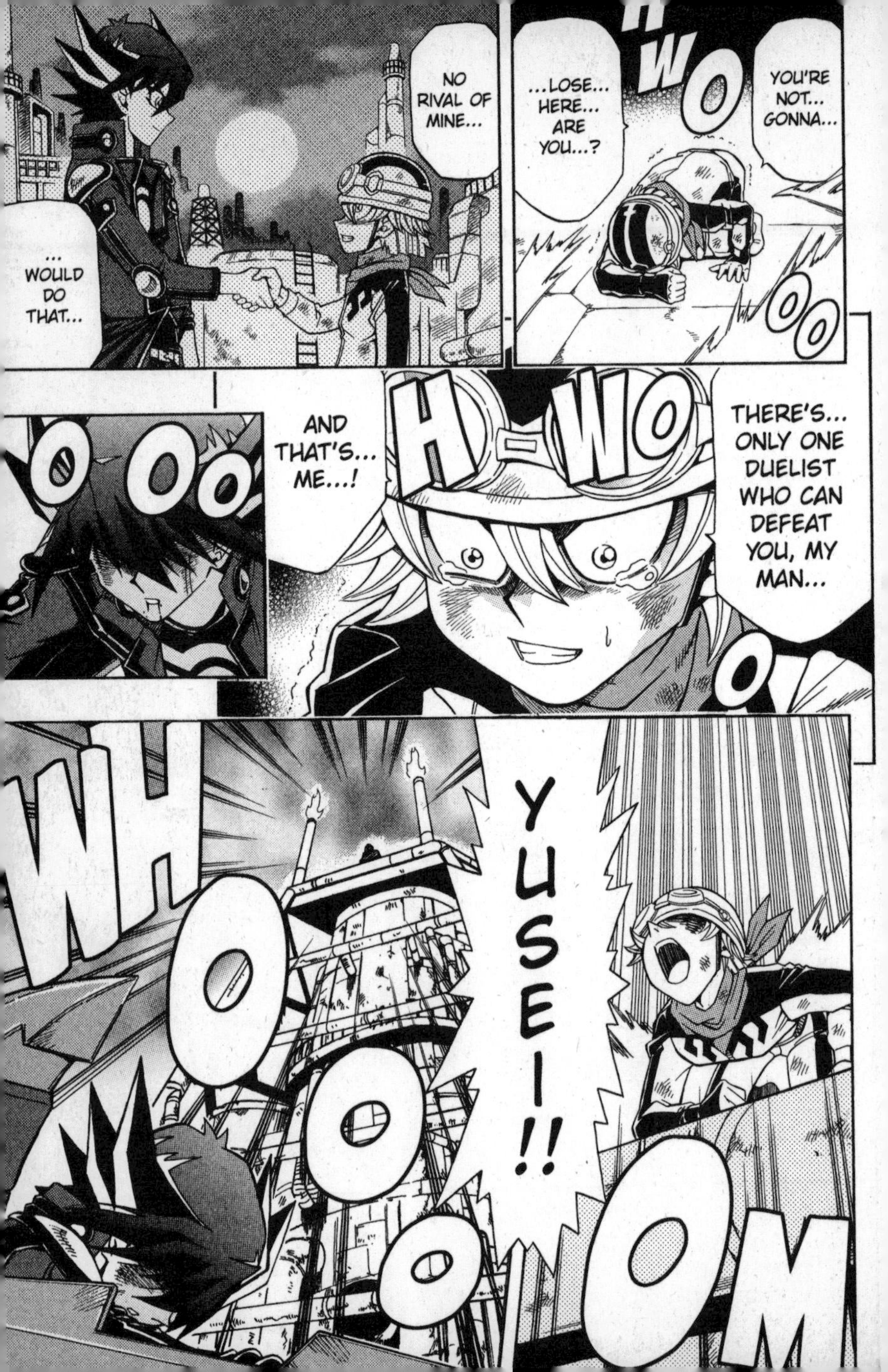
YOU'RE NOT... GONNA...
...LOSE... HERE... ARE YOU...?
NO RIVAL OF MINE...
... WOULD DO THAT...
THERE'S... ONLY ONE DUELIST WHO CAN DEFEAT YOU, MY MAN...
AND THAT'S... ME...!
H-WOOOO
YUSEI!!
WHOOOOOOM

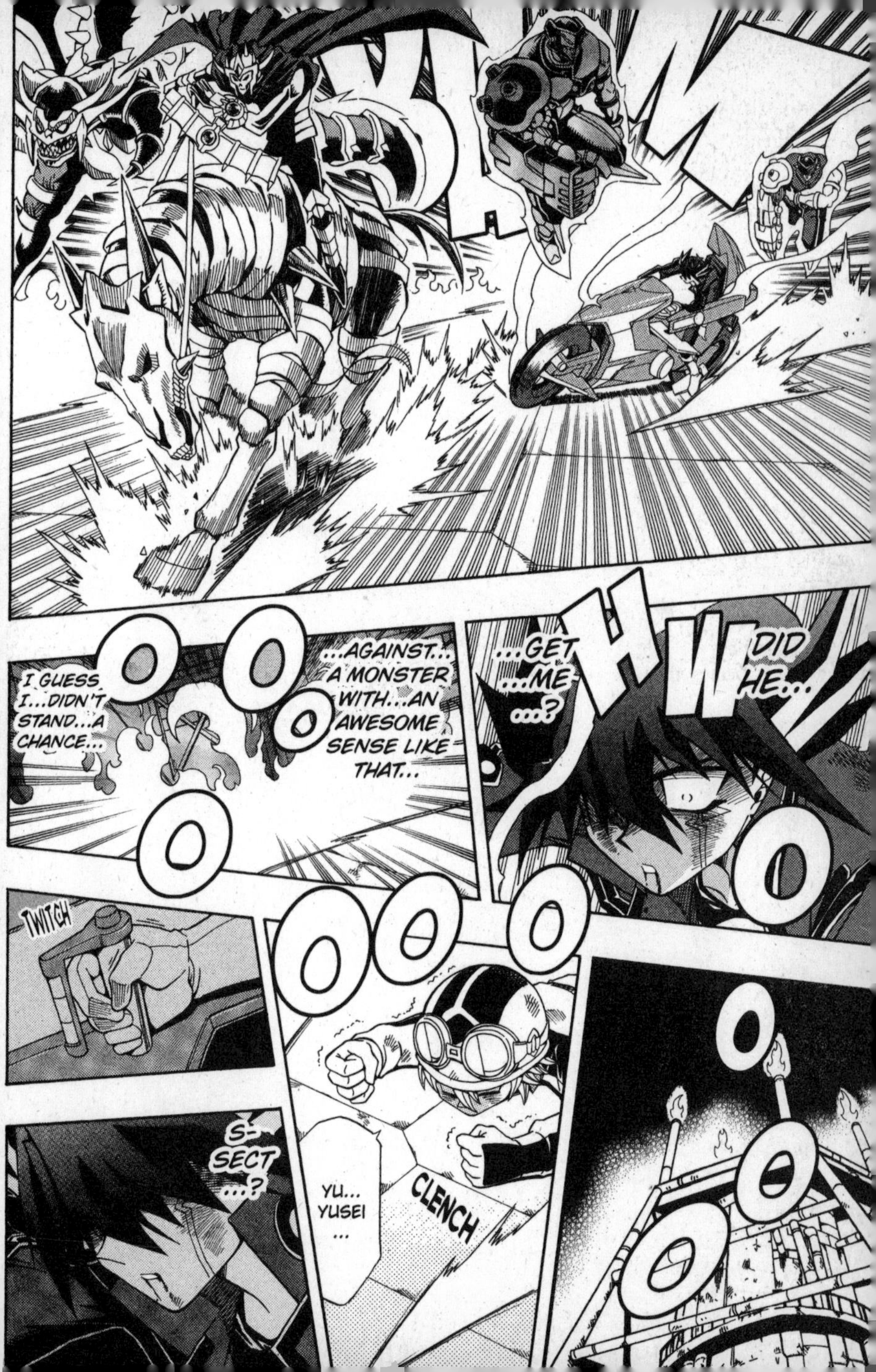
DID HE...
...GET ...ME ...?
I GUESS I...DIDN'T STAND...A CHANCE...
...AGAINST... A MONSTER WITH...AN AWESOME SENSE LIKE THAT...
CLENCH
YU... YUSEI ...
TWITCH
S- SECT ...?

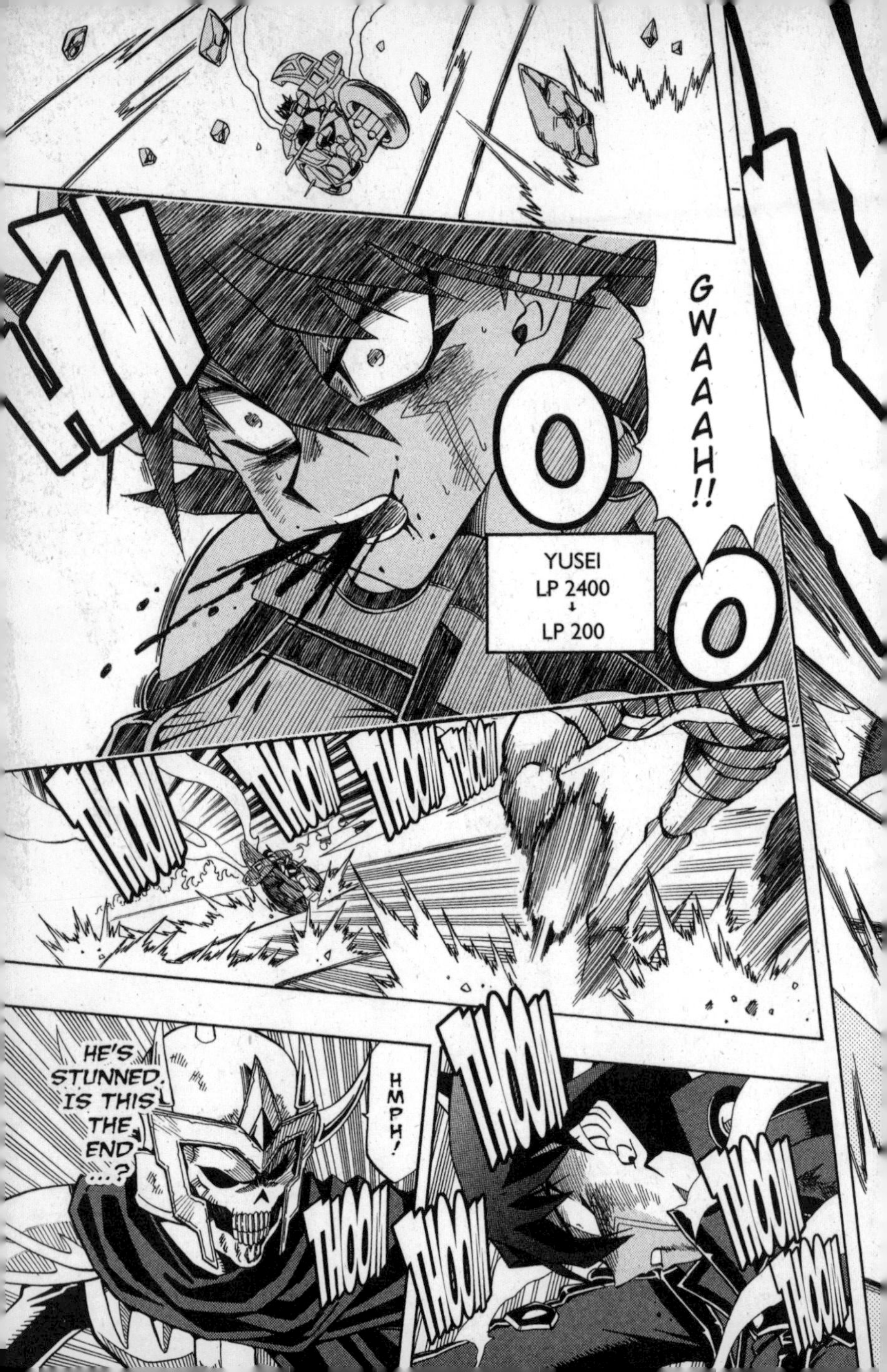
GWAAAAH!!
YUSEI
LP 2400
↓
LP 200
THOOM THOOM THOOM THOOM
THOOM
THOOM THOOM THOOM THOOM
HMPH!
HE'S STUNNED. IS THIS THE END...?

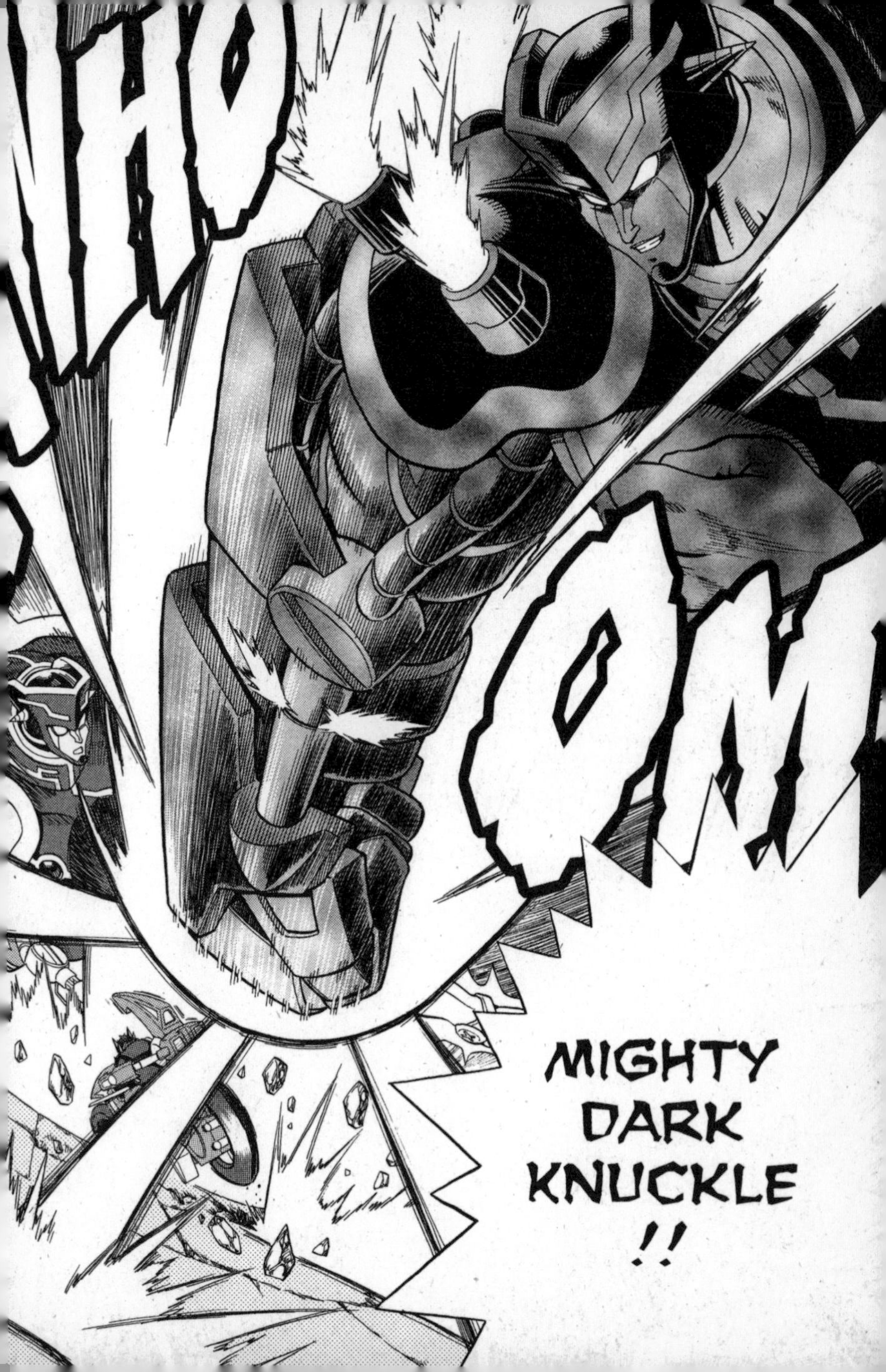
MIGHTY DARK KNUCKLE !!

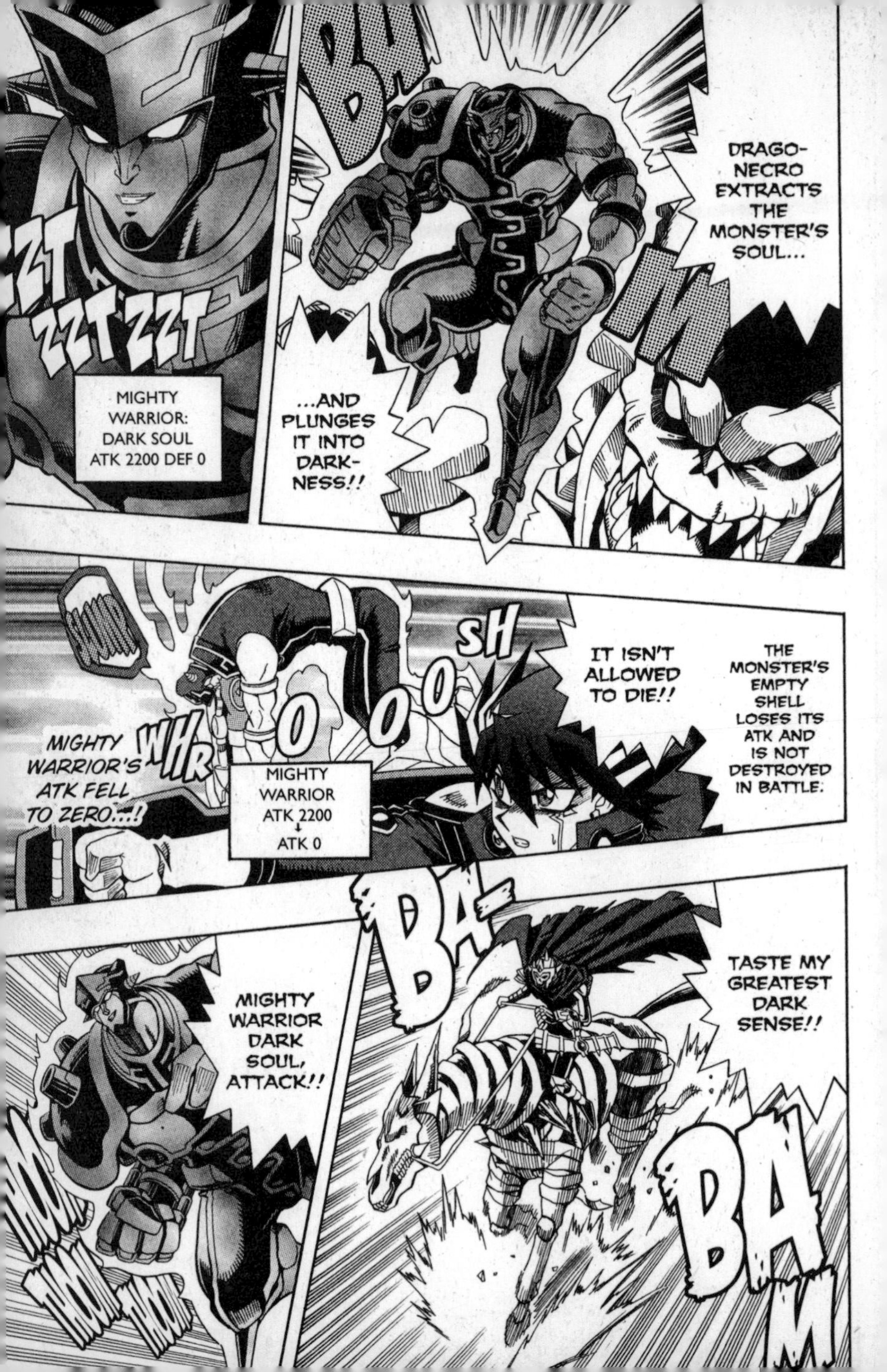
BA
DRAGO-NECRO EXTRACTS THE MONSTER'S SOUL...
...AND PLUNGES IT INTO DARKNESS!!
M
ZZT
ZZT ZZT
MIGHTY WARRIOR: DARK SOUL ATK 2200 DEF 0
SH
THE MONSTER'S EMPTY SHELL LOSES ITS ATK AND IS NOT DESTROYED IN BATTLE.
IT ISN'T ALLOWED TO DIE!!
WHR
MIGHTY WARRIOR ATK 2200 ↓ ATK 0
MIGHTY WARRIOR'S ATK FELL TO ZERO...!
BA-
TASTE MY GREATEST DARK SENSE!!
BA
M
MIGHTY WARRIOR DARK SOUL, ATTACK!!

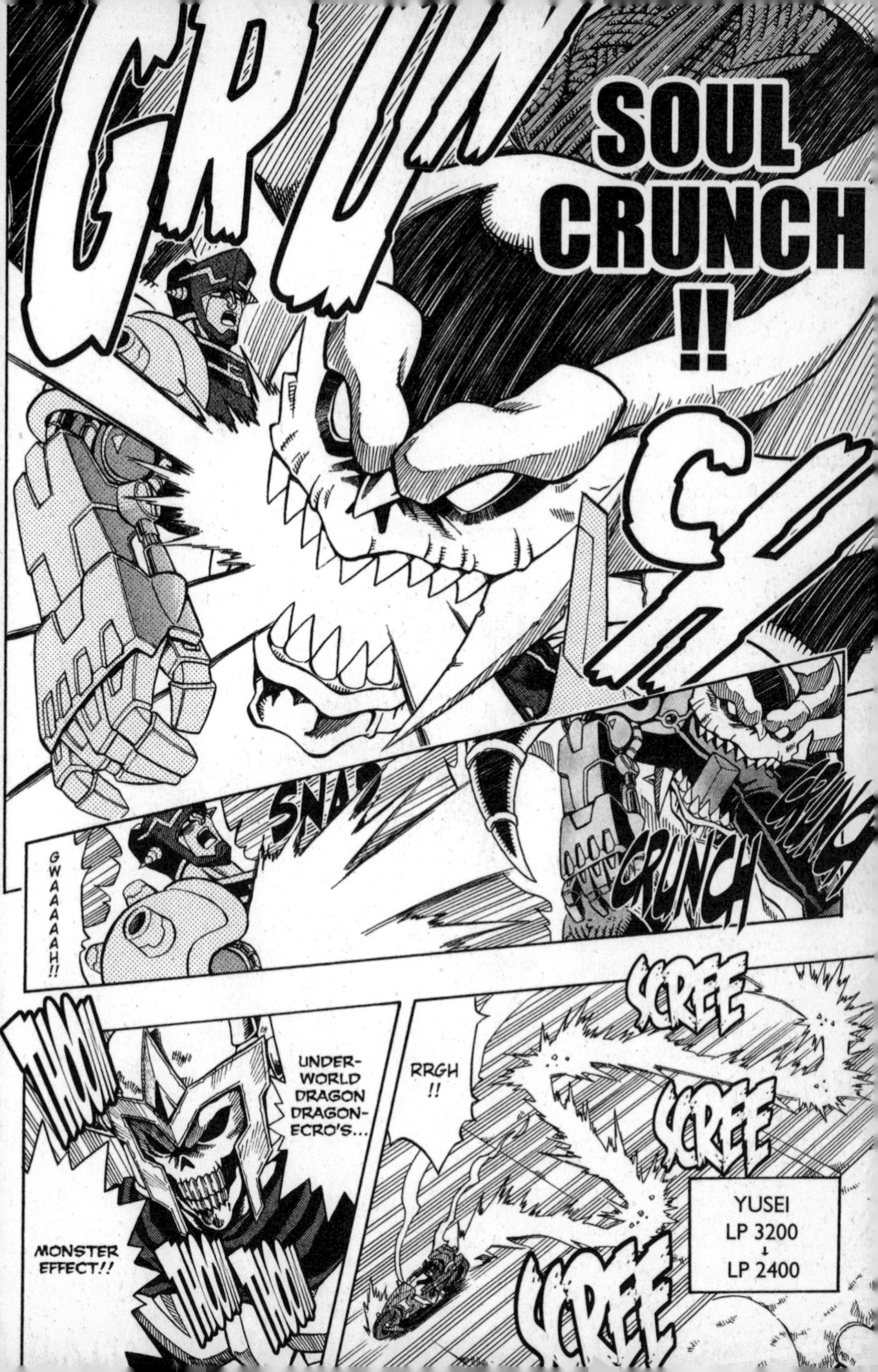
SOUL CRUNCH !!
CRUNCH
CRUNCH
GWAAAAAAAH!!
SCREE
SCREE
SCREE
RRGH !!
YUSEI LP 3200 ↓ LP 2400
UNDER-WORLD DRAGON DRAGON-ECRO'S...
MONSTER EFFECT!!

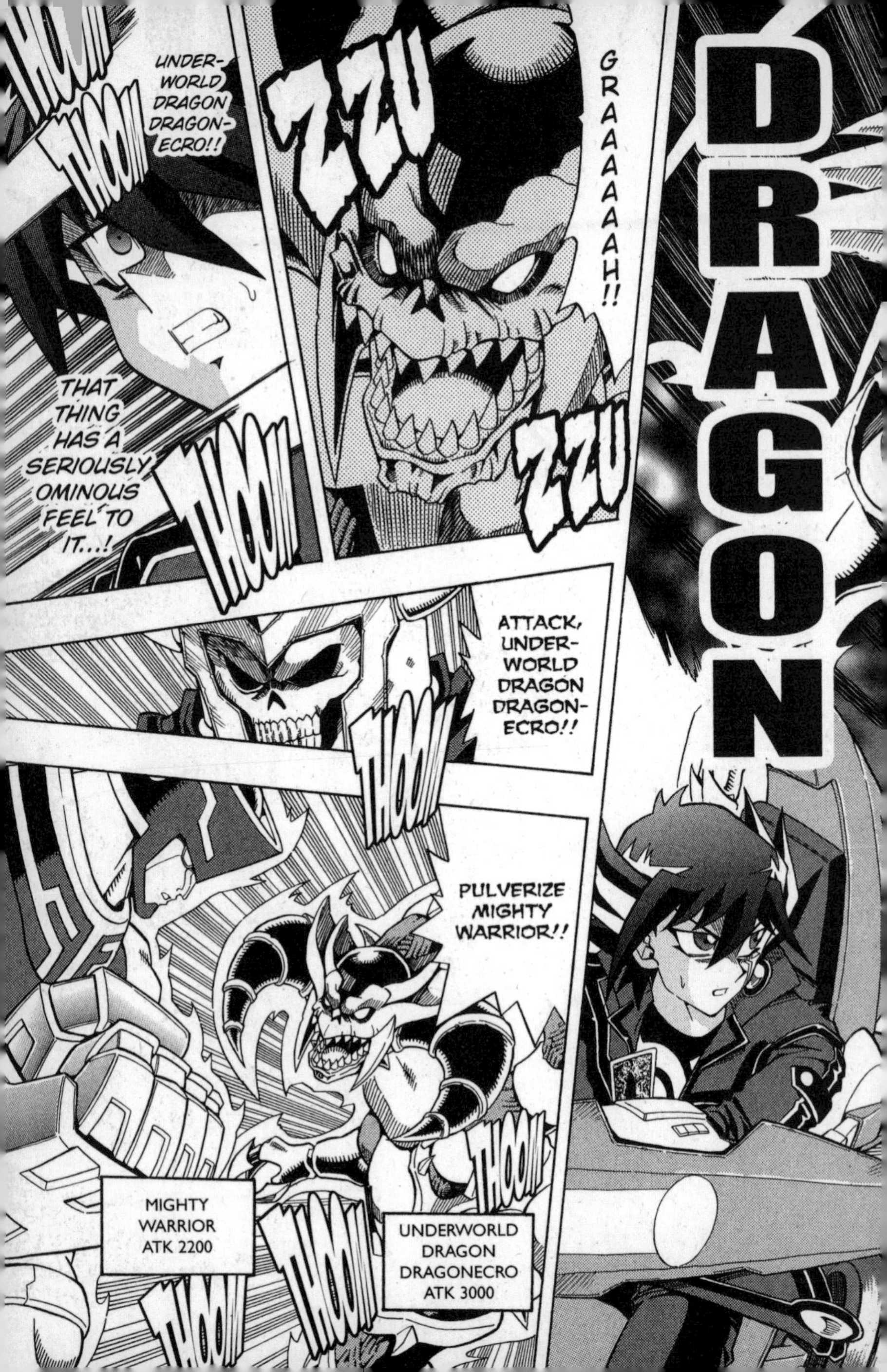
DRAGON
GRAAAAAAAAH!!
ZZZU
ZZZU
THOOM
THOOM
UNDERWORLD DRAGON DRAGONECRO!!
THAT THING HAS A SERIOUSLY OMINOUS FEEL TO IT...!
THOOM
ATTACK, UNDERWORLD DRAGON DRAGONECRO!!
THOOM
PULVERIZE MIGHTY WARRIOR!!
THOOM
UNDERWORLD DRAGON DRAGONECRO ATK 3000
MIGHTY WARRIOR ATK 2200
THOOM
THOOM

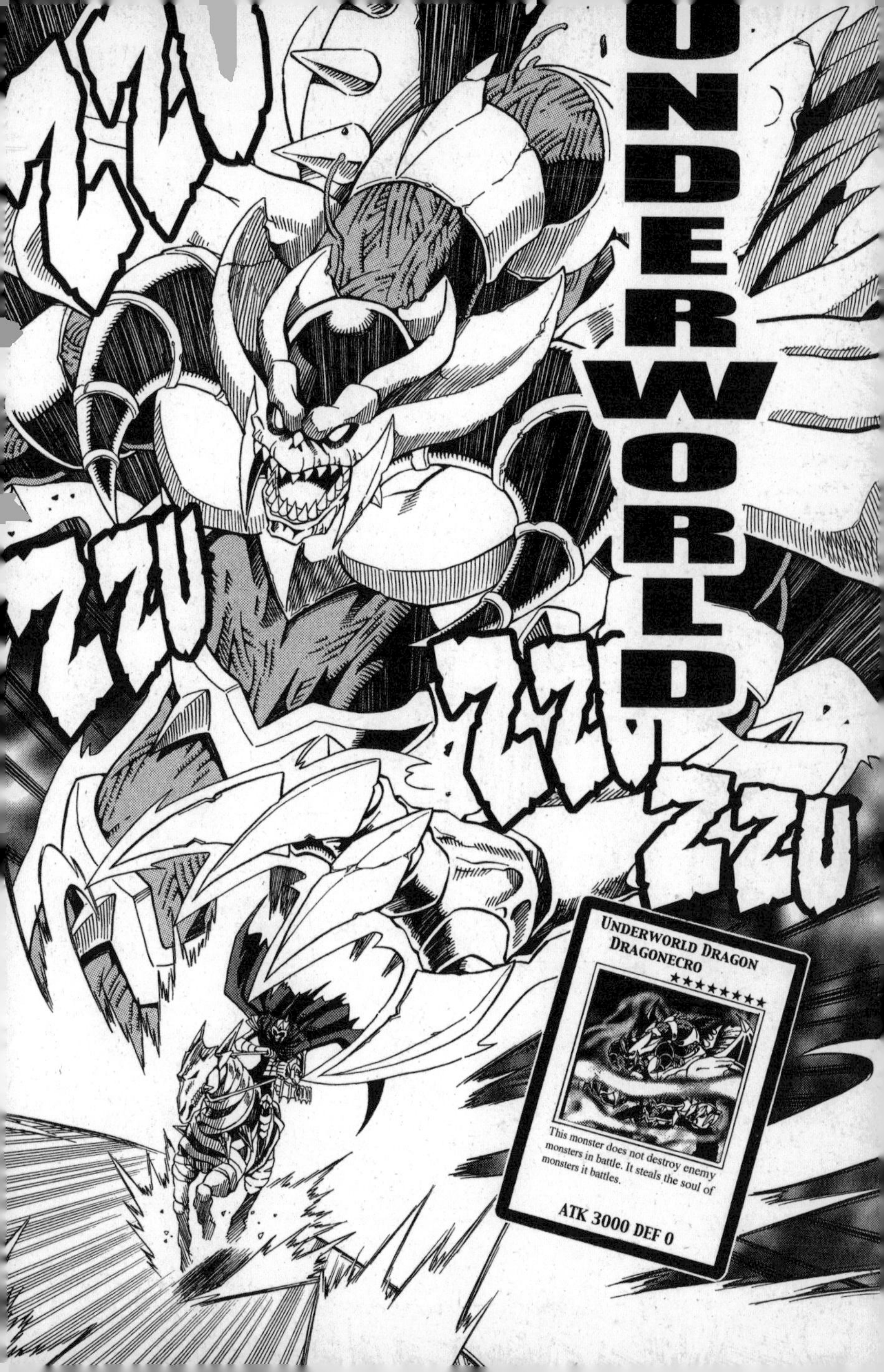
UNDERWORLD
ZZU
ZZU
ZZU
ZZU
UNDERWORLD DRAGON DRAGONECRO
This monster does not destroy enemy monsters in battle. It steals the soul of monsters it battles.
ATK 3000 DEF 0

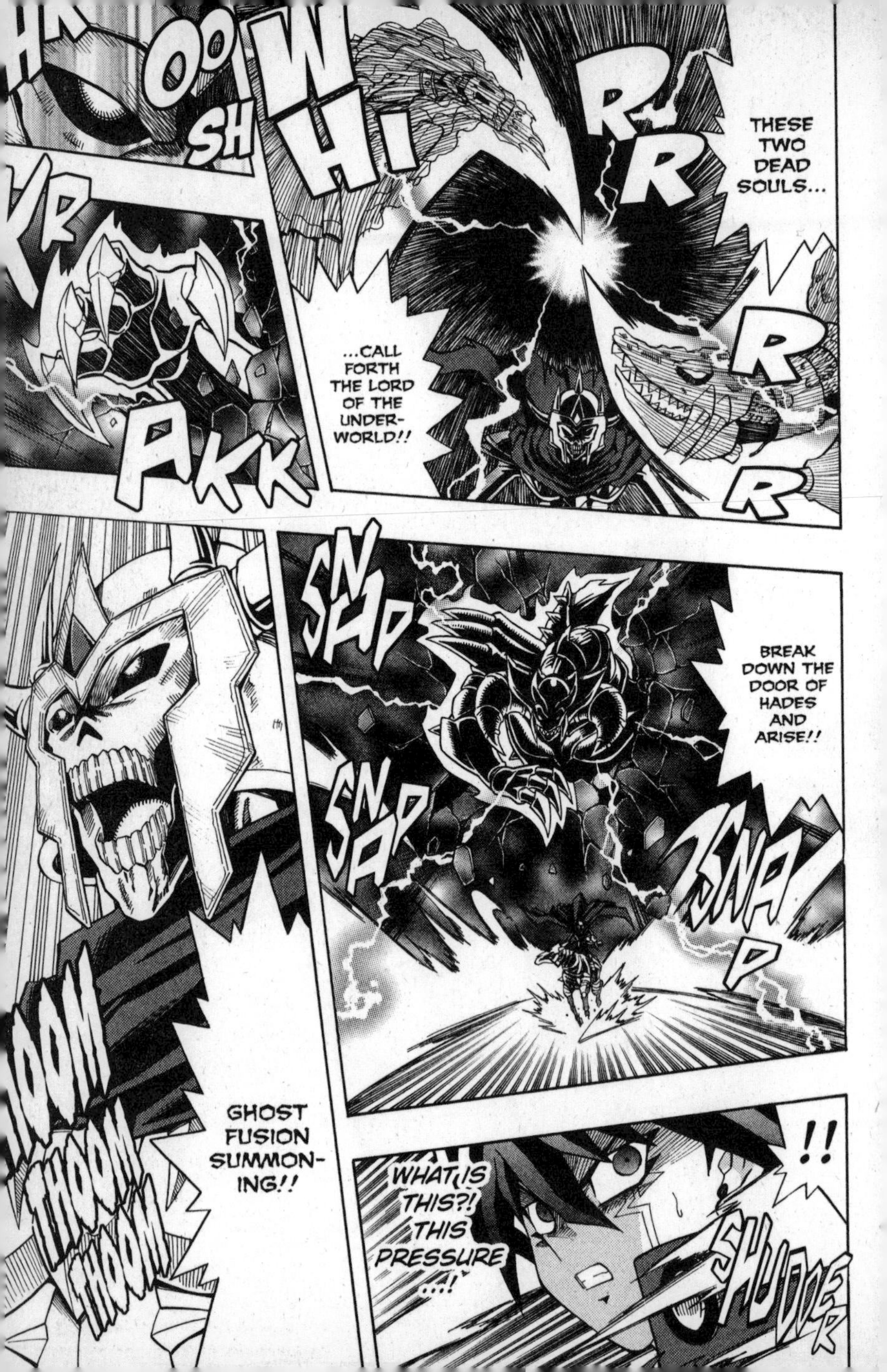
WHIRRR
THESE TWO DEAD SOULS...
...CALL FORTH THE LORD OF THE UNDERWORLD!!
RRR
WHOOOSH
KRAKK
SNAP
SNAP
BREAK DOWN THE DOOR OF HADES AND ARISE!!
SNAP
SNAP
!!
WHAT IS THIS?! THIS PRESSURE ...!
SHUDDER
GHOST FUSION SUMMONING!!
THOOM THOOM THOOM

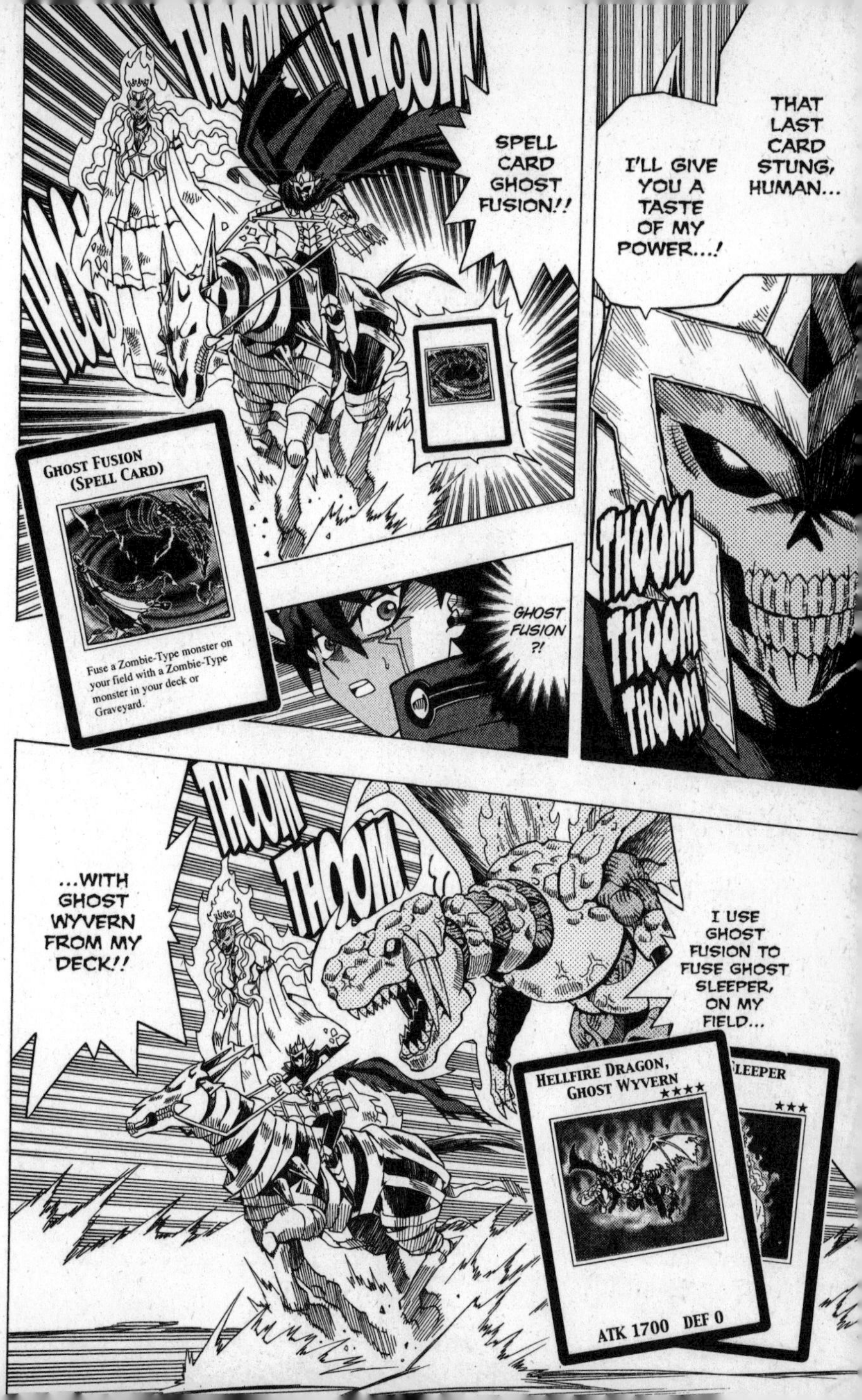
THAT LAST CARD STUNG, HUMAN...
I'LL GIVE YOU A TASTE OF MY POWER...!
THOOM THOOM THOOM
THOOM THOOM
SPELL CARD GHOST FUSION!!
GHOST FUSION (SPELL CARD)
Fuse a Zombie-Type monster on your field with a Zombie-Type monster in your deck or Graveyard.
GHOST FUSION?!
THOOM THOOM
I USE GHOST FUSION TO FUSE GHOST SLEEPER, ON MY FIELD...
...WITH GHOST WYVERN FROM MY DECK!!
HELLFIRE DRAGON, GHOST WYVERN ★★★★
ATK 1700 DEF 0

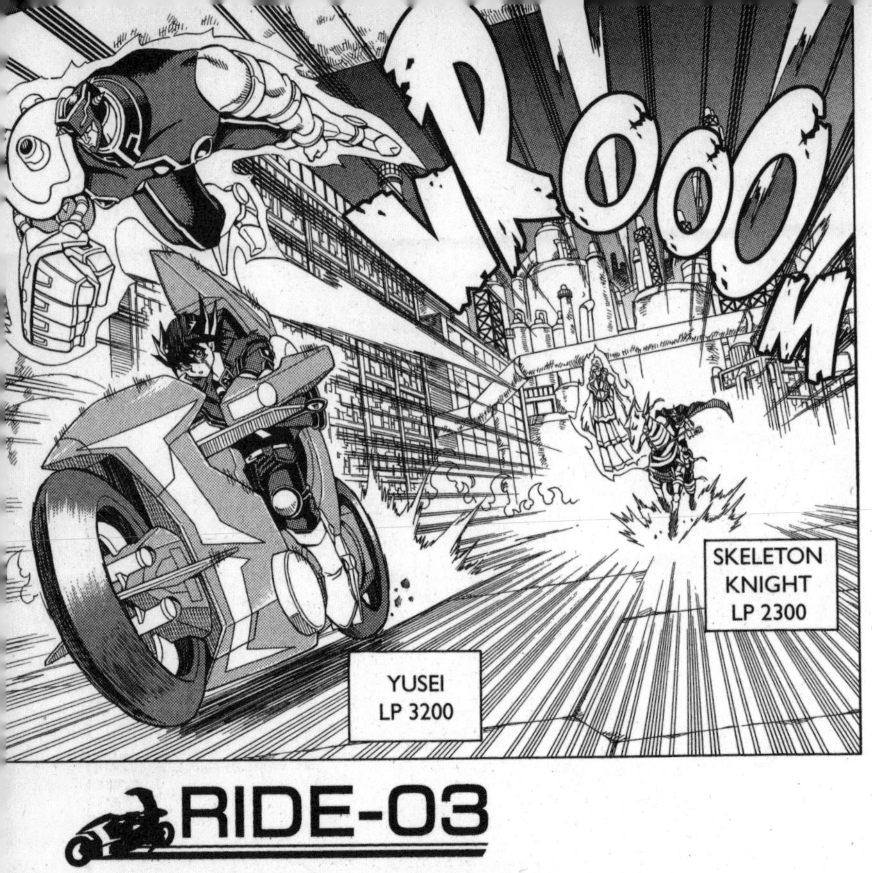
SKELETON KNIGHT LP 2300
YUSEI LP 3200

RIDE-03

LORD OF THE UNDERWORLD!!

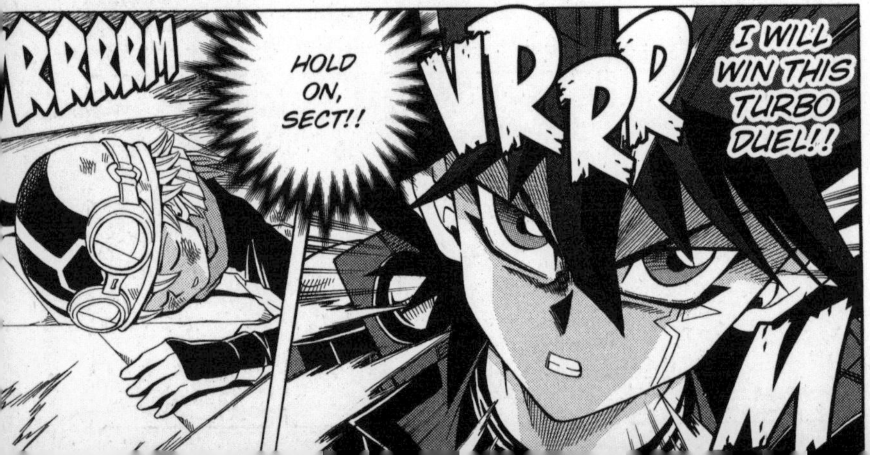
I WILL WIN THIS TURBO DUEL!!
HOLD ON, SECT!!
RRRRM

5D's TRACKS

THE 2ND

BY SATOMASA

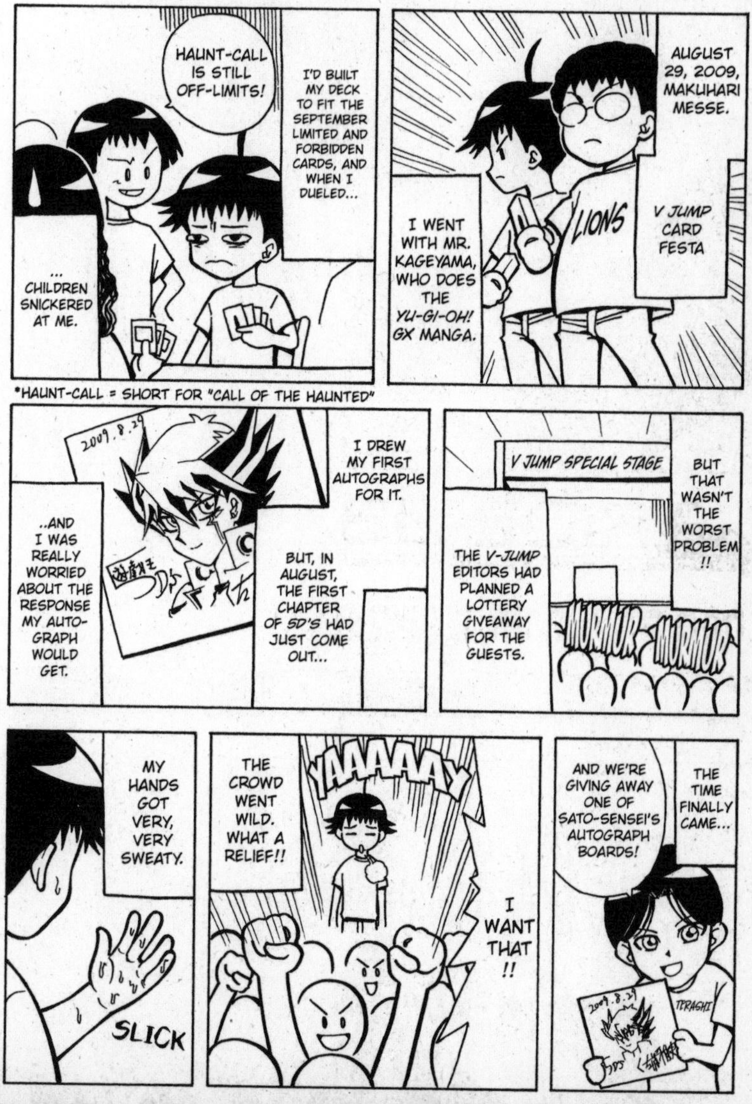
AUGUST 29, 2009, MAKUHARI MESSE.
V JUMP CARD FESTA
LIONS
I WENT WITH MR. KAGEYAMA, WHO DOES THE YU-GI-OH! GX MANGA.
I'D BUILT MY DECK TO FIT THE SEPTEMBER LIMITED AND FORBIDDEN CARDS, AND WHEN I DUELED...
HAUNT-CALL IS STILL OFF-LIMITS!
... CHILDREN SNICKERED AT ME.
*HAUNT-CALL = SHORT FOR "CALL OF THE HAUNTED"
V JUMP SPECIAL STAGE
BUT THAT WASN'T THE WORST PROBLEM!!
THE V-JUMP EDITORS HAD PLANNED A LOTTERY GIVEAWAY FOR THE GUESTS.
MURMUR MURMUR
I DREW MY FIRST AUTOGRAPHS FOR IT.
2009.8.29
BUT, IN AUGUST, THE FIRST CHAPTER OF 5D'S HAD JUST COME OUT...
..AND I WAS REALLY WORRIED ABOUT THE RESPONSE MY AUTOGRAPH WOULD GET.
THE TIME FINALLY CAME...
AND WE'RE GIVING AWAY ONE OF SATO-SENSEI'S AUTOGRAPH BOARDS!
TERASHI
THE CROWD WENT WILD. WHAT A RELIEF!!
YAAAAAY
I WANT THAT!!
MY HANDS GOT VERY, VERY SWEATY.
SLICK

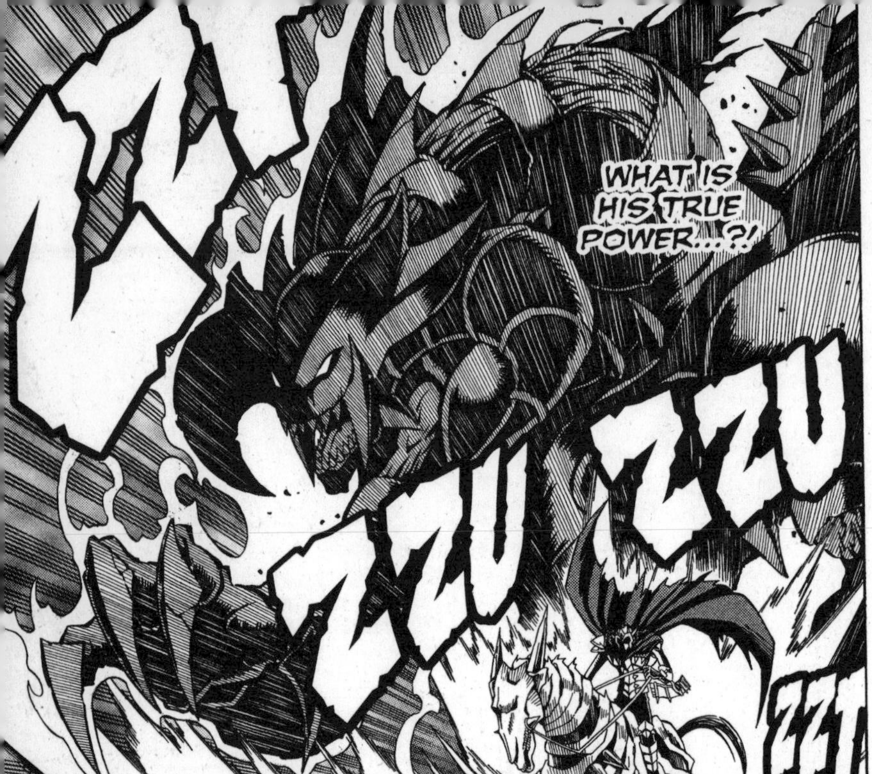
WHAT IS HIS TRUE POWER...?!
ZZU ZZU
ZZT
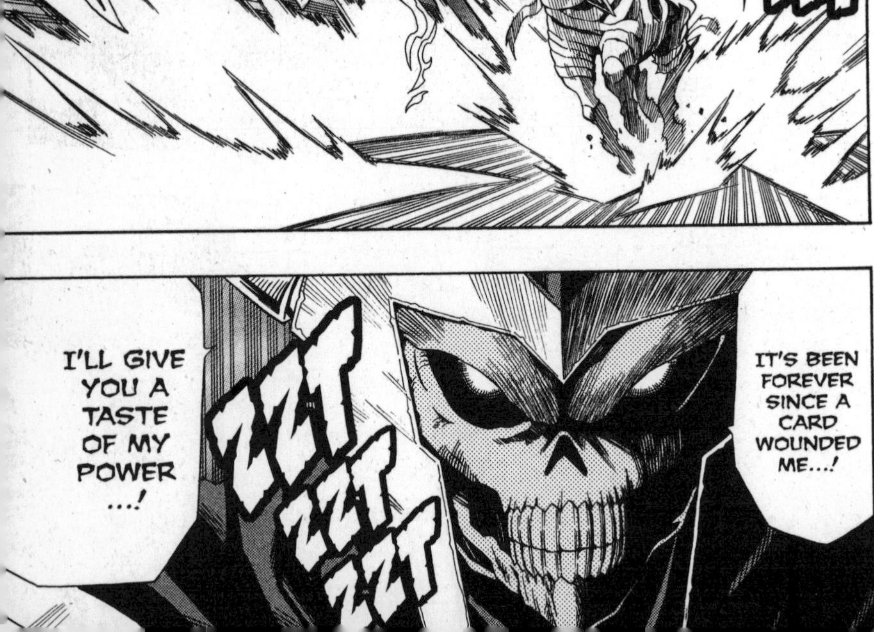
IT'S BEEN FOREVER SINCE A CARD WOUNDED ME...!
ZZT ZZT ZZT
I'LL GIVE YOU A TASTE OF MY POWER ...!

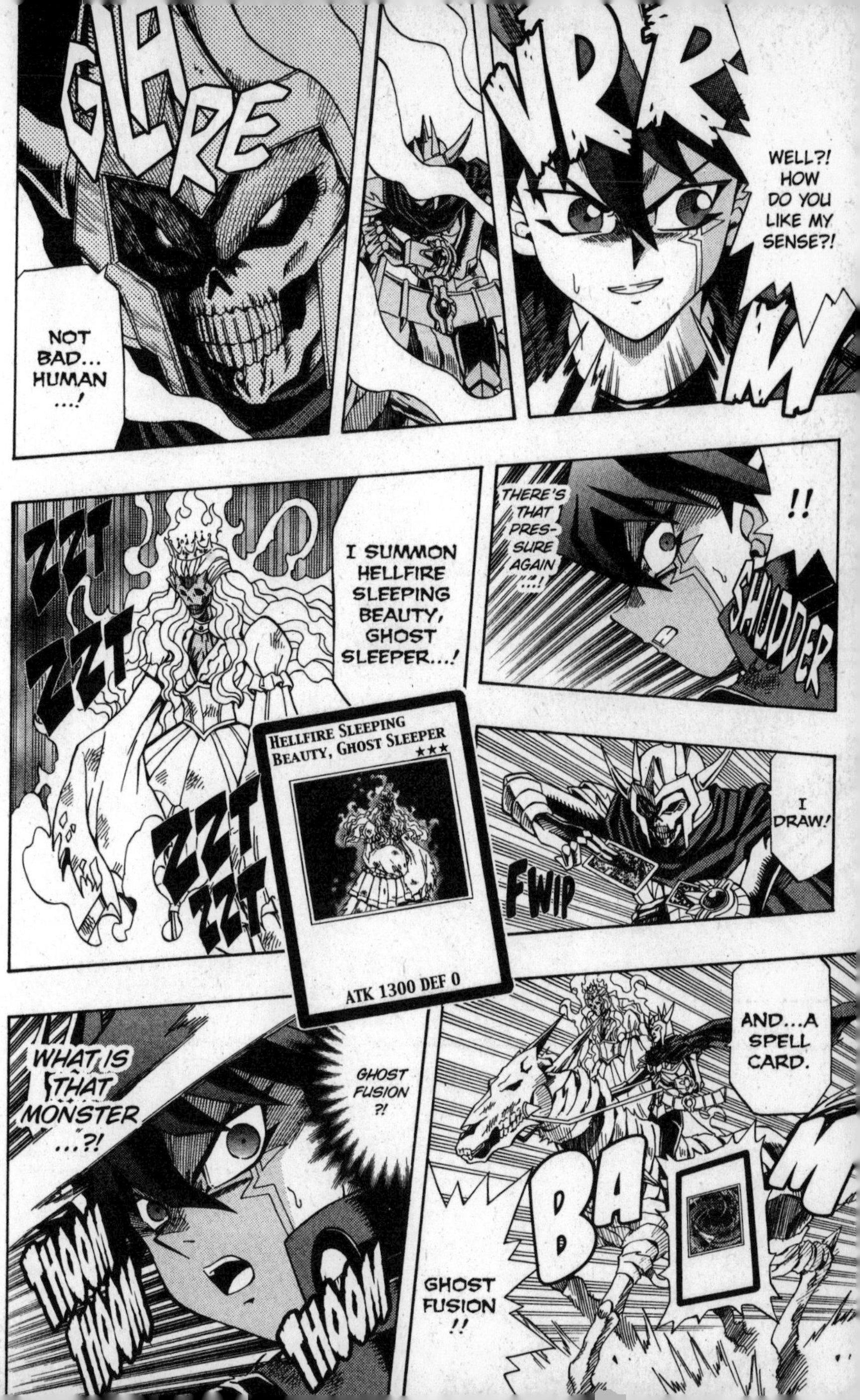
WELL?! HOW DO YOU LIKE MY SENSE?!
GLARE
NOT BAD... HUMAN ...!
THERE'S THAT PRES-SURE AGAIN ...!
!!
SHUDDER
I SUMMON HELLFIRE SLEEPING BEAUTY, GHOST SLEEPER...!
ZZT ZZT
ZZT ZZT
I DRAW!
FWIP
HELLFIRE SLEEPING BEAUTY, GHOST SLEEPER
ATK 1300 DEF 0
AND...A SPELL CARD.
BA
GHOST FUSION!!
GHOST FUSION?!
WHAT IS THAT MONSTER ...?!
THOOM THOOM
THOOM

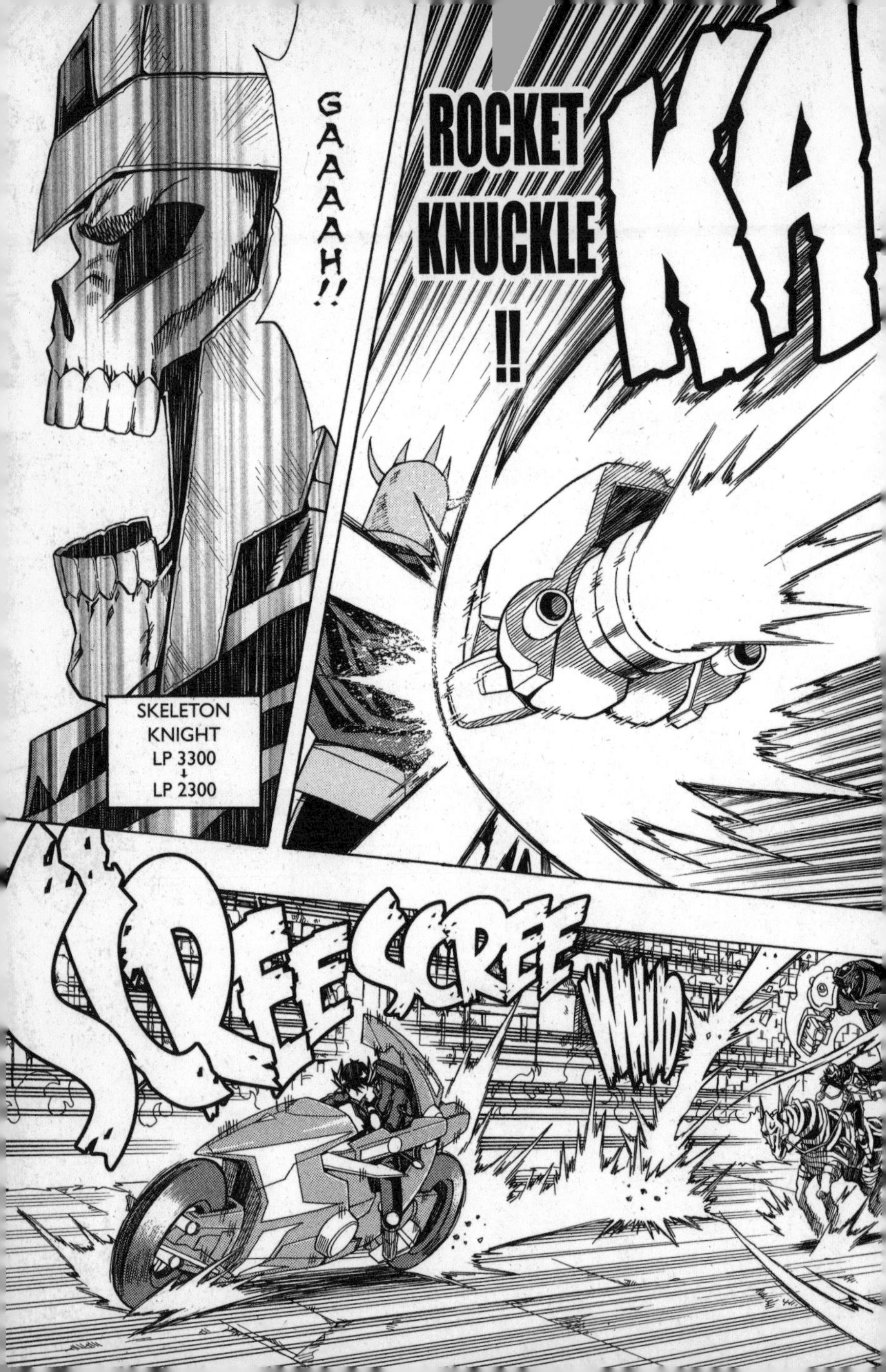
KA
ROCKET KNUCKLE!!
GAAAAAH!!
SKELETON KNIGHT LP 3300 ↓ LP 2300
SCREE

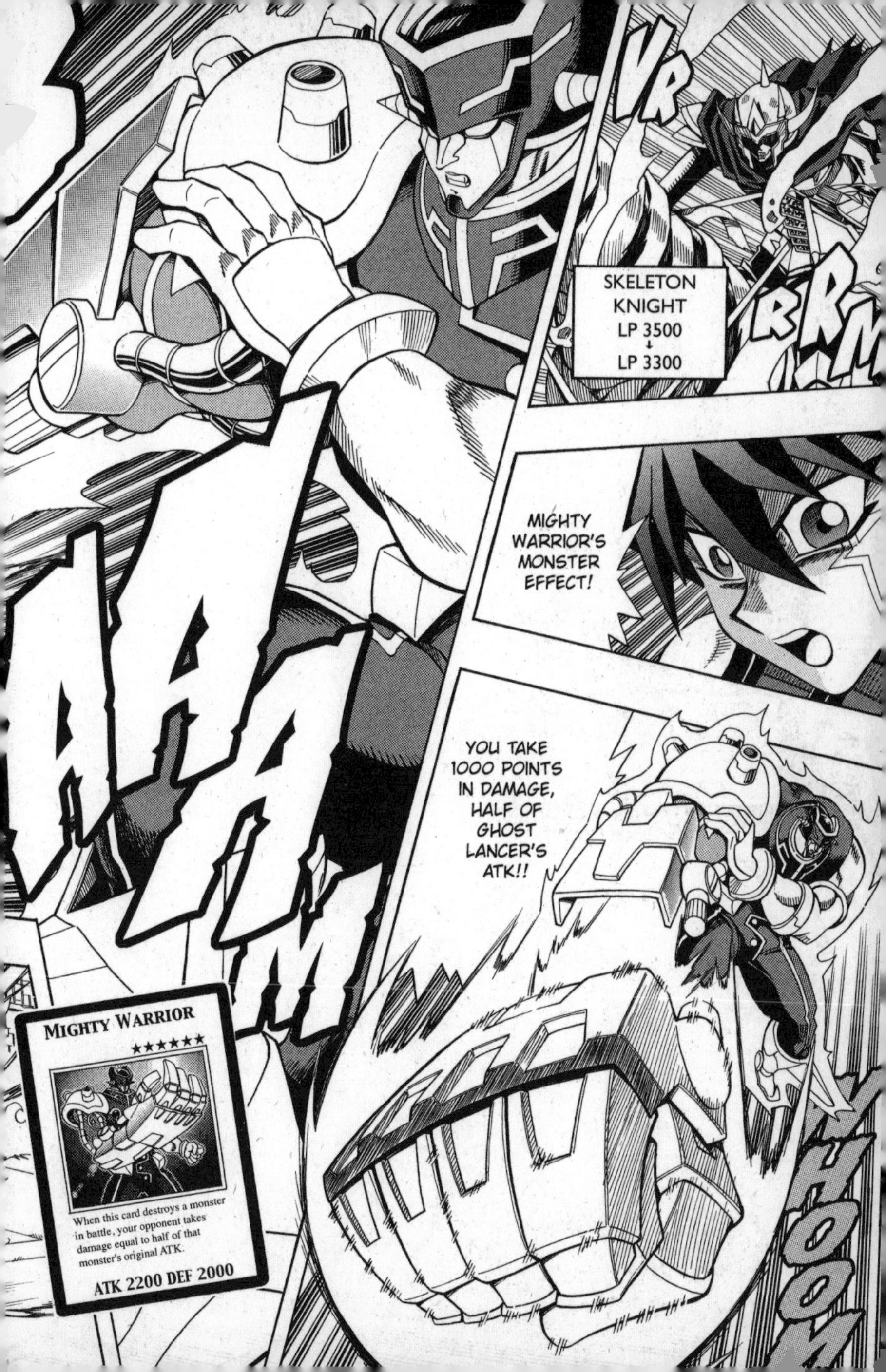

VR
RRM
SKELETON KNIGHT
LP 3500
LP 3300
MIGHTY WARRIOR'S MONSTER EFFECT!
YOU TAKE 1000 POINTS IN DAMAGE, HALF OF GHOST LANCER'S ATK!!
MIGHTY WARRIOR
★★★★★★
When this card destroys a monster in battle, your opponent takes damage equal to half of that monster's original ATK.
ATK 2200 DEF 2000

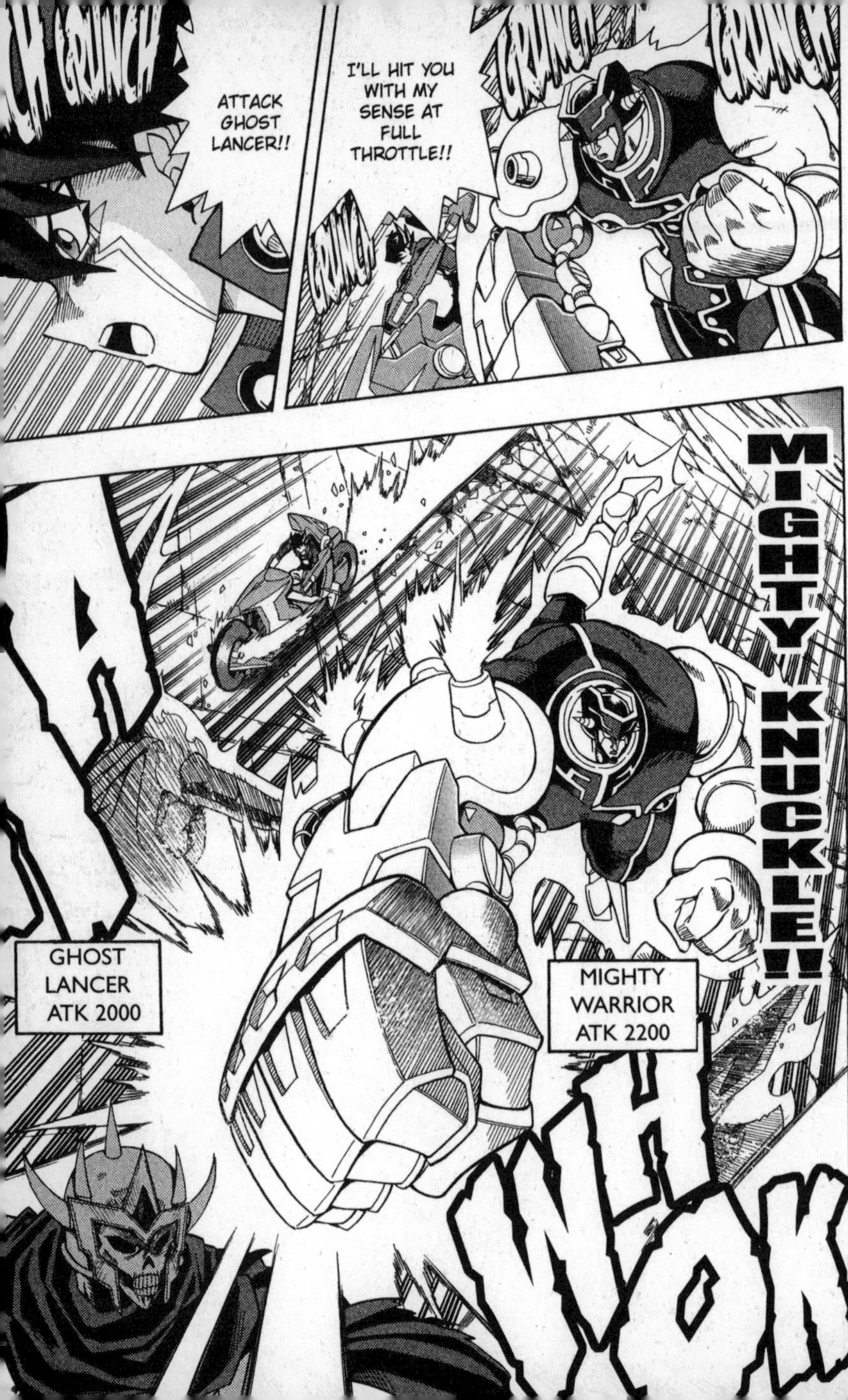
CRUNCH
CRUNCH
I'LL HIT YOU WITH MY SENSE AT FULL THROTTLE!!
CRUNCH
ATTACK GHOST LANCER!!
CH CRUNCH
MIGHTY KNUCKLE!!
MIGHTY WARRIOR ATK 2200
GHOST LANCER ATK 2000

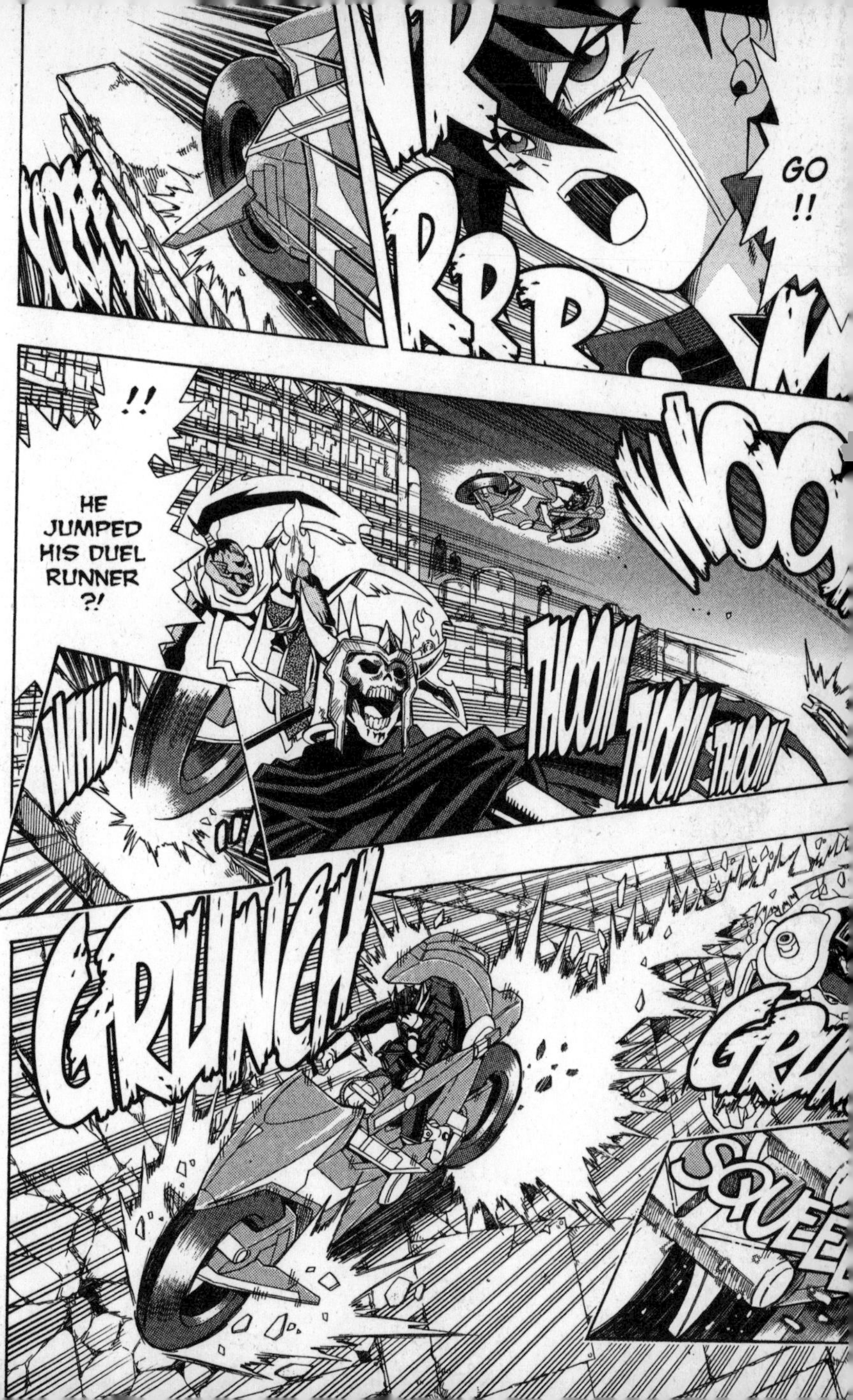
GO !!
VRRROOM
VROOM
!!
WOOO
HE JUMPED HIS DUEL RUNNER ?!
THOOM THOOM THOOM
WHUD
GRUNCH
GRU
SQUEEE

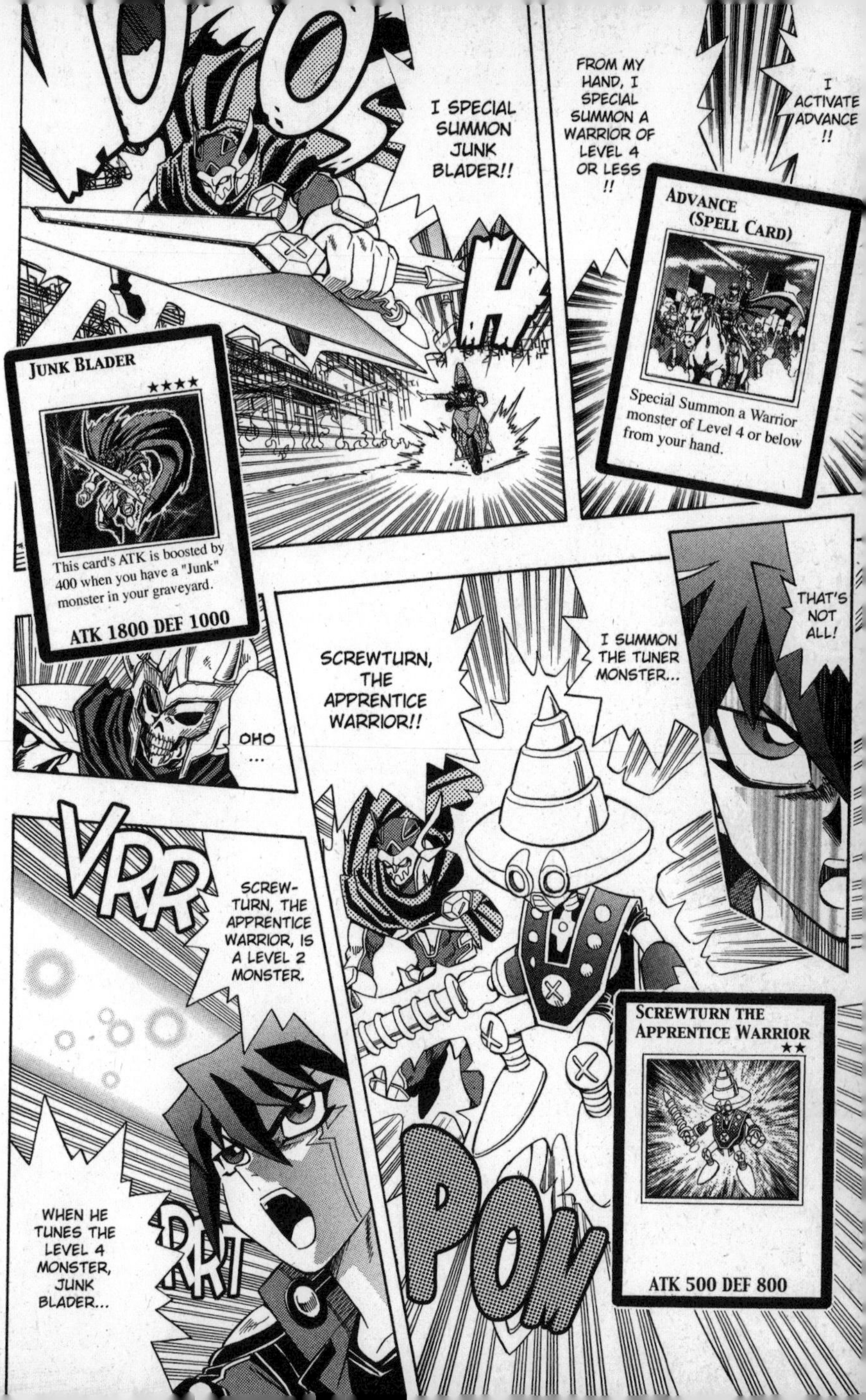
I ACTIVATE ADVANCE!!
FROM MY HAND, I SPECIAL SUMMON A WARRIOR OF LEVEL 4 OR LESS!!
ADVANCE (SPELL CARD)
Special Summon a Warrior monster of Level 4 or below from your hand.
I SPECIAL SUMMON JUNK BLADER!!
H
JUNK BLADER
★★★★
This card's ATK is boosted by 400 when you have a "Junk" monster in your graveyard.
ATK 1800 DEF 1000
THAT'S NOT ALL!
I SUMMON THE TUNER MONSTER...
SCREWTURN, THE APPRENTICE WARRIOR!!
OHO...
SCREWTURN THE APPRENTICE WARRIOR
★★
ATK 500 DEF 800
POW
VRR
SCREW-TURN, THE APPRENTICE WARRIOR, IS A LEVEL 2 MONSTER.
DRRT
WHEN HE TUNES THE LEVEL 4 MONSTER, JUNK BLADER...

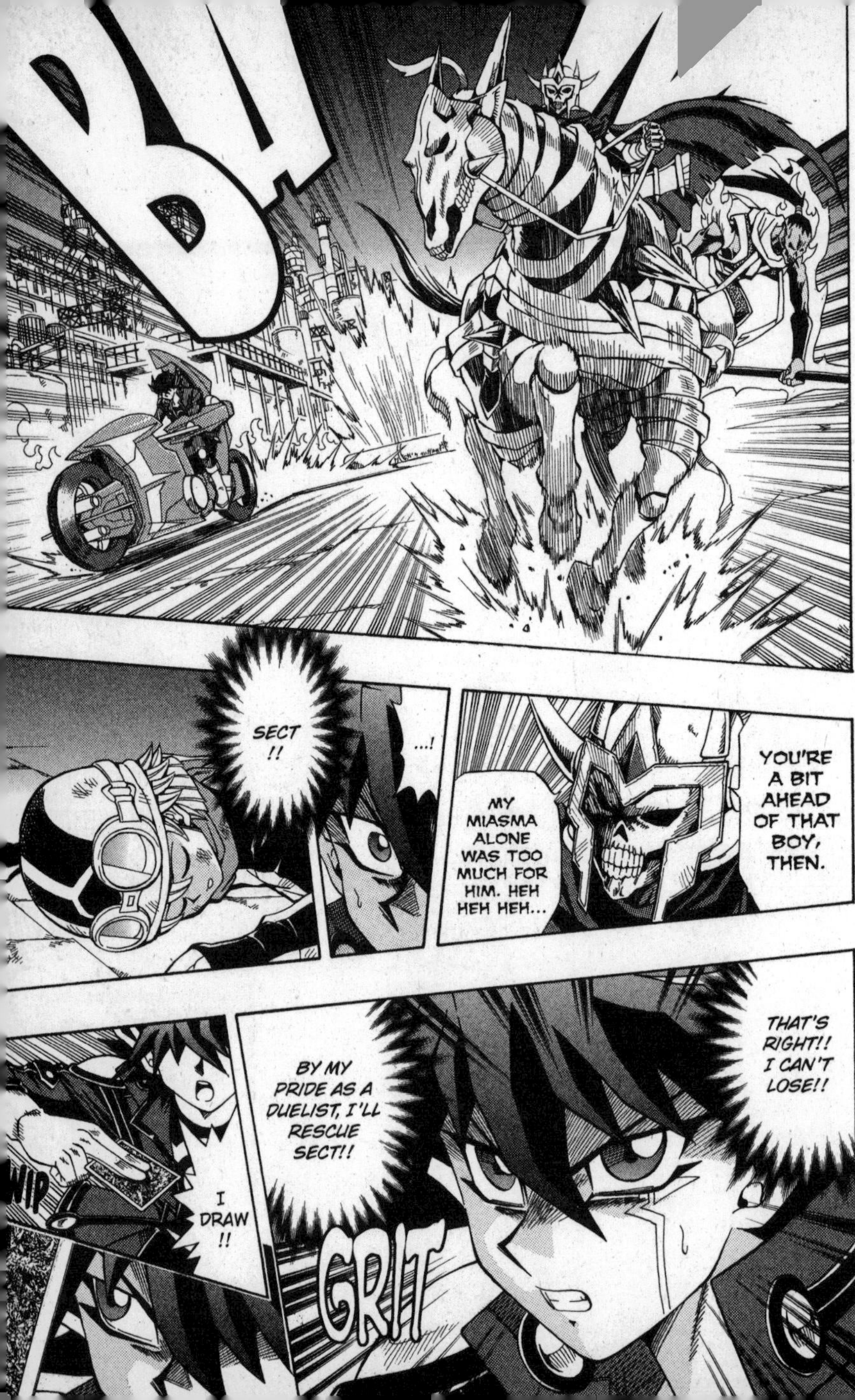
YOU'RE A BIT AHEAD OF THAT BOY, THEN.
MY MIASMA ALONE WAS TOO MUCH FOR HIM. HEH HEH HEH...
...!
SECT !!
THAT'S RIGHT!! I CAN'T LOSE!!
BY MY PRIDE AS A DUELIST, I'LL RESCUE SECT!!
GRIT
I DRAW !!

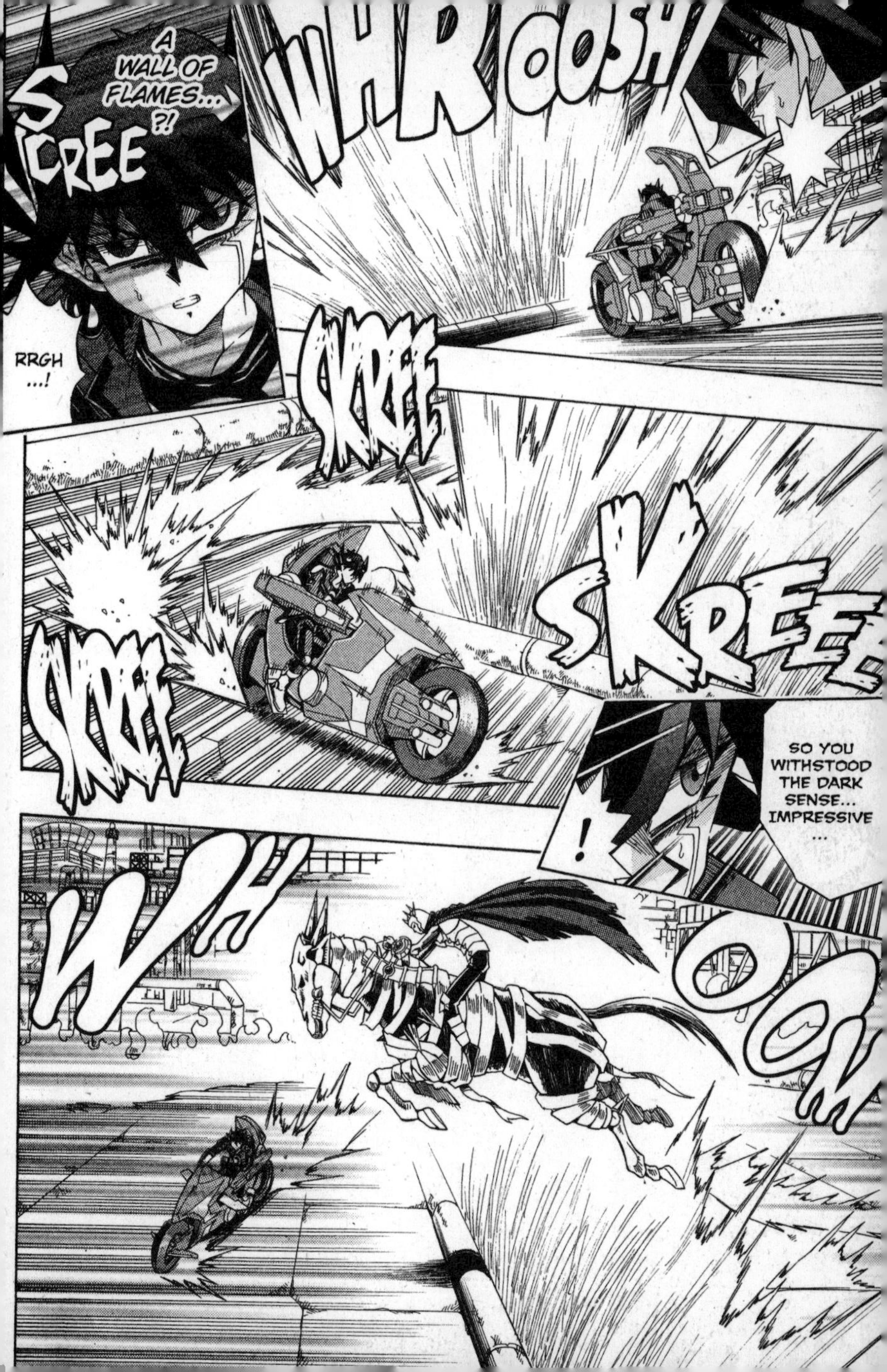
WHROOSH
A WALL OF FLAMES...?!
SCREE
RRGH ...!
SKREE
SKREE
SKREE
SO YOU WITHSTOOD THE DARK SENSE... IMPRESSIVE ...
!
WHOOOM

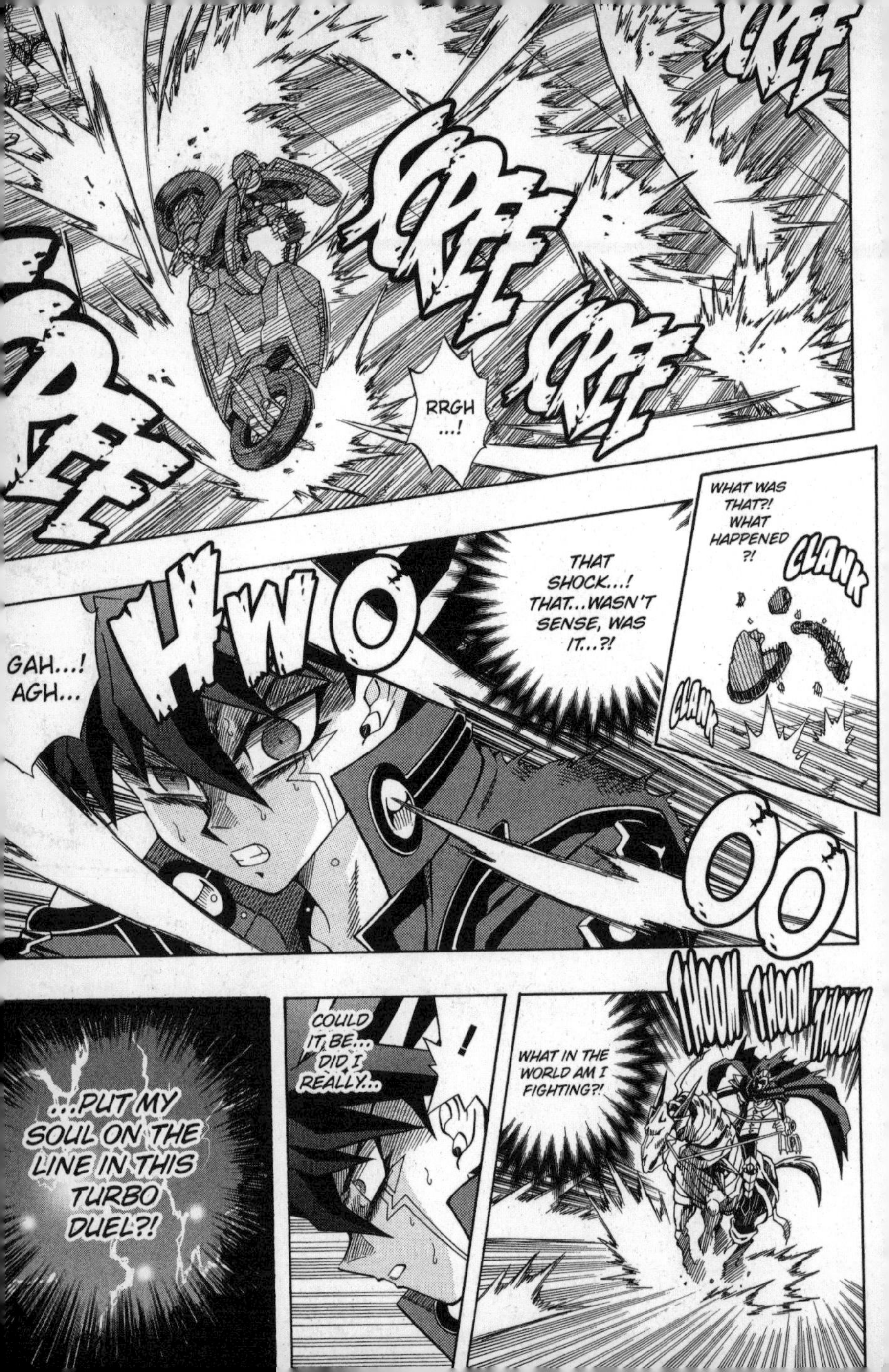
RRGH ...!
WHAT WAS THAT?! WHAT HAPPENED ?!
CLANK
CLANK
HWOOO
THAT SHOCK...! THAT...WASN'T SENSE, WAS IT...?!
GAH...! AGH...
THOOM THOOM THOOM
WHAT IN THE WORLD AM I FIGHTING?!
!
COULD IT BE... DID I REALLY...
...PUT MY SOUL ON THE LINE IN THIS TURBO DUEL?!

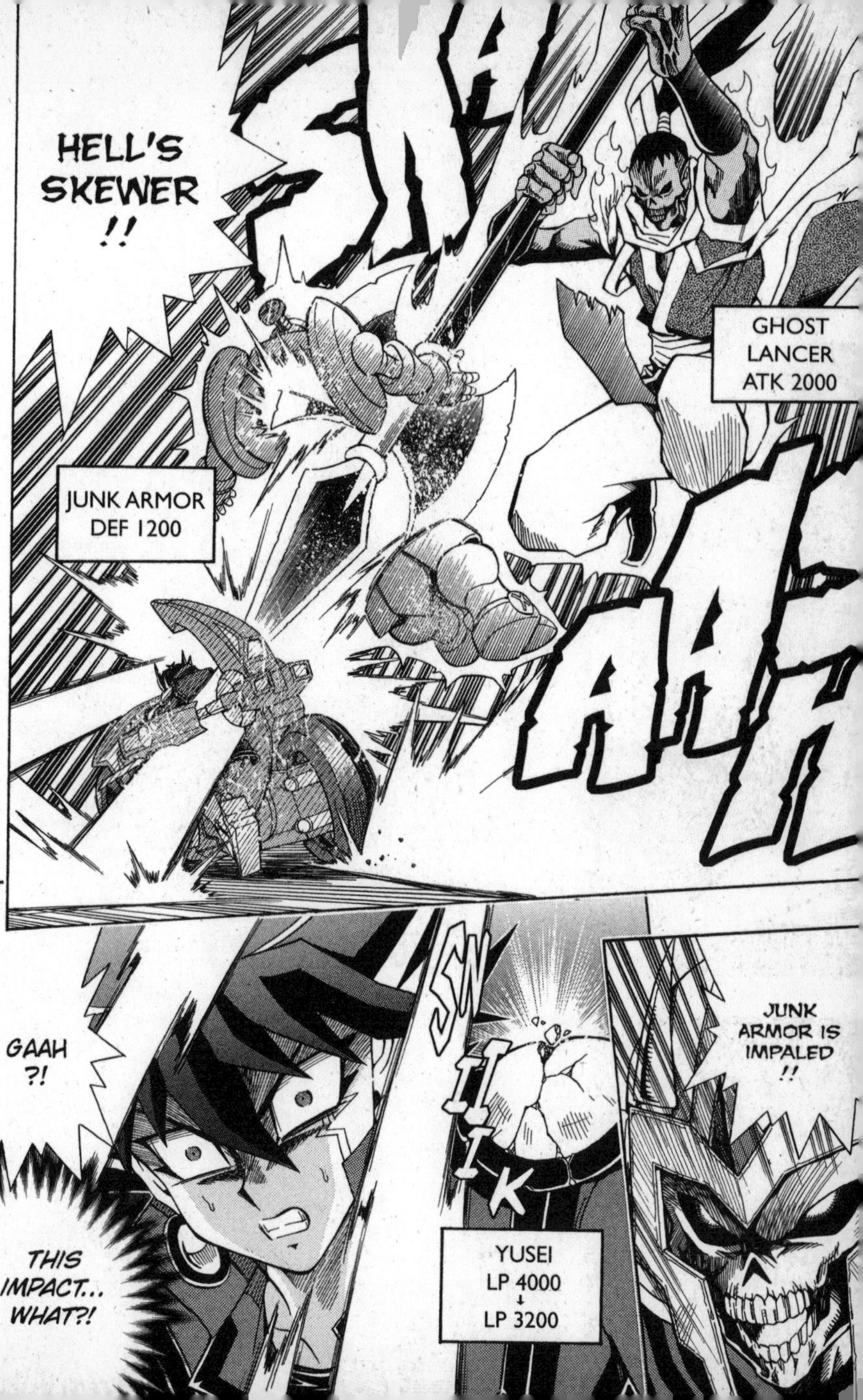
HELL'S SKEWER!!
GHOST LANCER ATK 2000
JUNK ARMOR DEF 1200
JUNK ARMOR IS IMPALED!!
YUSEI LP 4000 ↓ LP 3200
GAAH?!
THIS IMPACT... WHAT?!

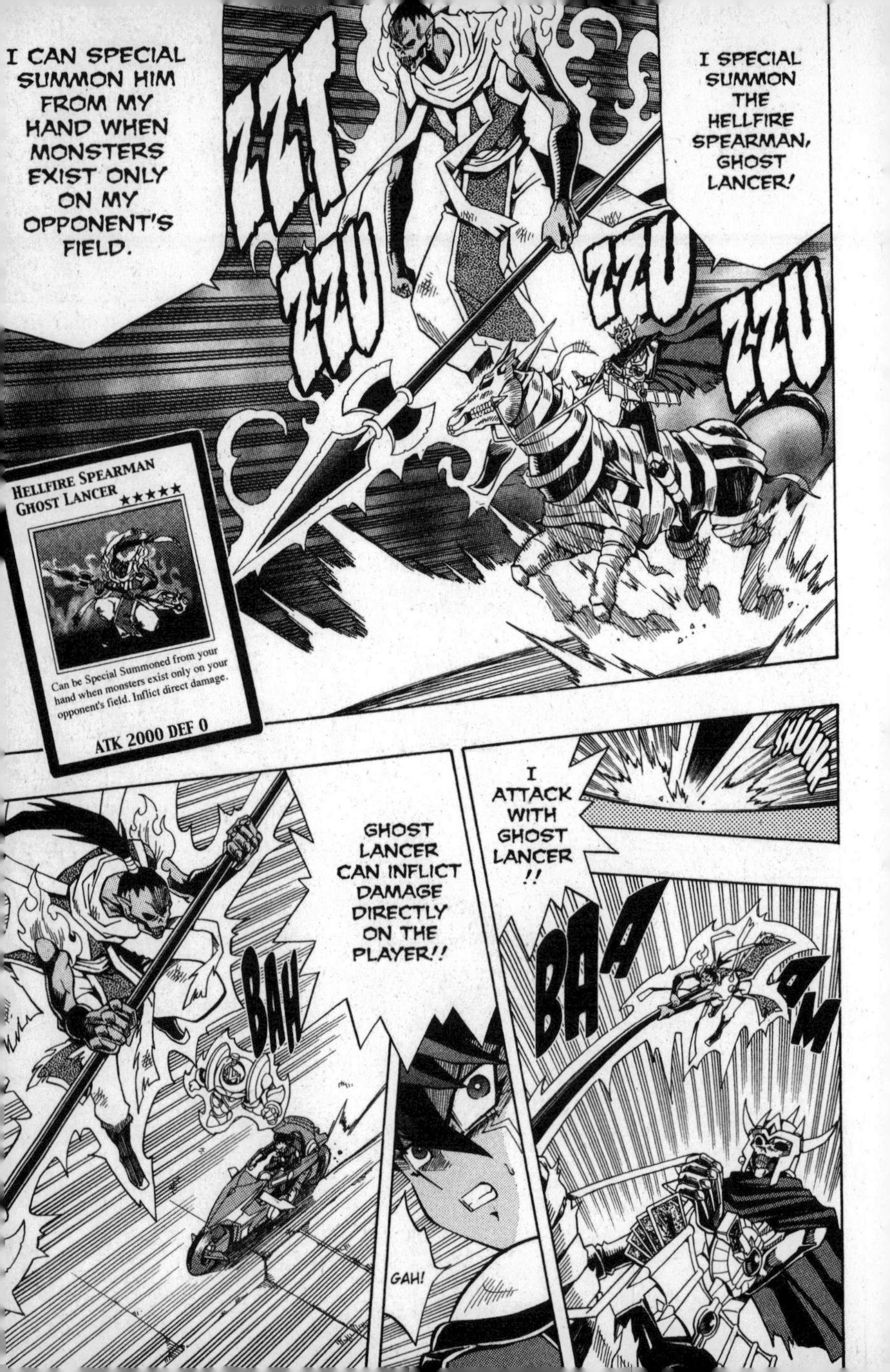
I SPECIAL SUMMON THE HELLFIRE SPEARMAN, GHOST LANCER!
I CAN SPECIAL SUMMON HIM FROM MY HAND WHEN MONSTERS EXIST ONLY ON MY OPPONENT'S FIELD.
ZZZT
ZZZU
ZZZU
ZZZU
HELLFIRE SPEARMAN GHOST LANCER ★★★★★
Can be Special Summoned from your hand when monsters exist only on your opponent's field. Inflict direct damage.
ATK 2000 DEF 0
SHUNK
I ATTACK WITH GHOST LANCER!!
BAAAM
GAH!
GHOST LANCER CAN INFLICT DAMAGE DIRECTLY ON THE PLAYER!!
BAH

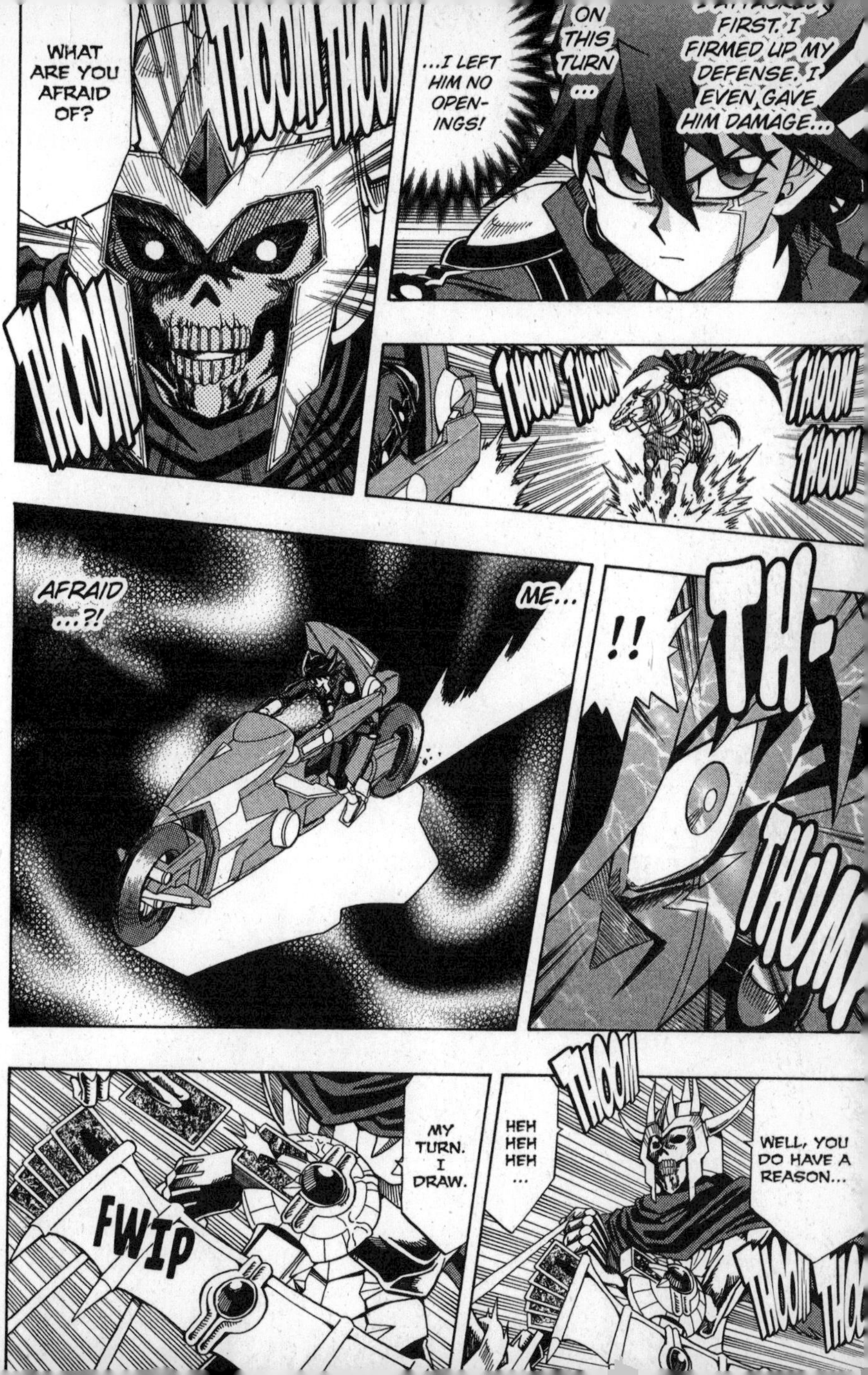
FIRST. I FIRMED UP MY DEFENSE. I EVEN GAVE HIM DAMAGE...
ON THIS TURN ...
...I LEFT HIM NO OPENINGS!
THOOM THOOM
THOOM THOOM
THOOM THOOM
WHAT ARE YOU AFRAID OF?
THOOM
TH-
THUM
!!
ME...
AFRAID ...?!
WELL, YOU DO HAVE A REASON...
THOOM
THOOM THO
HEH HEH HEH ...
MY TURN. I DRAW.
FWIP

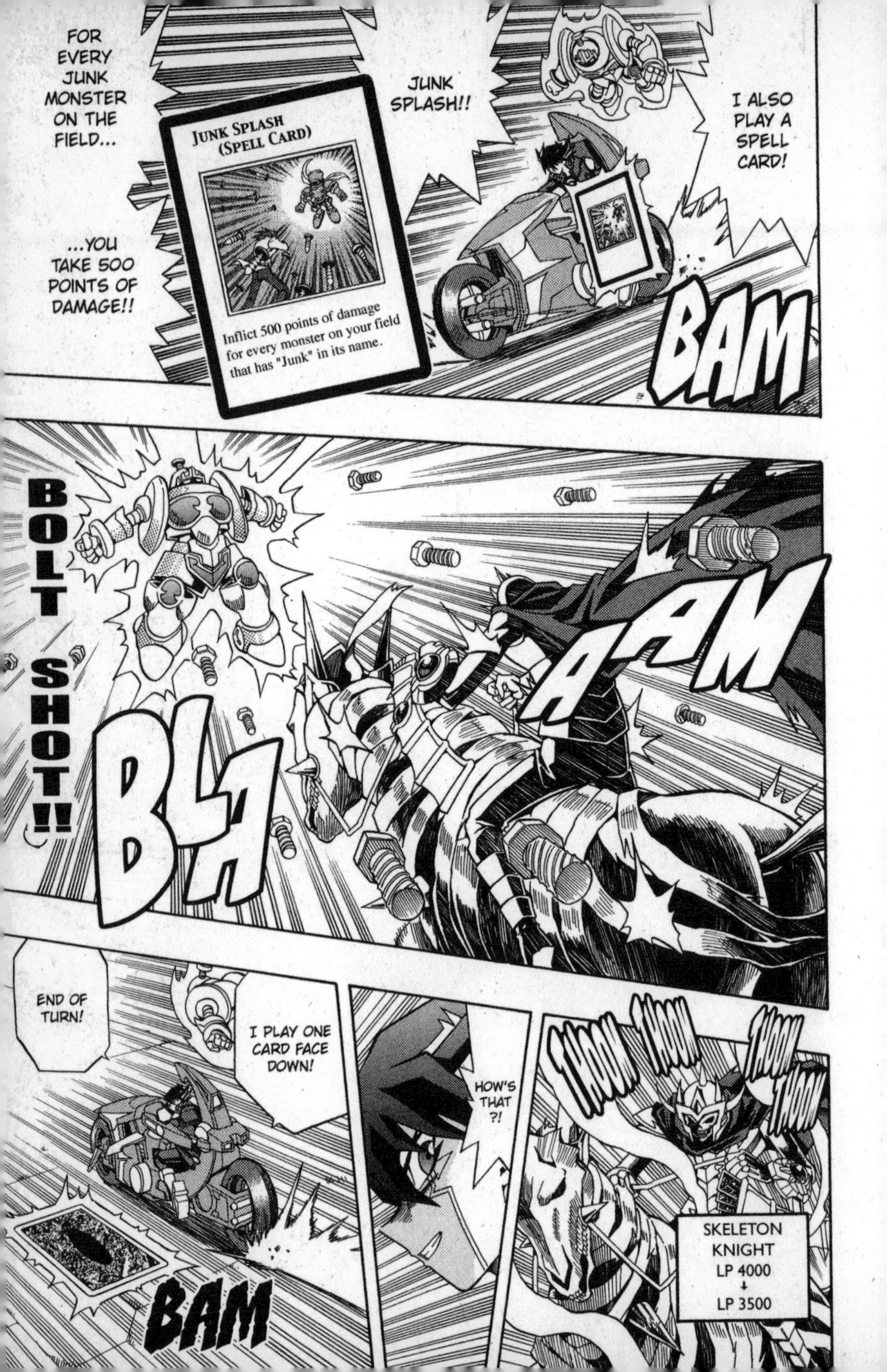
I ALSO PLAY A SPELL CARD!
JUNK SPLASH!!
JUNK SPLASH (SPELL CARD)
Inflict 500 points of damage for every monster on your field that has "Junk" in its name.
FOR EVERY JUNK MONSTER ON THE FIELD...
...YOU TAKE 500 POINTS OF DAMAGE!!
BAM
BLAAM
BOLT SHOT!!
SKELETON KNIGHT LP 4000 ↓ LP 3500
HOW'S THAT ?!
I PLAY ONE CARD FACE DOWN!
END OF TURN!
BAM

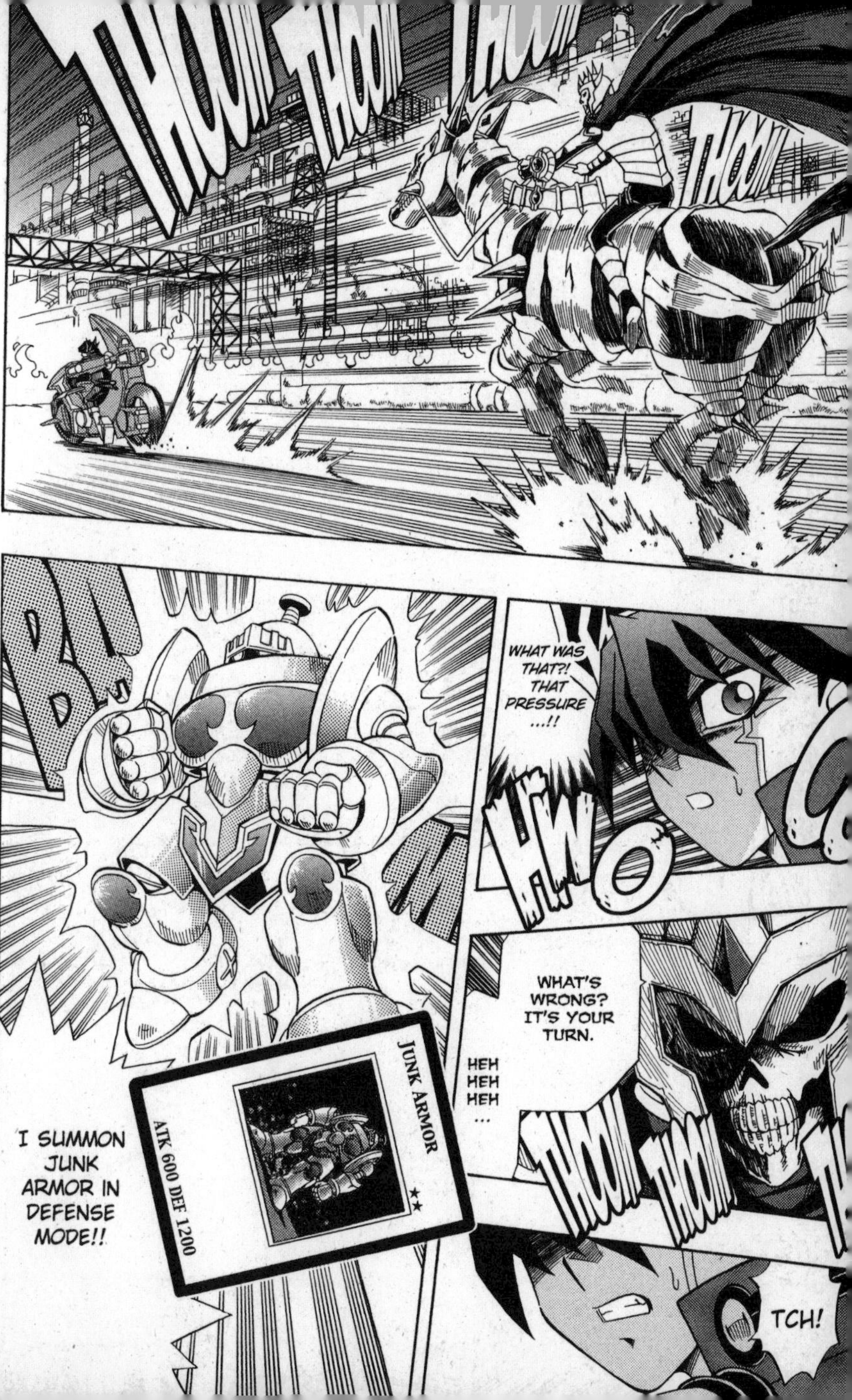
THOOM
THOOM
THOOM
THOOM
WHAT WAS THAT?! THAT PRESSURE ...!!
WHAT'S WRONG? IT'S YOUR TURN.
HEH HEH HEH ...
THOOM
THOOM
TCH!
JUNK ARMOR
ATK 600 DEF 1200
I SUMMON JUNK ARMOR IN DEFENSE MODE!!

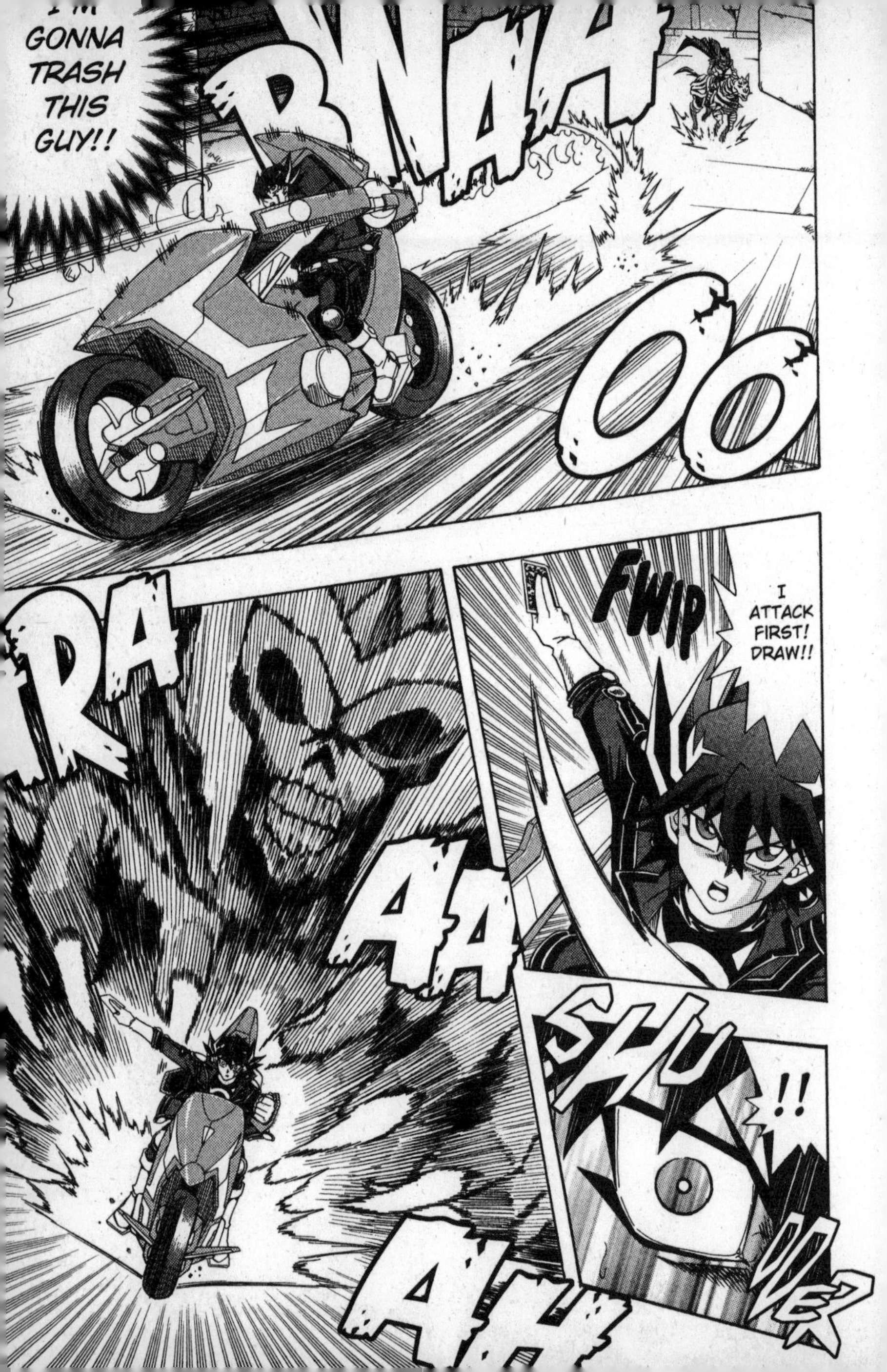
GONNA TRASH THIS GUY!!
BWA
OO
I ATTACK FIRST! DRAW!!
FWIP
RA
AA
AAH
SHU
!!
VER

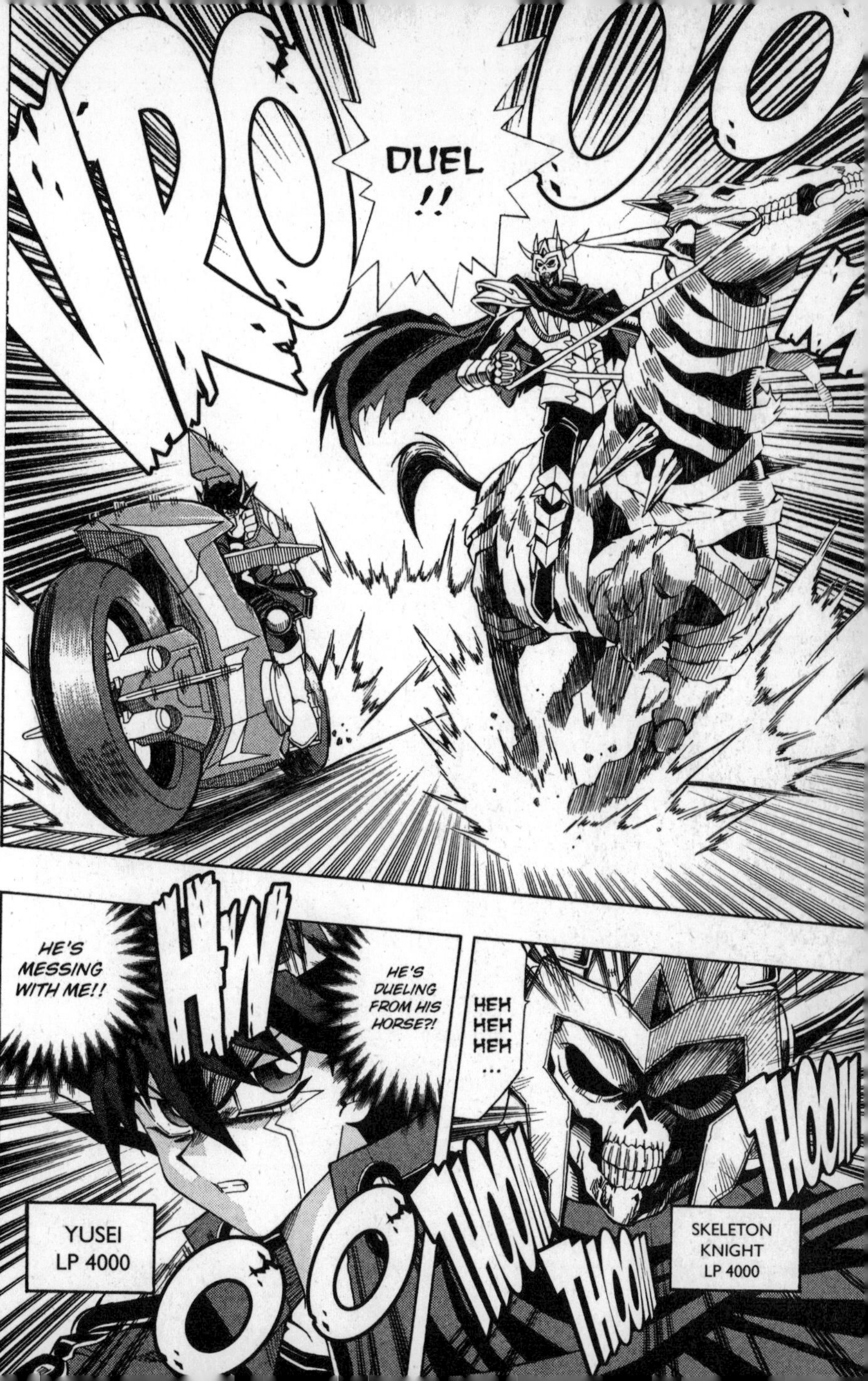
DUEL !!
HEH HEH HEH ...
SKELETON KNIGHT LP 4000
THOOM
THOOM
THOOM
HE'S DUELING FROM HIS HORSE?!
HE'S MESSING WITH ME!!
YUSEI LP 4000

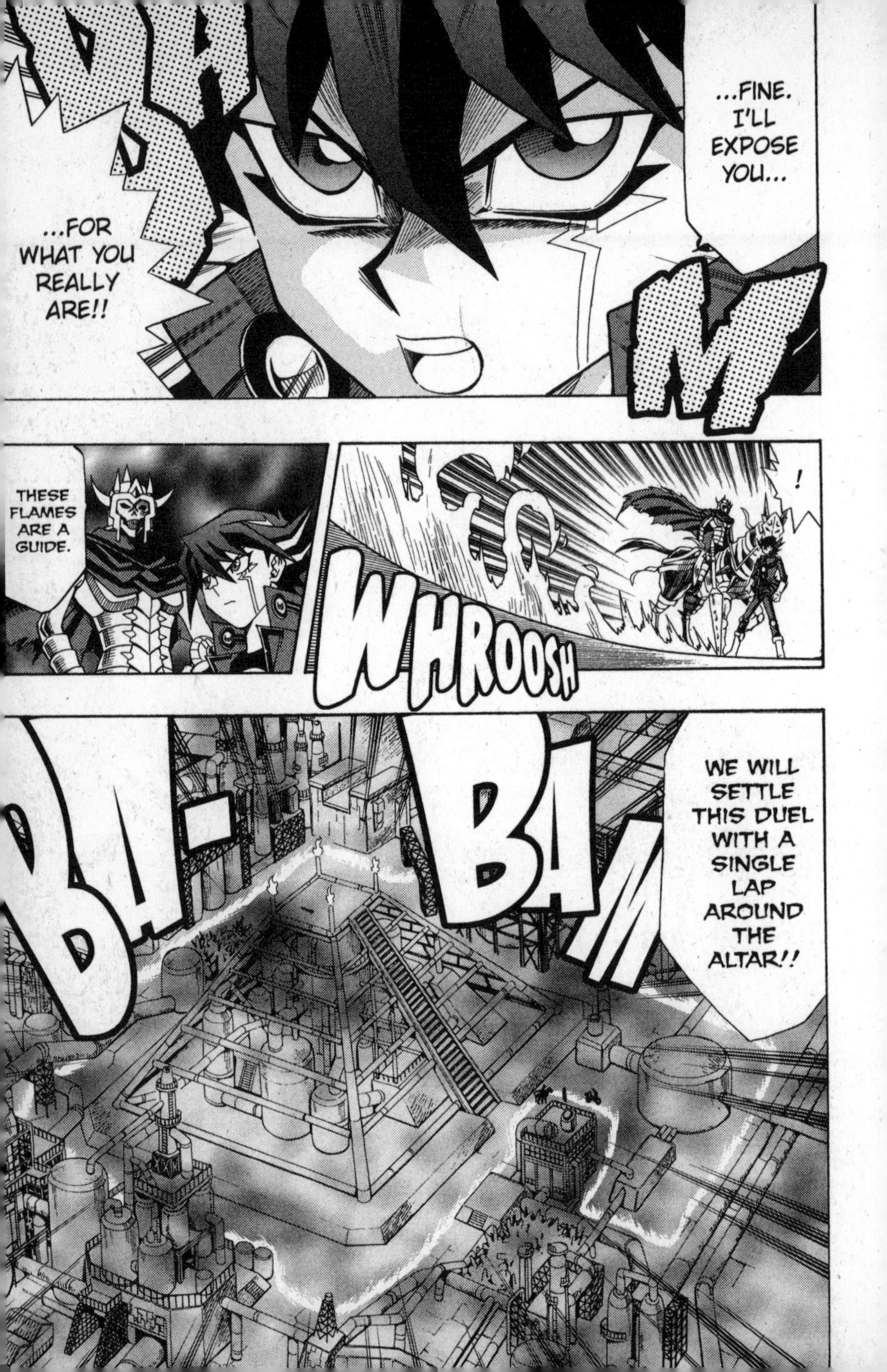
...FINE. I'LL EXPOSE YOU...
...FOR WHAT YOU REALLY ARE!!
!
WHROOSH
THESE FLAMES ARE A GUIDE.
WE WILL SETTLE THIS DUEL WITH A SINGLE LAP AROUND THE ALTAR!!
BA-BAM

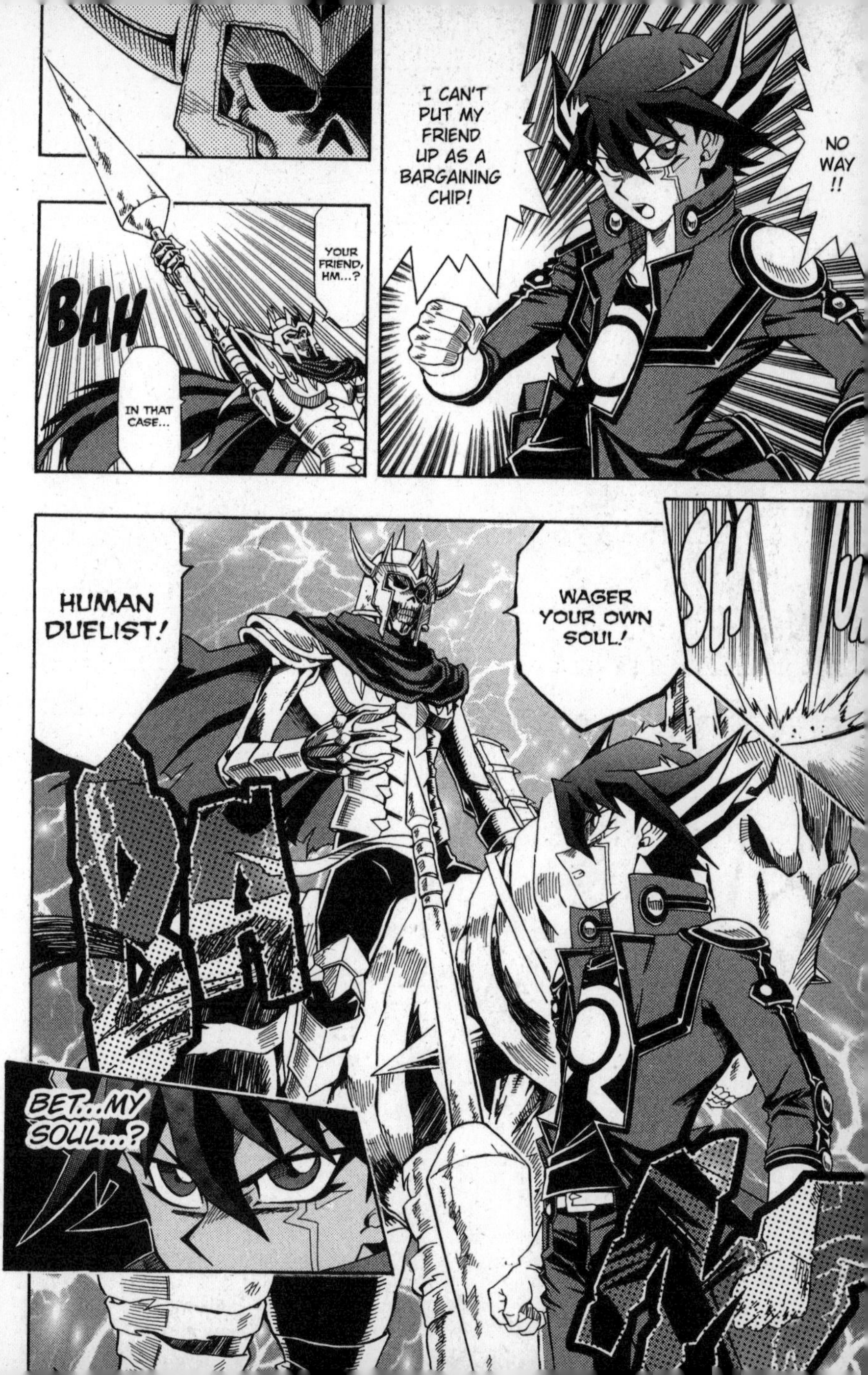
NO WAY!!
I CAN'T PUT MY FRIEND UP AS A BARGAINING CHIP!
YOUR FRIEND, HM...?
BAH
IN THAT CASE...
WAGER YOUR OWN SOUL!
HUMAN DUELIST!
BET...MY SOUL...?

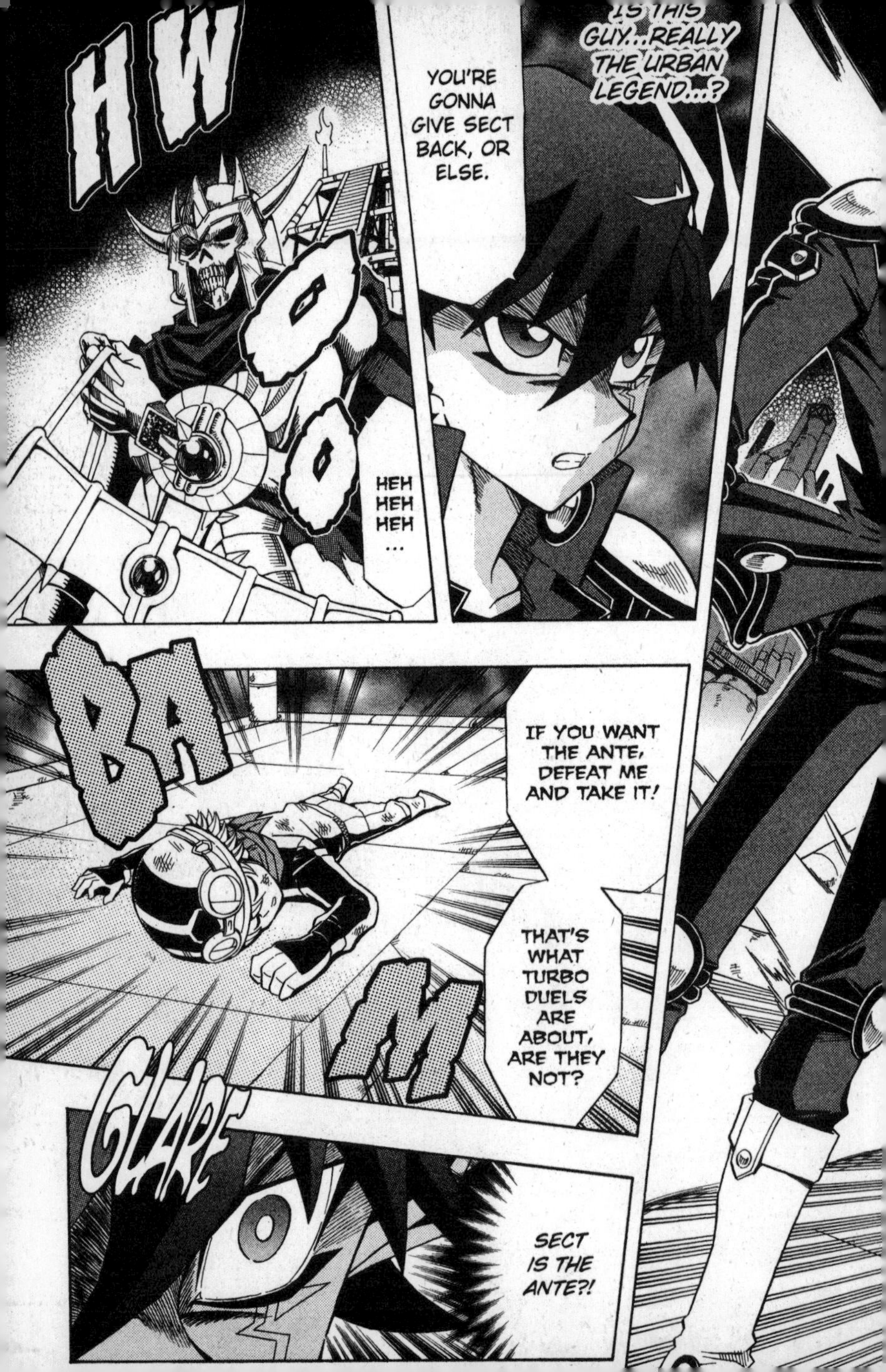
IS THIS GUY...REALLY THE URBAN LEGEND...?
YOU'RE GONNA GIVE SECT BACK, OR ELSE.
HWOOO
HEH HEH HEH ...
BAM
IF YOU WANT THE ANTE, DEFEAT ME AND TAKE IT!
THAT'S WHAT TURBO DUELS ARE ABOUT, ARE THEY NOT?
GLARE
SECT IS THE ANTE?!

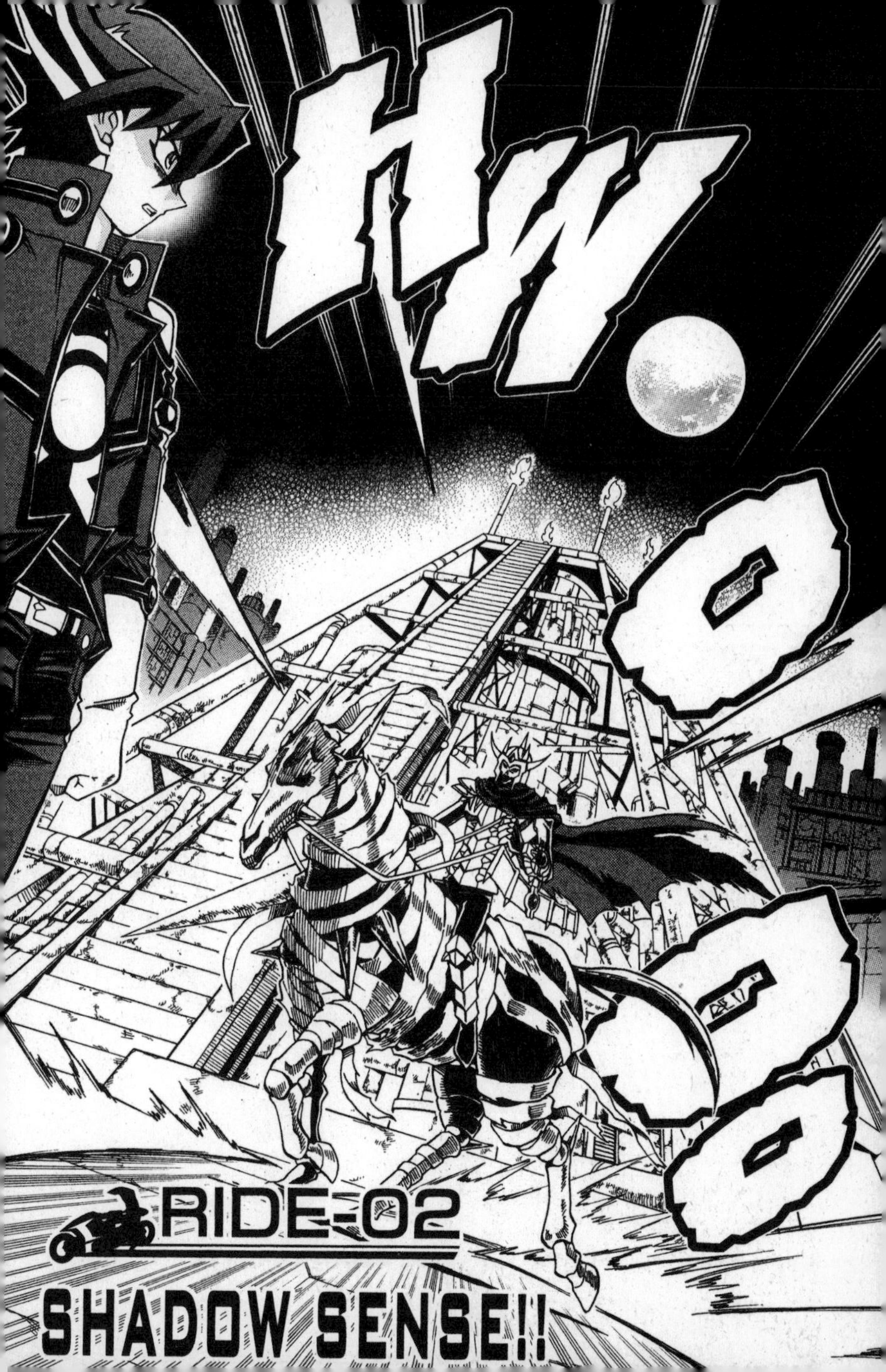
HWOOO
RIDE-02
SHADOW SENSE!!

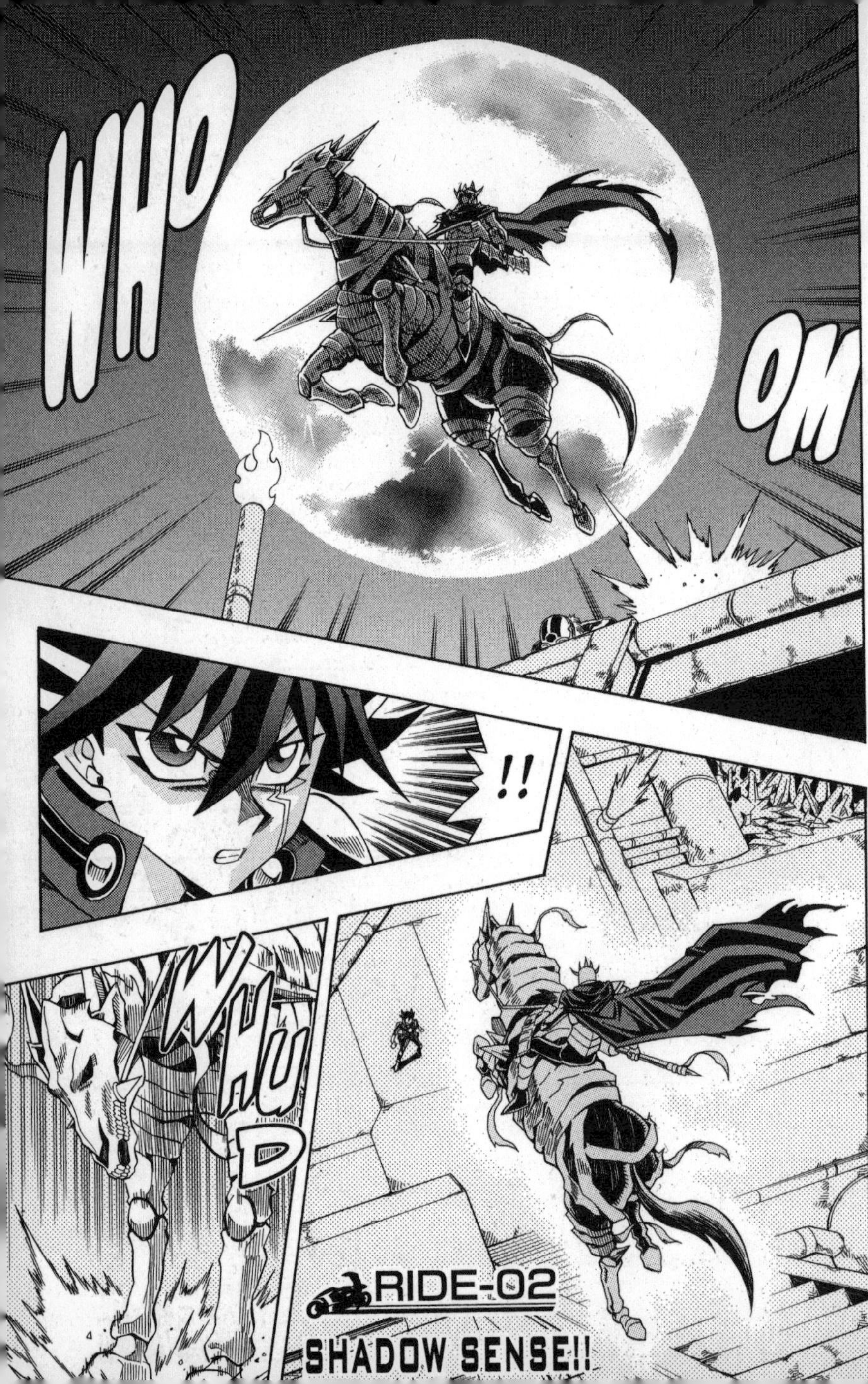
WHOOM
RIDE-02
SHADOW SENSE!!
!!
WHUD

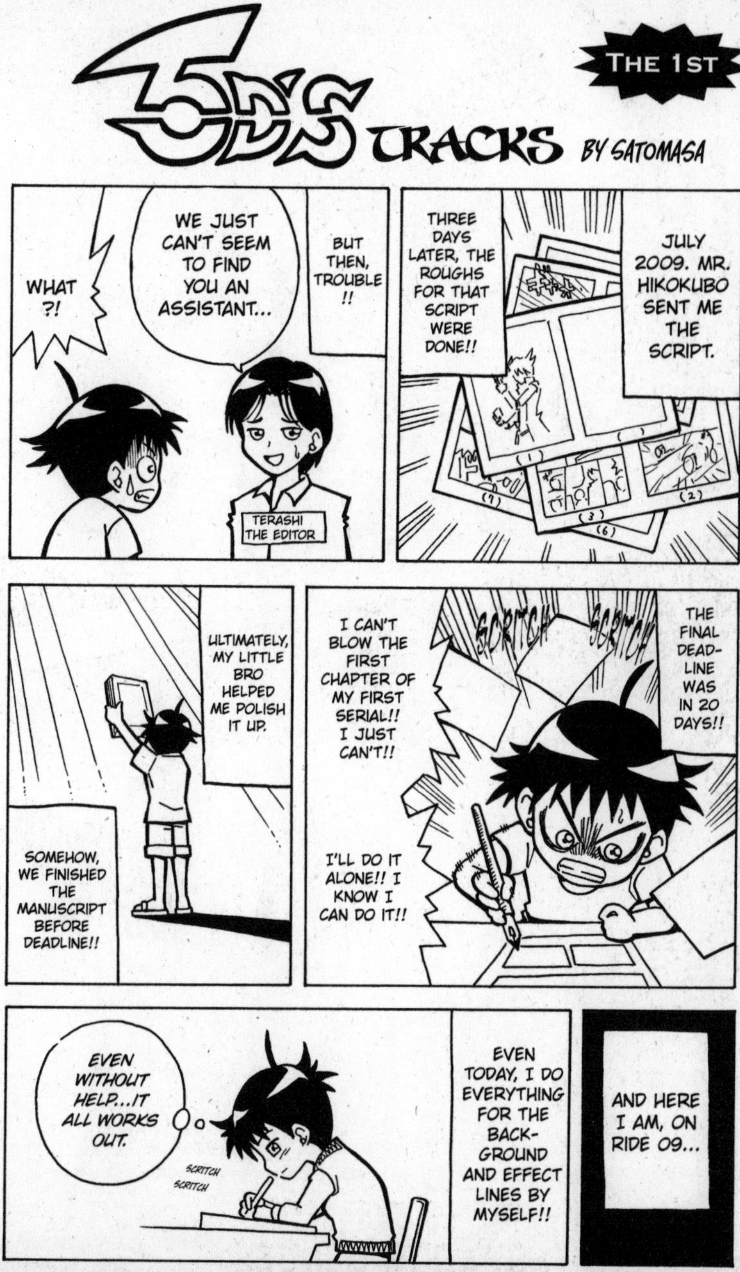
5D's TRACKS
THE 1ST
BY SATOMASA
JULY 2009. MR. HIKOKUBO SENT ME THE SCRIPT.
THREE DAYS LATER, THE ROUGHS FOR THAT SCRIPT WERE DONE!!
BUT THEN, TROUBLE!!
WE JUST CAN'T SEEM TO FIND YOU AN ASSISTANT...
WHAT?!
TERASHI THE EDITOR
THE FINAL DEAD-LINE WAS IN 20 DAYS!!
SCRITCH
SCRITCH
I CAN'T BLOW THE FIRST CHAPTER OF MY FIRST SERIAL!! I JUST CAN'T!!
I'LL DO IT ALONE!! I KNOW I CAN DO IT!!
ULTIMATELY, MY LITTLE BRO HELPED ME POLISH IT UP.
SOMEHOW, WE FINISHED THE MANUSCRIPT BEFORE DEADLINE!!
AND HERE I AM, ON RIDE 09...
EVEN TODAY, I DO EVERYTHING FOR THE BACK-GROUND AND EFFECT LINES BY MYSELF!!
EVEN WITHOUT HELP...IT ALL WORKS OUT.
SCRITCH
SCRITCH

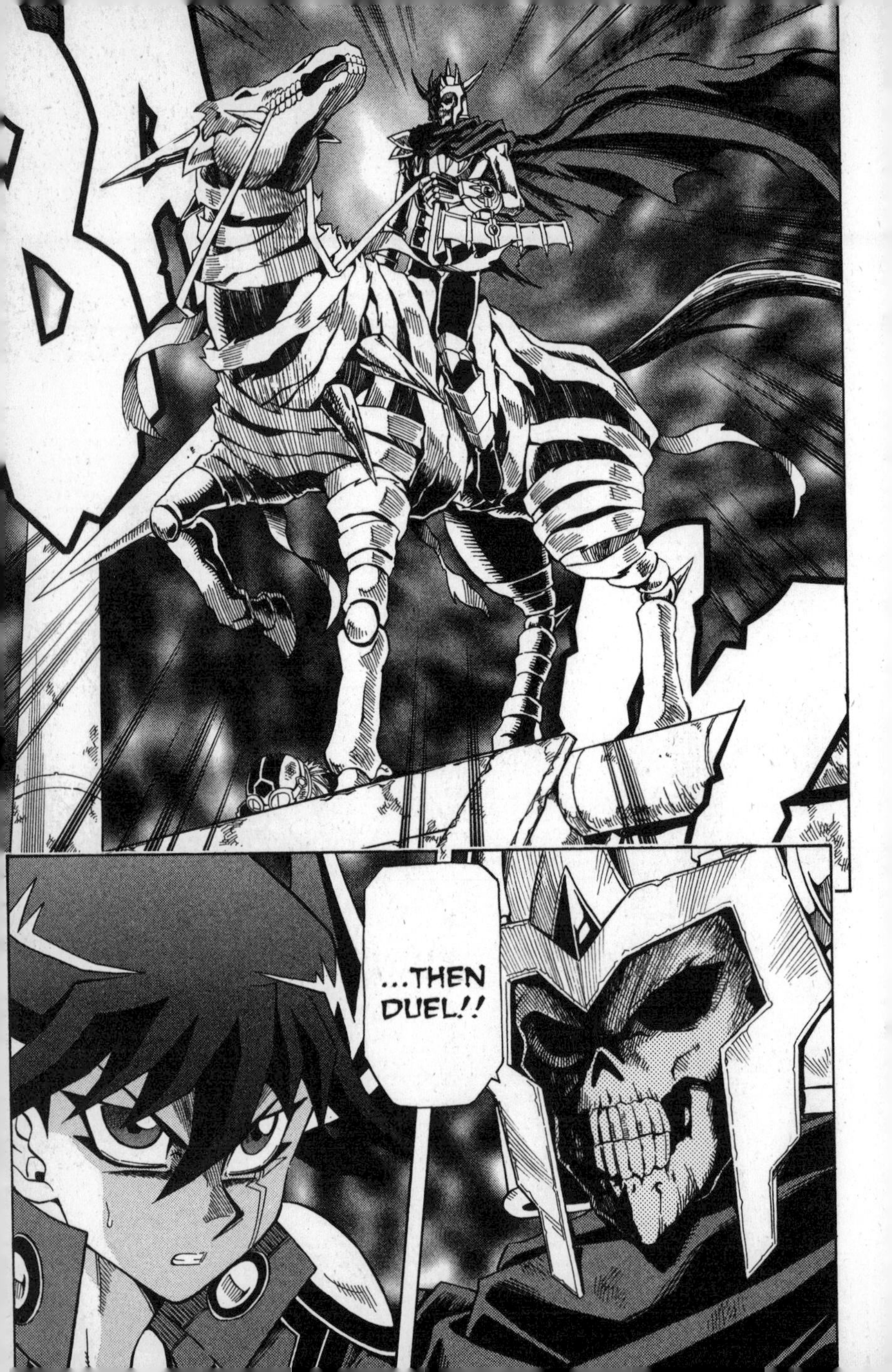
...THEN DUEL!!

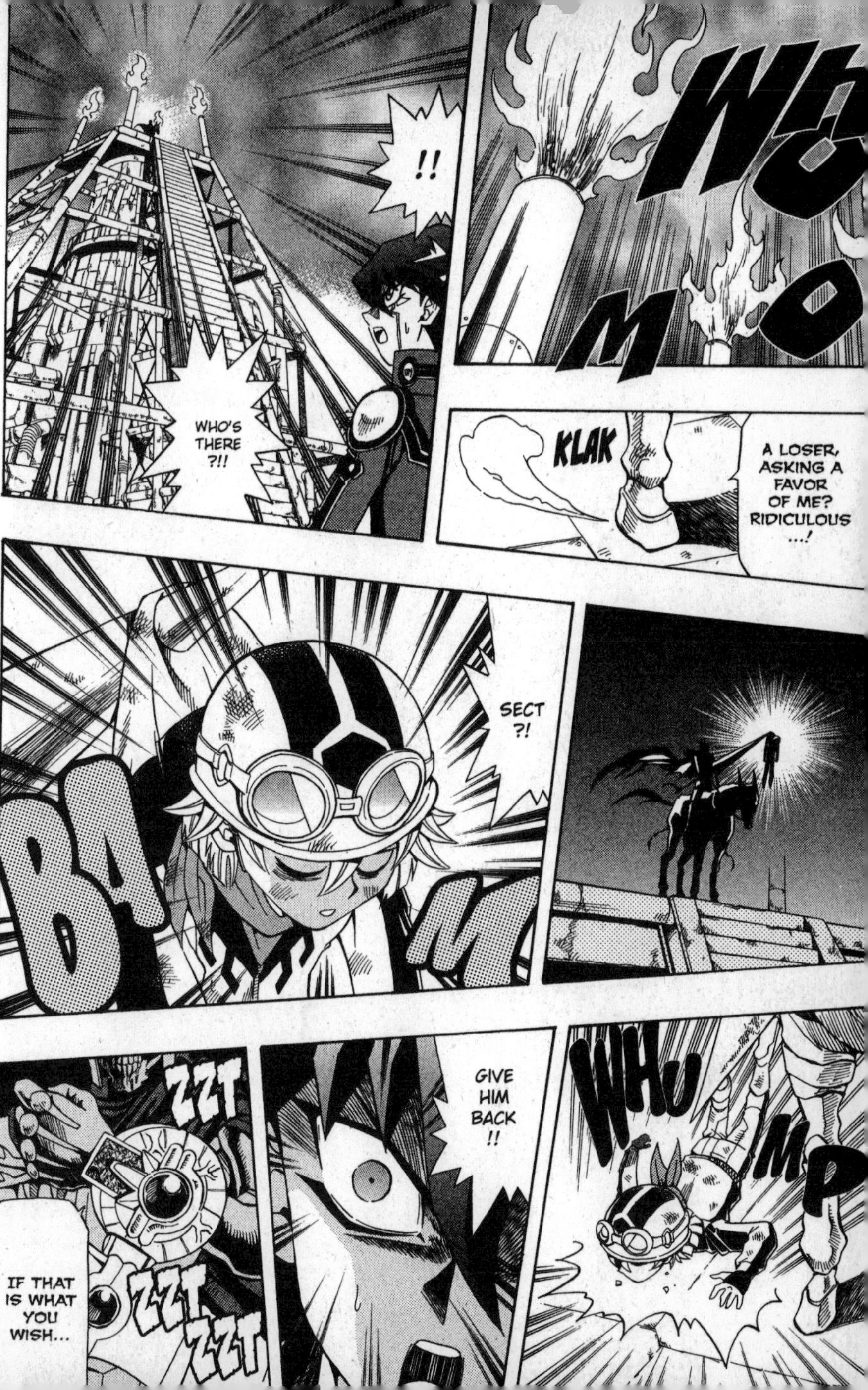
WHOOM
KLAK
A LOSER, ASKING A FAVOR OF ME? RIDICULOUS...!
!!
WHO'S THERE ?!!
SECT ?!
BAM
WHUMP
GIVE HIM BACK !!
ZZT
IF THAT IS WHAT YOU WISH...
ZZT
ZZT

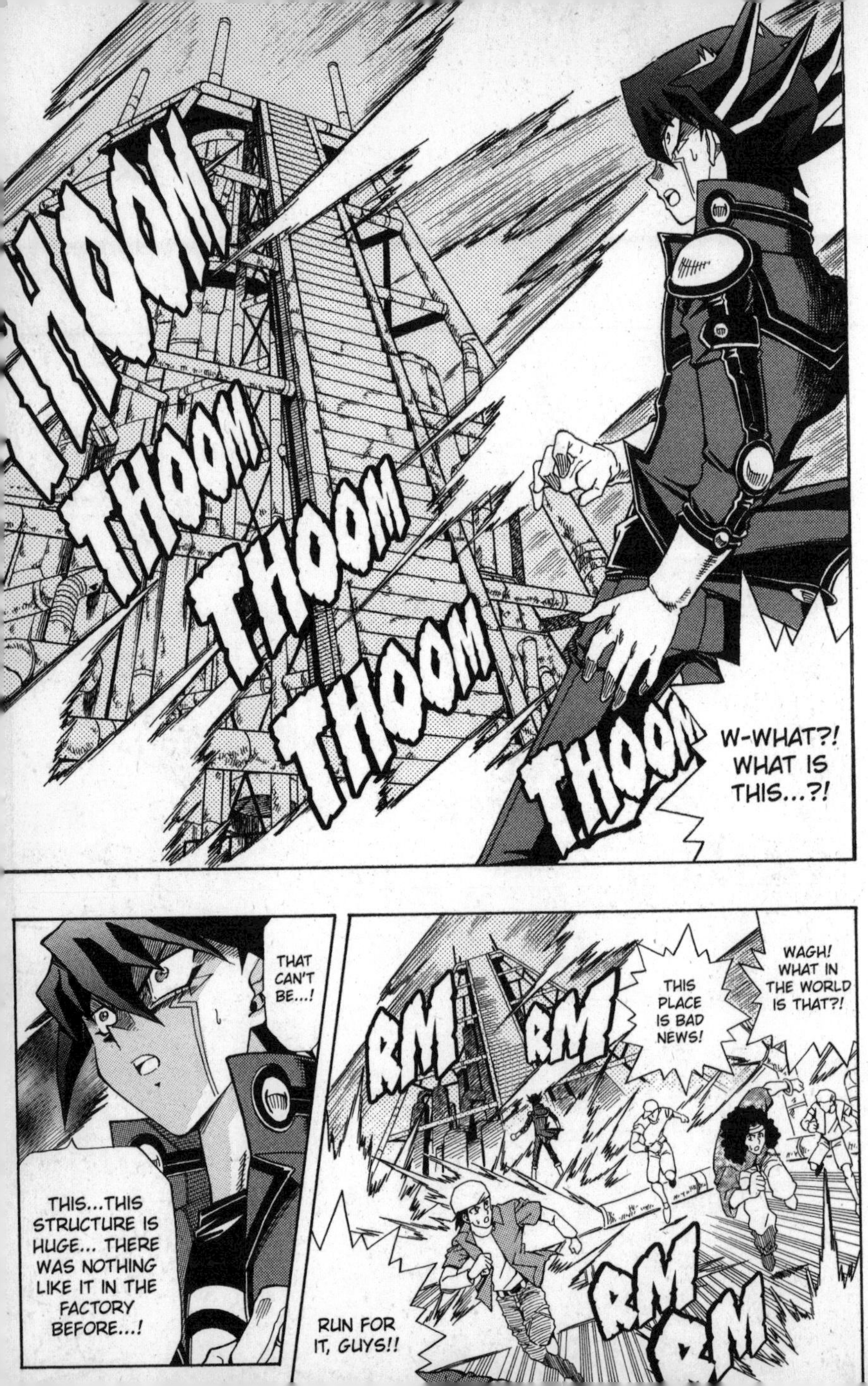
HOOM
THOOM
THOOM
THOOM
THOO
W-WHAT?! WHAT IS THIS...?!
WAGH! WHAT IN THE WORLD IS THAT?!
THIS PLACE IS BAD NEWS!
RM RM
RUN FOR IT, GUYS!!
RM RM
THAT CAN'T BE...!
THIS...THIS STRUCTURE IS HUGE... THERE WAS NOTHING LIKE IT IN THE FACTORY BEFORE...!

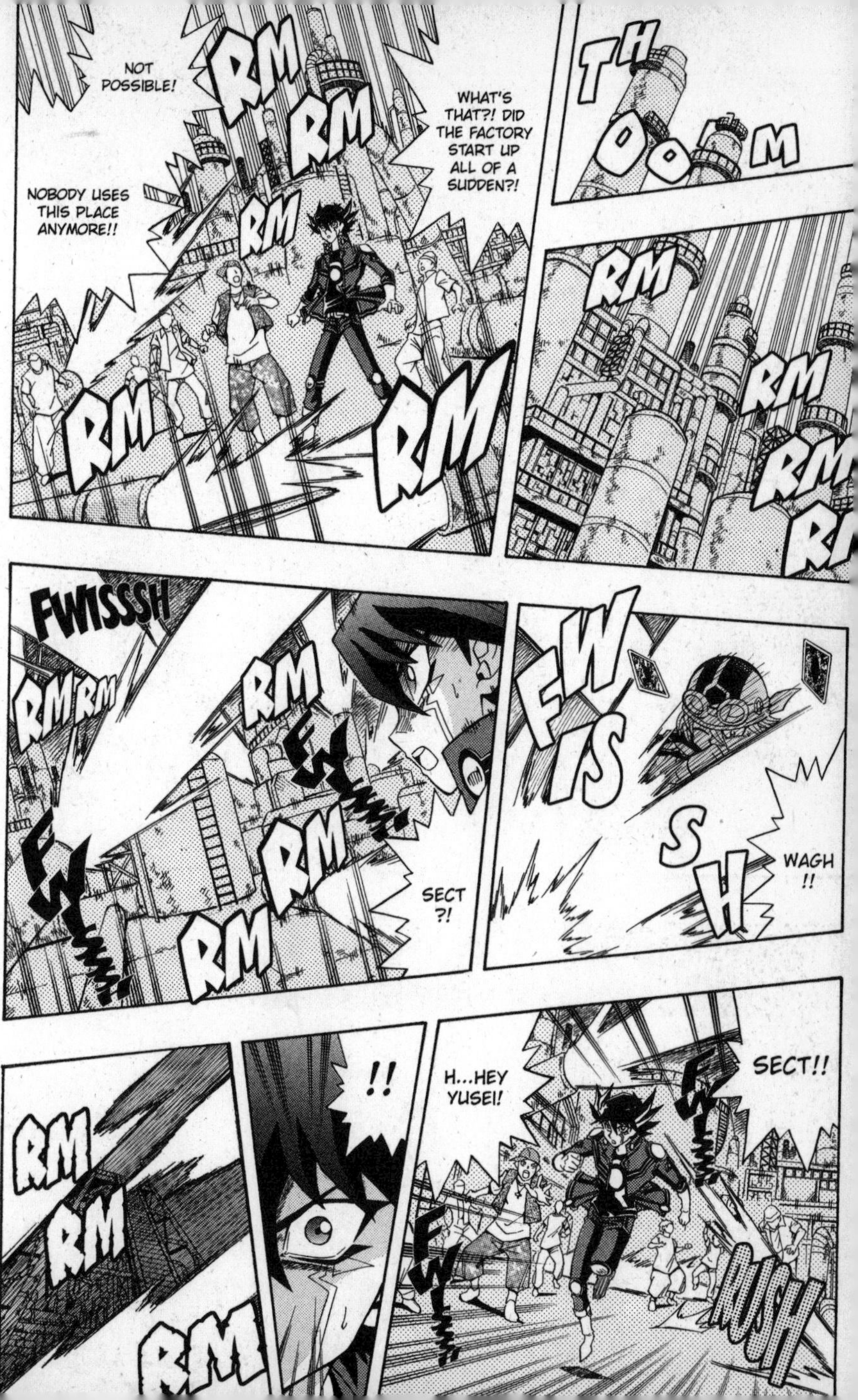
THOOOM
RM
RM
RM
WHAT'S THAT?! DID THE FACTORY START UP ALL OF A SUDDEN?!
RM
RM
NOT POSSIBLE!
NOBODY USES THIS PLACE ANYMORE!!
RM
RM
RM
FWISSSH
WAGH!!
RM
SECT?!
RM
RM
FWISSSH
RM RM
SECT!!
H...HEY YUSEI!
!!
RM
RM
RM

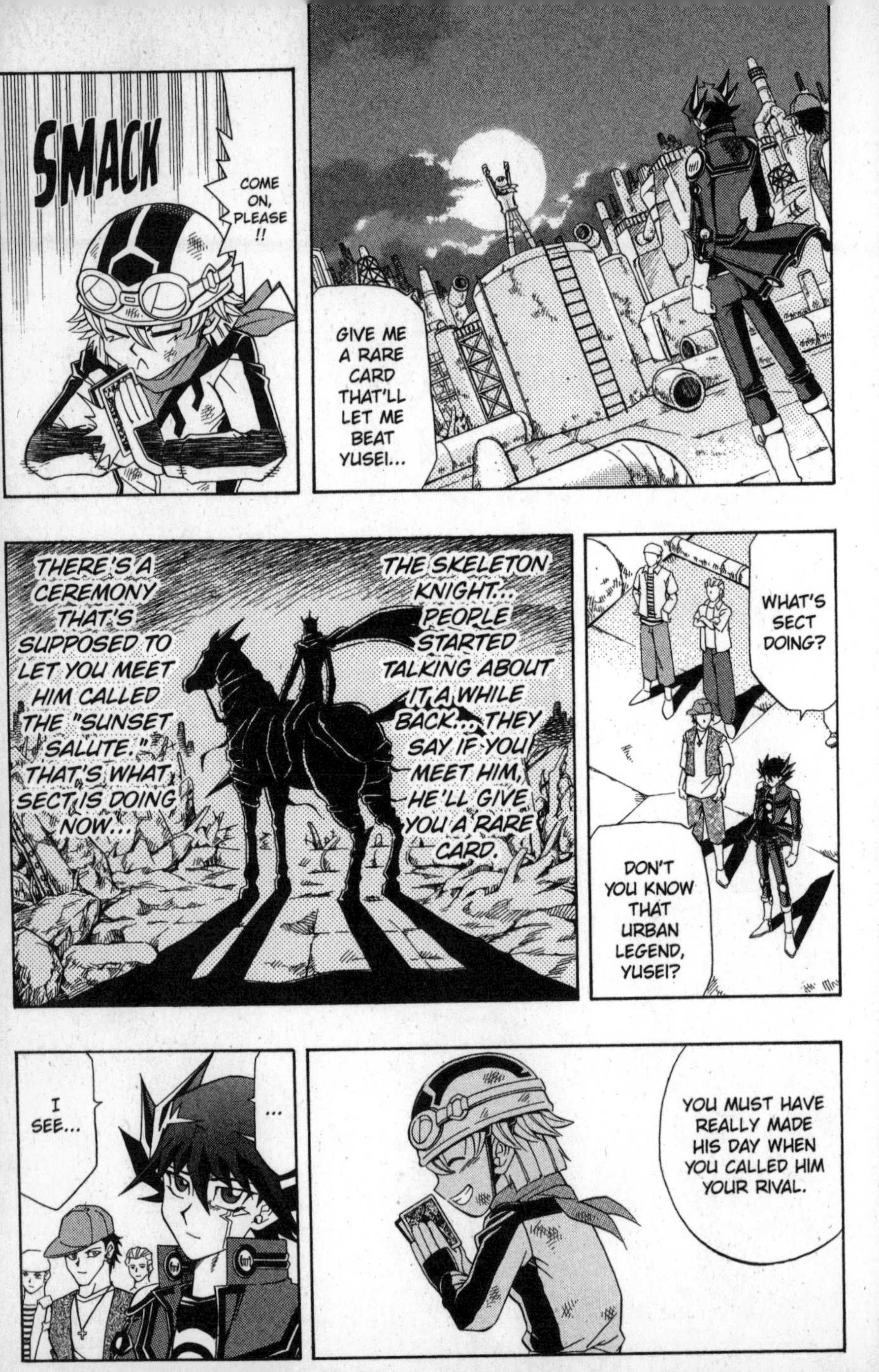
GIVE ME A RARE CARD THAT'LL LET ME BEAT YUSEI...
SMACK
COME ON, PLEASE !!
WHAT'S SECT DOING?
DON'T YOU KNOW THAT URBAN LEGEND, YUSEI?
THE SKELETON KNIGHT... PEOPLE STARTED TALKING ABOUT IT A WHILE BACK... THEY SAY IF YOU MEET HIM, HE'LL GIVE YOU A RARE CARD.
THERE'S A CEREMONY THAT'S SUPPOSED TO LET YOU MEET HIM CALLED THE "SUNSET SALUTE." THAT'S WHAT SECT IS DOING NOW...
YOU MUST HAVE REALLY MADE HIS DAY WHEN YOU CALLED HIM YOUR RIVAL.
...
I SEE...

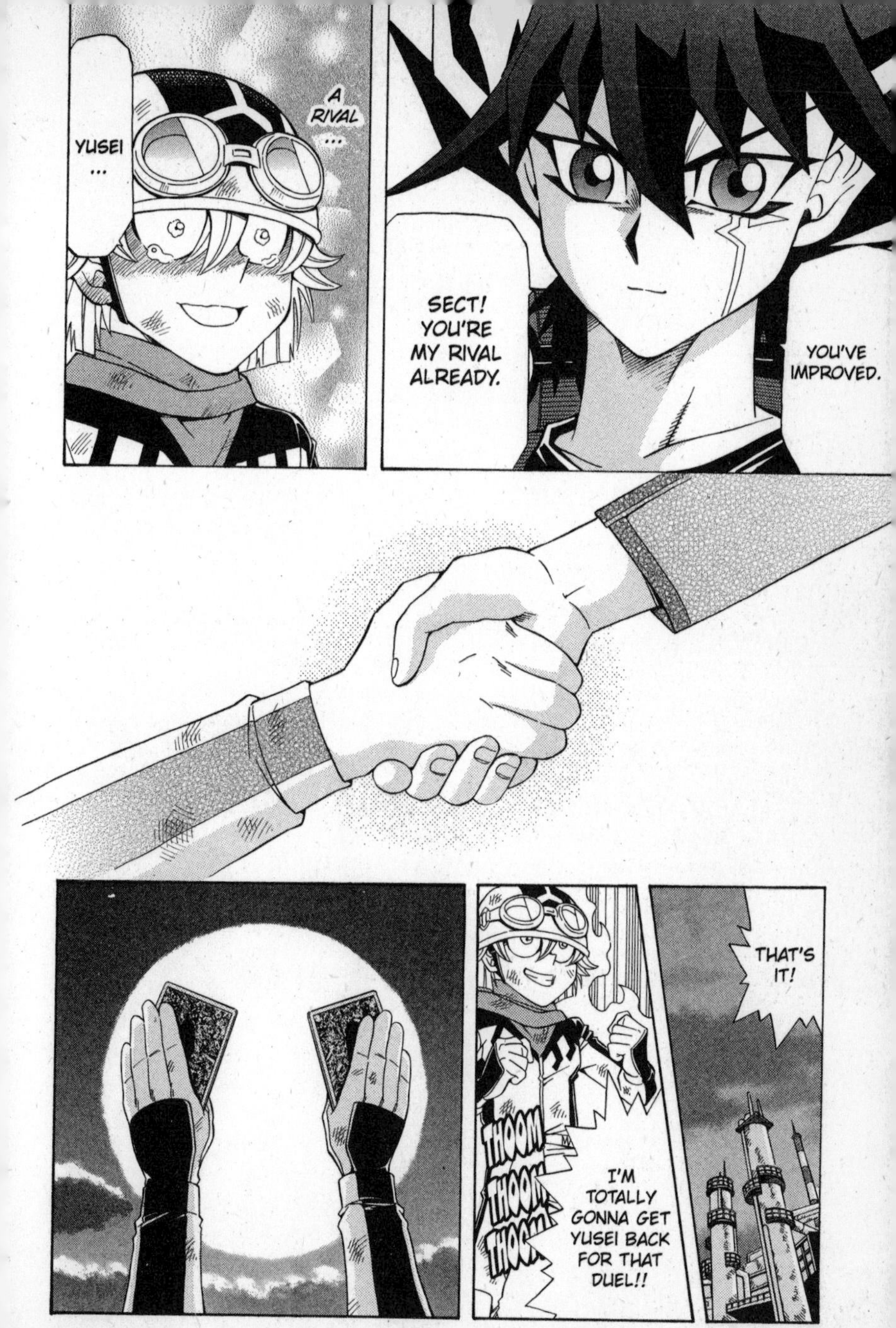
YOU'VE IMPROVED.
SECT! YOU'RE MY RIVAL ALREADY.
A RIVAL ...
YUSEI ...
THAT'S IT!
I'M TOTALLY GONNA GET YUSEI BACK FOR THAT DUEL!!
THOOM
THOOM
THOOM

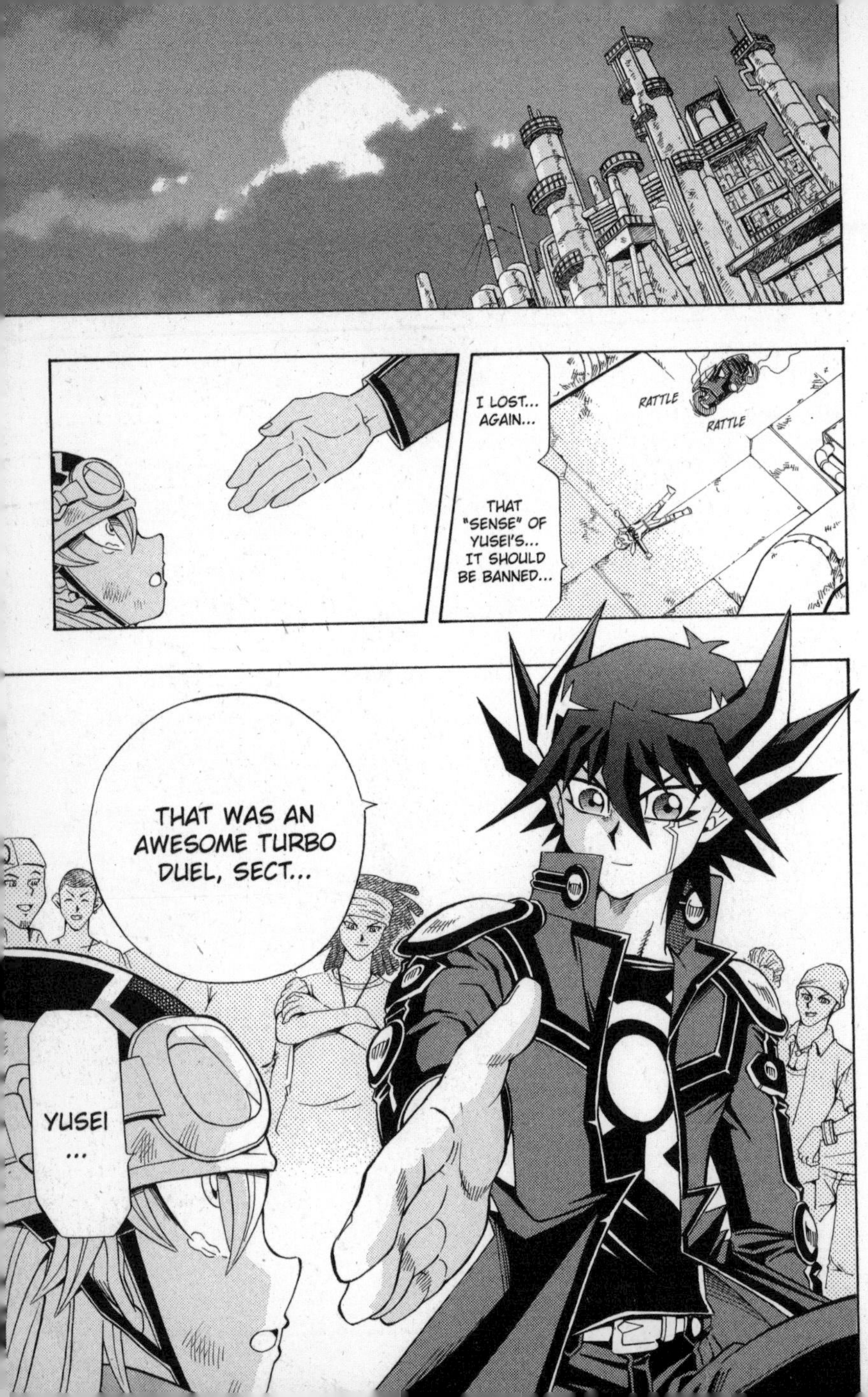
I LOST... AGAIN...
RATTLE
RATTLE
THAT "SENSE" OF YUSEI'S... IT SHOULD BE BANNED...
THAT WAS AN AWESOME TURBO DUEL, SECT...
YUSEI ...

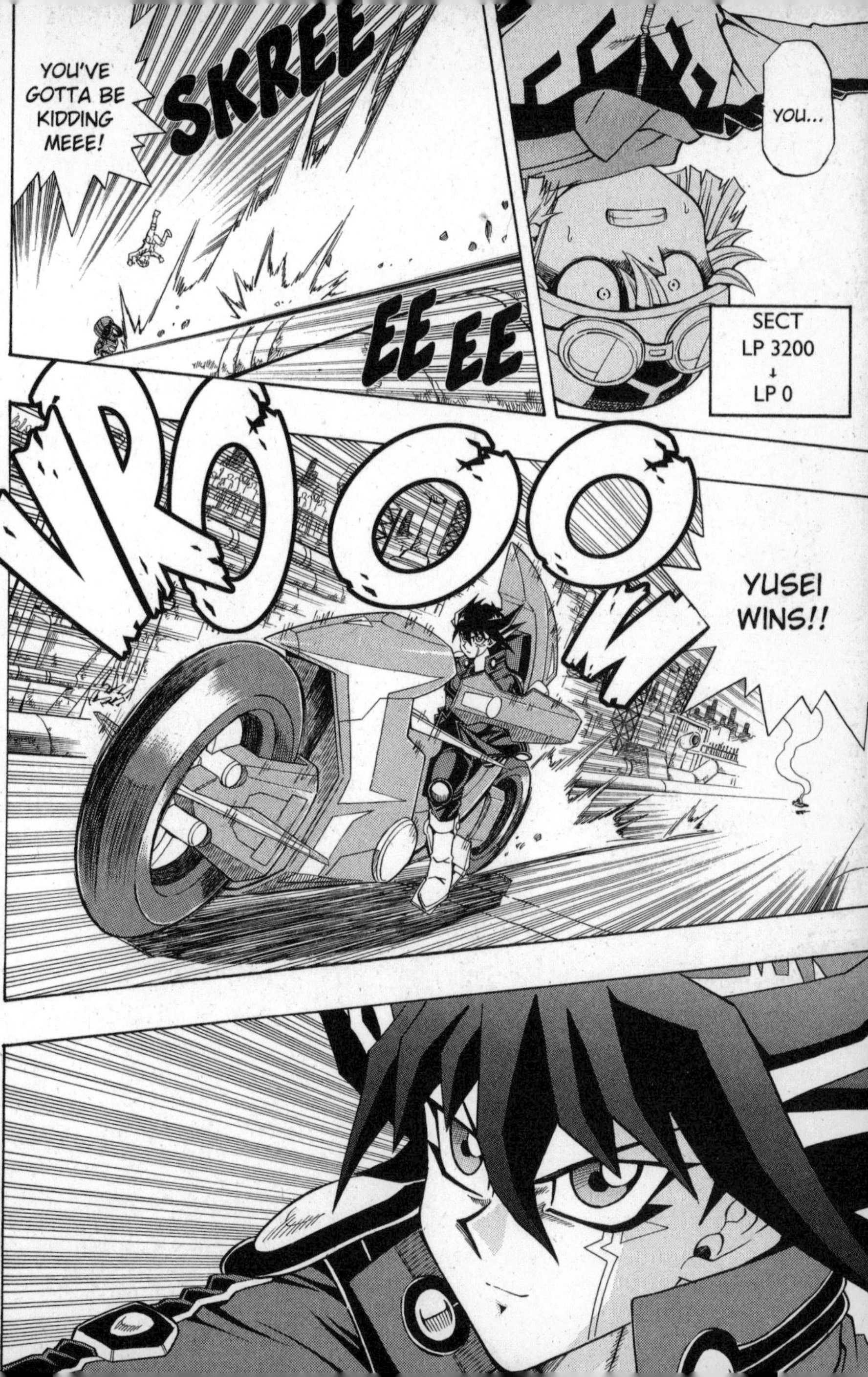
YOU...
SECT
LP 3200
↓
LP 0
SKREE
YOU'VE GOTTA BE KIDDING MEEE!
EEEE
VROOOM
YUSEI WINS!!

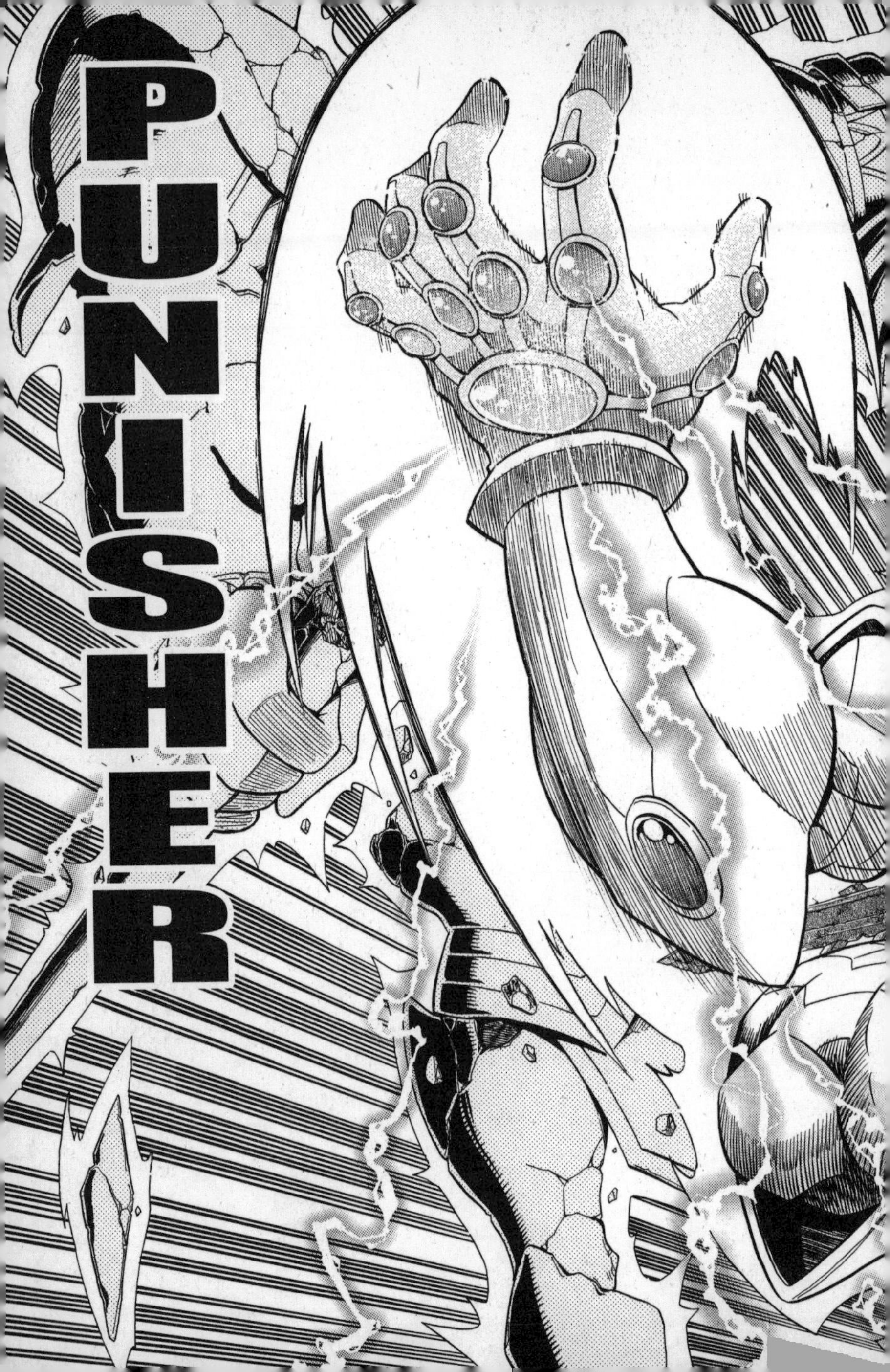
PUNISHER

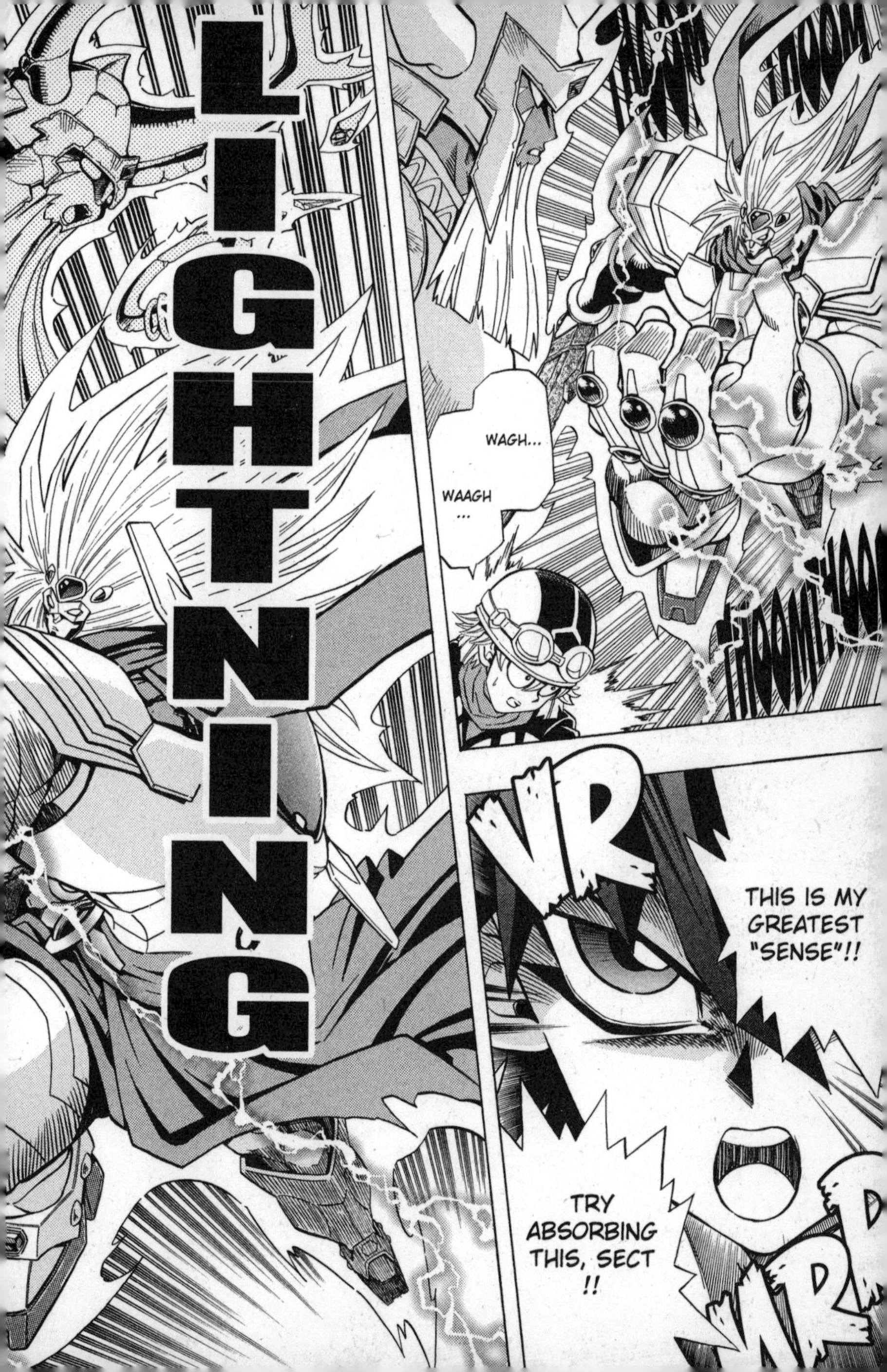
WAGH...
WAAGH ...
THIS IS MY GREATEST "SENSE"!!
TRY ABSORBING THIS, SECT !!
LIGHTNING

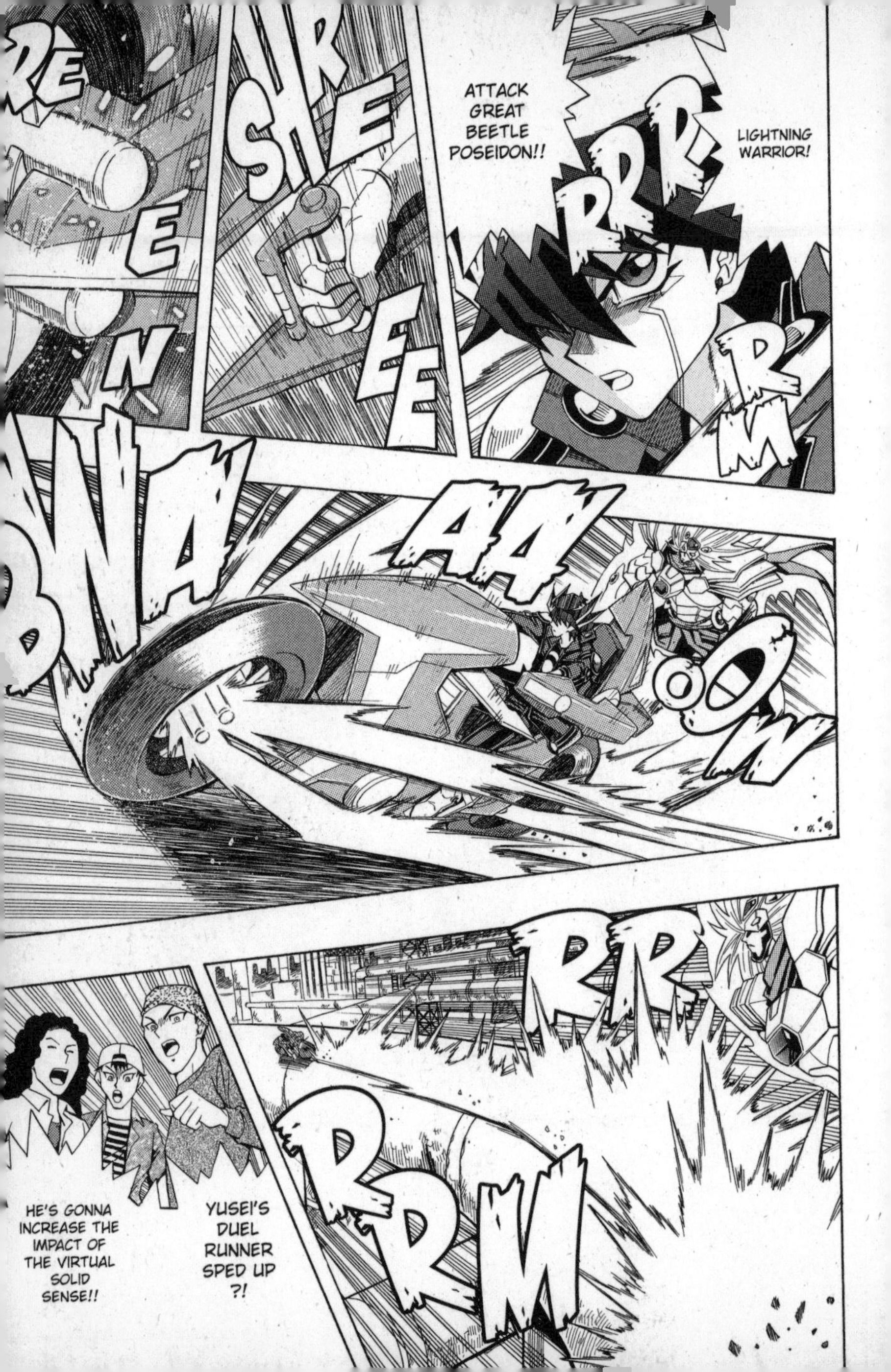
LIGHTNING WARRIOR!
ATTACK GREAT BEETLE POSEIDON!!
RRRR
RRM
SHREEE
REEN
BWAAOON
RRRRM
YUSEI'S DUEL RUNNER SPED UP ?!
HE'S GONNA INCREASE THE IMPACT OF THE VIRTUAL SOLID SENSE!!

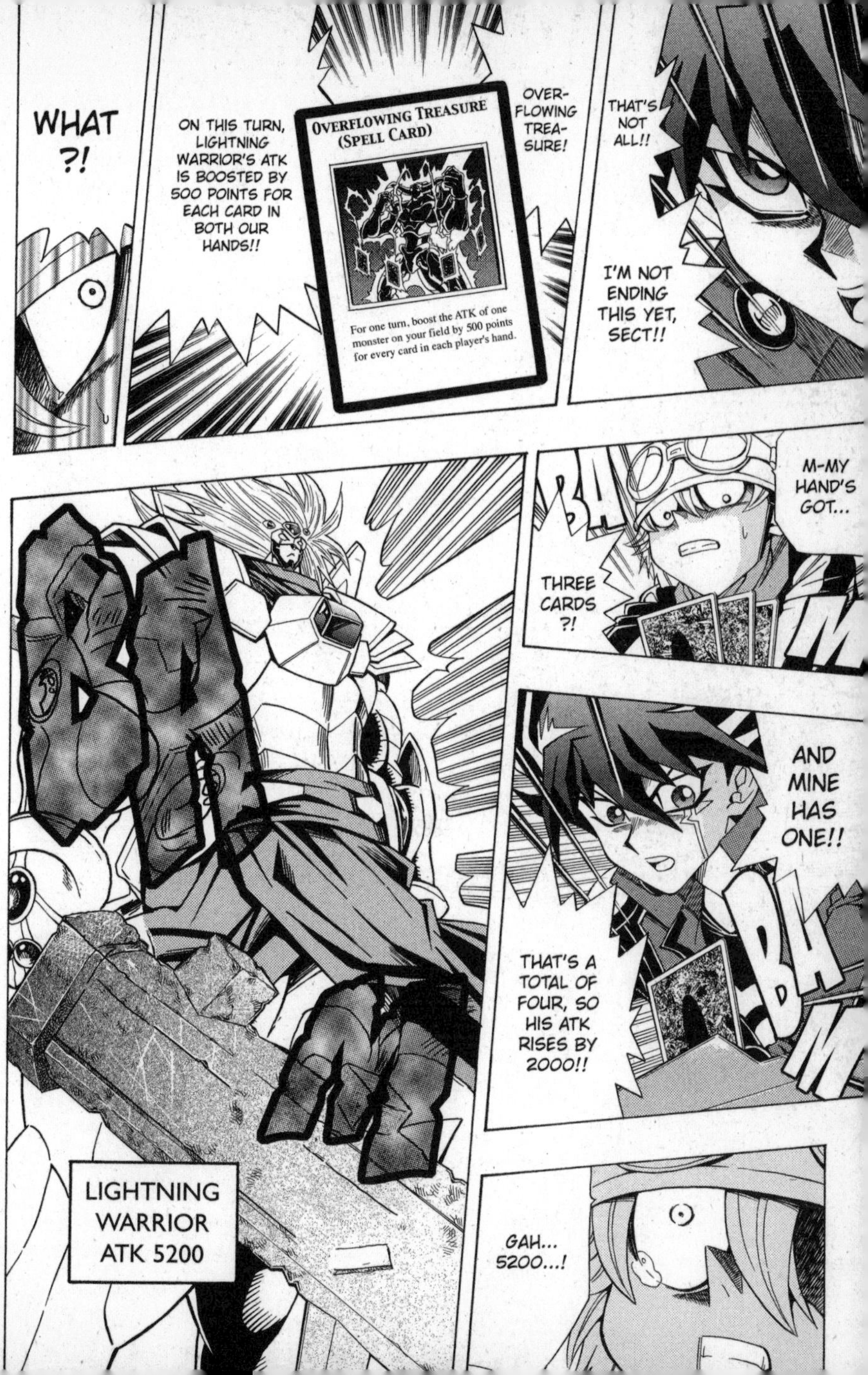
THAT'S NOT ALL!!
I'M NOT ENDING THIS YET, SECT!!
OVER-FLOWING TREA-SURE!
OVERFLOWING TREASURE (SPELL CARD)
For one turn, boost the ATK of one monster on your field by 500 points for every card in each player's hand.
ON THIS TURN, LIGHTNING WARRIOR'S ATK IS BOOSTED BY 500 POINTS FOR EACH CARD IN BOTH OUR HANDS!!
WHAT ?!
M-MY HAND'S GOT...
THREE CARDS ?!
AND MINE HAS ONE!!
THAT'S A TOTAL OF FOUR, SO HIS ATK RISES BY 2000!!
GAH... 5200...!
LIGHTNING WARRIOR ATK 5200

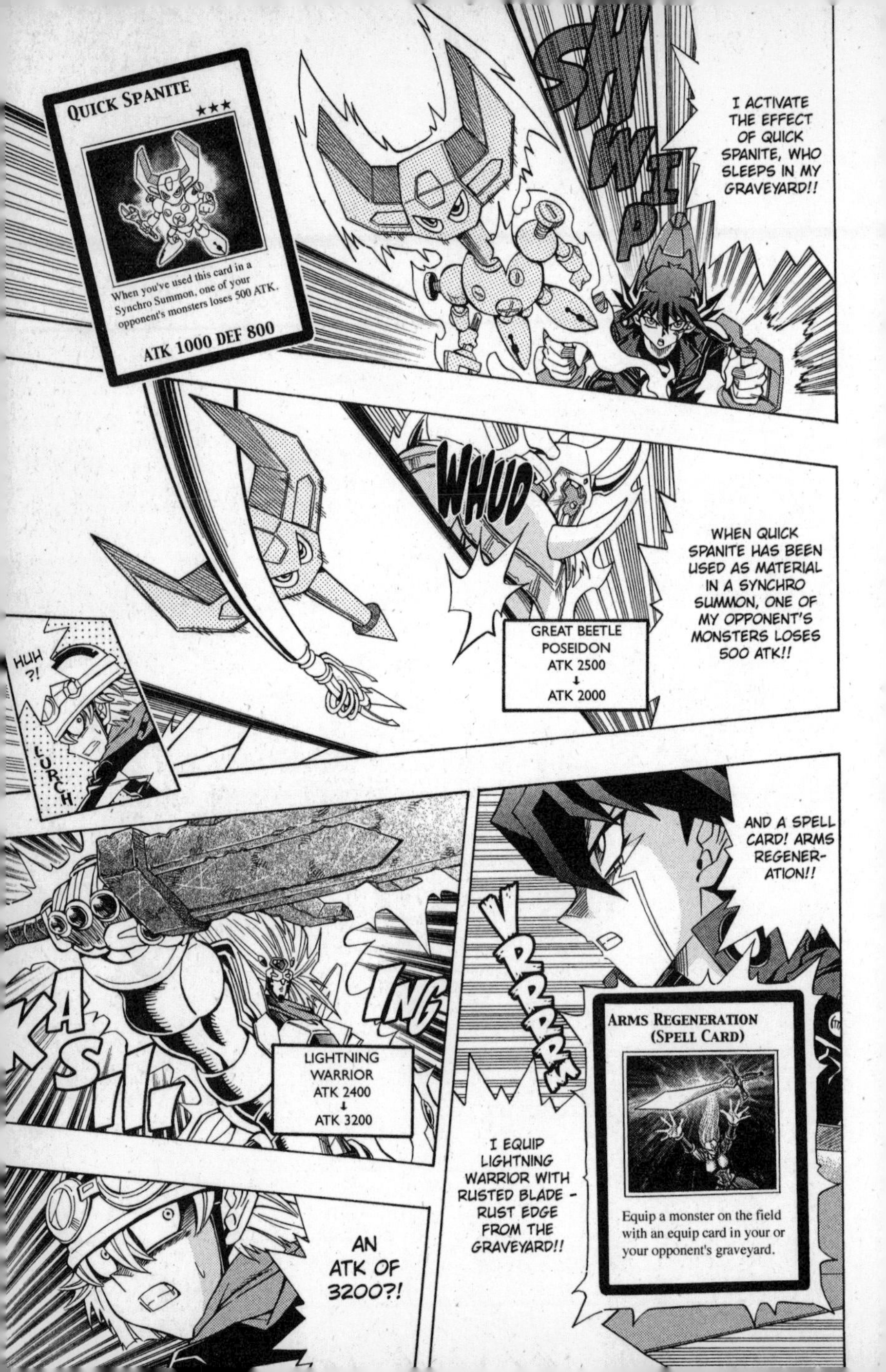
SHWIP
I ACTIVATE THE EFFECT OF QUICK SPANITE, WHO SLEEPS IN MY GRAVEYARD!!
QUICK SPANITE ★★★
When you've used this card in a Synchro Summon, one of your opponent's monsters loses 500 ATK.
ATK 1000 DEF 800
WHUD
WHEN QUICK SPANITE HAS BEEN USED AS MATERIAL IN A SYNCHRO SUMMON, ONE OF MY OPPONENT'S MONSTERS LOSES 500 ATK!!
GREAT BEETLE POSEIDON ATK 2500 ↓ ATK 2000
HUH ?!
LURCH
AND A SPELL CARD! ARMS REGENER-ATION!!
VRRRM
ARMS REGENERATION (SPELL CARD)
Equip a monster on the field with an equip card in your or your opponent's graveyard.
I EQUIP LIGHTNING WARRIOR WITH RUSTED BLADE - RUST EDGE FROM THE GRAVEYARD!!
KASHING
LIGHTNING WARRIOR ATK 2400 ↓ ATK 3200
AN ATK OF 3200?!

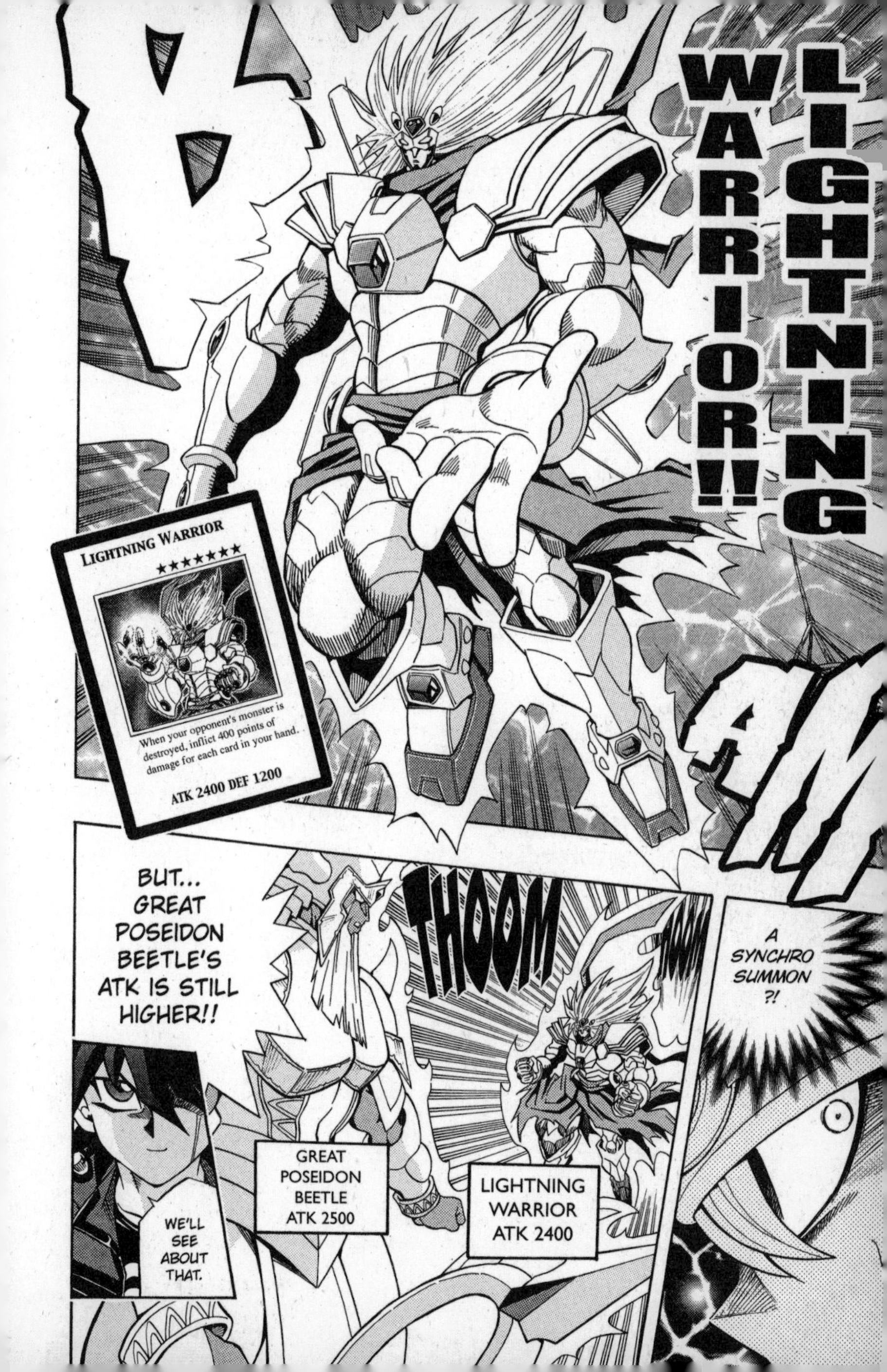
LIGHTNING WARRIOR!!
LIGHTNING WARRIOR
When your opponent's monster is destroyed, inflict 400 points of damage for each card in your hand.
ATK 2400 DEF 1200
A SYNCHRO SUMMON?!
BUT... GREAT POSEIDON BEETLE'S ATK IS STILL HIGHER!!
THOOM
GREAT POSEIDON BEETLE ATK 2500
LIGHTNING WARRIOR ATK 2400
WE'LL SEE ABOUT THAT.

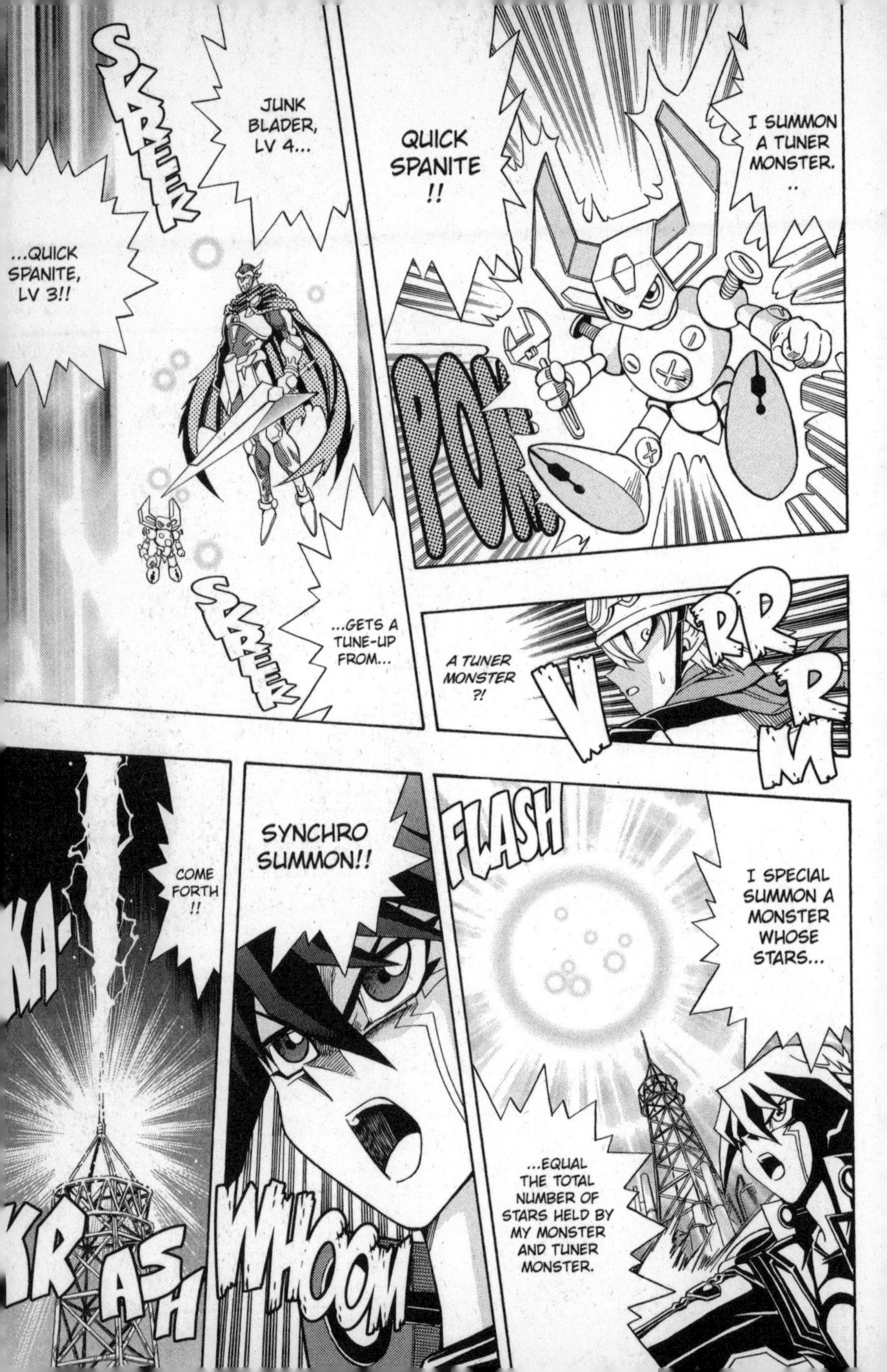
I SUMMON A TUNER MONSTER...
QUICK SPANITE!!
POK
A TUNER MONSTER?!
VRRRM
JUNK BLADER, LV 4...
...GETS A TUNE-UP FROM...
...QUICK SPANITE, LV 3!!
FLASH
I SPECIAL SUMMON A MONSTER WHOSE STARS...
...EQUAL THE TOTAL NUMBER OF STARS HELD BY MY MONSTER AND TUNER MONSTER.
SYNCHRO SUMMON!!
WHOOM
COME FORTH!!
KA-KRASH

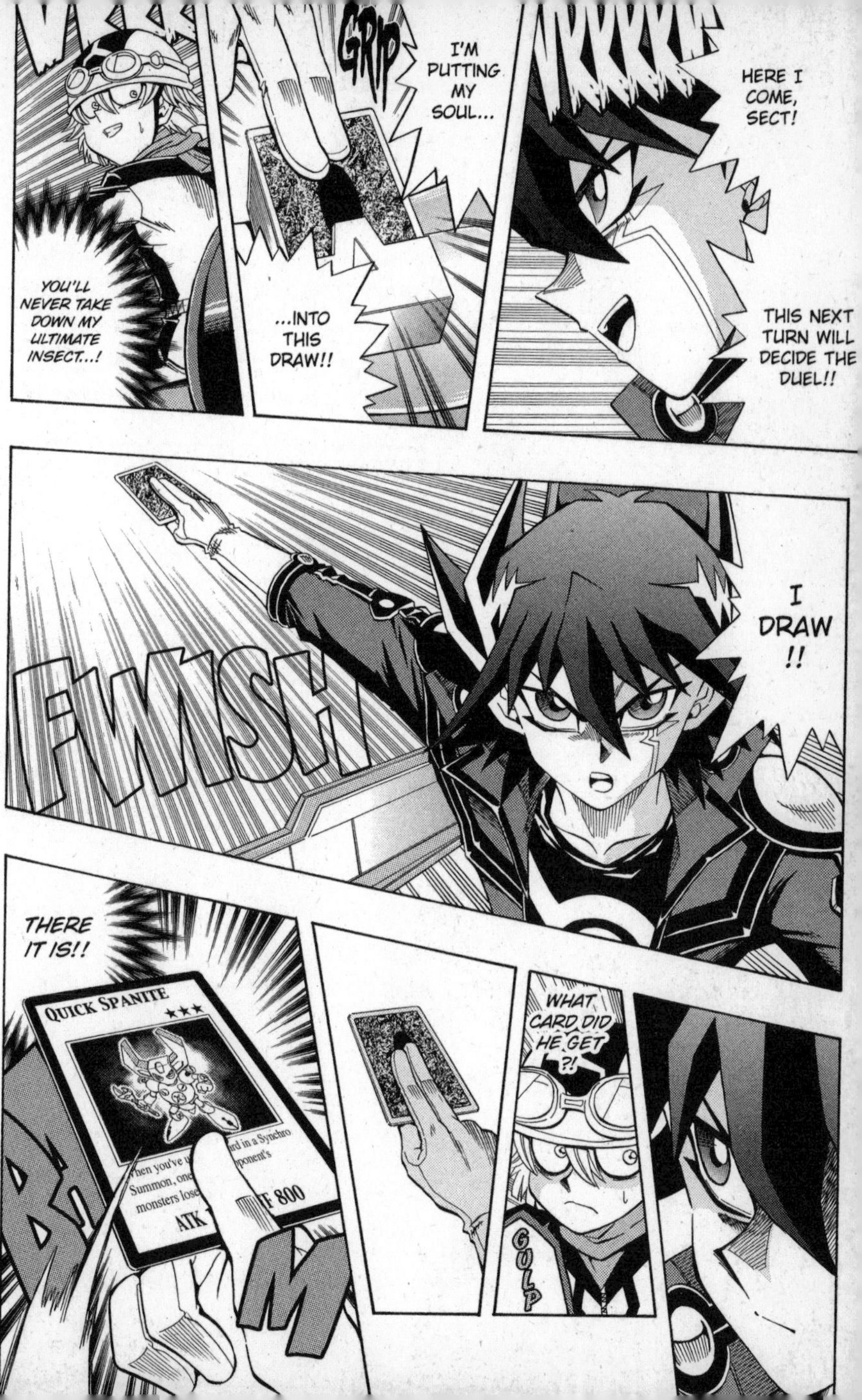
HERE I COME, SECT!
THIS NEXT TURN WILL DECIDE THE DUEL!!
GRIP
I'M PUTTING MY SOUL...
...INTO THIS DRAW!!
YOU'LL NEVER TAKE DOWN MY ULTIMATE INSECT...!
I DRAW!!
FWISH
WHAT CARD DID HE GET?!
GULP
THERE IT IS!!
QUICK SPANITE

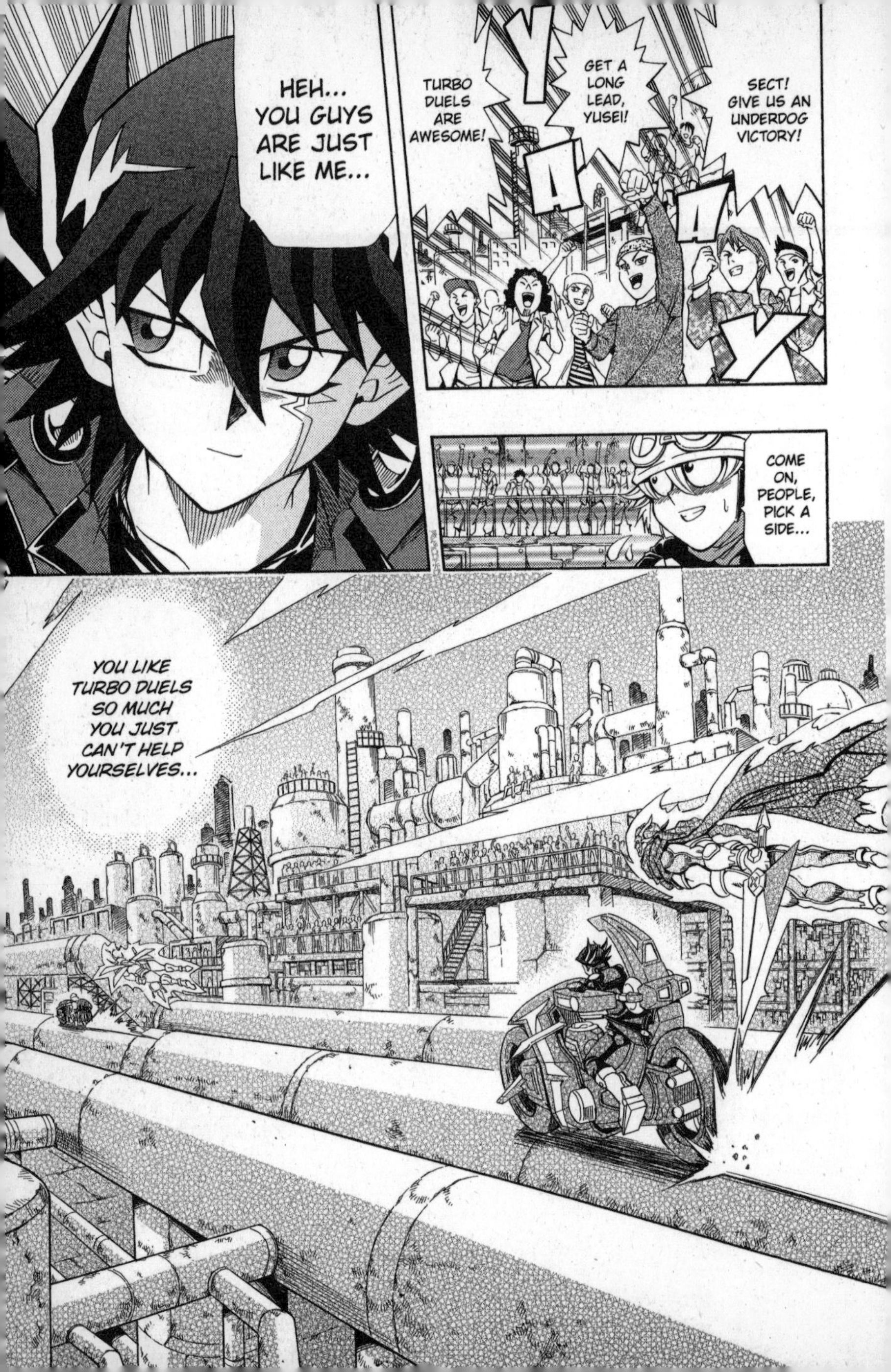
SECT! GIVE US AN UNDERDOG VICTORY!
GET A LONG LEAD, YUSEI!
TURBO DUELS ARE AWESOME!
YAAY
COME ON, PEOPLE, PICK A SIDE...
HEH... YOU GUYS ARE JUST LIKE ME...
YOU LIKE TURBO DUELS SO MUCH YOU JUST CAN'T HELP YOURSELVES...

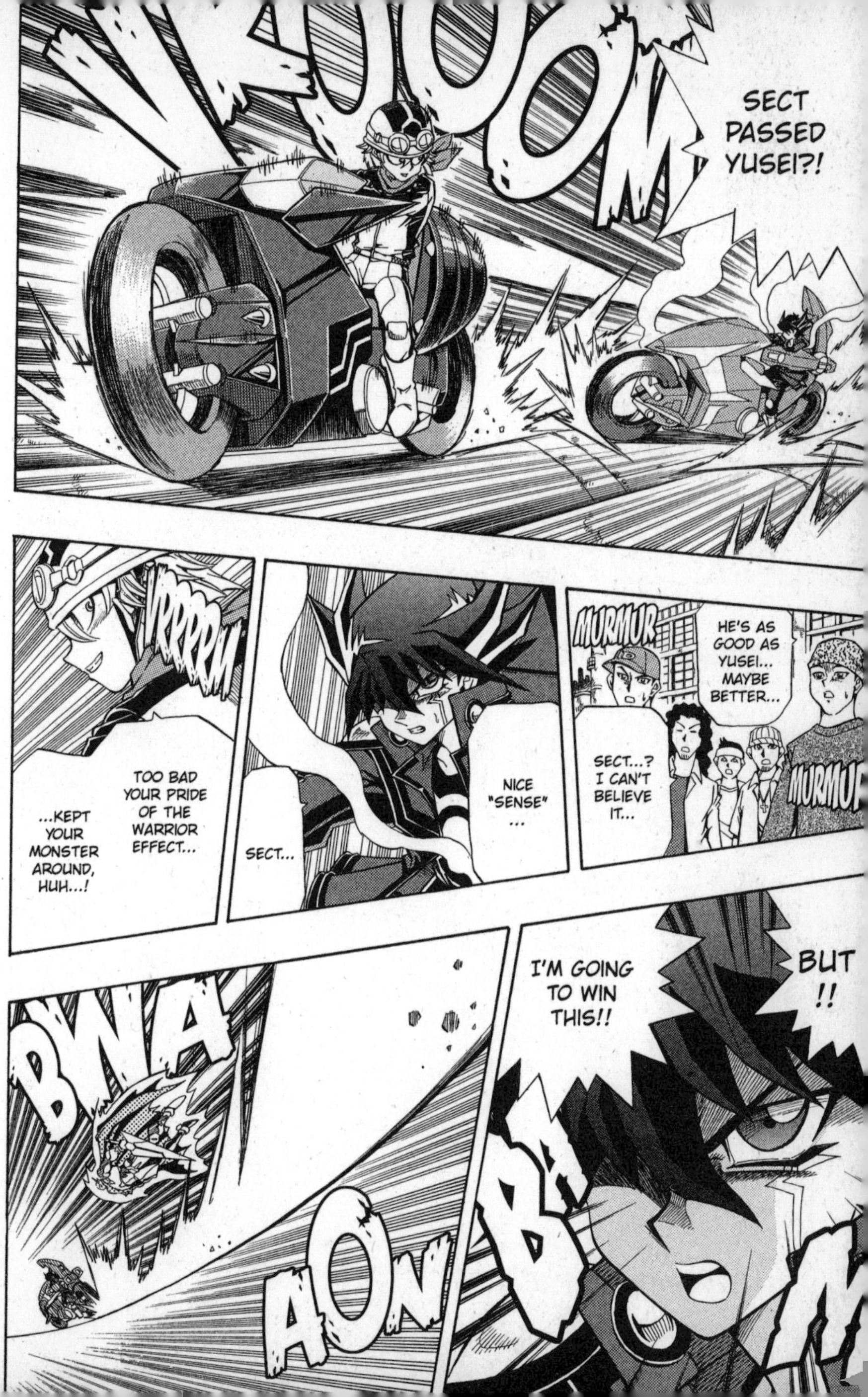
SECT PASSED YUSEI?!
MURMUR
HE'S AS GOOD AS YUSEI... MAYBE BETTER...
SECT...? I CAN'T BELIEVE IT...
NICE "SENSE" ...
SECT...
VRRRRM
TOO BAD YOUR PRIDE OF THE WARRIOR EFFECT...
...KEPT YOUR MONSTER AROUND, HUH...!
BUT !!
I'M GOING TO WIN THIS!!
BWA
AON

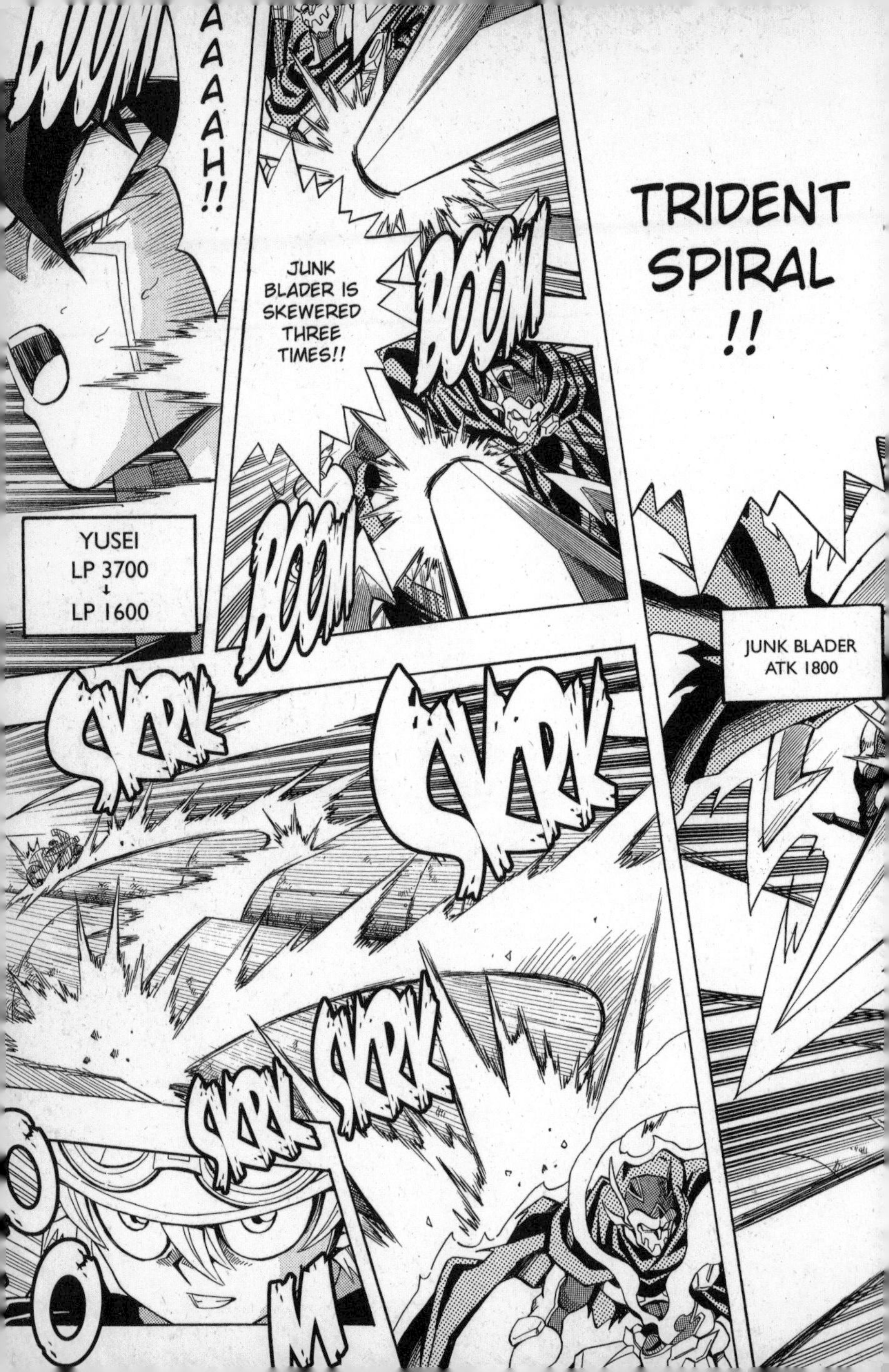
TRIDENT SPIRAL!!
JUNK BLADER ATK 1800
JUNK BLADER IS SKEWERED THREE TIMES!!
BOOM
BOOM
AAAAAH!!
YUSEI LP 3700 ↓ LP 1600
SKRK
SKRK
SKRK
SKRK

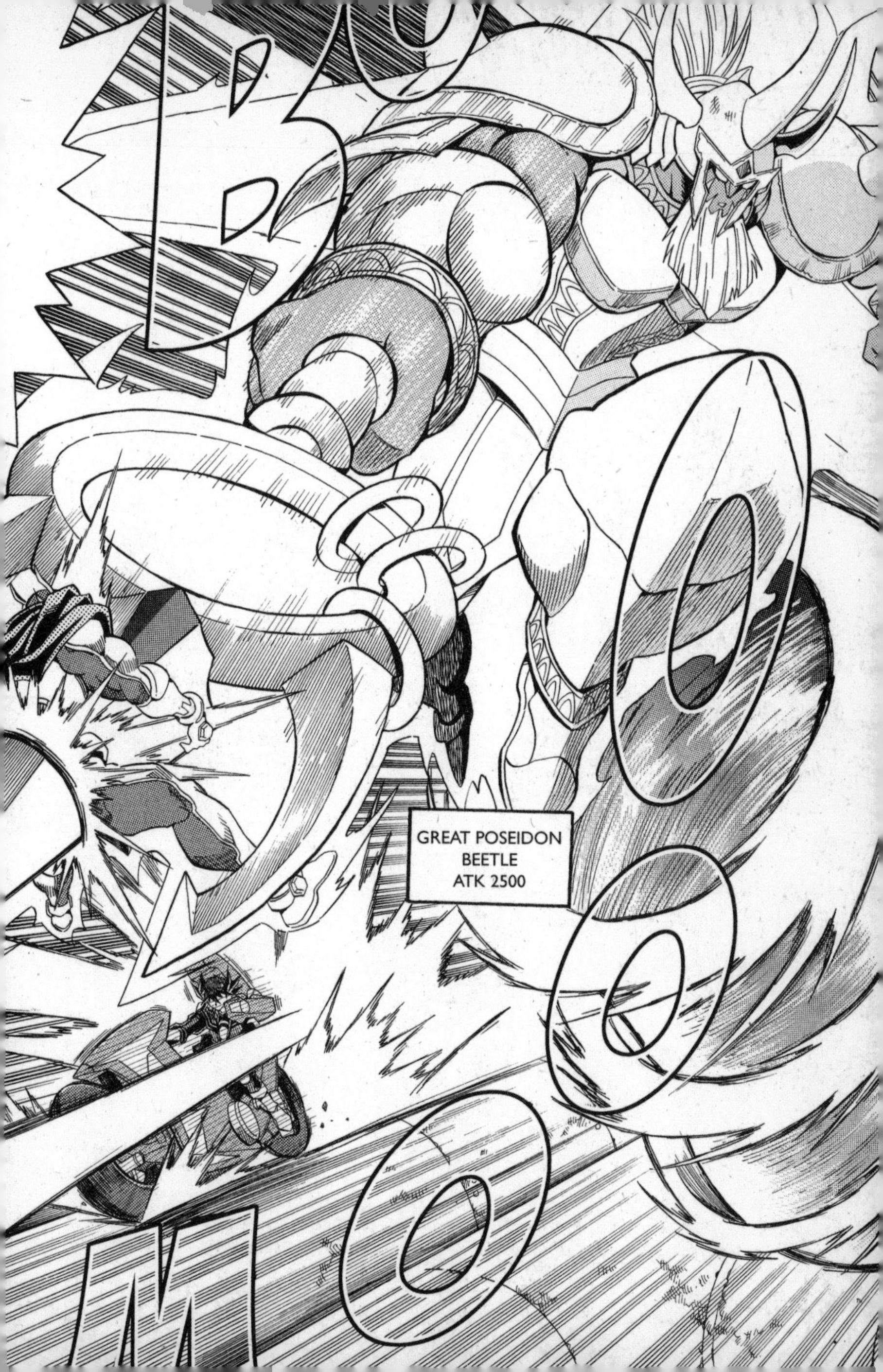
GREAT POSEIDON BEETLE ATK 2500

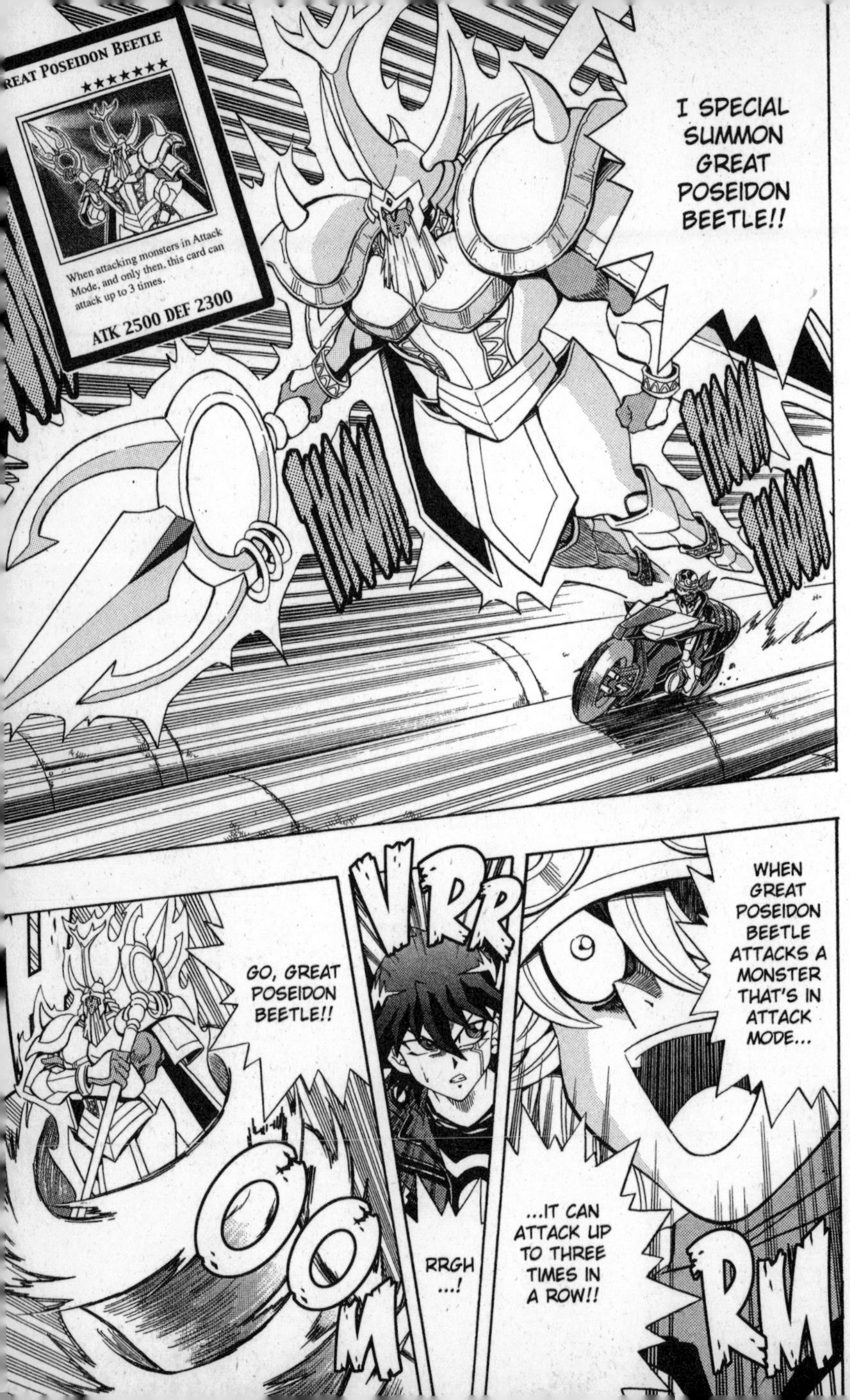
REAT POSEIDON BEETLE
When attacking monsters in Attack Mode, and only then, this card can attack up to 3 times.
ATK 2500 DEF 2300
I SPECIAL SUMMON GREAT POSEIDON BEETLE!!
WHEN GREAT POSEIDON BEETLE ATTACKS A MONSTER THAT'S IN ATTACK MODE...
...IT CAN ATTACK UP TO THREE TIMES IN A ROW!!
RM
VRR
RRGH ...!
GO, GREAT POSEIDON BEETLE!!
OOM

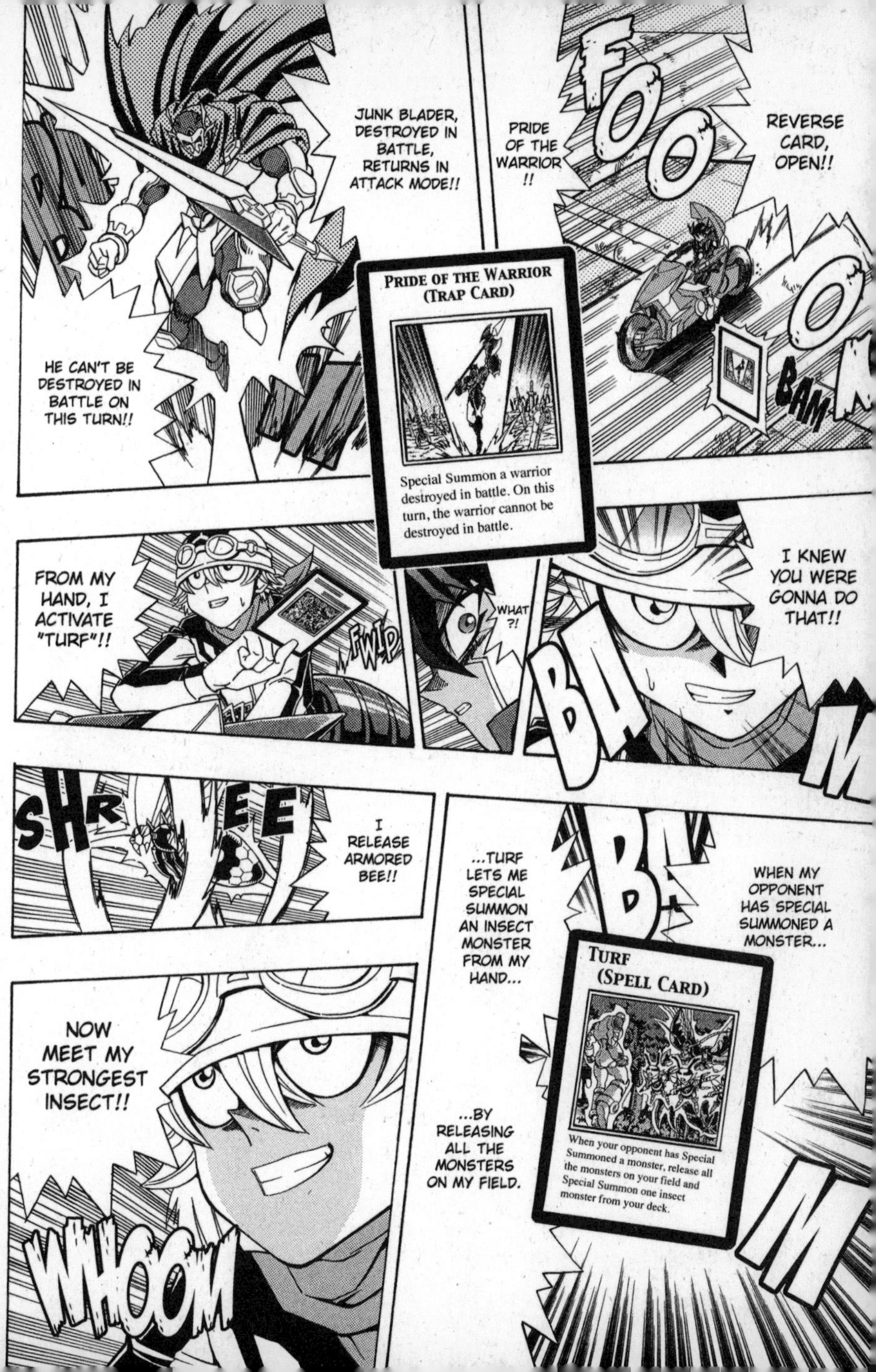
REVERSE CARD, OPEN!!
FOOOOM
PRIDE OF THE WARRIOR !!
BAM
JUNK BLADER, DESTROYED IN BATTLE, RETURNS IN ATTACK MODE!!
HE CAN'T BE DESTROYED IN BATTLE ON THIS TURN!!
PRIDE OF THE WARRIOR (TRAP CARD)
Special Summon a warrior destroyed in battle. On this turn, the warrior cannot be destroyed in battle.
I KNEW YOU WERE GONNA DO THAT!!
BOOM
WHAT ?!
FROM MY HAND, I ACTIVATE "TURF"!!
FWIP
WHEN MY OPPONENT HAS SPECIAL SUMMONED A MONSTER...
...TURF LETS ME SPECIAL SUMMON AN INSECT MONSTER FROM MY HAND...
...BY RELEASING ALL THE MONSTERS ON MY FIELD.
TURF (SPELL CARD)
When your opponent has Special Summoned a monster, release all the monsters on your field and Special Summon one insect monster from your deck.
BOOM
I RELEASE ARMORED BEE!!
SHREE
NOW MEET MY STRONGEST INSECT!!
WHOOM

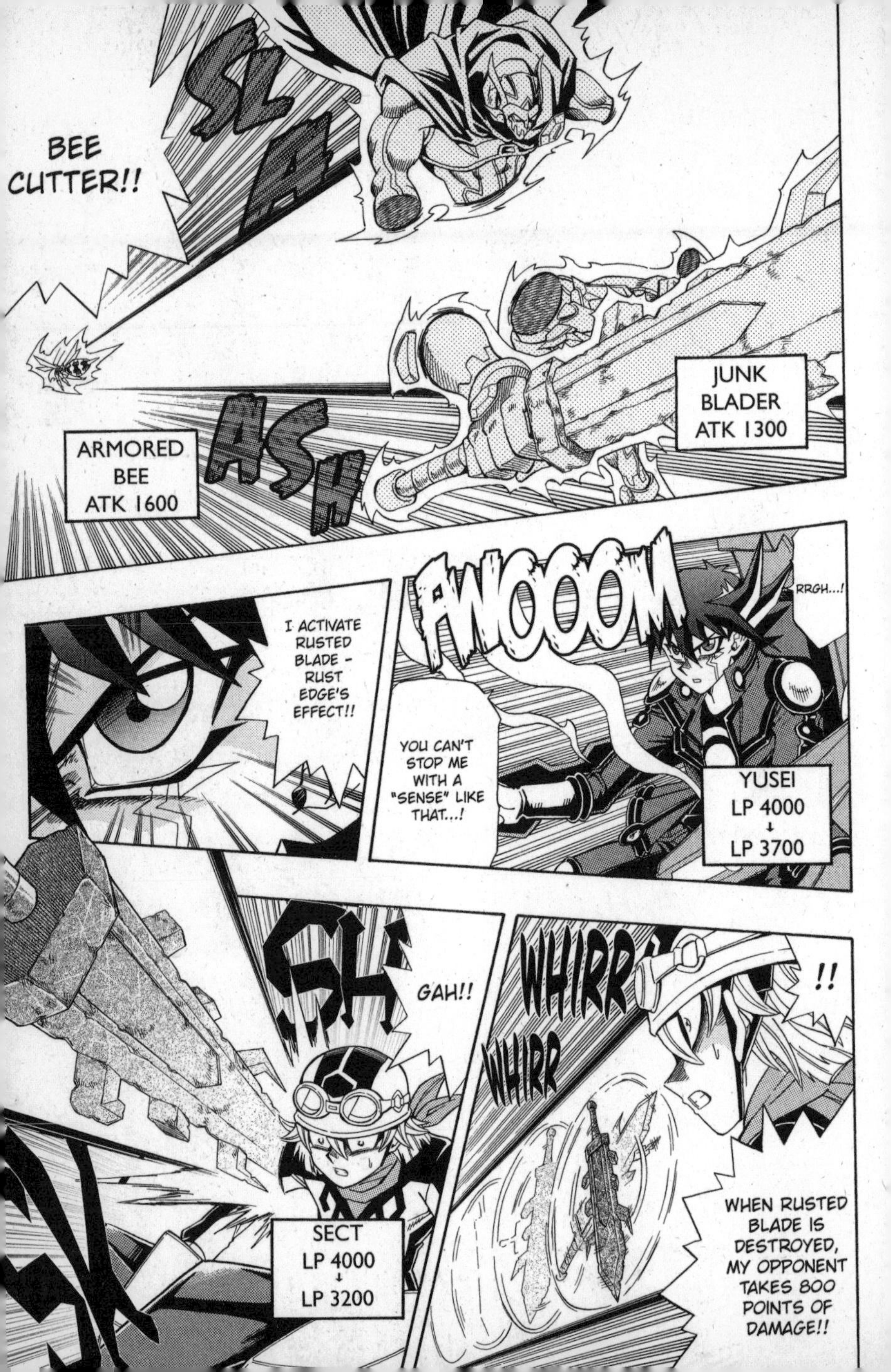
SLASH
BEE CUTTER!!
JUNK BLADER ATK 1300
ARMORED BEE ATK 1600
AWOOOM
RRGH...!
YUSEI LP 4000 ↓ LP 3700
YOU CAN'T STOP ME WITH A "SENSE" LIKE THAT...!
I ACTIVATE RUSTED BLADE - RUST EDGE'S EFFECT!!
WHIRR
!!
WHIRR
WHEN RUSTED BLADE IS DESTROYED, MY OPPONENT TAKES 800 POINTS OF DAMAGE!!
SHK
GAH!!
SECT LP 4000 ↓ LP 3200

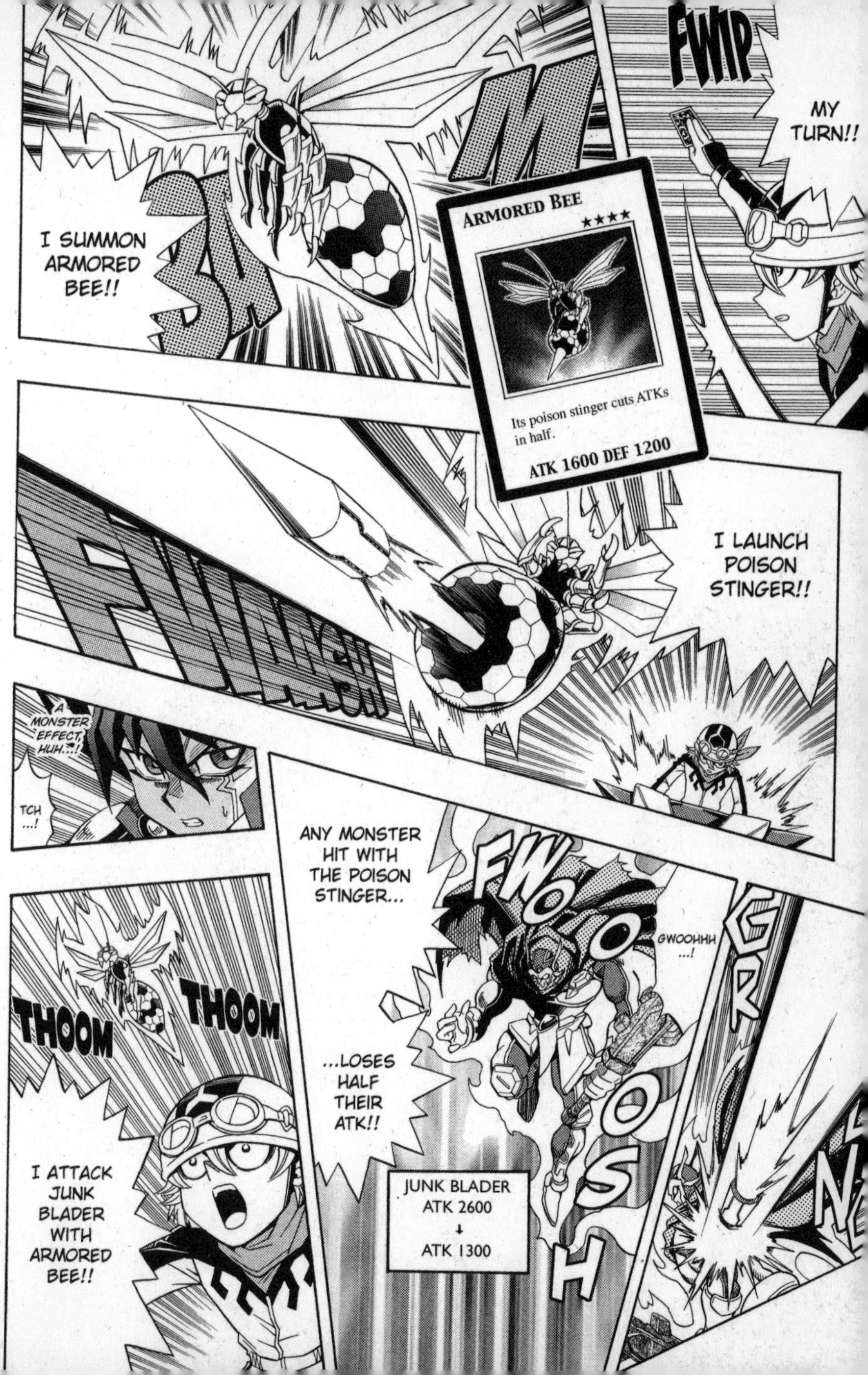
FWIP
MY TURN!!
M
SHA
I SUMMON ARMORED BEE!!
Armored Bee
★★★★
Its poison stinger cuts ATKs in half.
ATK 1600 DEF 1200
I LAUNCH POISON STINGER!!
A MONSTER EFFECT, HUH...!
TCH ...!
GR
GWOOHHH ...!
ANY MONSTER HIT WITH THE POISON STINGER...
FWOOOOSH
...LOSES HALF THEIR ATK!!
JUNK BLADER ATK 2600 ↓ ATK 1300
THOOM
THOOM
I ATTACK JUNK BLADER WITH ARMORED BEE!!

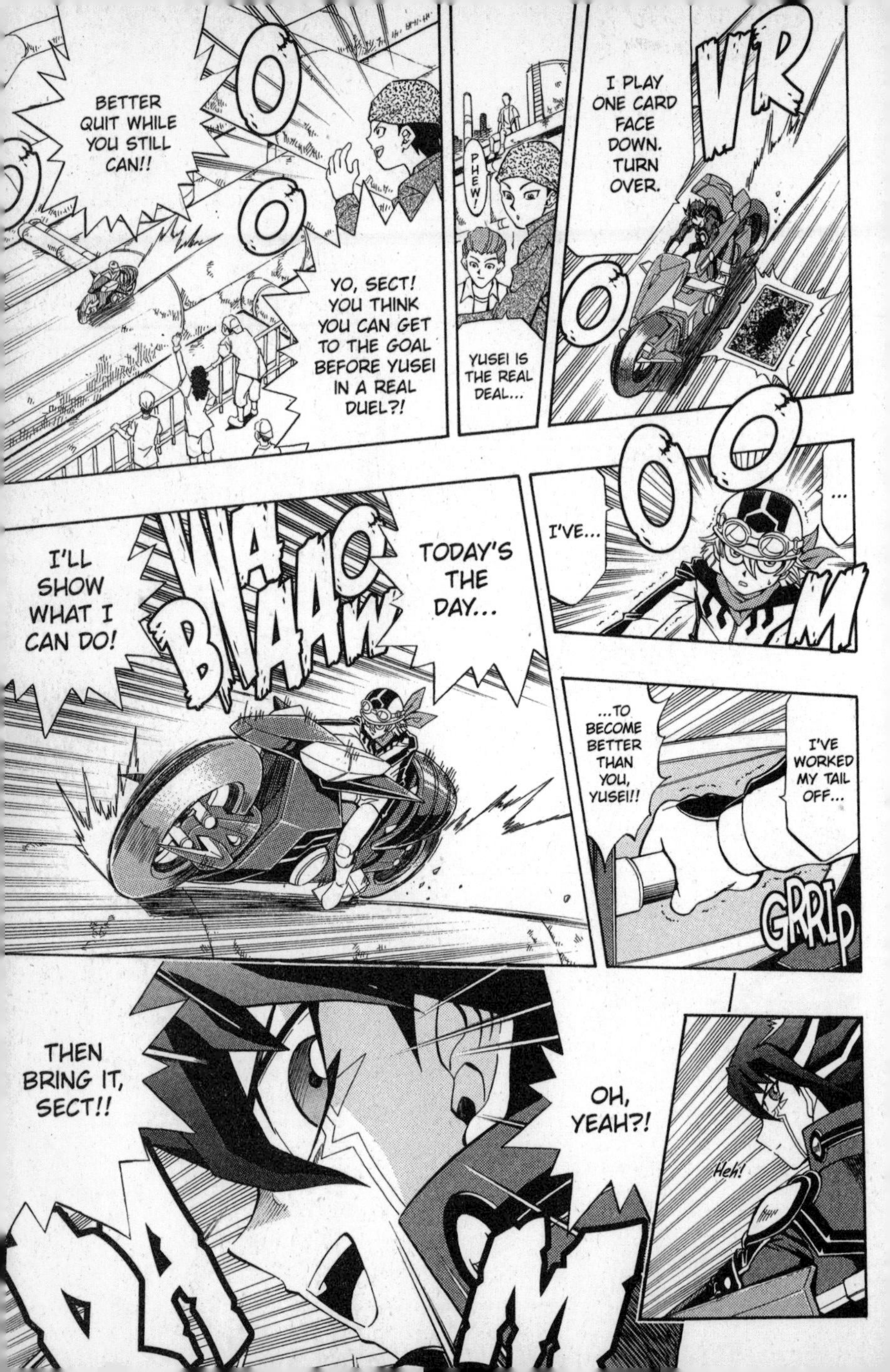
VR
I PLAY ONE CARD FACE DOWN. TURN OVER.
PHEW!
YUSEI IS THE REAL DEAL...
YO, SECT! YOU THINK YOU CAN GET TO THE GOAL BEFORE YUSEI IN A REAL DUEL?!
BETTER QUIT WHILE YOU STILL CAN!!
...
I'VE...
M
I'VE WORKED MY TAIL OFF...
...TO BECOME BETTER THAN YOU, YUSEI!!
GRRIP
TODAY'S THE DAY...
WAAC
BLAAW
I'LL SHOW WHAT I CAN DO!
Heh!
OH, YEAH?!
THEN BRING IT, SECT!!

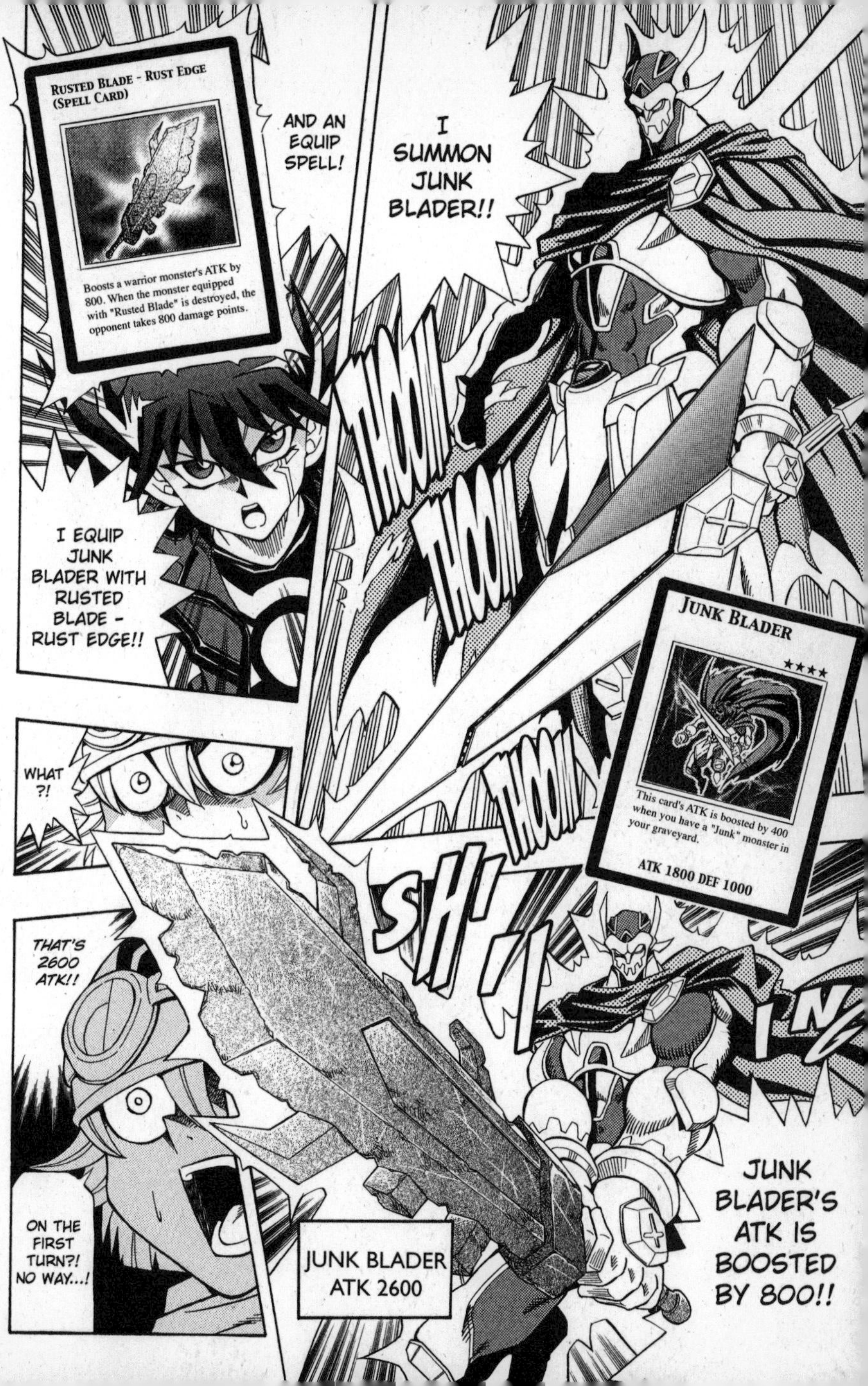

I SUMMON JUNK BLADER!!
THOOM
THOOM
THOOM
JUNK BLADER
This card's ATK is boosted by 400 when you have a "Junk" monster in your graveyard.
ATK 1800 DEF 1000
AND AN EQUIP SPELL!
RUSTED BLADE - RUST EDGE (SPELL CARD)
Boosts a warrior monster's ATK by 800. When the monster equipped with "Rusted Blade" is destroyed, the opponent takes 800 damage points.
I EQUIP JUNK BLADER WITH RUSTED BLADE - RUST EDGE!!
WHAT ?!
JUNK BLADER'S ATK IS BOOSTED BY 800!!
JUNK BLADER ATK 2600
THAT'S 2600 ATK!!
ON THE FIRST TURN?! NO WAY...!

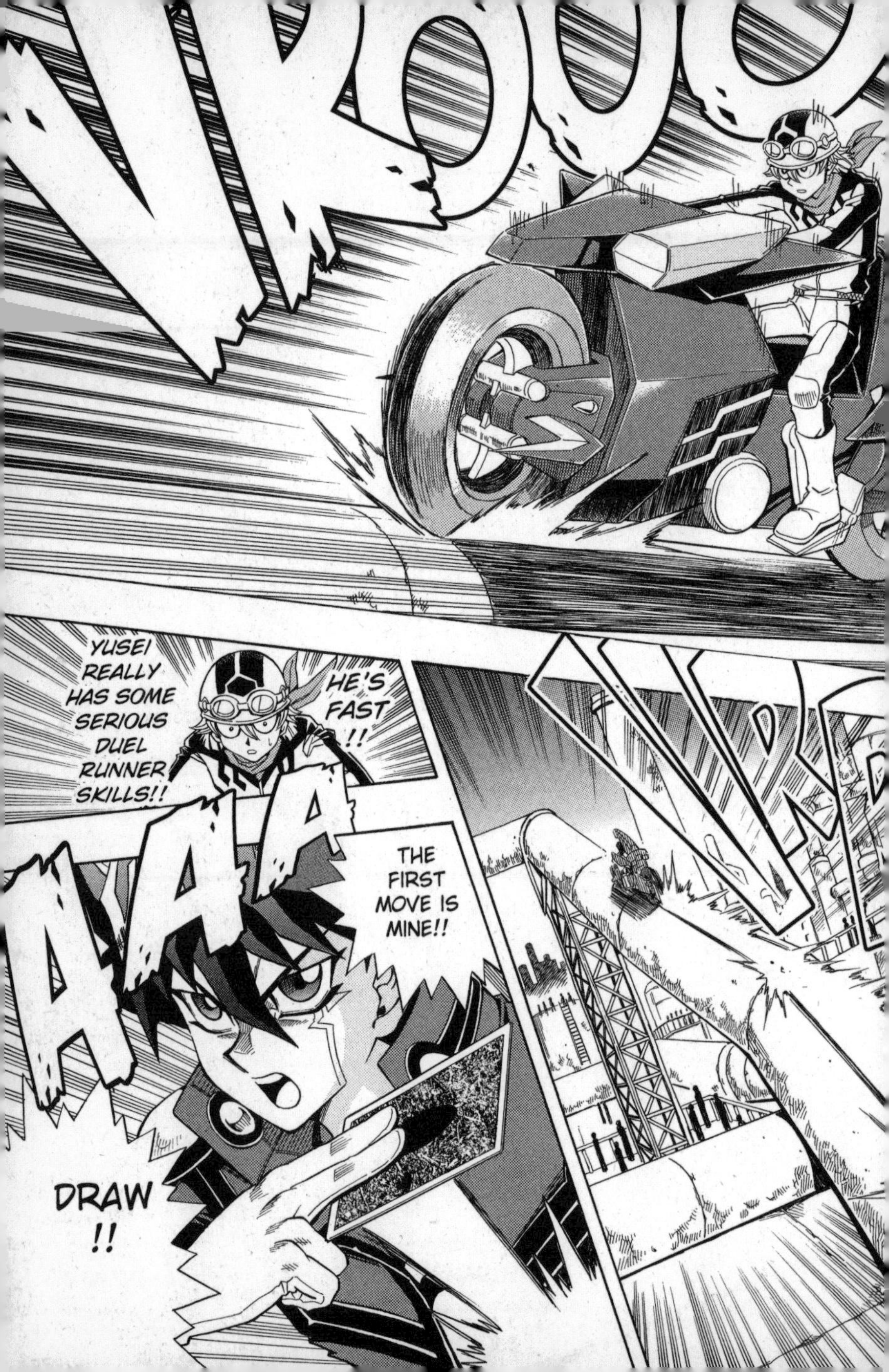
HE'S FAST!!
YUSEI REALLY HAS SOME SERIOUS DUEL RUNNER SKILLS!!
THE FIRST MOVE IS MINE!!
DRAW!!

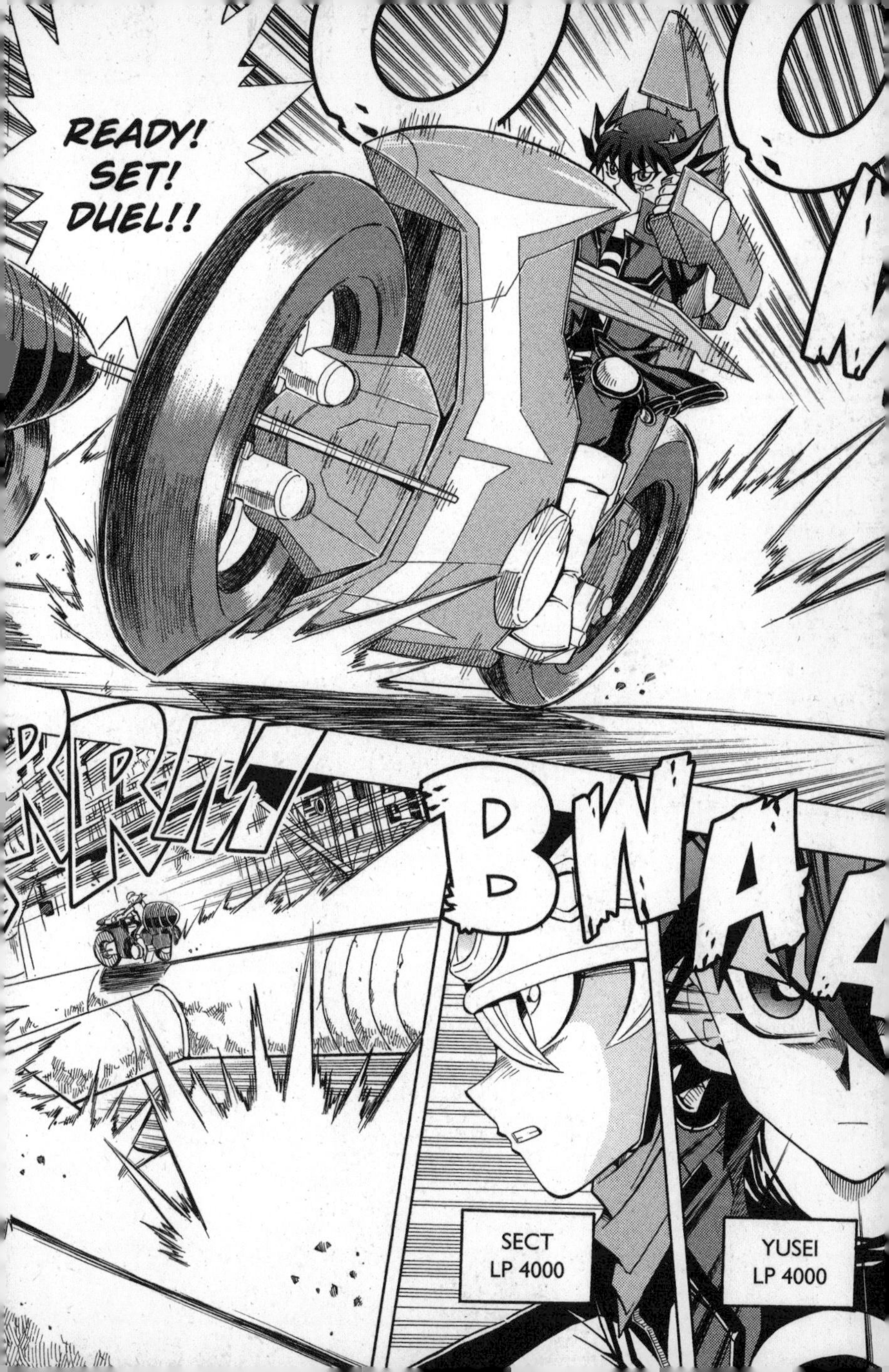
READY! SET! DUEL!!
BWA
SECT
LP 4000
YUSEI
LP 4000

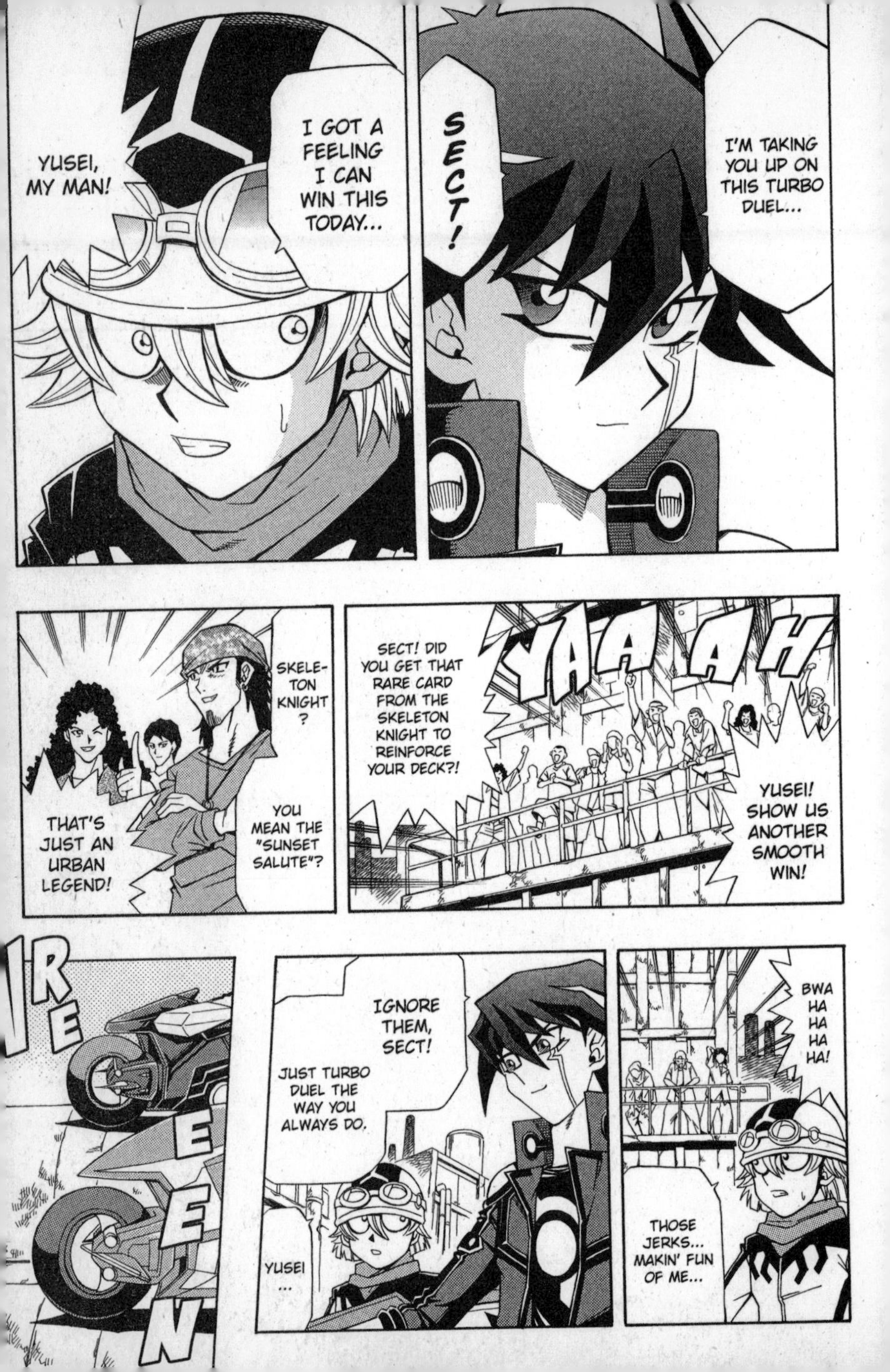
I'M TAKING YOU UP ON THIS TURBO DUEL...
SECT!
I GOT A FEELING I CAN WIN THIS TODAY...
YUSEI, MY MAN!
YAAAH
SECT! DID YOU GET THAT RARE CARD FROM THE SKELETON KNIGHT TO REINFORCE YOUR DECK?!
YUSEI! SHOW US ANOTHER SMOOTH WIN!
SKELE-TON KNIGHT?
YOU MEAN THE "SUNSET SALUTE"?
THAT'S JUST AN URBAN LEGEND!
BWA HA HA HA HA!
THOSE JERKS... MAKIN' FUN OF ME...
IGNORE THEM, SECT!
JUST TURBO DUEL THE WAY YOU ALWAYS DO.
YUSEI...
REEEN

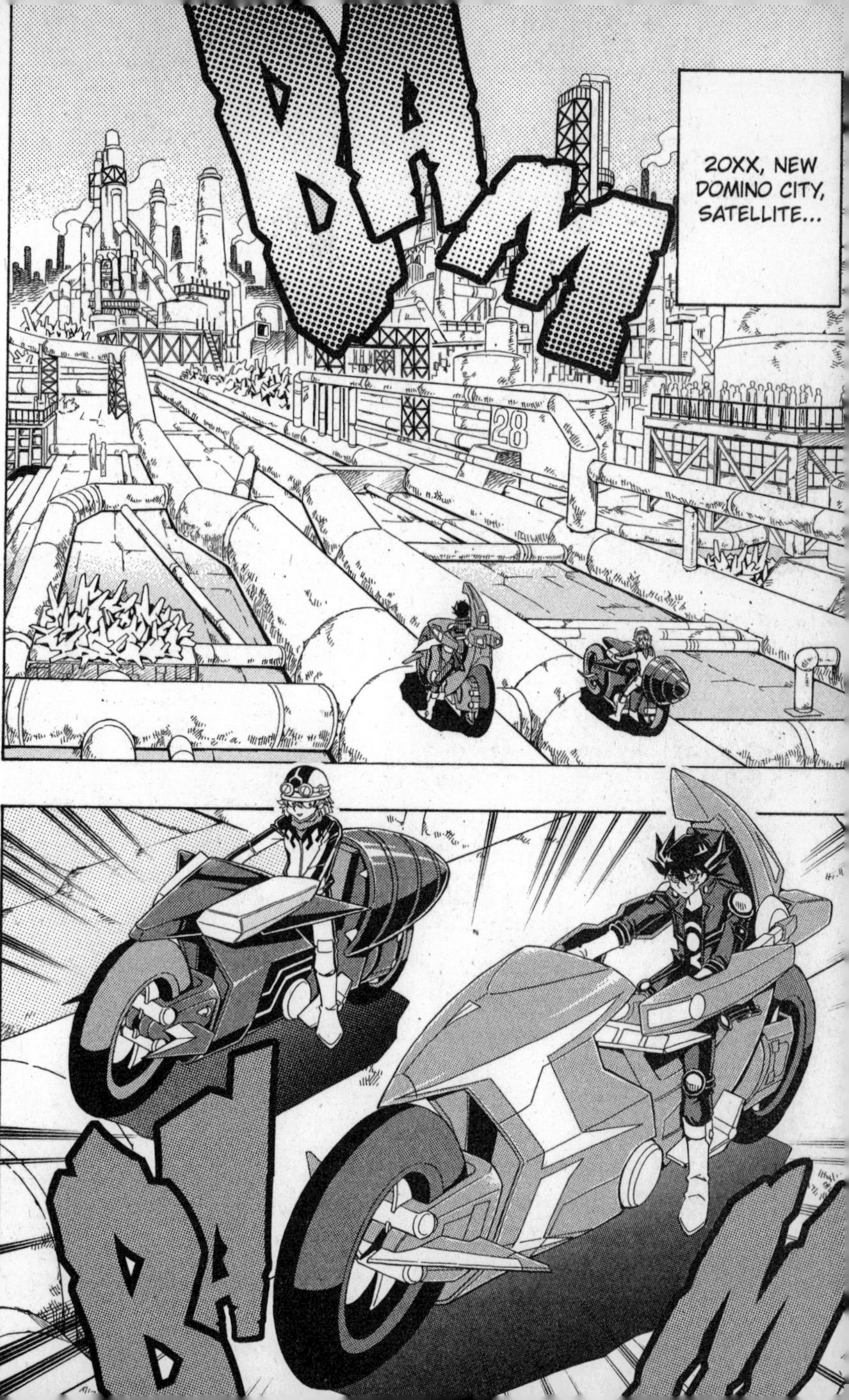
20XX, NEW DOMINO CITY, SATELLITE...
BAM
28
BAM

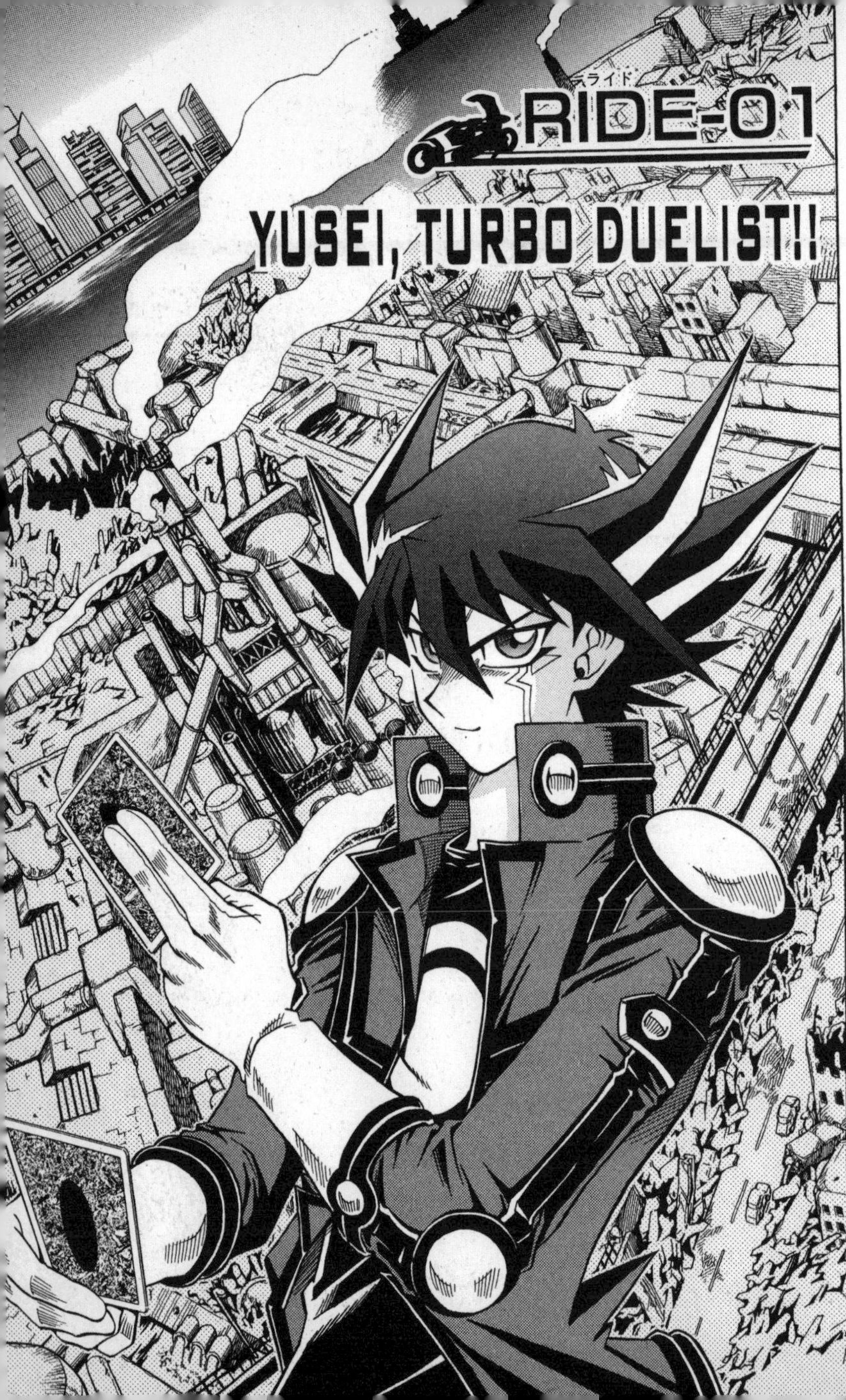
RIDE-01
YUSEI, TURBO DUELIST!!

VOLUME 1
YUSEI, TURBO DUELIST!!

JACK ATLAS
A Turbo Duelist known as "the King," and feared by all around him.

AKIZA IZINSKI
A Turbo Duelist who holds the title "Queen of Queens."

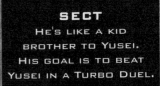

SECT
He's like a kid brother to Yusei. His goal is to beat Yusei in a Turbo Duel.

 **STORY**

New Domino City, in the year 20XX. Turbo Duels, fought from the seats of motorcycle-shaped duel disks called "Duel Runners," are the hottest game in town. Yusei Fudo and his sidekick Sect meet in Satellite, a district on the outskirts of New Domino City, and rev up for a duel. Start your engines—Yusei Fudo's Turbo Duel story begins now!!

CHARACTER

YUSEI FUDO

A Turbo Duelist who rides a Duel Runner. He's the toughest duelist in the Satellite district.

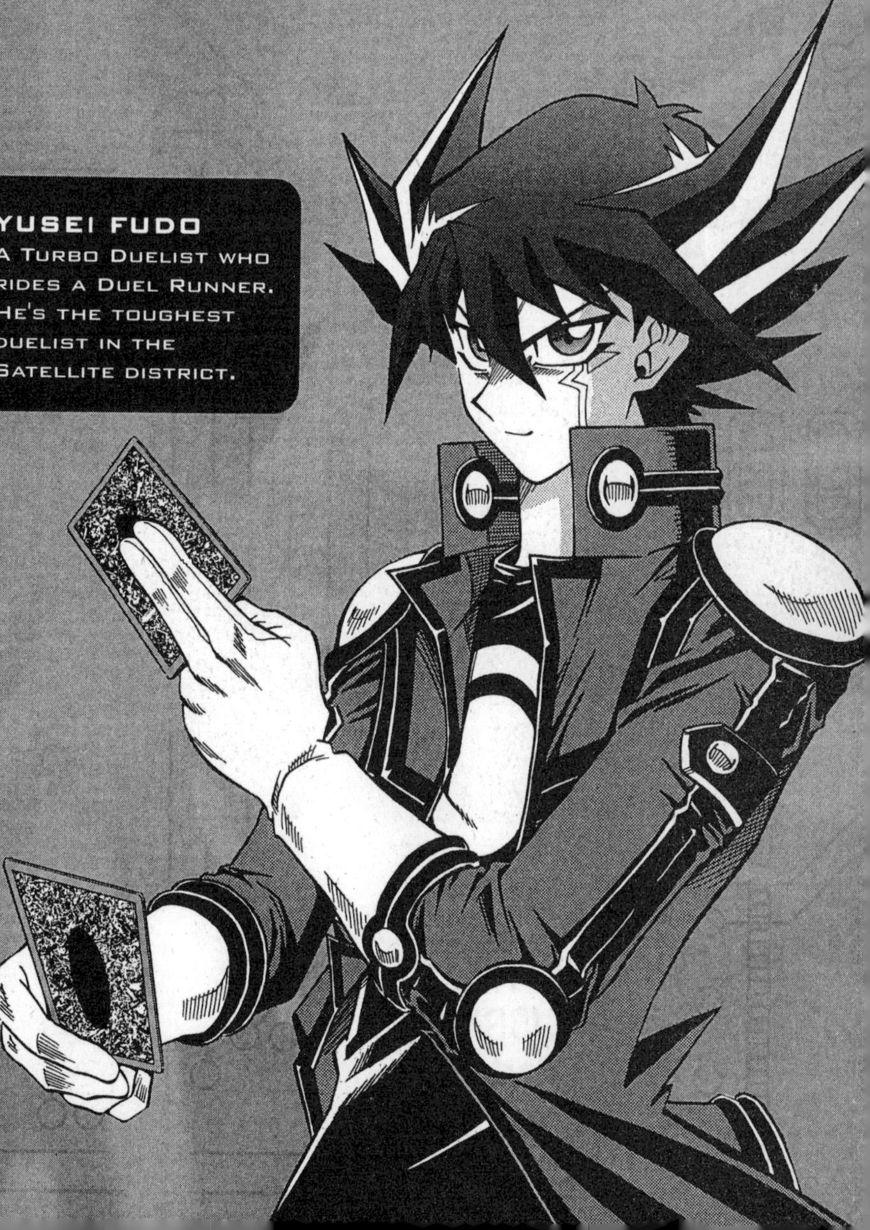

Yu-Gi-Oh! 5D's™

VOLUME 1

YUSEI, TURBO DUELIST!!

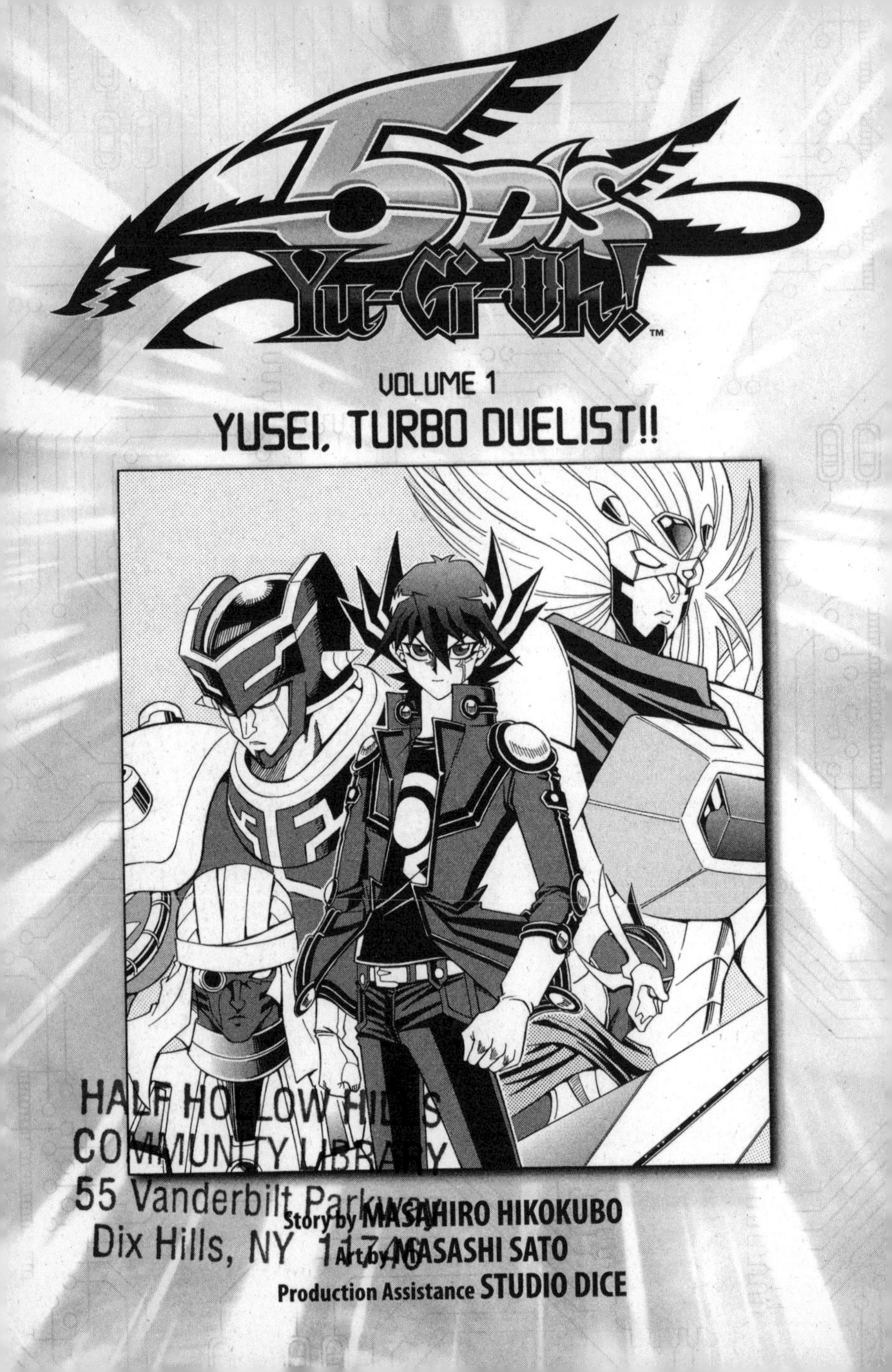

Story by MASAHIRO HIKOKUBO
Art by MASASHI SATO
Production Assistance STUDIO DICE

Volume 1
SHONEN JUMP Manga Edition

Story by **MASAHIRO HIKOKUBO**
Art by **MASASHI SATO**
Production Assistance **STUDIO DICE**

Translation & English Adaptation **TAYLOR ENGEL AND IAN REID, HC LANGUAGE SOLUTIONS**
Touch-up Art & Lettering **JOHN HUNT**
Designer **FAWN LAU**
Editor **MIKE MONTESA**

YU-GI-OH! 5D's © 2009 by Masahiro Hikokubo, Masashi Sato
All rights reserved.
First published in Japan in 2009 by SHUEISHA Inc., Tokyo.
English translation rights arranged by SHUEISHA Inc.

Based on Animation TV series YU-GI-OH! 5D's
© 1996 Kazuki Takahashi
© 2008 NAS • TV TOKYO

Printed in the U.S.A.

Published by VIZ Media, LLC
P.O. Box 77010
San Francisco, CA 94107

10 9 8 7 6 5 4 3 2 1
First printing, July 2011

www.viz.com

PARENTAL ADVISORY
YU-GI-OH! 5D's is rated T for Teen and
is recommended for ages 13 and up.
This volume contains fantasy violence.
ratings.viz.com

www.shonenjump.com

MASAHIRO HIKOKUBO

Umm, please enjoy this without saying
"THAT's not how it's supposed to be!"
(Actually, it's okay, you can say it! *laughs*)

MASASHI SATO

I've been involved with *Yu-Gi-Oh!* for
ten years. Who'd have thought the day
would come when I'd draw the manga!!
I'll work hard to earn your support!!